OECD/G20 Base Erosion and Profit Shifting Project

Addressing the Tax Challenges of the Digital Economy, Action 1 - 2015 Final Report

OECD
BETTER POLICIES FOR BETTER LIVES

Please cite this publication as:
OECD (2015), *Addressing the Tax Challenges of the Digital Economy, Action 1 - 2015 Final Report*, OECD/G20 Base Erosion and Profit Shifting Project, OECD Publishing, Paris.
http://dx.doi.org/10.1787/9789264241046-en

ISBN 978-92-64-24102-2 (print)
ISBN 978-92-64-24104-6 (PDF)

Series: OECD/G20 Base Erosion and Profit Shifting Project
ISSN 2313-2604 (print)
ISSN 2313-2612 (online)

Photo credits: Cover © ninog – Fotolia.com

Corrigenda to OECD publications may be found on line at: *www.oecd.org/about/publishing/corrigenda.htm*.

Foreword

International tax issues have never been as high on the political agenda as they are today. The integration of national economies and markets has increased substantially in recent years, putting a strain on the international tax rules, which were designed more than a century ago. Weaknesses in the current rules create opportunities for base erosion and profit shifting (BEPS), requiring bold moves by policy makers to restore confidence in the system and ensure that profits are taxed where economic activities take place and value is created.

Following the release of the report *Addressing Base Erosion and Profit Shifting* in February 2013, OECD and G20 countries adopted a 15-point Action Plan to address BEPS in September 2013. The Action Plan identified 15 actions along three key pillars: introducing coherence in the domestic rules that affect cross-border activities, reinforcing substance requirements in the existing international standards, and improving transparency as well as certainty.

Since then, all G20 and OECD countries have worked on an equal footing and the European Commission also provided its views throughout the BEPS project. Developing countries have been engaged extensively via a number of different mechanisms, including direct participation in the Committee on Fiscal Affairs. In addition, regional tax organisations such as the African Tax Administration Forum, the *Centre de rencontre des administrations fiscales* and the *Centro Interamericano de Administraciones Tributarias*, joined international organisations such as the International Monetary Fund, the World Bank and the United Nations, in contributing to the work. Stakeholders have been consulted at length: in total, the BEPS project received more than 1 400 submissions from industry, advisers, NGOs and academics. Fourteen public consultations were held, streamed live on line, as were webcasts where the OECD Secretariat periodically updated the public and answered questions.

After two years of work, the 15 actions have now been completed. All the different outputs, including those delivered in an interim form in 2014, have been consolidated into a comprehensive package. The BEPS package of measures represents the first substantial renovation of the international tax rules in almost a century. Once the new measures become applicable, it is expected that profits will be reported where the economic activities that generate them are carried out and where value is created. BEPS planning strategies that rely on outdated rules or on poorly co-ordinated domestic measures will be rendered ineffective.

Implementation therefore becomes key at this stage. The BEPS package is designed to be implemented via changes in domestic law and practices, and via treaty provisions, with negotiations for a multilateral instrument under way and expected to be finalised in 2016. OECD and G20 countries have also agreed to continue to work together to ensure a consistent and co-ordinated implementation of the BEPS recommendations. Globalisation requires that global solutions and a global dialogue be established which go beyond OECD and G20 countries. To further this objective, in 2016 OECD and G20 countries will conceive an inclusive framework for monitoring, with all interested countries participating on an equal footing.

A better understanding of how the BEPS recommendations are implemented in practice could reduce misunderstandings and disputes between governments. Greater focus on implementation and tax administration should therefore be mutually beneficial to governments and business. Proposed improvements to data and analysis will help support ongoing evaluation of the quantitative impact of BEPS, as well as evaluating the impact of the countermeasures developed under the BEPS Project.

Table of contents

Figures

Tables

Boxes

Abbreviations and acronyms

ANBPPI	Association des Bureaux pour la Protection de la Propriété Industrielle
API	Application programming interface
ASP	Application service provider
BEPS	Base erosion and profit shifting
BIAC	Business and Industry Advisory Committee to the OECD
BP	Business profit
B2B	Business-to-business
B2C	Business-to-consumer
CFA	Committee on Fiscal Affairs
CDS	Customs Declaration System
CFC	Controlled foreign company
CIT	Corporate income tax
CPA	Cost-per-action
CPC	Cost-per-click
CPM	Cost-per-mille
C2C	Consumer-to-consumer
DDME	Data-Driven Marketing Economy
EC	European Community
GRT	gross receipts tax
HTML	Hypertext Markup Language
HTTP	Hypertext Transfer Protocol
IaaS	Infrastructure as a service
ICT	Information and communication technology
IMAP	Internet Message Access Protocol
IP	Internet Protocol
ISP	Internet service provider
MLE	Multi-location enterprise
MNE	Multinational enterprise

NIST	National Institute of Standards and Technology
OECD	Organisation for Economic Co-operation and Development
OTT	Over-the-top
PE	Permanent establishment
POP	Post Office Protocol
RFID	Radio Frequency Identification
RKC	Revised Kyoto Convention
SDK	Software development kits
SME	Small and medium enterprise
SMTP	Simple Mail Transfer Protocol
TAG	Technical Advisory Group
TFDE	Task Force on the Digital Economy
UCC	User created content
UCR	Unique Consignment Reference Number
UPU	Universal Postal Union
VAT	Value added tax
VAT/GST	Value added tax/Goods and services tax
VLAN	Virtual local area network
WCO	World Customs Organization's
WP	Working Party
WT	withholding tax
WTO	World Trade Organisation
XaaS	X-as-a Service
XML	Extensible Markup Language

Executive summary

Action 1 of the base erosion and profit shifting (BEPS) Action Plan deals with the tax challenges of the Digital Economy.

Political leaders, media outlets, and civil society around the world have expressed growing concern about tax planning by multinational enterprises (MNEs) that makes use of gaps in the interaction of different tax systems to artificially reduce taxable income or shift profits to low-tax jurisdictions in which little or no economic activity is performed. In response to this concern, and at the request of the G20, the Organisation for Economic Co-operation and Development (OECD) published an *Action Plan on Base Erosion and Profit Shifting* (BEPS Action Plan, OECD, 2013) in July 2013. Action 1 of the BEPS Action Plan calls for work to address the tax challenges of the digital economy.

The Task Force on the Digital Economy (TFDE), a subsidiary body of the Committee on Fiscal Affairs (CFA) in which non-OECD G20 countries participate as Associates on an equal footing with OECD countries, was established in September 2013 to develop a report identifying issues raised by the digital economy and detailed options to address them by September 2014. The TFDE consulted extensively with stakeholders and analysed written input submitted by business, civil society, academics, and developing countries. It issued an interim report in September 2014 and continued its work in 2015. The conclusions regarding the digital economy, the BEPS issues and the broader tax challenges it raises, and the recommended next steps are contained in this final report.

The digital economy is the result of a transformative process brought by information and communication technology (ICT), which has made technologies cheaper, more powerful, and widely standardised, improving business processes and bolstering innovation across all sectors of the economy.

Because the digital economy is increasingly becoming the economy itself, it would be difficult, if not impossible, to ring-fence the digital economy from the rest of the economy for tax purposes. The digital economy and its business models present however some key features which are potentially relevant from a tax perspective. These features include mobility, reliance on data, network effects, the spread of multi-sided business models, a tendency toward monopoly or oligopoly and volatility. The types of business models include several varieties of e-commerce, app stores, online advertising, cloud computing, participative networked platforms, high speed trading, and online payment services. The digital economy has also accelerated and changed the spread of global value chains in which MNEs integrate their worldwide operations.

BEPS issues in the digital economy

While the digital economy and its business models do not generate unique BEPS issues, some of its key features exacerbate BEPS risks. These BEPS risks were identified and the work on the relevant actions of the BEPS Project was informed by these findings and took these issues into account to ensure that the proposed solutions fully address BEPS in the digital economy. Accordingly,

- It was agreed to modify the list of exceptions to the definition of PE to ensure that each of the exceptions included therein is restricted to activities that are otherwise of a "preparatory or auxiliary" character, and to introduce a new anti-fragmentation rule to ensure that it is not possible to benefit from these exceptions through the fragmentation of business activities among closely related enterprises. For example, the maintenance of a very large local warehouse in which a significant number of employees work for purposes of storing and delivering goods sold online to customers by an online seller of physical products (whose business model relies on the proximity to customers and the need for quick delivery to clients) would constitute a permanent establishment for that seller under the new standard.
- It was also agreed to modify the definition of PE to address circumstances in which artificial arrangements relating to the sales of goods or services of one company in a multinational group effectively result in the conclusion of contracts, such that the sales should be treated as if they had been made by that company. For example, where the sales force of a local subsidiary of an online seller of tangible products or an online provider of advertising services habitually plays the principal role in the conclusion of contracts with prospective large clients for those products or services, and these contracts are routinely concluded without material modification by the parent company, this activity would result in a permanent establishment for the parent company.
- The revised transfer pricing guidance makes it clear that legal ownership alone does not necessarily generate a right to all (or indeed any) of the return that is generated by the exploitation of the intangible, but that the group companies performing the important functions, contributing the important assets and controlling economically significant risks, as determined through the accurate delineation of the actual transaction, will be entitled to an appropriate return. Specific guidance will also ensure that the transfer pricing analysis is not weakened by information asymmetries between the tax administration and the taxpayer in relation to hard-to-value intangibles, or by using special contractual relationships, such as a cost contribution arrangement.
- The recommendations on the design of effective CFC include definitions of CFC income that would subject income that is typically earned in the digital economy to taxation in the jurisdiction of the ultimate parent company.

It is expected that the implementation of these measures, as well as the other measures developed in the BEPS Project (e.g. minimum standard to address treaty shopping arrangements, best practices in the design of domestic rules on interest and other deductible financial payments, application to IP regimes of a substantial activity requirement with a "nexus approach"), will substantially address the BEPS issues exacerbated by the digital economy at the level of both the market jurisdiction and the jurisdiction of the ultimate parent company, with the aim of putting an end to the phenomenon of so-called stateless income.

Broader tax challenges raised by the digital economy

The digital economy also raises broader tax challenges for policy makers. These challenges relate in particular to nexus, data, and characterisation for direct tax purposes, which often overlap with each other. The digital economy also creates challenges for value added tax (VAT) collection, particularly where goods, services and intangibles are acquired by private consumers from suppliers abroad. The TFDE discussed and analysed a number of potential options to address these challenges, including through an analysis of their economic incidence, and concluded that:

- The option to modify the exceptions to PE status in order to ensure that they are available only for activities that are in fact preparatory or auxiliary in nature that was adopted as a result of the work on Action 7 of the BEPS Project is expected to be implemented across the existing tax treaty network in a synchronised and efficient manner via the conclusion of the multilateral instrument that modifies bilateral tax treaties under Action 15.
- The collection of VAT/GST on cross-border transactions, particularly those between businesses and consumers, is an important issue. Countries are thus recommended to apply the principles of the International VAT/GST Guidelines and consider the introduction of the collection mechanisms included therein.
- None of the other options analysed by the TFDE, namely *(i)* a new nexus in the form of a significant economic presence, *(ii)* a withholding tax on certain types of digital transactions, and *(iii)* an equalisation levy, were recommended at this stage. This is because, among other reasons, it is expected that the measures developed in the BEPS Project will have a substantial impact on BEPS issues previously identified in the digital economy, that certain BEPS measures will mitigate some aspects of the broader tax challenges, and that consumption taxes will be levied effectively in the market country.
- Countries could, however, introduce any of these three options in their domestic laws as additional safeguards against BEPS, provided they respect existing treaty obligations, or in their bilateral tax treaties. Adoption as domestic law measures would require further calibration of the options in order to provide additional clarity about the details, as well as some adaptation to ensure consistency with existing international legal commitments.

Next steps

Given that these conclusions may evolve as the digital economy continues to develop, it is important to continue working on these issues and to monitor developments over time. To these aims, the work will continue following the completion of the other follow-up work on the BEPS Project. This future work will be done in consultation with a broad range of stakeholders, and on the basis of a detailed mandate to be developed during 2016 in the context of designing an inclusive post-BEPS monitoring process. A report reflecting the outcome of the continued work in relation to the digital economy should be produced by 2020.

Chapter 1

Introduction to tax challenges of the digital economy

This chapter discusses the background leading to the adoption of the BEPS Action Plan, including the work to address the tax challenges of the digital economy. It then summarises the work of the Task Force on the Digital Economy leading to the production of the report. Finally, it provides an overview of the contents of the report.

1. Political leaders, media outlets, and civil society around the world have expressed growing concern about tax planning by multinational enterprises (MNEs) that makes use of gaps in the interaction of different tax systems to artificially reduce taxable income or shift profits to low-tax jurisdictions in which little or no economic activity is performed. In response to this concern, and at the request of the G20, the Organisation for Economic Co-operation and Development (OECD) published an *Action Plan on Base Erosion and Profit Shifting* (BEPS Action Plan, OECD, 2013) in July 2013. The BEPS Action Plan identifies 15 actions to address BEPS in a comprehensive manner, and sets deadlines to implement those actions.

2. As noted in the BEPS Action Plan, "the spread of the digital economy also poses challenges for international taxation. The digital economy is characterised by an unparalleled reliance on intangibles, the massive use of data (notably personal data), the widespread adoption of multi-sided business models capturing value from externalities generated by free products, and the difficulty of determining the jurisdiction in which value creation occurs. This raises fundamental questions as to how enterprises in the digital economy add value and make their profits, and how the digital economy relates to the concepts of source and residence or the characterisation of income for tax purposes. At the same time, the fact that new ways of doing business may result in a relocation of core business functions and, consequently, a different distribution of taxing rights which may lead to low taxation is not per se an indicator of defects in the existing system. It is important to examine closely how enterprises of the digital economy add value and make their profits in order to determine whether and to what extent it may be necessary to adapt the current rules in order to take into account the specific features of that industry and to prevent BEPS."

3. Against this background, the BEPS Action Plan includes the following description of the work to be undertaken in relation to the digital economy:

Action 1 – Address the tax challenges of the digital economy

Identify the main difficulties that the digital economy poses for the application of existing international tax rules and develop detailed options to address these difficulties, taking a holistic approach and considering both direct and indirect taxation. Issues to be examined include, but are not limited to, the ability of a company to have a significant digital presence in the economy of another country without being liable to taxation due to the lack of nexus under current international rules, the attribution of value created from the generation of marketable location relevant data through the use of digital products and services, the characterisation of income derived from new business models, the application of related source rules, and how to ensure the effective collection of VAT/GST with respect to the cross-border supply of digital goods and services. Such work will require a thorough analysis of the various business models in this sector.

4. At their meeting in St. Petersburg on 5-6 September 2013, the G20 Leaders fully endorsed the BEPS Action Plan, and issued a declaration that included the following paragraph related to BEPS:

In a context of severe fiscal consolidation and social hardship, in many countries ensuring that all taxpayers pay their fair share of taxes is more than ever a priority. Tax avoidance, harmful practices and aggressive tax planning have to be tackled. The growth of the digital economy also poses challenges for international taxation. We fully endorse the ambitious and comprehensive Action Plan – originated in the OECD – aimed at addressing base erosion and profit shifting with mechanism to enrich the Plan as appropriate. We welcome the establishment of the G20/OECD BEPS project and we encourage all interested countries to participate. Profits should be taxed where economic activities deriving the profits are performed and where value is created […] (G20, 2013).

5. The Task Force on the Digital Economy (TFDE), a subsidiary body of the Committee on Fiscal Affairs (CFA) was established in September 2013 to carry out the work, with the aim of developing a report identifying issues raised by the digital economy and possible actions to address them by September 2014.

6. The TFDE discussed the scope of the work and heard presentations from experts on the digital economy. The Task Force also discussed the relevance of the work done in the past on this topic. In particular, the Task Force discussed the outcomes of the 1998 Ottawa Ministerial Conference on Electronic Commerce where Ministers welcomed the 1998 CFA Report "Electronic Commerce: Taxation Framework Conditions" (OECD, 2001) setting out the following taxation principles that should apply to electronic commerce.

Box 1.1. **Ottawa Taxation Framework Conditions – Principles**

Neutrality: Taxation should seek to be neutral and equitable between forms of electronic commerce and between conventional and electronic forms of commerce. Business decisions should be motivated by economic rather than tax considerations. Taxpayers in similar situations carrying out similar transactions should be subject to similar levels of taxation.

Efficiency: Compliance costs for taxpayers and administrative costs for the tax authorities should be minimised as far as possible.

Certainty and Simplicity: The tax rules should be clear and simple to understand so that taxpayers can anticipate the tax consequences in advance of a transaction, including knowing when, where and how the tax is to be accounted.

Effectiveness and Fairness: Taxation should produce the right amount of tax at the right time. The potential for tax evasion and avoidance should be minimised while keeping counteracting measures proportionate to the risks involved.

Flexibility: The systems for taxation should be flexible and dynamic to ensure that they keep pace with technological and commercial developments.

7. These principles are still relevant today and, supplemented as necessary, can constitute the basis to evaluate options to address the tax challenges of the digital economy. In addition, the Task Force discussed the post-Ottawa body of work and in particular the work of the Technical Advisory Group on Business Profits (TAG BP) relating to the attribution of profits to permanent establishments (PEs), the place of effective management concept and treaty rules in the context of e-commerce. For an overview of this prior work, please refer to Annex A.

8. Considering the importance of stakeholders' input, the OECD issued a public request for input on 22 November 2013. Input received was discussed at the second meeting of the TFDE on 2-3 February 2014. The Task Force discussed the evolution and pervasiveness of the digital economy as well as the key features of the digital economy and tax challenges raised by them. The Task Force heard presentations from delegates outlining possible options to address the BEPS and tax challenges of the digital economy and agreed

on the importance of publishing a discussion draft for public comments and input. The input received was discussed by the Task Force and contributed to the finalisation of an interim report, which was published in September 2014. In accordance with the interim report, the Task Force continued its work until September 2015 in order to *(i)* ensure that work carried out in other areas of the BEPS Project tackles BEPS issues in the digital economy, and that it can assess the outcomes of that work; and *(ii)* continue the work on the broader tax challenges related to nexus, data, and characterisation, so as to refine the technical details of the potential options and enable their evaluation in light of the outcomes of the BEPS project.

9. This final report first provides an overview of the fundamental principles of taxation, focusing on the difference between direct and indirect taxes and the concepts that underlie them as well as double tax treaties (Chapter 2). It then examines the evolution over time of information and communication technology (ICT), including emerging and possible future developments (Chapter 3) and discusses the spread and impact of ICT across the economy, providing examples of new business models and identifying the key features of the digital economy (Chapter 4). It then provides a detailed description of the core elements of BEPS strategies in the digital economy (Chapter 5) and discusses how they will be addressed by the measures developed through the work on the BEPS Action Plan and the OECD work on indirect taxation (Chapter 6). It identifies also the broader tax challenges raised by the digital economy and summarises the potential options to address them that have been discussed and analysed by the Task Force, both in the areas of corporate income tax (Chapter 7) and of indirect tax (Chapter 8). Finally, it provides an evaluation of the broader direct and indirect tax challenges raised by the digital economy and of the options to address them (Chapter 9), taking into consideration not only the impact on BEPS issues of the measures developed in the course of the BEPS Project, but also the economic incidence of the different options to tackle these broader tax challenges. The conclusions of the Task Force, together with determination of the next steps, are included at the end of the report (Chapter 10).

Bibliography

G20 (2013), *Leaders' Declaration*, St. Petersburg, Russia, https://www.g20.org/sites/default/files/g20_resources/library/Saint_Petersburg_Declaration_ENG_0.pdf (accessed on 09 July 2014).

OECD (2013), *Action Plan on Base Erosion and Profit Shifting*, OECD Publishing, Paris, http://dx.doi.org/10.1787/9789264202719-en.

Chapter 2

Fundamental principles of taxation

This chapter discusses the overarching principles of tax policy that have traditionally guided the development of tax systems. It then provides an overview of the principles underlying corporate income tax, focusing primarily on the taxation of cross-border income both under domestic laws and in the context of tax treaties. Finally, it provides an overview of the design features of value-added tax (VAT) systems.

2.1. Overarching principles of tax policy

10. In a context where many governments have to cope with less revenue, increasing expenditures and resulting fiscal constraints, raising revenue remains the most important function of taxes, which serve as the primary means for financing public goods such as maintenance of law and order and public infrastructure. Assuming a certain level of revenue that needs to be raised, which depends on the broader economic and fiscal policies of the country concerned, there are a number of broad tax policy considerations that have traditionally guided the development of taxation systems. These include neutrality, efficiency, certainty and simplicity, effectiveness and fairness, as well as flexibility. In the context of work leading up to the report on the Taxation of Electronic Commerce (see Annex A for further detail), these overarching principles were the basis for the 1998 Ottawa Ministerial Conference, and are since then referred to as the Ottawa Taxation Framework Conditions (OECD, 2001). At the time, these principles were deemed appropriate for an evaluation of the taxation issues related to e-commerce. Although most of the new business models identified in Chapter 4 did not exist yet at the time, these principles, with modification, continue to be relevant in the digital economy, as discussed in Chapter 8. In addition to these well-recognised principles, equity is an important consideration for the design of tax policy.

- **Neutrality:** Taxation should seek to be neutral and equitable between forms of business activities. A neutral tax will contribute to efficiency by ensuring that optimal allocation of the means of production is achieved. A distortion, and the corresponding deadweight loss, will occur when changes in price trigger different changes in supply and demand than would occur in the absence of tax. In this sense, neutrality also entails that the tax system raises revenue while minimising discrimination in favour of, or against, any particular economic choice. This implies that the same principles of taxation should apply to all forms of business, while addressing specific features that may otherwise undermine an equal and neutral application of those principles.
- **Efficiency:** Compliance costs to business and administration costs for governments should be minimised as far as possible.
- **Certainty and simplicity:** Tax rules should be clear and simple to understand, so that taxpayers know where they stand. A simple tax system makes it easier for individuals and businesses to understand their obligations and entitlements. As a result, businesses are more likely to make optimal decisions and respond to intended policy choices. Complexity also favours aggressive tax planning, which may trigger deadweight losses for the economy.
- **Effectiveness and fairness:** Taxation should produce the right amount of tax at the right time, while avoiding both double taxation and unintentional non-taxation. In addition, the potential for evasion and avoidance should be minimised. Prior discussions in the Technical Advisory Groups (TAGs) considered that if there is a class of taxpayers that are technically subject to a tax, but are never required to pay the tax due to inability to enforce it, then the taxpaying public may view the tax as unfair and ineffective. As a result, the practical enforceability of tax rules is an important consideration for policy makers. In addition, because it influences the collectability and the administrability of taxes, enforceability is crucial to ensure efficiency of the tax system.

- **Flexibility:** Taxation systems should be flexible and dynamic enough to ensure they keep pace with technological and commercial developments. It is important that a tax system is dynamic and flexible enough to meet the current revenue needs of governments while adapting to changing needs on an ongoing basis. This means that the structural features of the system should be durable in a changing policy context, yet flexible and dynamic enough to allow governments to respond as required to keep pace with technological and commercial developments, taking into account that future developments will often be difficult to predict.

11. Equity is also an important consideration within a tax policy framework. Equity has two main elements; horizontal equity and vertical equity. Horizontal equity suggests that taxpayers in similar circumstances should bear a similar tax burden. Vertical equity is a normative concept, whose definition can differ from one user to another. According to some, it suggests that taxpayers in better circumstances should bear a larger part of the tax burden as a proportion of their income. In practice, the interpretation of vertical equity depends on the extent to which countries want to diminish income variation and whether it should be applied to income earned in a specific period or to lifetime income. Equity is traditionally delivered through the design of the personal tax and transfer systems.

12. Equity may also refer to inter-nation equity. As a theory, inter-nation equity is concerned with the allocation of national gain and loss in the international context and aims to ensure that each country receives an equitable share of tax revenues from cross-border transactions (OECD, 2001). The tax policy principle of inter-nation equity has been an important consideration in the debate on the division of taxing rights between source and residence countries. At the time of the Ottawa work on the taxation of electronic commerce, this important concern was recognised by stating that "any adaptation of the existing international taxation principles should be structured to maintain fiscal sovereignty of countries, [...] to achieve a fair sharing of the tax base from electronic commerce between countries..." (OECD, 2001: 228).

13. Tax policy choices often reflect decisions by policy makers on the relative importance of each of these principles and will also reflect wider economic and social policy considerations outside the field of tax.

2.2. Taxes on income and consumption

14. Most countries impose taxes on both income and consumption. While income taxes are levied on net income (i.e. from labour and capital) over an annual tax period, consumption taxes operate as a levy on expenditure relating to the consumption of goods and services, imposed at the time of the transaction.

15. There are a variety of forms of income and consumption taxes. Income tax is generally due on the net income realised by the taxpayer over an income period. In contrast, consumption taxes find their taxable event in a transaction, the exchange of goods and services for consideration either at the last point of sale to the final end user (retail sales tax and VAT), or on intermediate transactions between businesses (VAT) (OECD, 2011), or through levies on particular goods or services such as excise taxes, customs and import duties. Income taxes are levied at the place of source of income while consumption taxes are levied at the place of destination (i.e. the importing country).

16. It is also worth noting that the tax burden is not always borne by those who are legally required to pay the tax. Depending on the price elasticity of the factors of production (which in turn depends on the preferences of consumers, the mobility of factors of production,

the degree of competition etc.), the tax burden may be shifted and thus both income and consumption taxes can have a similar tax incidence. In general, it is said that the tax incidence falls upon capital, labour and/or consumption. For example, if capital were more mobile than labour and the market is a highly competitive and well-functioning one, most of the tax burden would be borne by workers.

2.3. Corporate income tax

17. Although the tax base can be defined in a great variety of ways, corporate income tax (CIT) generally relies on a broad tax base, formulated to encompass all types of income derived by the corporation whatever their nature,[1] which encompasses the normal return on equity capital in addition to what can be described as "pure" or "economic rents" i.e. what the enterprise earns from particular competitive advantages which may be related to advantageous production factors (such as natural resources that are easily exploitable or low labour costs) or advantages related to the market in which the products will be sold (e.g. a monopolistic position).

18. At the time CIT systems were introduced, one of their primary objectives was to act as a prepayment of personal income taxes due by the shareholders (i.e. the "gap-filling" function (Bird, 2002), also referred to as the "deferral justification"), thereby preventing potentially indefinite deferral of personal income tax (Vann, 2010). As a result, the corporate tax base was seen as a proxy for the return on equity capital. It follows that corporate taxes are generally imposed on net profits, that is receipts minus expenses. Two basic models, different in their approach but similar in their practical result, are used to assess this taxable income:

- The receipts-and-outgoings system (or profit and loss method): net income is determined as the difference between all recognised income derived by a corporation in the tax period and all deductible expenses incurred by the corporation in the same tax period.
- The balance-sheet system (or net-worth comparison method): net income is determined by comparing the value of the net assets in the balance sheet of the taxpayer at the end of the tax period (plus dividends distributed) with the value of the net assets in the balance sheet of the taxpayer at the beginning of the tax period.

19. Some countries have achieved substantial uniformity, except for some differences where the accounting treatment may be vulnerable to manipulations intended to distort the measurement of taxable income (e.g. denial of deduction of certain expenses, different method of recognition of capital expenditures, different timing in recognition of gains on certain fixed assets). In other countries tax and financial accounting are substantially independent, with tax law provisions addressing to a large extent the treatment of the transactions entered into by a corporation.

2.3.1. The taxation of cross-border income under domestic corporate income tax laws

20. It is commonly accepted that there are two aspects to a state's sovereignty: the power over a territory ("enforcement jurisdiction") and the power over a particular set of subjects ("political allegiance"). This binary nature of sovereignty was strongly rooted in the minds of the people during the 19th and 20th century and exercised a significant influence in the fashioning of one State's jurisdiction to tax. Conscious that taxes ought to be confined to taxable subjects and objects that have some sort of connection with the imposing State, policy makers reached the conclusion that a legitimate tax claim ought

to be either based on the relationship to a person (i.e. a "personal attachment") or on the relationship to a territory (i.e. a "territorial attachment") (Schon, 2010; Beale, 1935).

21. Along the same line, the dual nature of sovereignty has also contributed to the formulation of the realistic doctrine, which is driven by concerns for the enforcement, administration, collection of taxes and came to limit the traditional notion of sovereignty (Tadmore, 2007). While a state's right to levy income taxes relies on territory or residence, the realistic doctrine advances that without the power to tax, there is no jurisdiction to tax and is more concerned with the exercise of taxing rights by the State in an effective manner (Tadmore, 2007). Under the realistic doctrine, a distinction is made between jurisdiction to impose taxes and jurisdiction to enforce them, also called "the enforcement jurisdiction" (Hellerstein, 2009) and emphasis is placed on practicality over theory.

22. Domestic tax rules for the taxation of cross-border income generally address two situations: the taxation of outbound investments of resident companies, and the taxation of inbound investments of non-resident companies. With respect to the former category, the definition of residence is a key notion. Some countries determine the residence of a corporation based on formal criteria such as place of incorporation. In other countries, the residence of a corporation is determined by reference factual criteria such as place of effective management or similar concepts. Some countries have mixed systems, where there is both a place of incorporation test and a place of effective management test.

23. With respect to taxation of outbound investments of resident companies, two broad models can be identified: the worldwide system and the territorial system. It should be noted that these categories are simplifications, as most countries in practice apply a combination of both systems.

24. A country employing a worldwide system subjects its residents to tax on their worldwide income whether derived from sources in or outside its territory. In order to implement the residence principle, the tax administration in the country of residence has to

Box 2.1. **Controlled foreign company (CFC) rules**

CFC rules provide for the taxation of profits derived by non-resident companies in the hands of their resident shareholders. They can be thought of as a category of anti-avoidance rules, or an extension of the tax base, designed to tax shareholders on passive or highly mobile income derived by non-resident companies in circumstances where, in the absence of such rules, that income would otherwise have been exempt from taxation (e.g. under a territorial system) or only taxed on repatriation (e.g. under a worldwide tax system with a deferral regime).

CFC rules vary substantially in approach. In some instances, they seek to reduce tax incentives to undertake business or investment through a non-resident company. But they may also include provisions (such as the exclusion of active income) intended to ensure that certain types of investment in a foreign jurisdiction by residents of the country applying the CFC regime will be subject to no greater overall tax burden than investment in the same foreign jurisdiction by shareholders that are not residents. Most systems of CFC rules have the character of anti-avoidance rules targeting diverted income, and are not intended to deter genuine foreign investment.

CFC rules require some or all of the foreign company's profits to be included in the income of the resident shareholder, and thus may also have the effect of protecting the tax base of the source country by discouraging investments that erode its tax base or that are designed to shift profit to low-tax jurisdictions.

collect information with respect to the foreign-source income of their residents. As a result, countries rarely, if ever, adopt pure worldwide systems of taxation. Instead, under most of these systems foreign-sourced profits of foreign subsidiaries are taxed upon repatriation (the deferral system), and not on an accrual basis. In addition, the credit for tax paid on profits generated abroad is usually limited to the amount of taxation that would have been imposed on the foreign earnings by the residence country, thereby ensuring that the worldwide system does not impair the residence state's taxation of its own domestic source income.

25. A country applying a territorial CIT system subjects its residents to tax only on the income derived from sources located in its territory. This means that resident companies are taxed only on their local income – i.e. income deemed to have their source inside the country. Determining the source of business income is therefore key in a territorial system.

26. With respect to the taxation of inbound investments of non-resident companies, both a worldwide tax system and a territorial tax system impose tax on income arising from domestic sources. Hence, the determination of source of the income is key. Sourcing rules vary from country to country. With respect to business income, the concept of source under domestic law often parallels the concept of permanent establishment (PE) as defined under tax treaties. Such income is typically taxed on a net basis. For practical reasons however, it may be difficult for a country to tax certain items of income derived by non-resident corporations. It may also be difficult to know what expenses a non-resident incurred in earning such income. As a result, taxation at source of certain types of income (e.g. interest, royalties, dividends) derived by non-resident companies commonly occurs by means of withholding taxes at a gross rate. To allow for the fact that no deductions are allowed, gross-based withholding taxes are imposed at rates that are usually lower than standard corporate tax rates.

2.3.2. The taxation of cross-border income under double tax treaties

27. The exercise of tax sovereignty may entail conflicting claims from two or more jurisdictions over the same taxable amount, which may lead to juridical double taxation, which is the imposition of comparable taxes in two (or more) states on the same taxpayer in respect of the same income. Double taxation has harmful effects on the international exchange of goods and services and cross-border movements of capital, technology and persons. Bilateral tax treaties address instances of double taxation by allocating taxing rights to the contracting states. Most existing bilateral tax treaties are concluded on the basis of a model, such as the OECD Model Tax Convention or the United Nations Model, which are direct descendants of the first Model of bilateral tax treaty drafted in 1928 by the League of Nations. As a result, while there can be substantial variations between one tax treaty and another, double tax treaties generally follow a relatively uniform structure, which can be viewed as a list of provisions performing separate and distinct functions: *(i)* articles dealing with the scope and application of the tax treaty, *(ii)* articles addressing the conflict of taxing jurisdiction, *(iii)* articles providing for double taxation relief, *(iv)* articles concerned with the prevention of tax avoidance and fiscal evasion, and *(v)* articles addressing miscellaneous matters (e.g. administrative assistance).

2.3.2.1. A historical overview of the conceptual basis for allocating taxing rights

28. As global trade increased in the early 20th century, and concerns around instances of double taxation grew, the League of Nations appointed in the early 1920s four economists (Bruins et al., 1923) to study the issue of double taxation from a theoretical

and scientific perspective. One of the tasks of the group was to determine whether it is possible to formulate general principles as the basis of an international tax framework capable of preventing double taxation, including in relation to business profits.[2] In this context the group identified the concept of economic allegiance as a basis to design such international tax framework. Economic allegiance is based on factors aimed at measuring the existence and extent of the economic relationships between a particular state and the income or person to be taxed. The four economists identified four factors comprising economic allegiance, namely *(i)* origin of wealth or income, *(ii) situs* of wealth or income, *(iii)* enforcement of the rights to wealth or income, and *(iv)* place of residence or domicile of the person entitled to dispose of the wealth or income.

29. Among those factors, the economists concluded that in general, the greatest weight should be given to "the origin of the wealth [i.e. source] and the residence or domicile of the owner who consumes the wealth". The origin of wealth was defined for these purposes as all stages involved in the creation of wealth: "the original physical appearance of the wealth, its subsequent physical adaptations, its transport, its direction and its sale". In other words, the group advocated that tax jurisdiction should generally be allocated between the state of source and the state of residence depending on the nature of the income in question. Under this approach, in simple situations where all (or a majority of) factors of economic allegiance coincide, jurisdiction to tax would go exclusively with the state where the relevant elements of economic allegiance have been characterised. In more complex situations in which conflicts between the relevant factors of economic allegiance arise, jurisdiction to tax would be shared between the different states on the basis of the relative economic ties the taxpayer and his income have with each of them.

30. On the basis of this premise, the group considered the proper place of taxation for the different types of wealth or income. Business profits were not treated separately, but considered under specific classes of undertakings covering activities nowadays generally categorised as "bricks and mortar" businesses, namely "Mines and Oil Wells", "Industrial Establishments" or "Factories", and "Commercial Establishments".[3] In respect of all those classes of activities, the group came to the conclusion that the place where income was produced is "of preponderant weight" and "in an ideal division a preponderant share should be assigned to the place of origin". In other words, in allocating jurisdiction to tax on business profits, greatest importance was attached to the nexus between business income and the various physical places contributing to the production of the income.

31. Many of the report's conclusions proved to be controversial and were not entirely followed in double tax treaties. In particular, the economists' preference for a general exemption in the source state for all "income going abroad" as a practical method of avoiding double taxation[4] was explicitly rejected by the League of Nations, who chose as the basic structure for its 1928 Model the "classification and assignment of sources" method – i.e. attach full or limited source taxation to certain classes of income and assign the right to tax other income exclusively to the state of residence. Nevertheless, the theoretical background enunciated in the 1923 Report has survived remarkably intact and is generally considered as the "intellectual base" (Ault, 1992: 567) from which the various League of Nations models (and consequently virtually all modern bilateral tax treaties) developed (Avi-Yonah, 1996).

32. Before endorsing the economic allegiance principle, the group of four economists briefly discussed other theories of taxation, including the benefit principle (called at the time the "exchange theory"), and observed that the answers formulated by this doctrine had to a large extent been supplanted by the theory of ability to pay. Several authors consider

that the decline of the benefit theory is undeniable as far as determination of the amount of tax liability is concerned, but not in the debate on taxing jurisdiction in an international context (Vogel, 1988). Under the benefit theory, a jurisdiction's right to tax rests on the totality of benefits and state services provided to the taxpayer that interacts with a country (Pinto, 2006), and corporations, in their capacity as agents integrated into the economic life of a particular country, ought to contribute to that country's public expenditures. In other words, the benefit theory provides that a state has the right to tax resident and non-resident corporations who derive a benefit from the services it provides. These benefits can be specific or general in nature. The provision of education, police, fire and defence protection are among the more obvious examples. But the state can also provide conducive and operational legal structures for the proper functioning of business, for example in the form of a stable legal and regulatory environment, the protection of intellectual property and the knowledge-based capital of the firm, the enforcement of consumer protection laws, or well-developed transportation, telecommunication, utilities and other infrastructure (Pinto, 2006).

2.3.2.2. Allocation of taxing rights under tax treaties

33. At the time the four economists presented their report, various jurisdictions had already started addressing juridical double taxation through bilateral and unilateral measures. The League of Nations Tax Committees built upon the practical experience of government experts with negotiating and administering contemporary treaties. Partly as a result of historic path dependence, and partly due to the need for an effective way to allocate taxing rights between tax systems that may diverge significantly, avoidance of double taxation was not addressed by an alternative system such as formulary apportionment, or another system based on the principles identified by the four economists. Instead, supported by the development of the OECD and UN Model treaties, the international tax framework developed around a vast network of bilateral tax treaties following the so-called "classification and assignment of sources" method, in which different types of income are subject to different distributive rules. This schedular nature of distributive rules entails a preliminary step, whereby the income subject to conflicting claims is first classified into one of the categories of income defined by the treaty. Where an item of income falls under more than one category of income, double tax treaties resolve the conflict through ordering rules. Once the income is characterised for treaty purposes, the treaty provides distributive rules that generally either grant one contracting state the exclusive right to exercise domestic taxing rights or grant one contracting state priority to exercise its domestic taxing right while reserving a residual taxing right to the other contracting state.

34. Treaty rules provide that business profits derived by an enterprise are taxable exclusively by the state of residence unless the enterprise carries on business in the other state through a PE situated therein. In the latter situation, the source state may tax only the profits that are attributable to the PE. The PE concept is thus used to determine whether or not a contracting state is entitled to exercise its taxing rights with respect to the business profits of a non-resident taxpayer. Special rules apply, however, to profits falling into certain enumerated categories of income, such as dividends, interest, royalties, and capital gains.

35. The PE concept effectively acts as a threshold which, by measuring the level of economic presence of a foreign enterprise in a given State through objective criteria, determines the circumstances in which the foreign enterprise can be considered sufficiently integrated into the economy of a state to justify taxation in that state (Holmes, 2007; Rohatgi, 2005). A link can thus reasonably be made between the requirement of a sufficient level of economic presence under the existing PE threshold and the economic allegiance factors developed by the group of economists more than 80 years ago. This legacy is regularly emphasised in literature (Skaar,

1991), as well as reflected in the existing OECD Commentaries when it is stated that the PE threshold "has a long history and reflects the international consensus that, as a general rule, until an enterprise of one State has a permanent establishment in another State, it should not properly be regarded as participating in the economic life of that other State to such an extent that the other State should have taxing rights on its profits".[5] By requiring a sufficient level of economic presence, this threshold is also intended to ensure that a source country imposing tax has enforcement jurisdiction, the administrative capability to enforce its substantive jurisdiction rights over the non-resident enterprise.

36. The PE definition initially comprised two distinct thresholds: *(i)* a fixed place through which the business of the enterprise is wholly or partly carried on or, where no place of business can be found, *(ii)* a person acting on behalf of the foreign enterprise and habitually exercising an authority to conclude contracts in the name of the foreign enterprise. In both situations a certain level of physical presence in the source jurisdiction is required, either directly or through the actions of a dependent agent. Some extensions have been made over time to address changes in business conditions. For example, the development of the service industry has led to the inclusion in many existing bilateral treaties of an additional threshold whereby the performance of services by employees (or other persons receiving instructions) of a non-resident enterprise may justify source-based taxation as soon as the duration of such services exceeds a specific period of time, irrespective of whether the services are performed through a fixed place of business (Alessi, Wijnen and de Goede, 2011).

37. Treaty rules on business profits provide that only the profits "attributable" to the PE are taxable in the jurisdiction where the PE is located. These are the profits that the PE would be expected to make if it were a distinct and separate enterprise.

38. By virtue of separate distributive rules which take priority over the PE rule, some specific items of income may be taxed in the source jurisdiction even though none of the alternative PE thresholds are met in that country. These include:

- Income derived from immovable property (and capital gains derived from the sale thereof), which generally may be taxed by the country of source where the immovable property is located.
- Business profits that include certain types of payments which, depending on the treaty, may include dividends, interest, royalties or technical fees, on which the treaty allows the country of source to levy a limited withholding tax.

39. In the case of outbound payments of dividends, interest, and royalties, countries commonly impose tax under their domestic law on a gross basis (i.e. not reduced by the deduction of expenses) by means of a withholding tax. Bilateral tax treaties commonly specify a maximum rate at which the source state may impose such a withholding tax, with the residual right to tax belonging to the state of residence.[6] However, where the asset giving rise to such types of income is effectively connected to a PE of the non-resident enterprise in the same state, the rules for attribution of profits to a PE control (Article 10(4), 11(4) and 12(3) of the OECD Model Tax Convention).

40. Where priority is given by bilateral tax treaties to the taxing rights of the source jurisdiction, the resident state must provide double taxation relief. Two mechanisms are generally available in bilateral tax treaties, namely the exemption method and the credit method. But in practice many jurisdictions, and accordingly existing bilateral tax treaties, use a mixture of these approaches – i.e. exemption method for income attributable to a PE, and credit method for items of income subject to a withholding – in relation to business profits (Rohatgi, 2005).

2.4. Value added taxes and other indirect consumption taxes

41. Value added taxes (VAT) and other consumption taxes are generally designed to be indirect taxes. While they are generally intended to tax the final consumption of goods and services, they are collected from the suppliers of these goods and services rather than directly from the consumers. The consumers bear the burden of these taxes, in principle, as part of the market price of the goods or services purchased.

42. Two categories of consumption taxes are generally distinguished (OECD, 2013):

- General taxes on goods and services, consisting of VAT and its equivalent in several jurisdictions, sales taxes and other general taxes on goods and services.
- Taxes on specific goods and services, consisting primarily of excise taxes, customs and import duties, and taxes on specific services (e.g. taxes on insurance premiums and financial services).

43. This section focuses mainly on VAT, which is the primary form of consumption tax for countries around the world. The combination of the global spread of VAT and the rapid globalisation of economic activity, which resulted in increased interaction between VAT systems, and increasing VAT rates (OECD, 2012) have raised the profile of VAT as a significant issue in cross-border trade.

2.4.1. Main design features of a VAT

2.4.1.1. Overarching purpose of a VAT – A broad-based tax on final consumption

44. The term VAT is used here to cover all value added taxes, by whatever name, in whatever language, they are known. Note, for instance, that many countries refer to their value added taxes as a "goods and services tax" (GST) (e.g. Australia, Canada, India, New Zealand and Singapore). While there is considerable diversity in the structure of the VAT systems currently in place, most of these systems are grounded on certain fundamental design principles that are described in this section, at least in theory if not in practice. The overarching purpose of a VAT is to impose a broad-based tax on consumption, which is understood to mean final consumption by households.

45. In principle only private individuals, as distinguished from businesses, engage in the consumption at which a VAT is targeted. In practice, however, many VAT systems impose VAT burden not only on final household consumption, but also on various entities that are involved in non-business activities or in VAT-exempt activities. In such situations, VAT can be viewed alternatively as treating such entities as if they were end consumers, or as "input taxing" the supplies made by such entities on the presumption that the burden of the VAT imposed will be passed on in the prices of the outputs of those non-business activities.

2.4.1.2. The central design feature of a VAT – Staged collection process

46. The central design feature of a VAT, and the feature from which it derives its name, is that the tax is collected through a staged process. Each business (taxable person) in the supply chain is responsible for collecting the tax on its outputs (supplies) and remitting the proportion of tax corresponding to its margin, i.e. the value added, in a particular tax period. This means that the taxable person remits the difference between the VAT imposed on its taxed outputs (output tax) and the VAT imposed on its taxed inputs (input tax) for this period. Thus, the tax is in principle collected on the "value added" at each stage of production and

distribution. In this respect, the VAT differs from a retail sales tax, which taxes consumption through a single-stage levy imposed in theory only at the point of final sale.

47. This central design feature of the VAT, coupled with the fundamental principle that the burden of the tax should not rest on businesses, requires a mechanism for relieving businesses of the burden of the VAT they pay when they acquire goods or services. There are two principal approaches to implementing the staged collection process while relieving businesses of the VAT burden. Under the invoice-credit method, each taxable person charges VAT at the rate specified for each supply and passes to the customer an invoice showing the amount of tax charged. If the customer is also a taxable person, it will be able to credit that input tax against the output tax charged on its sales, each being identified at the transaction level, remitting the balance to the tax authorities or receiving a refund of any excess credits. Under the subtraction method, the tax is levied directly on an accounts-based measure of value added, which is determined for each business by subtracting the taxable person's allowable expenditure on inputs for the tax period from taxable outputs for that period and applying the tax rate to the resulting amount (Cockfield et al., 2013). Almost all jurisdictions that operate a VAT use the invoice-credit method, the Japanese system being the most notable example of a subtraction method consumption tax.

48. VAT exemptions create an important exception to the neutrality of VAT. When a supply is VAT-exempt, this means that no output tax is charged on the supply and that the supplier is not entitled to credit the related input tax. Many VAT systems apply exemptions for activities that are hard to tax (the exemption for financial services being the most notable example) and/or to pursue distributional objectives (agricultural and fuel exemptions and exemptions for basic health and education are commonly encountered). One adverse consequence of VAT exemptions is that they create "cascading" when applied in a business-to-business (B2B) context. The business making an exempt supply can be expected to pass on the uncreditable input tax in the price of this supply, while this "hidden tax" can subsequently not be credited by the recipient business.

2.4.2. VAT on cross-border transaction – The destination principle

49. The fundamental policy issue in relation to the international application of the VAT is whether the levy should be imposed by the jurisdiction of origin or by the jurisdiction of destination. Under the destination principle, tax is ultimately levied only on the final consumption that occurs within the taxing jurisdiction. Under the origin principle, the tax is levied in the various jurisdictions where the value was added.

50. Under the destination principle, no VAT is levied on exports and the associated input tax is refunded to the exporting business (this is often called "free of VAT" or "zero-rated"), while imports are taxed on the same basis and at the same rates as domestic supplies. Accordingly, the total tax paid in relation to the supply is determined by the rules applicable in the jurisdiction of its consumption and all revenue accrues to the jurisdiction where the supply to the final consumer occurs. The application of the destination principle in VAT thus achieves neutrality in international trade, as there is no advantage in buying from a low or no-tax jurisdiction, nor do high and/or multiple VAT rates distort the level or composition of a country's exports.

51. By contrast, under the origin principle each jurisdiction would levy VAT on the value created within its own borders. Under an origin-based regime, exporting jurisdictions would tax exports on the same basis and at the same rate as domestic supplies, while importing jurisdictions would give a credit against their own VAT for the hypothetical tax that would have been paid at the importing jurisdiction's own rate. This approach runs counter to the

core features of a tax on consumption, in which the revenue should accrue to the jurisdiction where the final consumption takes place. Under the origin principle, these revenues are shared amongst jurisdictions where value is added. By imposing tax at the various rates applicable in the jurisdictions where value is added, the origin principle could influence the economic or geographical structure of the value chain and undermine neutrality in international trade.

52. For these reasons, there is widespread consensus that the destination principle, with revenue accruing to the country where final consumption occurs, is preferable to the origin principle from both a theoretical and practical standpoint. In fact, the destination principle is the international norm and is sanctioned by World Trade Organisation (WTO) rules. Footnote 1 of the WTO's *Agreement on Subsidies and Countervailing Measures* provides that "…the exemption of an exported product from duties or taxes borne by the like product when destined for domestic consumption, or the remission of such duties or taxes in amounts not in excess of those which have accrued, shall not be deemed to be a subsidy."

2.4.3. Implementing the destination principle

53. While the destination principle has been widely accepted as the basis for applying VAT to international trade, its implementation is nevertheless diverse across jurisdictions. This can lead to double taxation or unintended non-taxation and to complexity and uncertainty for businesses and tax administrations. In order to apply the destination principle, VAT systems must have a mechanism for identifying the destination of supplies. Because VAT is generally applied on a transaction-by-transaction basis, VAT systems contain "place of taxation" rules that address all transactions, building on "proxies" that indicate where the good or service supplied is expected to be used by a business in the production and distribution process (if the supply is made to a business) or consumed (if the supply is made to a final consumer).

54. The following paragraphs provide a concise overview of the mechanisms for identifying the destination of a supply, first looking at supplies of goods and subsequently at supplies of services.

2.4.3.1. Implementing the destination principle – Goods

55. The term "goods" generally means "tangible property" for VAT purposes. The VAT treatment of supplies of goods normally depends on the location of the goods at the time of the transaction and/or their location as a result of the transaction. The supply of a good is in principle subject to VAT in the jurisdiction where the good is located at the time of the transaction. When a transaction involves goods being moved from one jurisdiction to another, the exported goods are generally free of VAT in the seller's jurisdiction (and are freed of any input VAT via successive businesses' deductions of input tax), whilst the imports are subject to the same VAT as equivalent domestic goods in the purchaser's jurisdiction. The VAT on imports is generally collected from the importer at the same time as customs duties, before the goods are released from customs control, although in some jurisdictions collection is postponed until declared on the importer's next VAT return. Allowing deduction of the VAT incurred at importation in the same way as input tax deduction on a domestic supply ensures neutrality and limits distortions in relation to international trade.

56. Many VAT systems apply an exemption for the importation of relatively low value goods. These exemptions are generally motivated by the consideration that the administrative costs of bringing these low value items into the customs system are likely to outweigh the revenue gained. If these additional costs would be passed on to consumers, the charges could

be disproportionally high compared to the value of the goods. Most OECD countries apply such a VAT relief arrangement, with thresholds varying widely across countries.

2.4.3.2. Implementing the destination principle – Services

57. The VAT legislation in many countries tends to define a "service" negatively as "anything that is not otherwise defined", or to define a "supply of services" as anything other than a "supply of goods". While this generally also includes a reference to intangibles, some jurisdictions regard intangibles as a separate category. For the purposes of this section references to "services" include "intangibles" unless otherwise stated.[7]

58. A wide range of proxies can be used by VAT systems to identify the place of taxation of services, including the place of performance of the service, the place of establishment or actual location of the supplier, the residence or the actual location of the consumer, and the location of tangible property (for services connected with tangible property, such as repair services). Many systems use multiple proxies before the place of taxation is finally determined and may use different rules for inbound, outbound, wholly foreign, and wholly domestic supplies (Cockfield et al., 2013).

59. The application of these principles for identifying the place of taxation has become increasingly difficult as volumes of cross-border services are growing. VAT systems have considerable difficulties to determine where services are deemed to be consumed, to monitor this and to ensure collection of the tax, particularly where businesses sell services in jurisdictions where they do not have a physical presence. In practice, broadly two approaches can be distinguished for applying VAT to cross-border supplies of services (Ebrill et al., 2001):

- The first approach focuses on the jurisdiction where the customer is resident (established, located). Under this approach, when the customer is resident in another jurisdiction than the supplier, the supply is free of VAT ("zero-rated") in the jurisdiction of the supplier and is subject to VAT in the jurisdiction of the customer. In principle, the supplier needs to register in the customer's jurisdiction and collect and remit the tax there. In practice, when the customer is a VAT-registered business, the VAT is often collected through a "reverse charge" mechanism. This is a tax mechanism that switches the liability to pay the tax from the supplier to the customer. The business customer will generally be able to credit the input tax on the acquired service immediately against the output tax liability. Some VAT systems therefore do not require the reverse charge to be made if the customer is entitled to a full input tax credit in respect of the purchase.
- Under the second approach, the supply of the service is subjected to VAT in the jurisdiction where the supplier is resident (established, located). Supplies of services are then subject to VAT in the supplier's jurisdiction, even when they are performed abroad or supplied to foreign customers. Customers that are taxable businesses are generally able to apply for a refund of the VAT paid on business inputs in the supplier's jurisdiction, from the tax authorities of that jurisdiction.

60. For B2B supplies, both approaches have ultimately the same effect, in that "exported" services are relieved from any VAT burden in the origin country and subject to VAT in the jurisdiction where the service is deemed to be used by the business customer. The first approach, which identifies the place of taxation by reference to the location of the customer, is recommended as the main rule for applying VAT to B2B supplies of services by the OECD's *International VAT/GST Guidelines* (OECD, 2014). It was also the recommended approach for

"cross-border supplies of services and intangibles that are capable of delivery from a remote location" under the OECD's 2003 E-commerce Guidelines (OECD, 2003a). A key advantage of this approach is that it avoids the need for cross-border refunds of VAT to businesses that have acquired services abroad, which often involve considerable administrative and compliance burden and costs for tax administrations and businesses. In practice, however, many VAT systems apply the second approach, taxing services by reference to the location of the supplier, mainly to minimise the risk of fraud through claims of exported services which are typically difficult to verify.

61. Whereas both approaches lead to a result that is consistent with the destination principle in a B2B context, the situation is more complicated for business-to-consumer (B2C) supplies. Implementing the destination principle by zero-rating cross-border supplies to non-resident final consumers and relying on self-assessment by the consumer in its jurisdiction of residence, is likely to result in widespread non-taxation of these supplies in practice. While reverse charge methods operate relatively well in a B2B context, they are generally viewed as ineffectual for B2C supplies. Such a method would require final consumers to self-assess their VAT liability on services purchased abroad, e.g. through their income tax returns. The level of voluntary compliance can be expected to be low, as private consumers have no incentive to voluntarily declare and pay the tax due, unlike taxable persons who can credit input tax paid against output tax (Lamensch, 2012). Collecting and enforcing this VAT, which may be small amounts in many cases, from large numbers of people is likely to involve considerable complexity and costs for tax payers and tax authorities.

62. Most VAT systems therefore tax supplies of services to private consumers in the jurisdiction where the supplier is resident (established, located). Many jurisdictions that zero-rate cross-border supplies of services to non-resident customers, limit the application of this regime to B2B supplies, notably by applying it only to services that are typically supplied to businesses (advertising, consultancy, etc.) Supplies to foreign private consumers are then subject to VAT in the supplier's jurisdiction while services acquired from abroad by resident final consumers are not subject to VAT in the consumer's jurisdiction. While this approach, which effectively results in origin taxation, is likely to be less vulnerable to fraud, it may create an incentive for suppliers to divert their activities to jurisdictions where no or a low VAT is applied and to sell remote services into foreign markets VAT-free or at a low VAT rate. This potential distortion and the associated revenue losses become increasingly significant as volumes of cross-border supplies of services keep growing.

63. More and more jurisdictions therefore consider ways to implement a destination based approach for both B2B and B2C cross-border supplies of services, thereby relying on a system that would require suppliers to collect and remit the tax in line with what was recommended by the OECD's E-commerce Guidelines. As self-assessment methods are unlikely to offer an effective solution for collecting the tax at destination in a B2C-context, a system that requires suppliers to collect and remit the tax may appear the only realistic alternative. This was notably the conclusion of the OECD's Consumption Tax Guidance Series, which provided guidance for the implementation of the E-commerce Guidelines (OECD, 2003b-c-d). This guidance indicated that countries may consider it necessary for non-resident vendors to register and account for the tax in the jurisdiction of consumption, and it recommended the use of simplified registration regimes and registration thresholds to minimise the potential compliance burden. The most notable application of a destination-based approach for taxing B2C cross-border supplies of services relying on a simplified registration system for non-resident suppliers, is the European Union's "One Stop Shop" scheme.

Notes

1. This global approach is generally co-ordinated with specific tax regimes applying to items of income derived from specific types of assets (e.g. participation shares, patents and trademarks).

2. Noteworthy, at the time the study was performed most of the industrialised countries had not yet introduced in their domestic legislation a modern corporate income tax system integrated with personal income taxes.

3. Professional earnings were considered separately, unless the concerned activity gives rise to a branch in another country, in which case the occupation becomes a commercial enterprise and, according to the economist, ought to fall under the same allocation rule as other businesses.

4. The predominant argument put forward by the economists to reach a conclusion (i.e. exclusive taxation in the state of residence) was convenience and practicability.

5. OECD Commentaries on Art. 7, par. 11; see also in relation to service activities, Commentaries on Art. 5, par. 42.11.

6. These limitations on withholding at source generally do not apply, however, to excessive payments of interest or royalties to related parties. For instance, paragraph 6 of Article 11 of the OECD Model Convention provides that, if there is a special relationship between the payer and the recipient as a result of which the interest is higher than that which they would have agreed upon in the absence of such a relationship, the excess part remains taxable according to the laws of both the source state and the residence state. Similar rules apply with respect to excessive royalties under paragraph 4 of Article 12 of the OECD Model Tax Convention.

7. Many VAT systems define a "service" negatively as "anything that is not otherwise defined", or a "supply of services" as anything other than a "supply of goods". While this generally also includes a reference to intangibles, some jurisdictions regard intangibles as a separate category, and this is explicitly recognised in this report where relevant. It should be noted that the term "intangibles" when used for transfer pricing and direct tax purposes has a different meaning than that used under certain VAT legislations.

Bibliography

Alessi, A., J. de Goede and W. Wijnen (2011), "The Treatment of Services in Tax Treaties", *Bulletin for International Taxation*, 2012, Vol. 66, No. 1.

Ault, H.J. (1992), "Corporate Integration, Tax Treaties and the Division of the International Tax Base: Principles and Practice", 47 *Tax L. Review*, p. 567.

Avi-Yonah, R.S. (1996), "The Structure of International Taxation: A Proposal for Simplification", *74 Tax L. Review*, p. 1301.

Beale, J.H (1935), *A Treatise on the Conflict of Laws*, Vol. 1, p. 275.

Bird, R.M. (2002), "Why Tax Corporations?" *Bulletin for International Tax*, Vol. 56, No. 5, IBFD, Amsterdam.

Bruins et al. (1923), *Report on Double Taxation submitted to the Financial Committee*, No. E.F.S. 73.F.19, League of Nations, Geneva.

Cockfield, A. et al. (2013), *Taxing Global Digital Commerce*, Kluwer Law International BV, the Netherlands.

Ebrill.L. et al. (2001), *The Modern VAT*, International Monetary Fund, Washington, DC.

Hellerstein, W. (2009), "Jurisdiction to Impose and Enforce Income and Consumption Taxes: Towards a Unified Conception of Nexus in Value Added Tax and Direct Tax: Similarities and Differences", IBFD, the Netherlands.

Holmes, K. (2007), *International Tax Policy and Double Tax Treaties*, IBFD Publications, the Netherlands.

Lamensch, M. (2012), "Are 'reverse charging' and the 'one shop scheme' efficient ways to collect VAT on digital supplies?" in World Journal of VAT Law, Vol 1, Isssue 1.

OECD (2014), *International VAT/GST Guidelines*, OECD, Paris, www.oecd.org/ctp/consumption/international-vat-gst-guidelines.htm.

OECD (2013), *Revenue Statistics 1965-2012*, OECD Publishing, Paris, http://dx.doi.org/10.1787/rev_stats-2013-en-fr.

OECD (2012), Model Tax Convention on Income and Capital 2010 (updated 2010), OECD Publishing, Paris, http://dx.doi.org/10.1787/9789264175181-en.

OECD (2011), "Taxing Consumption" in *Consumption Tax Trends 2010: VAT/GST and Excise Rates, Trends and Administration Issues*, OECD Publishing, Paris, http://dx.doi.org/10.1787/ctt-2010-en.

OECD (2003a), *Consumption Taxation of Cross Border Services and Intangible Property in the context of E-commerce, Guidelines on the Definition of Place of Consumption*, OECD, Paris.

OECD (2003b), *Electronic Commerce-Commentary on Place of Consumption for Business to Business Supplies (Business Presence)*, OECD, Paris.

OECD (2003c), *Electronic Commerce-Simplified Registration Guidance*, OECD, Paris.

OECD (2003d), *Verification of Customer Status and Jurisdiction*, OECD, Paris.

OECD (2001), *Taxation and Electronic Commerce-Implementing the Ottawa Framework Conditions*, OECD Publishing, Paris, http://dx.doi.org/10.1787/9789264189799-en.

Pinto, D. (2006), "The Need to Reconceptualise the Permanent Establishment Threshold", Bulletin for International Taxation. IBFD pp. 266-279.

Rohatgi, R. (2005), *Basic International Taxation, Volume I: Principles*, Second Edition, Richmond Law and Tax Ltd, United Kingdom.

Schon, W. (2010), "Persons and territories: on international allocation of taxing rights", *British Tax Review*, pp. 554-562.

Skaar, A.A. (1991), *Permanent Establishment, Erosion of a Tax Treaty Principle*, Series on International Taxation, Kluwer Law and Taxation Publishers, The Netherlands.

Tadmore, N. (2007), "Source Taxation of Cross-Border Intellectual Supplies-Concepts, History and Evolution into the Digital Age", *Bulletin for International Taxation*, pp. 2-16.

Vann, R.J. (2010), "Taxing International Business Income: Hard-Boiled Wonderland and the End of the World", *World Tax Journal*, Vol. 2, No. 3.

Vogel, K. (1988), "Worldwide vs. source taxation of income – A review and re-evaluation of arguments (Part 3)", *Intertax*, Vol. 11, pp. 393-402.

WTO's *Agreement on Subsidies and Countervailing Measures*, https://www.wto.org/english/docs_e/legal_e/24-scm.pdf.

Chapter 3

Information and communication technology and its impact on the economy

This chapter examines the evolution over time of information and communication technology (ICT), including emerging and possible future developments. It then provides a conceptual overview, highlighting interactions between various layers of information and communication technology.

3.1. The evolution of information and communication technology

64. The development of ICT has been characterised by rapid technological progress that has brought prices of ICT products down rapidly, ensuring that technology can be applied throughout the economy at low cost. In many cases, the drop in prices caused by advances in technology and the pressure for constant innovation have been bolstered by a constant cycle of commoditisation that has affected many of the key technologies that have led to the growth of the digital economy. As products become successful and reach a greater market, their features have a tendency to solidify, making it more difficult for original producers to change those features easily. When features become more stable, it becomes easier for products to be copied by competitors. This is stimulated further by the process of standardisation that is characteristic of the ICT sector, which makes components interoperable, making it more difficult for individual producers to distinguish their products from others. Unless the original producer can differentiate its product from the copies (for example, by bundling its product with services or other features that are not easily duplicated), or otherwise find a way to maintain a dominant position in the market, it will be forced to compete solely on price or move to other market segments.

65. This process tends to cause prices of the commoditised goods or services to fall, and innovation to move elsewhere in the value chain. This does not necessarily mean that every single component of the commoditised product becomes a commodity. A producer of a component of the overall product can maintain or create a proprietary advantage by enhancing some elements or subsystems of that component. This can "decommoditise" those elements or subsystems of the commoditised product, creating new opportunities at a different stage of the value chain.

3.1.1. Personal computing devices

66. Early in the life of the digital economy, many manufacturers of computing hardware used proprietary hardware components, which meant that the computers of different manufacturers operated on entirely different standards. When the architecture of personal computers was largely standardised thirty years ago, however, many market participants started competing on price. That, combined with rapid technological progress, resulted in substantial drops in the price of personal computing hardware. In the period that followed, the most successful manufacturers succeeded in large part because their products integrated best with other products or because they developed the strongest marketing and distribution strategies, rather than primarily because the hardware they produced was distinguishable from those of their competitors. As mentioned above, this cycle has been paralleled at various points throughout the evolution of the digital economy, resulting in substantial changes in the digital value chain over time.

67. A relatively recent development is the advent of innovative integrated packages of hardware and software, such as smartphones and tablets (and increasingly, connected wearable devices). Designing, manufacturing and selling these devices has allowed companies to improve their position in the value chain and on the market. There appear to be two major trends that confirm the growing importance of devices. The first trend is the diversification of devices. Consumers initially accessed the Internet almost exclusively through personal computers. Now the industry has designed a wide variety of devices providing access to the web, such as smartphones, tablets, and connected TVs. The second trend is the growing specialisation in devices of businesses formerly specialised in software or other parts of the value chain. Several businesses have launched their own tablets or other devices. These devices allow them to establish a closer relationship with their

customers, allowing them to collect more detailed information so that they may provide customised service with even more relevance and added value.

68. Over time, hardware devices have both multiplied and diversified in terms of features and technical characteristics. As shown in Figure 3.1, the number of mobile devices connected to the Internet keeps rising, forming an interconnected infrastructure colloquially referred to as the Internet of Things (see Section 3.2 on discussion of emerging and potential future developments below). After a long period of personal computer commoditisation, hardware has regained importance in the value chain. At the same time, the price of devices continues to fall over time. Devices connected through the Internet operate within certain standards that accelerate their commoditisation, if only because individuals own more and more devices that must be synchronised around the same set of content and data. In addition, connected objects and devices facilitate sales of intangible goods and services (for example, a connected car becomes a point of sale for services based on geo-location, including driving assistance). For this reason, a number of businesses now use hardware devices as loss leaders in their business model, aimed at expanding the market of customers for goods and services available through those devices, or at otherwise leveraging their growing network of end users. Assuming these trends continue, it appears that for many businesses, revenue from connected devices may ultimately flow primarily from the operation rather than the continued sales of these devices.

Figure 3.1. **Percentage of fibre connections in total fixed broadband subscriptions, June 2014**

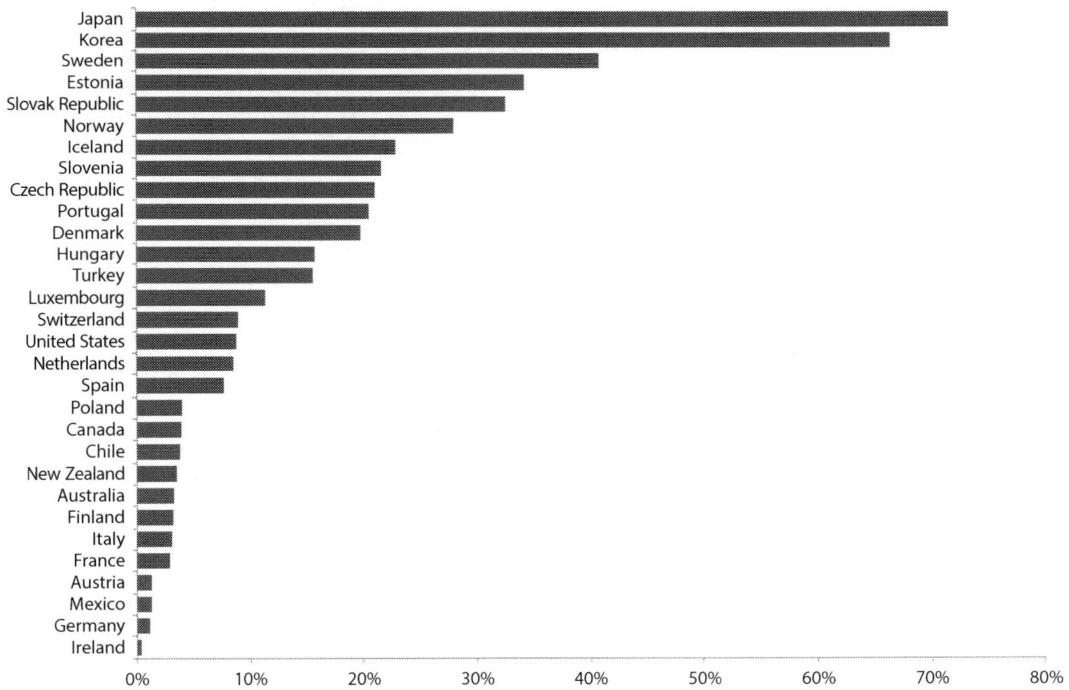

StatLink http://dx.doi.org/10.1787/9789264232440-graph47-en.

Source: OECD (2015), *OECD Digital Economy Outlook 2015*, OECD Publishing, Paris, http://dx.doi.org/10.1787/9789264232440-en.

Figure 3.2. **Total fixed, mobile and broadband access paths subscriptions (millions)**

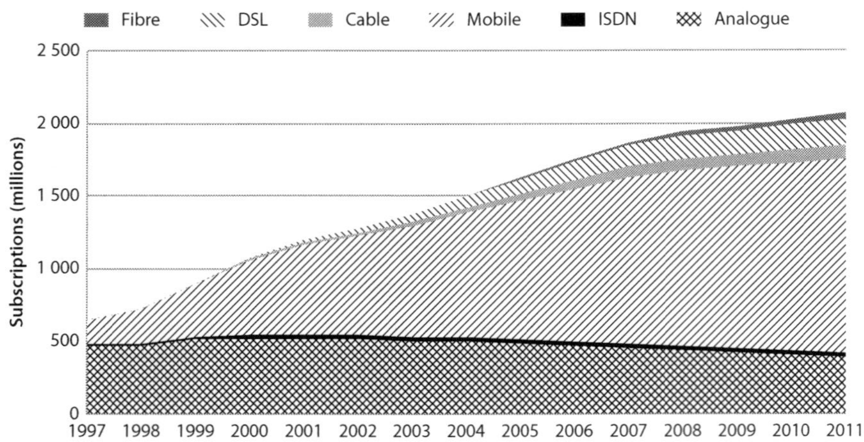

StatLink http://dx.doi.org/10.1787/comms _ outlook-2013-graph44-en.

Source: OECD (2013a), *OECD Communications Outlook 2013*, OECD Publishing, Paris, http://dx.doi.org/10.178/comms_outlook-2013-en.

3.1.2. Telecommunications networks

69. As the Internet turned into a major business phenomenon and adoption rates accelerated, the network component providers, infrastructure intermediaries, and Internet service providers (ISPs) that powered and operated the infrastructure of the telecommunications networks that form the Internet became central to the digital economy. The interconnection of networks initially gave birth to a specific economy organised around the status of such infrastructure providers as the primary points of contact with the ultimate end users, through peering points, data centres, and the data routes that form the Internet backbone.

70. The strength of ISPs, however, has traditionally been primarily in providing network access rather than in providing services across these networks. As a result, unless the ISPs could leverage their control of access to telecommunications networks, they had difficulty maintaining their status as the sole access point to the end user against competition from third-party businesses that provided content and services directly to users over the Internet. The providers of this content (sometimes called over-the-top (OTT) content), were able to deliver services more responsive to demand. Thus, while ISPs remain privileged points of contact with end users and have in general been able to maintain high profit margins, leveraging control of network access was not possible in most cases because ISPs were generally operating in increasingly competitive markets due to sector regulation and were essentially local in their reach (although some ISPs operated across borders, and many, such as mobile network providers, still do).

71. In contrast, OTT content providers could offer an unified experience to users at scale, since their reach was global, unlike network providers whose reach was limited to the length of their network. As a result, providers of OTT content increasingly took on a direct relationship with the end users. The development of open source software accelerated the pace of innovation on top of the networks. As a consequence, while the success of OTT content providers has increased aggregate demand for networks, in markets where there is sufficient competition, prices have declined. While a compelling hardware

device or new network service can still give a particular firm a short term lead and introduce new business models (such as "app stores", for example), experience has shown that no single player in the value chain can entirely control access to customers as long as there is sufficient competition.

3.1.3. Software

72. The World Wide Web, initially made of websites and webpages, marked the emergence of Internet-powered software applications. Software has therefore been regarded from the beginning as an important component of the value chain. Even some software, however, is becoming commoditised. This commoditisation has, once again, been driven by standards, starting with those of the Internet: the Hypertext Transfer Protocol (HTTP), the Hypertext Markup Language (HTML) and later Extensible Markup Language (XML) data formats, email exchange protocols such as Simple Mail Transfer Protocol (SMTP), Post Office Protocol (POP), and Internet Message Access Protocol (IMAP). On top of these standards, communities of open source developers needed to accelerate the speed to market and constantly iterate newer versions of their software. In order to innovate at this pace, they chose to share their source code rather than redevelop it. Although some major software vendors have countered the process of commoditisation with innovation and differentiation, large-scale differentiation and advanced positions have become increasingly difficult to sustain.

73. As growing competition in the development of operating systems, databases, web servers, and browsers reduced profits in many companies' core business, it also created new opportunities. Just as commoditisation in the hardware market cut profit margins for traditional manufacturers while creating new opportunities for low-cost low-margin manufacturers, growing competition in the software market has forced software companies to become more creative and more responsive to consumers' needs, all of which benefited the consumer.

3.1.4. Content

74. Content gained attention at the end of the 1990s, when content production, consumption and, above all, indexation appeared to drive the digital economy's growth. It saw the rise of first content portals and then search engines as the main gatekeepers to accessible content on the Internet. Today, many major players in the digital economy are content providers.

75. The definition of content in that regard is quite large: it includes both copyrighted content produced by professionals, enterprise-generated content, and non-copyrighted user-generated content (such as consumer reviews or comments in online forums). The importance of content flows from the fact that it is important to attract an audience and provoke interactions between users. In addition, more content updated more frequently increases a website's visibility in search results. Content has hence been a driving force behind the advertising industry: it has become a key asset to attract an audience and monetise it with advertisers. Content has also become a way to advertise in and of itself, with classification into three categories: owned content (content distributed by the brand on its own channels), paid content (content distributed by other media in exchange of a payment by the brand), and earned content (content willingly created and shared by customers without direct payment by the brand, such as customer product reviews, videos, and social media sharing).

76. Content is more and more often produced by users, resulting in greater volumes of content. The success of sites predicated on massive online collaboration by users, such as

Wikipedia and YouTube, has proven that an entire experience can be built around content primarily generated by individual users. Further, the emergence of the social networking phenomenon, and the success of major applications in which links and interactions between users matter more than any primary content put forward to attract an audience show the same path. Even advertising relies increasingly on user-generated content, through the concept of earned content, one of the pillars of content marketing. The sophistication of techniques designed to customise services, including cookies (technical tools used by businesses to collect user data, notably for commercial purposes such as behavioural advertising), targeting and retargeting, and collaborative filtering, is also relevant. The amount of content available online has become so vast that relatively few businesses have succeeded online by offering premium content, unless they can leverage that content through a service that prevents competition on volume.

3.1.5. Use of data

77. Users of applications provide businesses with access to substantial amounts of data, which are often personal and are used in a variety of ways that continue to be developed.[1] Collected data can be used not only to customise the experience, but also to generate productivity and quality gain at scale, through controlled experimentation. Personal data is acquired in multiple ways; it can be: provided voluntarily by users (for example, when registering for an online service); observed (for example, by recording Internet browsing activities, location data, etc.), or inferred (for example, based on analysis of online activities). Figure 3.3, which is non-exhaustive, provides illustrations of the ways in which

Figure 3.3. **Personal data**

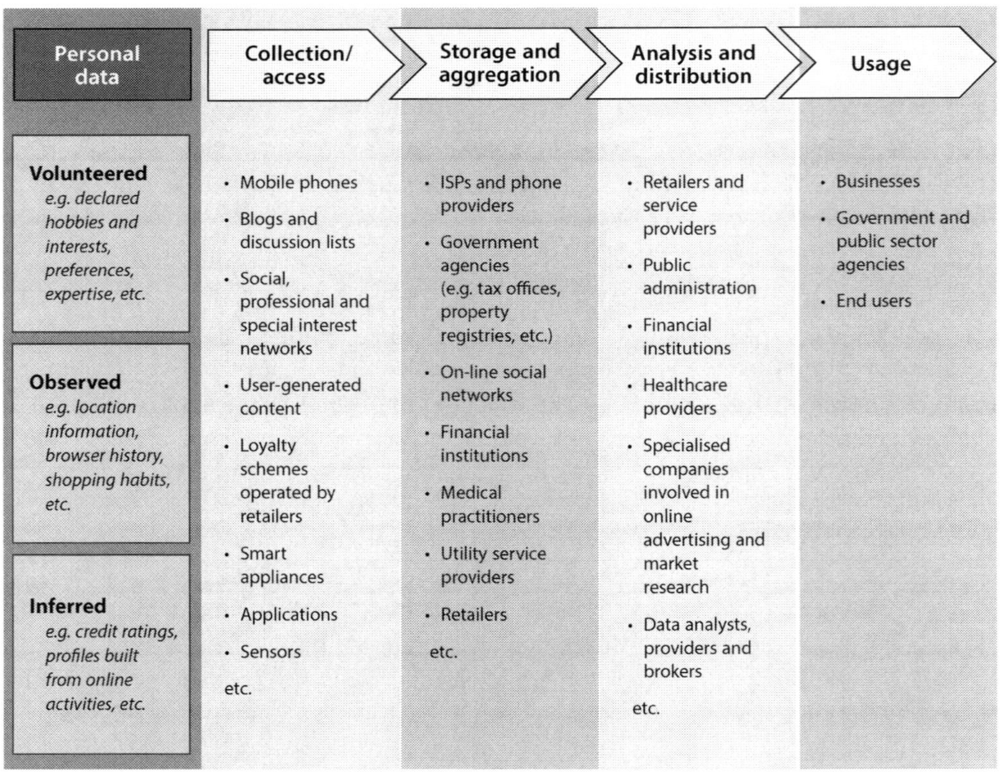

Source: OECD, based on World Economic Forum (2011), *Personal Data: The Emergence of a New Asset Class*, www3.weforum.org/docs/WEF_ITTC_PersonalDataNewAsset_Report_2011.pdf.

data is collected, stored, analysed, and used. Capacity to collect useful data is increasing as the number of Internet-connected devices increases. Businesses of all sorts make use of user data, as it allows them to tailor their offerings to customers. As increasing amounts of potentially useful data are collected, more and more sophisticated techniques must be developed in order to collect, usefully process and analyse that data.

3.1.6. Cloud-based processes

78. As a result of the standardisation and commoditisation of different individual resources, such as hardware, network infrastructure, and software, some businesses have been able to combine those resources and make them available through the Internet as services.

79. Centralised hosting of software resources dates back to the 1960s, when mainframe providers conducted a service bureau business, also referred to as time-sharing or utility computing. Such services included offering computing power and database storage to banks and other large organisations from their worldwide data centres. Cloud computing at scale is the result of several trends related to both technology and business models: growing availability of high-capacity networks, low-cost computers and storage devices as well as the widespread adoption of hardware virtualisation, service-oriented architecture, and utility computing. As a result, value has migrated to new proprietary applications that are not stand-alone software products, but Internet-based applications that combine executable code, dynamically updated databases, and user participation. Although the term "cloud computing" has become commonplace, these applications have also at various points been referred to as "infoware", "computing on demand" or "pervasive computing".

80. The X-as-a Service (XaaS) acronym has been introduced to refer to the trending transformation of software products from goods to services. The Internet essentially accelerated a transition from traditional software business to XaaS models. A website is essentially a software application providing a service delivered over the Internet rather than provided locally or on-site. The service can be about providing access to content (as a portal), or about providing access to executable code performing certain features. Thus the expansion of the Internet brought a new class of centralised computing providers, called application service providers (ASP). ASPs provided businesses with the service of hosting and managing specialised business applications, with the goal of reducing costs through central administration and through the ASP's specialisation in a particular business application.

81. As of today, many business-to-consumer (B2C) applications are also delivered as software as a service: search engines, social networking applications are mainly used through a web browser, without any need to download any executable code beforehand. Although applications continue to be downloaded and installed locally, this is done primarily when there is a frequent need to use them offline. Even some locally-installed applications, however, require an Internet connection to provide full functionality. The growing popularity of smart phones and other devices that use frequently interrupted mobile Internet connections, however, has made downloading applications prominent again.

82. Focusing on value created through cloud-based processes is particularly useful to analyse the ultimate development of the Internet of Things (discussed below), which refers to the Internet as a network connecting individuals, content, and things in everyday lives. At the centre of this complex network of interconnections are powerful software-powered processes whose resources can only be stored and executed in the cloud.

3.2. Emerging and potential future developments

83. The rapid technological progress that has characterised the development of ICT has led to a number of emerging trends and potential developments that may prove influential in the near future. Although this rapid change makes it difficult to predict future developments with any degree of reliability, some of these potential developments are discussed below.

3.2.1. Internet of Things

84. While use of the Internet as a digital platform has enabled the creation of the sharing economy (see below), the ability to connect any smart device or object over time to a network of networks is enabling the "Internet of Things". The term refers to a series of components of equal importance including machine-to-machine communication, cloud computing, big data analysis, sensors and actuators, the combination of which leads to further developments in machine learning and remote control (see Figure 3.4).

Figure 3.4. **Main enablers of the Internet of Things**

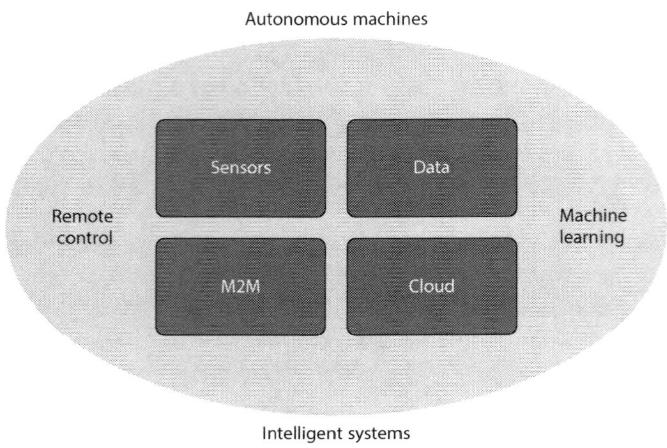

Source: OECD (2015), *OECD Digital Economy Outlook*, OECD Publishing, Paris, http://dx.doi.org/10.1787/9789264232440-en.

85. The number of devices connected to the Internet is expanding rapidly, but substantial room for expansion remains. While Cisco has estimated that between 10 and 15 billion devices are currently connected to the Internet, that figure represents less than 1% of the total devices and things that could ultimately be connected (Evans, 2012). Within the area of the Organisation for Economic Co-operation and Development (OECD), households alone currently have approximately 1.8 billion connected devices. This figure could reach as many as 5.8 billion by 2017, and as many as 14 billion by 2022 (OECD, 2013a). As increasing numbers of connected devices are developed and sold, the expansion of machine-to-machine communication appears likely to dramatically expand and improve the ability of businesses to collect and analyse relevant data.

86. A major feature of the Internet of Things is the widened ability to collect and share data through powerful information systems connected to a multitude of devices, sensors, and cloud computing components. The analysis and use of the data collected and transmitted by connected devices can help individuals and organisations use their resources more accurately, make informed purchasing decisions, ramp up productivity, and respond faster to

changing environments. As devices increasingly transmit more detailed data, the processing of this data can be used automatically to change the behaviour of those devices in real time. It can also make training workers for skilled positions an easier and more cost-effective process. This trend, so far primarily contained in data-intensive industries such as finance, advertising, or entertainment, is likely to penetrate more traditional industries in the future. In addition, while the Internet of Things still generally requires human interaction, remote-controlled machines and systems combined with machine learning may ultimately lead to autonomous machines and intelligent systems, in particular robotic machines (see below).

3.2.2. Virtual currencies

87. Recent years have been marked by the appearance and development of "virtual currencies", meaning digital units of exchange that are not backed by government-issued legal tender. These currencies have taken various forms. Some virtual currencies are specific to a single virtual economy, such as an online game, where they are used to purchase in-game assets and services. In some cases, these economy-specific virtual currencies can be exchanged for real currencies or used to purchase real goods and services, through exchanges which may be operated by the creators of the game or by third parties.

Figure 3.5. **How bitcoins enter circulation and are used in transactions**

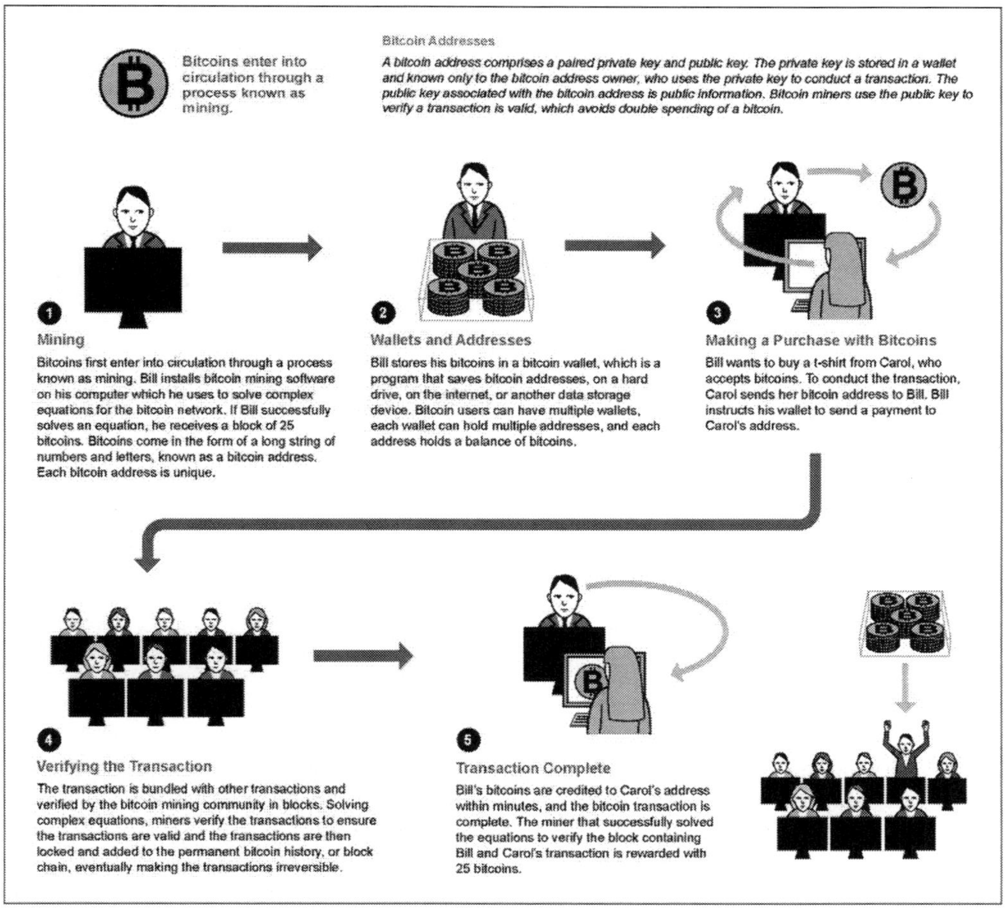

Source: U.S. Government Accountability Office (2013), *Virtual Economies and Currencies*, Report to the Committee on Finance, US Senate.

88. Other virtual currencies were developed primarily to allow the purchase of real goods and services. The most prominent example of this type are the various "cryptocurrencies", including in particular bitcoins, which rely on cryptography and peer-to-peer verification to secure and verify transactions. Many private operators have chosen to accept payment in bitcoins.

89. As virtual currencies increasingly acquire real economic value, they raise substantial policy issues. Some of these stem from the anonymous nature of transactions. In the case of bitcoins, for example, transactions can be made on an entirely anonymous basis, since no personally identifying information is required to be provided to acquire or transact in bitcoins.

3.2.3. Advanced robotics

90. The development of new connected and smart robots is changing manufacturing profoundly. The increased productivity of new automated factories is already making it possible for some multinational enterprises (MNEs) that had previously moved manufacturing offshore to take advantage of lower labour costs to consider moving their manufacturing activities back to where most of their customers are.

91. Manufacturing will be further changed by the progress in robotics, as robots have the potential to make factories less labour intensive and force MNEs to think about production and distribution at the same time. This trend has the potential to be felt particularly strongly in already machine-intensive industries, as automation increasingly centres on artificial cognition, sensors, machine learning, and distributed smart networks. It will also have a potential impact where automation has been scarce so far, especially in small factories and workshops, because software can help improve security and allow humans to work alongside automated systems. Also, as robots embed more software and are connected to cloud-based resources, it will become both easier and cheaper to programme them, which could lead to lowered prices, making them more accessible to small and middle-size operations. These lower costs have the potential to bring manufacturing and other business activities increasingly closer to customers.

92. In the future, progress in artificial intelligence and the emergence of cognitive computing may expand the influence of robots beyond the manufacturing sector and into broader segments of the economy, as well as into household applications such as assisting the elderly or disabled with manual tasks. As robots learn to do jobs that previously were solely done by humans, they can potentially generate productivity, help lower prices for customers, contribute to scaling up operations at a global level, and create innovation opportunities which will lead to the emergence of new activities that will require new skills and potentially create new jobs.

3.2.4. 3D Printing

93. Advances in 3D printing have the potential to enable manufacturing closer to the customer, with direct interaction with consumers impacting the design of product features. As a result, manufacturing could gradually move away from mass production of standardised products, and instead focus on shorter product lifecycle by adopting a strategy of constant experimentation at scale. In the healthcare industry, 3D printing of custom health products such as hearing aid earpieces is already heavily used. In addition, 3D printing has the potential to reduce environmental impact relative to traditional manufacturing, by reducing the number of steps involved in production, transportation, assembly, and distribution, and

can reduce the amount of material wasted as well (Manika, 2013). The size of the 3D printing market is growing rapidly, with further implications for the digital economy. The global 3D printing market is estimated to increase from USD 2.2 billion in 2012 to USD 6 billion by 2017. Many companies are incorporating 3D printing into their R&D activities with the majority of manufacturers using the technology for prototyping. According to a survey conducted by PricewaterhouseCoopers in 2014, 25% of manufacturers used 3D printing technology for prototyping only, and 10% used it for both prototyping and production of final parts, while just 1% used 3D printing expressly for final product production (PricewaterhouseCoopers, 2014). As 3D printing continues to advance, it is conceivable that some manufacturers could eventually transition away from assembling products themselves, and could instead license plans and specifications to third party manufacturers or even retailers who will "print" the products on demand, closer to the customers, but at their own risks and with a very low margin. Alternatively, consumers may be able to assemble products themselves by using 3D printers, further increasing the possibility of locating business activities at a location that is physically remote from the ultimate customer.

3.2.5. The sharing economy and collaborative production

94. The sharing economy, or collaborative consumption, is another potentially significant trend within the digital economy. The "sharing economy" refers to peer-to-peer sharing of goods and services. The sharing economy is not new, but advances in technology have reduced transaction costs, increased availability of information, and provided greater reliability and security. Recent years have seen the emergence of numerous innovative sharing applications using different business models and focusing on one particular service or product, such as cars, spare rooms, food, clothes, and private jets. Most individuals who participate in the sharing economy do not do so mainly to make a living, but to entertain relationships with others, to serve a cause that inspires them, or simply to make ends meet. Because the supplementary income is a net benefit and often does not involve much quantitative cost-benefit analysis, amateur providers have a tendency to share their available resources at a lower price than what a professional might have billed, thus bringing down overall prices, including those of the professionals. Through time, as certain platforms attract substantial number of individuals, these platforms become the prime access point for customers on the online market and have the potential to provide substantial competition for traditional e-commerce applications operated by professionals, which may cut their profit margins further.

95. While the sharing economy concerns "collective consumption", crowdsourcing and crowdfunding are manifestations of "collaborative production". Both large companies and entrepreneurs make increasing use of these practices, for example, for capital peer-to-peer lending. The term crowdfunding is increasingly being used for different types of platforms, enabling lending, donations or reward-based funding, and equity crowdfunding (investment). The crowdfunding market has grown strongly over the past years, driven mainly by non-equity crowdfunding. Crowdfunding is most developed in the United States and Europe, which accounted for 60% and 35%, respectively, of the market in 2012 (OECD Outlook, 2015).

3.2.6. Access to government data

96. Governments are making progress at making machine-readable resources, notably data, publicly available in what has been alternatively labelled as open data policy, open government or government as a platform. There are three main goals assigned to open government policies:

- **Accountability:** Making government resources available allows the public to have direct access to these resources in order to track, document, and evaluate public policy cost, efficiency, and effectiveness. When it comes to accountability, open government strategies are meant to providing tools for transparency and to improving democracy as a whole.
- **Better performance:** Opening government resources also is intended to provide the means for government agencies to better co-operate with one another using cross-agency software applications.
- **Participation of third parties in government business:** When government resources are made available to others outside government, third parties can combine these resources with their own to create hybrid applications that allow better and more personalised service.

3.2.7. Reinforced protection of personal data

97. Under most legal systems, personal data supplied by users is protected by privacy rules and remains the property of those users. Personal data is regarded as an asset owned by the individual to whom it relates, such that it is considered their choice, rather than that of the organisation that holds it, to use, exchange, or make this information available. Data protection rules usually specify what constitutes personal data, how it is gathered, the standards companies must follow with respect to secure storage and the requirement to notify individuals of the personal data held and their rights of access to it. In many countries, rules require adequate data security provisions in regard to transfer of personal data to third countries. Compliance costs are usually borne by the public authorities, companies and other organisations that collect data from individuals.

98. As individuals become more sensitive to the use of their personal data and expect their privacy to be protected, discussions are ongoing in a number of countries to strengthen applicable laws and regulate data collection and exploitation by organisations (OECD, 2012, 2013b). Increasingly, these rules are imposing requirements as to how and where data is stored and processed. As exemplified by the bills currently discussed in the European Union, and in several countries, this trend could lead to a significant change in business models that rely on the use of personal data. For example, the obligation to make sure an individual has expressed consent for the collection of anonymous data, notably in cookies, could affect the user experience while surfing on web pages and make it more difficult to target or retarget advertising banners or clicks.

3.3. The interactions between various layers of information and communication technology (ICT): a conceptual overview

99. One way to picture the ICT sector is to focus on interactions between different layers, each characterised by a mix of both hardware and software. This approach is illustrated in Figure 3.6.

100. At the base lies the *infrastructure* of the Internet, which consists of the cables, tubes, routers, switches, and data centres that are designed and manufactured by firms specialised in network interconnection, and operated by ISPs, carriers, and network operators. Content delivery network operators, whose goal is to serve content to end users with high availability and high performance, pay ISPs, carriers, and network operators for hosting servers in their data centres. Internet protocol (IP) addresses and domain names are managed at this level.

Figure 3.6. **A layered view of ICT**

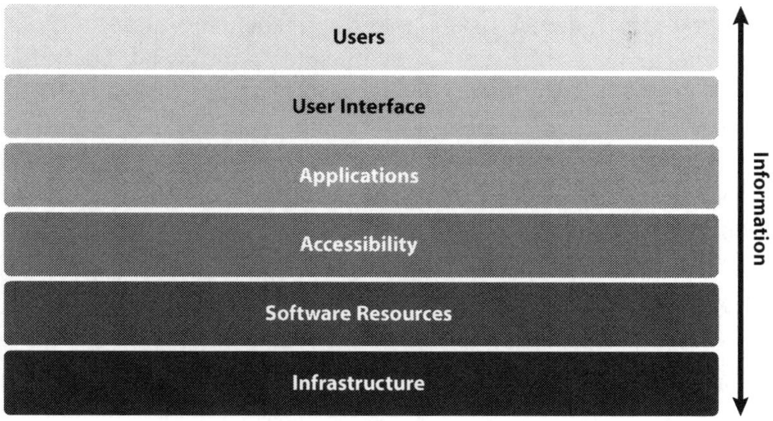

101. Immediately above, stored in servers that are located in data centres and organisations all around the world, are the core *software resources* that enable organisations to create applications, which can consist of raw data, digital content, or executable code. These can include both resources produced by organisations and resources derived from individual users and collected and stored by organisations for later use.

102. On top of these core resources is a layer of tools providing the fundamental *accessibility* necessary to allow software resources to be combined on top of the infrastructure to create applications usable by individual or business end users. This layer effectively provides the structure necessary for software applications to take advantage of the underlying infrastructure and core software resources of the Internet. This accessibility can be provided in many forms. An operating system that makes it possible to run applications on digital devices, for example, is one of the most familiar ways in which accessibility is provided: it allows a developer to design an application to be run on a certain device. The core higher-level protocols that allow communication of data between applications, such as the HTTP that forms the foundation of data communication on the World Wide Web, or the SMTP that provides a standard for email transmission, are another form of accessibility. Other ways to provide accessibility include web services, application programming interfaces (API), and software development kits (SDKs), all of which provide ways for applications usable by end users to connect with the resources necessary to connect to underlying resources.

103. The accessibility layer effectively provides platforms for the creation of *applications* that are usable by end users, and that are able to access the core software resources on top of the infrastructure. Those applications form the fourth layer of the digital economy. An application is a combination of software resources creating value for the end user through the provision of goods or services. Applications can fit together or link to one another: for instance, a web browser is an application, and it gives access to websites that are themselves web-based applications; an app store is also an application with a value proposal that is to allow users to discover and purchase other applications. Within the application layer are applications performing a gatekeeping function, retaining user information and allowing it to be combined with other resources only when necessary and with the express consent of the end user. These gatekeeping activities include authentication of users, payment, and geolocation, all of which involve collection and use of data so sensitive that a certain level of trust is required between the organisation and the user.

104. The next conceptual layer is the machine-to-human *interface* layer. An interface represents the user experience. The interface is displayed through a physical point of contact that can be either a device or a whole place (such as a store). Devices are of two kinds: they are generic when they support many applications; they are non-generic when only one application can run on them. For instance, a computer, a smartphone or a tablet are generic devices. A connected thermostat is a non-generic device. Certain devices, like connected cars, were generally non-generic in the early stages of their development, but become progressively more generic as they are equipped with more accessibility features (such as an operating system).

105. At the top of the chart, above the layers of functions, sit the *users*, who can be either individuals acting in their personal capacity or on behalf of a business. These individuals interact directly with the interface layer to access applications, either directly or through the services of another application acting as a gatekeeper.

106. Each layer is provided with hardware resources, software resources, and network connectivity. Resources can be stored at multiple levels: in data centres at the infrastructure level; in virtual servers located in the cloud; and on user devices (a computer or a tablet for instance). The business relationships between the layers are generally relationships between clients and providers: a company that operates a business in only one layer is generally paid by a company operating a business in the layer above. For instance, cloud computing operators that provide accessibility make payments to infrastructure operators and are paid by application developers. A company operating at the top layer derives payments directly from its interactions with end users, either by charging them money or through generation of value that can then be monetised by the company to derive income from another customer or business. The organisations that are paid at the top level are those operating connected devices, gate-keeping activities or an application that is tethered neither to a device nor to a gate-keeping capacity.

107. In general terms, several business models in the digital economy can be described in terms of vertical integration between layers. For example, traditional web businesses use software resources (layer 2) and rely on open protocols (like HTTP) (layer 3) to combine those resources into a web application (layer 4). They pay operators of the bottom layer to put their application on line, and their interactions with users generate revenue either directly from the user in the form of payment (which can be received directly or through a gatekeeping operator), or indirectly through the generation of value that can then be monetised elsewhere in the business model.

108. These interactions explain why some companies consider it critical to operate at the top, especially by providing applications performing gatekeeping functions. In fact gatekeepers are able to collect data from their users, analyse them and eventually make them available for developers to power even more applications (and collect even more data), or market them to other companies (advertising). This also explains the creation of large ecosystems based on a dominant position in the market of gatekeeping, accessibility and sometimes the operation of devices.

Note

1. User sensitivity has triggered waves of protest against certain features, practices or terms of service carried out by some companies with respect to personal data. In reaction, companies have often rolled back the features and even set up new ones to help their users control and protect their private information. It is worth noting as well that the collection and use of personal data is a closely regulated area across the OECD, with most legislation tracking the main elements of the OECD Privacy Guidelines.

Bibliography

Evan, D. (2012), *The Internet of Everything. How more Relevant and Valuable Connections Will Change the World,* Cisco IBSG.

Manika J. et al. (2013), *Disruptive technologies: Advances that will transform life, business and the global economy,* McKinsey Global Institute.

OECD (2015), OECD Digital Economy Outlook 2015, OECD Publishing Paris, http://dx.doi.org/10.1787/9789264232440-en.

OECD (2013a), *OECD Communications Outlook 2013*, OECD Publishing, Paris, http://dx.doi.org/10.1787/comms_outlook-2013-en.

OECD (2013b), "Protecting and Empowering Consumers in the Purchase of Digital Content Products", OECD Digital Economy Papers, No. 219, OECD Publishing, Paris. http://dx.doi.org/10.1787/5k49czlc7wd3-en.

OECD (2012), "Report on Consumer Protection in Online and Mobile Payments", OECD Digital Economy papers, No. 2014, OECD Publishing, Paris. http://dx.doi.org/10.1787/5k9490gwp7f3-en.

Pricewaterhouse Coopers (2014), "3D Printing and the New Shape of Industrial Manufacturing" www.pwc.com/us/en/industrial-products/assets/3d-printing-next_manufacturing-pwc.pdf (accessed on August 10, 2015).

Rosenstock, E. (n.d), "Paid, Owned, Earned Media Model will Disappear...It Will Just Be Called Marketing" http://elyrosenstock.com/blog/2011/05/13/earned-media-will-disappear-it-will-just-be-called-marketing/ (accessed on May 15 2014).

U.S. Government Accountability Office (2013), *Virtual Economies and Currencies, Report to the Committee on Finance*, US Senate.

World Economic Forum (2011), Personal Data: The Emergence of a New Asset Class, www3.weforum.org/docs/WEF_ITTC_PersonalDataNewAsset_Report_2011.pdf.

Chapter 4

The digital economy, new business models and key features

This chapter discusses the spread of information and communication technology (ICT) across the economy, provides examples of business models that have emerged as a consequence of the advances in ICT, and provides an overview of the key features of the digital economy that are illustrated by those business models.

4.1. The spread of ICT across business sectors: the digital economy

109. All sectors of the economy have adopted ICT to enhance productivity, enlarge market reach, and reduce operational costs. This adoption of ICT is illustrated by the spread of broadband connectivity in businesses, which in almost all countries of the Organisation for Economic Co-operation and Development (OECD) is universal for large enterprises and reaches 90% or more even in smaller businesses.

Figure 4.1. **Broadband connectivity, by size, 2010 and 2014.**

Percentage of enterprises in each employment size class

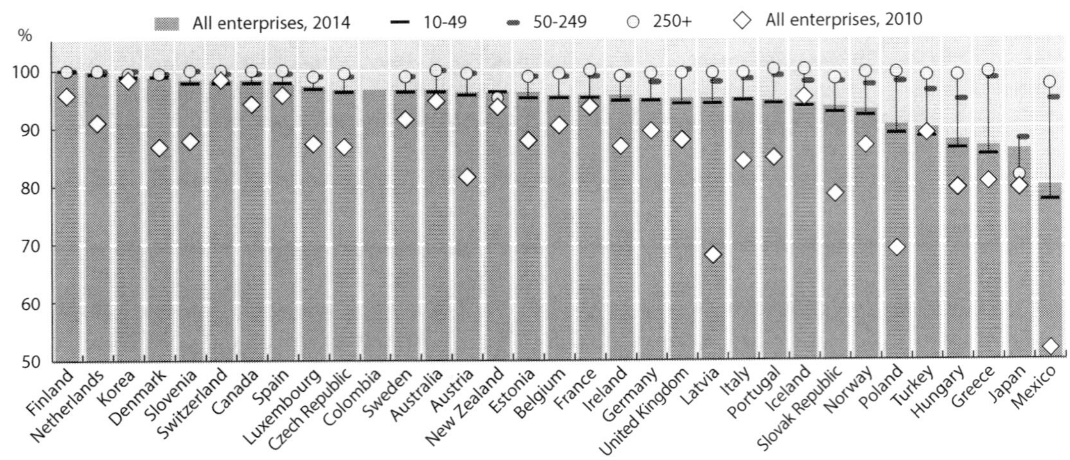

StatLink http://dx.doi.org/10.1787/9789264232440-graph71-en.

Source: OECD (2015), *OECD Digital Economy Outlook 2015*, OECD Publishing, Paris, http://dx.doi.org/10.1787/9789264232440-en.

110. The widespread adoption of ICT, combined with the rapid decline in price and increase in performance of these technologies, has contributed to the development of new activities in both the private and public sector. Together, these technologies have expanded market reach and lowered costs, and have enabled the development of new products and services. These technologies have also changed the ways in which such products and services are produced and delivered, as well as the business models used in companies ranging from multinational enterprises (MNEs) to start-ups. They also support activity by individuals and consumers, and have led to the creation of new payment mechanisms including new forms of digital currencies. The advent of the Internet brought major changes first to the entertainment, news, advertising, and retail industries. In those industries, the first major digital players initially started from traditional business models, adapting them to better end-user equipment (both inside and outside organisations) and more extensive interconnection through the Internet.

111. For example, online retailers initially adapted the business model of brick-and-mortar stores by selling traditional physical goods (for example, books) digitally. Online intermediaries that allowed the discovery, sale, and purchase of goods and services such as vehicles, homes, and jobs were another early category. Other digital players specialised in the online selling of traditional services (for example, online insurance brokers). Retailers then began selling digital products and services, like downloadable and streaming music and movies, executable code, games, and services based on data processing, increasingly

blurring the line between goods and services as businesses continued to develop. Online advertising similarly started from traditional advertising business models, becoming more sophisticated as the potential of digital technology became fully integrated into the industry. New online services enabling a sharing and service economy have also appeared, allowing people to rent out their homes, vehicles and skills to third parties.

112. As technology has advanced and costs of ICT have continued to fall, ICT has proven to be general-purpose technology that has become embedded in and central to the business models of firms operating across the economy. Businesses across all sectors are now able to design and build their operating models around technological capabilities, in order to improve flexibility and efficiency and extend their reach into global markets. Businesses across all sectors have changed the way their business is conducted by taking advantage of advances in communications and data processing capacity to lower transaction costs and extend their reach into global markets.

113. These advances, coupled with liberalisation of trade policy and reduction in transportation costs, have expanded the ability of businesses in all sectors to take advantage of global value chains in which production processes can be geographically dispersed in locations around the world to take advantage of the features of local markets. For example, in sectors relying heavily on technology and research and development, design and production can be managed centrally, while the assembly can be fragmented in different countries to take advantage of skilled labour and local resources.

114. Sectors as diverse as retail, logistics and education have changed and keep changing due to the spread of ICT:

- **Retail**: The digital economy has enabled retailers to allow customers to place online orders (often fulfilled from a local store) and has made it easier for retailers to gather and analyse data on customers, to provide personalised service and advertising. It has also enabled retailers to manage logistics and supply stores with products, which has had a significant, positive impact on productivity.
- **Transport and Logistics**: The logistics sector has been transformed by digital economy, which enables the tracking of both vehicles and cargo across continents, the provision of information to customers and facilitates the development of new operational processes such as Just In Time delivery in the manufacturing sector. Vehicle telemetry also helps maximise fuel efficiency, ensure efficient use of the transport network and support fleet maintenance activities. The information collected by fleets can also be used to create datasets with commercial value.
- **Financial Services**: Banks, insurance providers and other companies, including non-traditional payment service providers, increasingly enable customers to manage their finances, conduct transactions and access new products on line, although they still continue to support branch networks for operations. Better use of data also allows growth in customer insights and associated products, such as personalised spending analysis, which can be used to generate advertising revenue. The digital economy has also made it easier to track indices and manage investment portfolios and has enabled specialist businesses such as high-frequency trading.
- **Manufacturing and Agriculture**: The digital economy has enhanced design and development, as well as the ability to monitor production processes in factories and control robots, which has enabled greater precision in design and development and ongoing product refinement. The products being produced are also increasingly knowledge-intensive. In the automobile industry, for example, it is estimated that

90% of new features in cars have a significant software component. On farms, systems can monitor crops and animals, and soil/environmental quality. Increasingly, routine processes and agricultural equipment can be managed through automated systems.

- **Education:** As the digital economy spreads, universities, tutor services and other education service providers are able to provide courses remotely without the need for face to face interaction through technologies such as video conferencing and streaming and online collaboration portals, which enables them to tap into global demand and leverage brands in a way not previously possible.
- **Healthcare:** The digital economy is revolutionising the healthcare sector, from enabling remote diagnosis to enhancing system efficiencies and patient experience through electronic health records. It also allows opportunities for advertising, for example of drugs and other treatments.
- **Broadcasting and Media:** The digital economy has dramatically changed the broadcasting and media industry, with increasing broadband access in particular opening new avenues for delivery of content for traditional media players, while also enabling the participation in the news media of non-traditional news sources, and expanding user participation in media through user-generated content and social networking. The digital economy has also enhanced the ability of companies to collect and use information about the viewing habits and preferences of customers, to enable them to better target programming.

115. As digital technology is adopted across the economy, segmenting the digital economy is increasingly difficult. In other words, because the digital economy is increasingly becoming the economy itself, it would be difficult, if not impossible, to ring-fence the digital economy from the rest of the economy. Attempting to isolate the digital economy as a separate sector would inevitably require arbitrary lines to be drawn between what is digital and what is not. As a result, the tax challenges and base erosion and profit shifting (BEPS) concerns raised by the digital economy are better identified and addressed by analysing existing structures adopted by MNEs together with new business models and by focusing on the key features of the digital economy and determining which of those features raise or exacerbate tax challenges or BEPS concerns, and developing approaches to address those challenges or concerns.

4.2. The digital economy and the emergence of new business models

116. The digital economy has given rise to a number of new business models. Although many of these models have parallels in traditional business, modern advances in ICT have made it possible to conduct many types of business at substantially greater scale and over longer distances than was previously possible. This section discusses several prominent examples of these new business models. Some of these business models may complement each other and in some cases overlap with each other (for example, payment services could be described under e-commerce or under cloud computing). The business models discussed below are by no means exhaustive. Indeed, just as innovation in the digital economy allows the rapid development of new business models, it can also quickly cause existing businesses to become obsolete. The types of business discussed include several varieties of e-commerce, app stores, online advertising, cloud computing, participative networked platforms, high speed trading, and online payment services.

4.2.1. Electronic commerce

117. Electronic commerce, or e-commerce, has been defined broadly by the OECD Working Party on Indicators for the Information Society as "the sale or purchase of goods or services, conducted over computer networks[1] by methods specifically designed for the purpose of receiving or placing of orders. The goods or services are ordered by those methods, but the payment and the ultimate delivery of the goods or service do not have to be conducted online. An e-commerce transaction can be between enterprises, households, individuals, governments, and other public or private organisations" (OECD, 2011). E-commerce can be used either to facilitate the ordering of goods or services that are then delivered through conventional channels (indirect or offline e-commerce) or to order and deliver goods or services completely electronically (direct or on-line e-commerce). Although e-commerce covers a broad array of businesses, this section provides an illustration of some of the more prominent types.

4.2.1.1. Business-to-business models

118. The vast majority of e-commerce consists of transactions in which a business sells products or services to another business (so-called business-to-business (B2B)) (OECD, 2011). This can include online versions of traditional transactions in which a wholesaler purchases consignments of goods online, which it then sells to consumers from retail outlets. It can also include the provision of goods or services to support other businesses, including, among others: *(i)* logistics services such as transportation, warehousing, and distribution; *(ii)* application service providers offering deployment, hosting, and management of packaged software from a central facility; *(iii)* outsourcing of support functions for e-commerce, such as web-hosting, security, and customer care solutions; *(iv)* auction solutions services for the operation and maintenance of real-time auctions via the Internet; *(v)* content management services, for the facilitation of website content management and delivery; and *(vi)* web-based commerce enablers that provide automated online purchasing capabilities.

4.2.1.2. Business-to-consumer models

119. Business-to-consumer (B2C) models were among the earliest forms of e-commerce. A business following a B2C business model sells goods or services to individuals acting outside the scope of their profession. B2C models fall into several categories, including, for example, so-called "pureplay" online vendors with no physical stores or offline presence, "click-and-mortar" businesses that supplemented existing consumer-facing business with online sales, and manufacturers that use online business to allow customers to order and customise directly.

120. The goods or services sold by a B2C business can be tangible (such as a CD of music) or intangible (i.e. received by consumers in an electronic format). Through digitisation of information, including text, sound, and visual images, an increasing number of goods and services can be delivered digitally to customers increasingly remote from the location of the seller. B2C e-commerce can in many cases dramatically shorten supply chains by eliminating the need for many of the wholesalers, distributors, retailers, and other intermediaries that were traditionally used in businesses involving tangible goods. Partly because of this disintermediation, B2C businesses typically involve high investment in advertising and customer care, as well as in logistics. B2C reduces transaction costs (particularly search costs) by increasing consumer access to information. It also reduces market entry barriers, as the cost of maintaining a website is generally cheaper than installing a traditional brick-and-mortar retail shop.

4.2.1.3. Consumer-to-consumer models

121. Consumer-to-consumer (C2C) transactions are becoming more and more common. Businesses involved in C2C e-commerce play the role of intermediaries, helping individual consumers to sell or rent their assets (such as residential property, cars, motorcycles, etc.) by publishing their information on the website and facilitating transactions. These businesses may or may not charge the consumer for these services, depending on their revenue model. This type of e-commerce comes in several forms, including, but not limited to: *(i)* auctions facilitated at a portal that allows online bidding on the items being sold; *(ii)* peer-to-peer systems allowing sharing of files between users; and *(iii)* classified ads portals providing an interactive, online marketplace allowing negotiation between buyers and sellers.

4.2.1.4. Growth of e-commerce

122. The Internet facilitates transactions such as ordering goods and services. This means that many transactions that would have taken place without the Internet can be conducted more efficiently and at less expense. As a result, the number of firms carrying out business transactions over the Internet has increased dramatically over the last decade.

123. For example, e-commerce in the Netherlands has increased as a share of total company revenue from 3.4% in 1999 to 14.1% in 2009. Similarly, between 2004 and 2011 this share increased from 2.7% to 18.5% in Norway and from 2.8% to 11% in Poland. Based on comparable data, as illustrated in Figure 4.2, e-commerce is nearing 20% of total turnover in Finland, Hungary, and Sweden, and 25% in the Czech Republic (OECD, 2012).

124. In 2014, B2C e-commerce sales were estimated to exceed USD 1.4 trillion, an increase of nearly 20% from 2013. B2C sales are estimated to reach USD 2.356 trillion by 2018, with the Asia-Pacific region expected to surpass North America as the top market for B2C e-commerce sales in 2015 (Emarketer, 2014). According to the research firm Frost and Sullivan the B2B online retail market is expected to reach double the size of the B2C market, generating total revenues of USD 6.7 trillion by 2020. Such B2B online sales will comprise almost 27% of total manufacturing trade, which is estimated to reach USD 25 trillion by 2020 (Frost and Sullivan, 2014).

Figure 4.2. **Turnover from e-commerce, by size, 2008 and 2012**

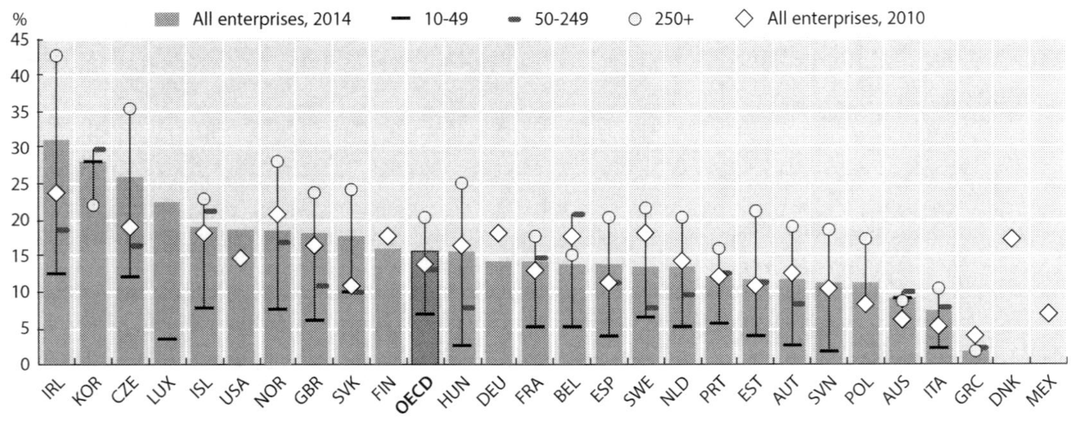

StatLink http://dx.doi.org/10.1787/9789264221796-graph104-en.

Source: OECD (2014), *Measuring the Digital Economy*, OECD Publishing, Paris, http://dx.doi.org/10.1787/9789264221796-en.

125. The Internet has also expanded the potential reach of smaller businesses, enabling them to reach markets that would not have been possible to reach without its existence. So far, however, overall uptake of e-commerce by small and medium enterprise (SMEs) has been moderate, especially across borders. Among other factors, consumer resistance to cross-border purchases, trade and regulatory barriers (e.g. high custom administration costs, high tariffs, inadequate property right protection) and lack of working capital to finance exports may explain this situation (OECD Outlook, 2015).

4.2.2. Payment services

126. Paying for online transactions traditionally required providing some amount of financial information, such as bank account or credit card information, to a vendor, which requires a high degree of trust that is not always present in the case of an unknown vendor, particularly in the case of a C2C transaction. Online payment service providers help address this concern by providing a secure way to enable payments online without requiring the parties to the transaction to share financial information with each other.

127. A payment service provider acts as an intermediary (typically using a software-as-a-service model) between online purchasers and sellers, accepting payments from purchasers through a variety of payment methods, including credit card payments or bank-based payments like direct debit or real-time bank transfers, processing those payments, and depositing the funds to the seller's account. Electronic payment systems offer a number of benefits for users, such as *(i)* protection against fraud, since the seller and buyer do not exchange sensitive information; *(ii)* faster delivery of payment compared with traditional payment methods; and *(iii)* in many cases, the ability to transact in multiple currencies. Payment service providers typically charge a fee for each transaction completed, which can be either a fixed charge or a percentage of the value of the transaction, though some payment service providers also charge monthly fees or setup fees for certain additional services.

128. A number of other alternative online payment options are in use as well, including:

- **Cash payment solutions**, in which a customer buys online, and pays in cash with a barcode or payment code at participating shops or settlement agencies, offering a way for customers unwilling to use other online payment methods to make online purchases in a secure manner.
- **E-wallets or cyber-wallets**, which are previously charged with credits and can be spent online as an alternative to the use of a credit card. These are often used for micropayments because the use of a credit card for frequent small payments is not economical.
- **Mobile payment solutions**, which encompass all types of technologies that enable payment using a mobile phone or smartphone, including, among others, mobile card processing using card readers connected to smartphones, in-app payments for virtual products, and near-field communications solutions which use short-range wireless technology to exchange information.

129. As discussed in Chapter 3, the digital economy has also given rise to virtual currencies that can be used to purchase goods and services from businesses that agree to accept them, acting as an alternative to payment services. In some cases, exchanges have arisen to allow purchase and sale of these virtual currencies for real currency.

4.2.3. App stores

130. The growth of Internet access through smartphones and tablets has caused an increase in the frequency of use of online services and the development of application stores, a type of digital distribution platform for software, often provided as a component of an operating system. Application stores typically take the form of central retail platforms, accessible through the consumer's device, through which the consumer can browse, view information and reviews, purchase and automatically download and install the application on his/her device.

131. Accessibility to application stores varies. Some application stores are only usable by consumers with a particular device. These stores may represent the sole way for users of that device to obtain applications, or may represent one of several possible means for users to obtain applications. Some application stores are accessible by consumers of any device using a particular operating system. Others are usable by consumers with service contracts with a particular network operator. Finally, certain others are freely accessible and are not dependent on the type of device, proprietary software, or service provider.

132. App stores will typically include both applications developed by the business operating the app store (typically, an operating system developer, device manufacturer, or telecommunications network provider), or by a third-party developer. Applications may be downloaded for free or for a fee. Free applications may be supported by advertising. In addition, applications are increasingly moving to a "freemium" model, in which basic functionality is provided for free, but customers may pay for additional content or features.

133. An application store will typically feature applications produced by developers in multiple countries. In addition, while many app stores are targeted at customers in particular geographic markets, applications are often cross listed on multiple app stores targeted at multiple geographic regions.

134. Use of application stores is growing rapidly. Gartner, Inc., an information technology research and advisory company, estimated that downloads from app stores would reach 102 billion in 2013, up from 64 billion in 2012.

135. Total revenue from app store purchases was expected to exceed USD 26 billion in 2013, an increase of 31% over the total in 2012. As noted above, free applications are becoming increasingly prevalent, and are expected by 2017 to account for 94.5% of total downloads, with in-app purchases accounting for 48% of total app store revenues.

4.2.4. Online advertising

136. Online advertising uses the Internet as a medium to target and deliver marketing messages to customers. Internet advertising offers a number of advantages over traditional advertising. For example, many Internet advertisers have developed sophisticated methods for segmenting consumers in order to allow more precise targeting of ads. Many Internet advertising publishers have also developed ways for clients to monitor performance of ads, tracking how users interact with their brands and learning what is of interest to current and prospective customers. Online advertising takes a number of forms, the most prominent of which are display ads, in which an advertiser pays to display ads linked to particular content or user behaviour, and search engine ads, in which an advertiser pays to appear among Internet search results.

137. Online advertising involves a number of players, including web publishers, who agree to integrate advertisements into their online content in exchange for compensation, advertisers, who produce advertisements to be displayed in the web publisher's content and advertising

network intermediaries, who connect web publishers with advertisers seeking to reach an online audience. Advertising network intermediaries include a range of players, including search engines, media companies, and technology vendors. These networks are supported by data exchanges, marketplaces in which advertisers bid for access to data about customers that has been collected through tracking and tracing of users' online activities. These data can be analysed, combined, and processed by specialist data analysers into a user profile.

138. In advertising-based business models, publishers of content are frequently willing to offer free or subsidised services to consumers in order to ensure a large enough audience to attract advertisers. The most successful advertising companies have been those that combine a large user base with sophisticated algorithms to collect, analyse, and process user data in order to allow targeted advertisements. While traditional advertising involved payment for display of ads for a specified period of time, with little way to monitor visibility or user response, online advertising has given rise to a number of new payment calculation methods, including cost-per-mille (CPM), in which advertisers pay per thousand displays of their message to users, cost-per-click (CPC), in which advertisers pay only when users click on their advertisements, and cost-per-action (CPA), in which advertisers only pay when a specific action (such as a purchase) is performed by a user.

139. Internet advertising is rapidly growing, both in terms of total revenues and in terms of share of the total advertising market. PwC estimates that Internet advertising reached USD 135.4 billion in 2014. The market for Internet advertising is projected to grow at a rate of 12.1% per year during the period from 2014 to 2019, reaching USD 239.8 billion in 2019. Internet advertising would by that point surpass television as the largest advertising medium. Within the online advertising market, search advertisement holds the greatest share. Paid search Internet advertising revenue is forecast to grow from USD 53.13 billion in 2014 to USD 85.41 billion in 2019, accounting for over 35% of total Internet advertising by then, although video and mobile advertising are experiencing rapid growth. While video Internet advertising only accounted for 4.7% of total Internet advertising revenue in 2014, it is expected to grow at over 19% a year, rising from USD 6.32 billion to USD15.39 billion in 2019. Similarly, mobile Internet advertising grew from just 5% of total Internet advertising in 2010 to 16.7% of the global share in 2014 and is expected to increase as mobile devices continue to proliferate (PwC, 2015).

4.2.5. Cloud computing

140. Cloud computing is the provision of standardised, configurable, on-demand, online computer services, which can include computing, storage, software, and data management, using shared physical and virtual resources (including networks, servers, and applications).[2] Because the service is provided online using the provider's hardware, users can typically access the service using various types of devices wherever they are located, provided they have a suitable Internet connection.

141. The resources to which cloud computing customers are granted access are not stored on a single computer. Instead, they are on many networked computers that are available to everyone who has access to that "cloud" of computing resources (which, depending on the cloud, could be a single organisation, a community of organisations, the general public, or some combination thereof). The system copies each user's data and software to other servers, which allows it to allocate requests for hardware resources to whatever physical location is best able to satisfy the demand efficiently. Each user has access to a large amount of computer resources when needed, and only when needed. This redundancy ensures that the failure of one machine will not lead to loss of data or software.

142. Cloud computing often provides customers with a cost effective alternative to purchasing and maintaining their own IT infrastructure, since the cost of the consumer resources is generally shared among a wide user base. The advantages of cloud computing are largely driven by economies of scale in setting up the infrastructure and maximising server usage by sharing space among clients whose needs for space and processing power may vary on a flexible basis.

143. The most common examples of cloud computing service models are:

- **Infrastructure-as-a-service**: In the most basic cloud-service model, providers of infrastructure as a service (IaaS) offer computers – physical or (more often) virtual machines – and other fundamental computing resources. IaaS clouds often offer additional resources such as a virtual-machine disk image library, raw (block) and file-based storage, firewalls, load balancers, Internet Protocol (IP) addresses, virtual local area networks (VLANs), and software bundles. The customer does not manage or control the underlying cloud infrastructure, but has control over the operating system, storage, and deployed applications, and may be given limited control of select networking components (e.g. host firewalls).

- **Platform-as-a-service**: Platform as a service is a category of cloud computing services that provides a computing platform and programming tools as a service for software developers. Software resources provided by the platform are embedded in the code of software applications meant to be used by end users. The client does not control or manage the underlying cloud infrastructure, including the network, servers, operating systems, or storage, but has control over the deployed applications.

- **Software-as-a-service**: A common form of cloud computing in which a provider allows the user to access an application from various devices through a client interface such as a web browser (e.g. web-based email). It can be provided either to business customers (B2B) or individual customers (B2C). Unlike in the old software vendor models, the code is executed remotely on the servers, thereby freeing the user of the necessity to upgrade when a new version is available – the executed version is always the latest, which means that new features go instantaneously to market without friction. The consumer generally does not manage or control the underlying cloud infrastructure, including the network, servers, operating systems, storage, or individual application capabilities, with the possible exception of limited user-specific application configuration settings.

144. Other X-as-a Service (XaaS) concepts include content or data:

- **Content-as-a-service**: Where rights are obtained and software is provided to allow content to be embedded by purchasers, content can be purchased as a service. This has been used particularly in the case of user-created content.

- **Data-as-a-service**: Data from multiple sources can be aggregated and managed by a service provider, so that controlled access to that data can be granted to entities that may be geographically and organisationally removed from each other, without each entity needing to develop or acquire the infrastructure necessary to prepare and process that data.

145. In the consumer markets, many cloud services (e.g. email, photo storage, and social networks) have been provided free of charge, with revenue generated through advertising or the sale of data on user behaviour, or on a "freemium" basis in which basic services are provided for free and expanded services require payment. Other consumer cloud services, such as web hosting or hard drive backup, are sold on a monthly subscription basis. In B2B

markets, cloud services are most typically sold by subscription, although "pay as you go" models are increasingly available.

146. In recent years, diffusion of different cloud computing applications and services among businesses has accelerated. For instance in 2014, 22% of companies relied on cloud computing services. In most countries, uptake is higher among large businesses compared to SMEs (OECD Outlook, 2015). Further, businesses more frequently invest in cloud computing services with a high level of sophistication, such as finance/accounting software, CRM software and computing power, than less sophisticated services such as emails, office software or file storage, as seen in Figure 4.4 (OECD Outlook, 2015).

Figure 4.3. **Use of cloud computing by enterprises, 2014**

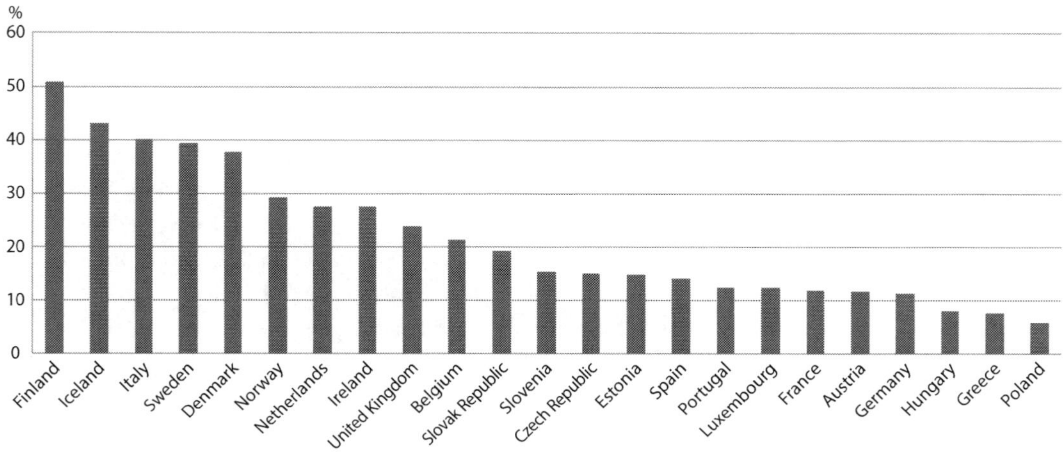

StatLink http://dx.doi.org/10.1787/9789264232440-graph14-en.

Source: Eurostat, Information Society Statistics, January 2015 in *OECD (2015), Digital Economy Outlook 2015*, OECD Publishing Paris, http://dx.doi.org/10.1787/9789264232440-en.

Figure 4.4. **Enterprises using cloud computing services by type of services, 2014**

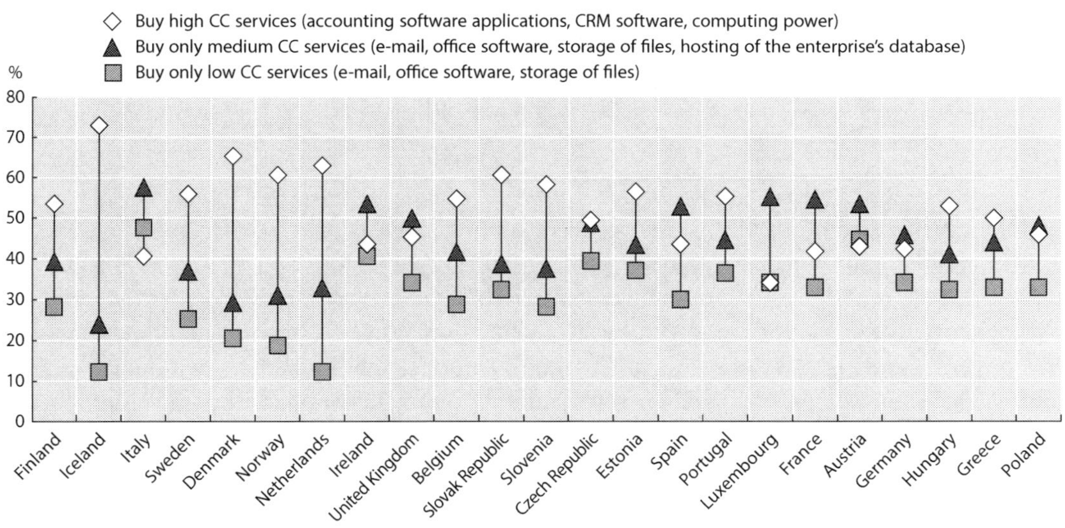

StatLink http://dx.doi.org/10.1787/9789264232440-graph76-en.

Source: Eurostat, Information Society Statistics, January 2015, in *OECD (2015) Digital Economy Outlook 2015*, OECD Publishing, Paris, http://dx.doi.org/10.1787/9789264232440-en.

4.2.6. High frequency trading

147. High frequency trading uses sophisticated technology, including complex computer algorithms, to trade securities at high speed. Large numbers of orders which are typically fairly small in size are sent into the markets at high speed, with round-trip execution times measured in microseconds. The parameters for the trades are set with algorithms run on powerful computers that analyse huge volumes of market data and exploit small price movements or opportunities for market arbitrage that may occur for only milliseconds. Typically, a high-frequency trader holds a position open for no more than a few seconds. In other words, high frequency trading firms profit mostly from small price changes exploited through small, but frequently executed trades.

148. Because trades are conducted entirely electronically, high frequency trading generally does not require personnel in the country where the infrastructure used to make trades is located. The implementation and execution of successful trading strategies depends on several factors, including the development of algorithms for trading, as well as writing programmes to monitor losses and performance and to automatically shut down trading to avoid fast-accruing losses. In addition, high frequency trading depends on the ability to be faster than competitors, which means that it is extremely sensitive to latency. As a result, the location of the server is extremely important to the business, with servers located close to the relevant exchange providing a meaningful advantage over servers located farther away. As a result, financial institutions offer installation of trading engines directly adjacent to their own infrastructure, minimising network latency.

4.2.7. Participative networked platforms

149. A participative networked platform is an intermediary that enables users to collaborate and contribute to developing, extending, rating, commenting on and distributing user-created content. User created content (UCC) comprises various forms of media and creative works (written, audio, visual, and combined) created by users. A range of different distribution platforms have been created, including text-based collaboration formats such as blogs or wikis, group-based aggregation and social bookmarking sites, social networking sites, podcasting, and virtual worlds. In general, UCC is created without the expectation of profit. The participative platform featuring the UCC, however, may monetise the UCC in a variety of ways, including through voluntary contributions, charging viewers for access on a per-item or subscription basis, advertising-based models, licensing of content and technology to third parties, selling goods and services to the community, and selling user data to market research or other firms.

150. Social networking applications are possibly the best known participative networked platform but the same model is also used in other areas, like fashion design, toy design, and computer games just to name a few. Collaborative production methods are not yet widespread in practice for product development, but some firms are using them intensively and with success, as illustrated below in Figure 4.5. The most common practice is to involve customers via social media and through feedback. In the 28 EU member countries, almost 10% of enterprises are currently involving customers in the development or innovation of goods and services (see Figure 4.6).

Figure 4.5. **Customer involvement in product development, 2013**

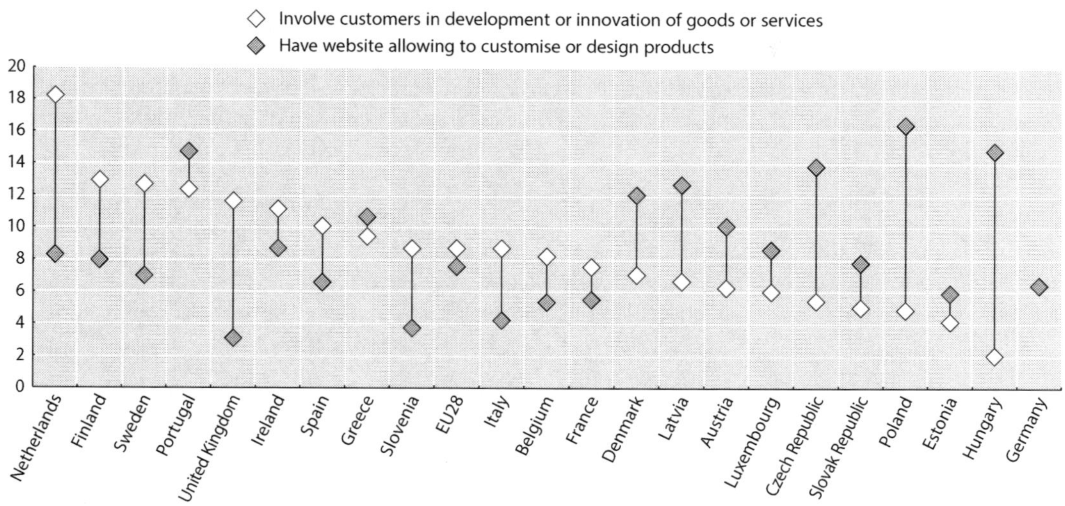

StatLink http://dx.doi.org/10.1787/9789264232440-graph19-en.

Note: Unless otherwise stated, sector coverage consists of all activities in manufacturing and non-financial market services. Only enterprises with ten or more persons employed are considered.

Source: Eurostat, Information Society Statistics, January 2015, in OECD (2015), *OECD Digital Economy Outlook 2015*, OECD Publishing, Paris, http://dx.doi.org/10.1787/9789264232440-en.

Figure 4.6. **Enterprises engaging with customers in product development, 2013**

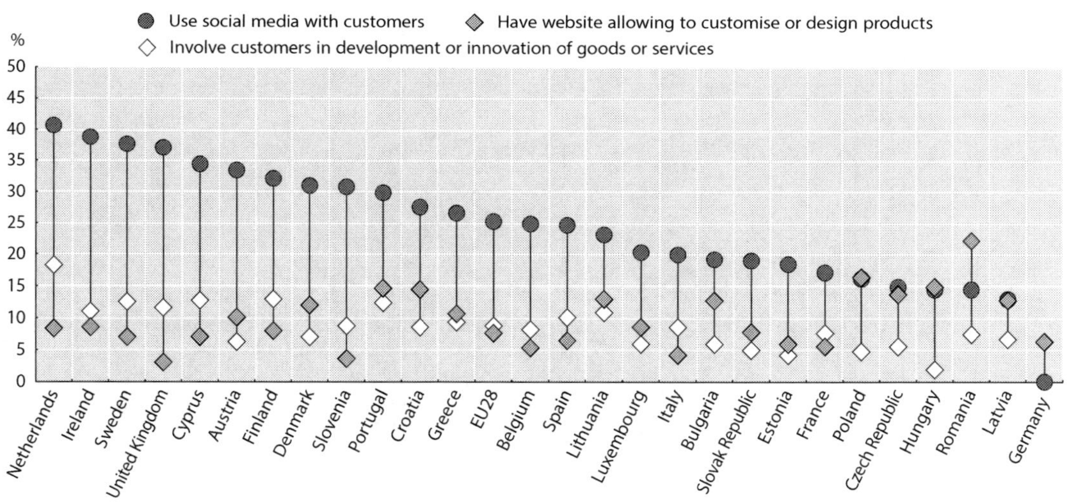

StatLink http://dx.doi.org/10.1787/9789264232440-graph94-en

Notes: 1. Unless otherwise stated, sector coverage consists of all activities in manufacturing and non-financial market services. Only enterprises with ten or more persons employed are considered.

2. Note by Turkey: The information in this document with reference to "Cyprus" relates to the southern part of the Island. There is no single authority representing both Turkish and Greek Cypriot people on the Island. Turkey recognises the Turkish Republic of Northern Cyprus (TRNC). Until a lasting and equitable solution is found within the context of United Nations, Turkey shall preserve its position concerning the "Cyprus issue".

Note by all the European Union Member States of the OECD and the European Union: The Republic of Cyprus is recognised by all members of the United Nations with the exception of Turkey. The information in this document relates to the area under the effective control of the Government of the Republic of Cyprus.

Source: Eurostat, Information Society Statistics, January 2015, in OECD (2015), *OECD Digital Economy Outlook 2015*, OECD Publishing, Paris, http://dx.doi.org/10.1787/9789264232440-en.

Box 4.1. **Diversity of revenue models**

The diversity of businesses in the current digital economy is illustrated by the variety of ways in which businesses turn value into revenue. The most common revenue models include the following:

i. Advertising-based revenues. One version of this model offers free or discounted digital content to users in exchange for requiring viewing of paid-for advertisements. Other models rely on providing advertising through mobile devices based on location or other factors. A third type concerns social media websites or platforms who typically build up a large online user community before monetising their captive audience through advertising opportunities.

ii. Digital content purchases or rentals. Users pay per item of download – for instance, e-books, videos, apps, games and music would fall into this category.

iii. Selling of goods (including virtual items). This category, which overlaps to a degree with (i), would include online retailers of tangible goods but could also cover online gaming, where users are offered a free or discounted introductory product but are also offered purchasable access to additional content or virtual items to enhance the experience.

iv. Subscription-based revenues. Examples include annual payments for "premium delivery" with online retailers, monthly payments for digital content including news, music, video-streaming, etc. It could also include regular payments for software services and maintenance such as anti-virus software, data storage, customer "help" services for operating systems, and payment for access to the Internet itself.

v. Selling of services. This category overlaps with (iv) but would include traditional services which can be delivered online such as legal services (e.g. e-conveyancing), financial services (e.g. brokerage), consultancy services, travel agency etc. It would also include a large range of B2B services linked to enterprises who provide core Internet access and act as Internet intermediaries (web hosting, domain registration, payment processing, platform access, etc.).

vi. Licensing content and technology. Again, this category overlaps with (iv) and (v) but might typically include access to specialist online content (e.g. publications and journals), algorithms, software, cloud based operating systems, etc., or specialist technology such as artificial intelligence systems.

vii. Selling of user data and customised market research. Examples include Internet service providers (ISPs), data brokers, data analytics firms, telemetrics and data gained from non-personal sources.

viii. "Hidden" fees and loss leaders. There may be instances in integrated businesses where profits or losses may be attributable to online operations but because of the nature of the business, cross-subsidy with physical operations occurs and it is difficult to separate and identify what should be designated as "online revenue". An example might include online banking, which is offered "free" but is subsidised through other banking operations and fees.

4.3. Key features of the digital economy

151. There are a number of features that are increasingly prominent in the digital economy and which are potentially relevant from a tax perspective. While these features may not all be present at the same time in any particular business, they increasingly characterise the modern economy. They include:

- Mobility, with respect to *(i)* the *intangibles* on which the digital economy relies heavily, *(ii) users*, and *(iii) business functions* as a consequence of the decreased need for local personnel to perform certain functions as well as the flexibility in many cases to choose the location of servers and other resources.

- Reliance on data, including in particular the use of so-called "big data".
- Network effects, understood with reference to user participation, integration and synergies.
- Use of multi-sided business models in which the two sides of the market may be in different jurisdictions.
- Tendency toward monopoly or oligopoly in certain business models relying heavily on network effects.
- Volatility due to low barriers to entry and rapidly evolving technology.

4.3.1. Mobility

4.3.1.1. Mobility of intangibles

152. Development and exploitation of intangibles is a key feature of the digital economy. This investment in and development of intangibles is a core contributor to value creation and economic growth for companies in the digital economy. For example, digital companies often rely heavily on software, and will expend substantial resources on research and development to upgrade existing software or to develop new software products.

153. This heavy reliance on intangibles can be present even where technology is incorporated into a business model primarily to manage wholly tangible resources. For example, an online retailer may develop a multi-layer digital activity to manage a logistic platform including warehouses and shipping capacity. As businesses evolve, the relative importance of these intangibles frequently grows, resulting in further concentration of value in the intangibles. Under existing tax rules, the rights to those intangibles can often be easily assigned and transferred among associated enterprises, with the result that the legal ownership of the assets may be separated from the activities that resulted in the development of those assets.

4.3.1.2. Mobility of users and customers

154. Advances in ICT and the increased connectivity that characterises the digital economy mean that users are increasingly able to carry on commercial activities remotely while traveling across borders. An individual can, for example, reside in one country, purchase an application while staying in a second country, and use the application from a third country. Challenges presented by the increasing mobility of consumers are exacerbated by the ability of many consumers to use virtual personal networks or proxy servers that may, whether intentionally or unintentionally, disguise the location at which the ultimate sale took place. The fact that many interactions on the Internet remain anonymous may add to the difficulty of the identity and location of users.

4.3.1.3. Mobility of business functions

155. As noted above, improved telecommunications, information management software, and personal computing have significantly decreased the cost of organising and co-ordinating complex activities over long distances. As a result, businesses are increasingly able to manage their global operations on an integrated basis from a central location that may be removed geographically from both the locations in which the operations are carried out and the locations in which their suppliers or customers are located.

156. One impact of these changes has been an expansion of the ability to access remote markets, which has substantially increased the ability to provide those goods and services across borders. This has been illustrated by the dramatic growth of international trade in ICT services in recent years. In particular, since 2000, the share of Computer and Information services on world exports of services doubled from 3% to 6%, while that of Telecommunication services increased from 2.2% to 2.3% (OECD, 2013). For the OECD, the combined share of Computer and Information and Communication services rose from 5.7% to 9.0% of total service exports.

157. Several important shifts in the provision of ICT services have occurred in recent years. India has quickly become the leading exporter of ICT services, followed by Ireland, the United States, Germany, and the United Kingdom. China as well became one of the major exporters. These six countries together represent about 60% of total exports of ICT services.

Figure 4.7. **Exporters of ICT services, 2013**

Percentage shares of total world services exports in USD billions

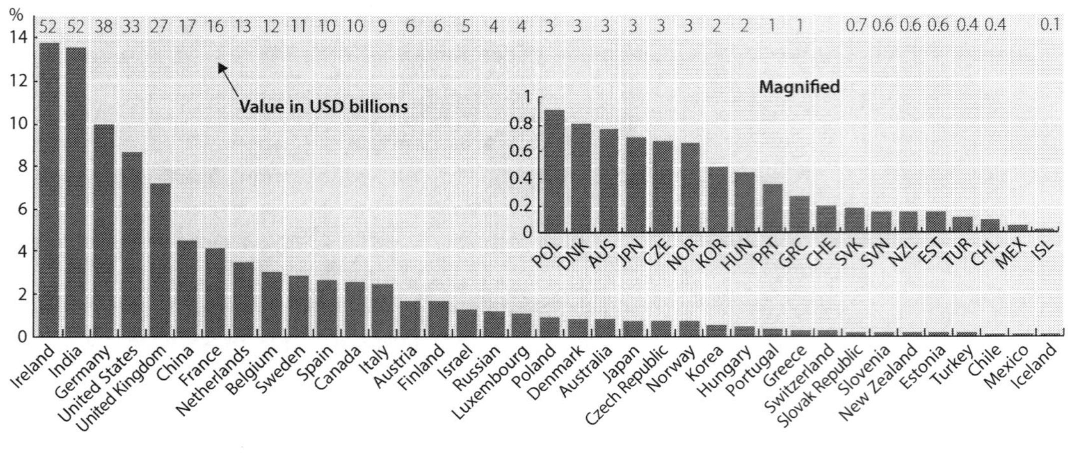

StatLink http://dx.doi.org/10.1787/9789264232440-graph5-en

For Denmark, data refer to 2004 instead of 2001. For Chile, Iceland and Israel, data refer to 2012. For Luxembourg, data refer to 2002 instead of 2001. For Mexico and Switzerland, ICT services only include communications services.

The statistical data for Israel are supplied by and under the responsibility of the relevant Israeli authorities. The use of such data by the OECD is without prejudice to the status of the Golan Heights, East Jerusalem and Israeli settlements in the West Bank under the terms of international law.

Source: OECD (2015), *OECD Digital Economy Outlook 2015*, OECD Publishing, Paris, http://dx.doi.org/10.1787/9789264232440-en.

158. In addition, technological advances increasingly make it possible for businesses to carry on economic activity with minimal need for personnel to be present. In many cases, businesses are able to increase substantially in size and reach with minimal increases in the number of personnel required to manage day-to-day operation of the businesses (so-called "scale without mass"). This has been particularly true in the case of Internet businesses, which have in many cases quickly amassed huge numbers of users while maintaining modest workforces. As a result, the average revenue per employee of top Internet firms, as shown in Figure 4.8, is substantially higher than in other types of businesses within the ICT sector.

Figure 4.8. **Average annual revenue per employee of the top 250 ICT firms by sector, 2000-11**[3]

USD thousands

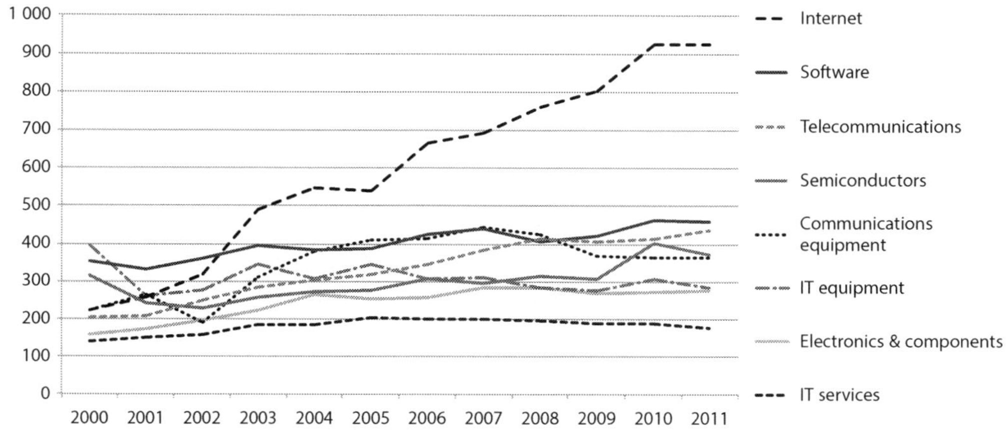

StatLink http://dx.doi.org/10.1787/888932692619

Source: OECD (2012), *OECD Internet Economy Outlook 2012*, OECD Publishing, Paris, http://dx.doi.org/10.1787/9789264086463-en.

159. The ability to manage business centrally while maintaining substantial flexibility over the location of business functions has increased the ability of businesses to spread functions and assets among multiple different countries. While such globalisation of business among larger organisations is certainly not a new phenomenon, the spread of the digital economy, combined with the growing importance of the service component, as well as reductions in trade costs due to trade and investment liberalisation and regulatory reforms, have helped to remove logistical barriers and increase the pace at which such globalisation is possible. Technological advances have also permitted greater integration of worldwide businesses, which has increased the flexibility of businesses to spread their activities among several locations worldwide, even if those locations may be distant from each other and from the physical location of their ultimate customers. In addition to improving the flexibility of larger, more established organisations, advances in information and communications technology have made it more possible for even small and mid-sized businesses to reach global markets from their inception. In short, global interconnectedness has grown to unprecedented levels.

160. Advances in technology have improved access to real-time market information and business analytics, and have improved communications within and between firms. These improvements have improved the capacity of businesses to manage their global operations on an integrated basis, with individual group companies exercising their functions within a framework of group policies and strategies set by the group as a whole and monitored centrally. Improved telecommunications, information management software, and personal computing have significantly decreased the cost of organising and co-ordinating complex activities over long distances, and enabled the creation of new and more efficient business models. This integration has made it easier for business to adopt global business models that centralise functions at a regional or global level, rather than at a country-by-country level. Even for SMEs, it has now become possible to be "micro-multinationals" that operate and have personnel in multiple countries and continents.

161. As worldwide operations have become more integrated, production processes increasingly take place as part of global value chains in which various stages of production are spread across multiple different countries, and are performed by a mix of independent

and affiliated suppliers. Businesses are increasingly able to choose the optimal location for productive activities and assets, even if that location may be distant from the location of customers or the location of other stages of production. In addition, rapid advances in information and communication technology have meant that services such as data entry, information processing, research, and consulting can increasingly be carried out remotely. These functions can be carried out by related parties, or, if a business determines that it is more advantageous to outsource the function, by an unrelated service provider.

162. There are limits to this flexibility, however. In general, fragmentation of activities among multiple locations involves trade-offs between lower costs for the activity itself and higher transaction and co-ordination costs. In addition, skills and talent remain a critical resource in the digital economy. Although many functions can be performed with limited personnel, managers, developers, software architects, and designers, among other key functions, remain instrumental. As a result, location of many of the substantial functions of a digital business must occur in locations in which these key people are willing to work. Further, although digital services can substantially expand the reach of businesses, these digital services often require a massive investment in infrastructure components. For example, cloud computing providers must build "server farms" of interconnected computers, and while there may be some flexibility as to where these resources are located, concerns like access to inexpensive and reliable sources of power and cooling may heavily influence the choice of location. In addition, in many businesses the user experience is meaningfully improved by proximity to the core infrastructure.

163. The result is that there are often compelling reasons for businesses to ensure that infrastructure resources are placed as close as possible to where key markets of users are, so that users experience less latency, shorter lag time, and higher quality. In addition, in some businesses, the need for a tangible presence in a jurisdiction for regulatory reasons may also limit choices about where to locate infrastructure and business activities.

4.3.2. Reliance on data and user participation

164. It is common in the digital economy for businesses to collect data about their customers, users, suppliers, and operations. For example, the use of a product or service by a user may provide data about the user that has value to the business as an input either in improving existing products and services or in providing products and services to another group of customers. Although businesses have always used information about interactions with customers to improve their business offerings, digital technologies and the shift to a participatory "culture" have greatly increased the ability of an enterprise to leverage and monetise such activities. As a result, data gathered from customers and users has increased in importance in certain businesses of the digital economy. In certain social networking-focused business models, for instance, companies frequently report to their investors that the active collaboration of their users is a key value-driver of the business.

165. Data can include both personalised data and data that is not personalised, and can be obtained in a number of ways. In the case of personal data, as mentioned in Chapter 3 (3.1.5 Use of data), it can be obtained directly from customers (for example, when registering for an online service), observed (for example, by recording Internet browsing preferences, location data, etc.), or inferred based on analysis in combination with other data. It is estimated that sources such as online or mobile financial transactions, social media traffic, and GPS co-ordinates generate in excess of 2.5 exabytes (billions of gigabytes) of data every day (World Economic Forum, 2012). The dividing line between personal and non-personal data is not always clear; however, as data obtained from multiple private and public sources

will frequently be combined in order to create value. A recent study quantifies the value of the Data-Driven Marketing Economy (DDME) and looks at the revenues generated for the US economy. The study found that the DDME added USD 156 billion in revenue to the United States economy in 2012 and notes that the real value of data is in its application and exchange across the DDME (Data-Driven Marketing Institute, 2013).

166. Although the use of data to improve products and services is not unique to the digital economy, the massive use of data has been facilitated by an increase in computing power and storage capacity and a decrease in data storage cost, as shown in Figures 4.9 and 4.10, which has greatly increased the ability to collect, store, and analyse data at a greater distance and in greater quantities than was possible before. The capacity to collect and analyse data is rapidly increasing as the number of sensors embedded in devices that are networked to computing resources increases. For example, while traditional data collection for utility companies was limited to yearly measurement, coupled with random samplings throughout the year, smart metering could increase that measurement rate to 15 minute samples, a 35 000 time increase in the amount of data collected (OECD, 2013). This has manifested itself in particular in the concept of "big data", meaning datasets large enough that they cannot be managed or analysed using typical database management tools. Data analytics, defined as the use of data storage and process techniques to support decisions, are becoming a driver for innovation in a number of scientific areas and are used increasingly in collaborative and crowd-based projects. In this regard, a text search performed on one of the largest repositories of scientific publications shows that articles related to data mining doubled during the last decade, as shown in Figure 4.11. The value of the ability to obtain and analyse data, and big data in particular, is increasingly well documented by market observers.

Figure 4.9. **Estimated worldwide data storage**

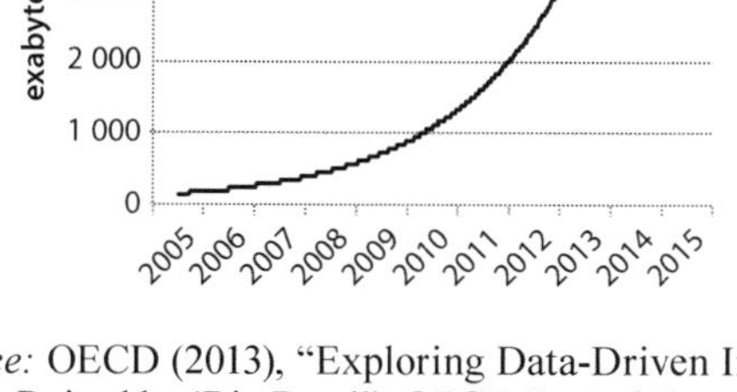

Figure 4.10. **Average data storage cost for consumers 1998-2012**

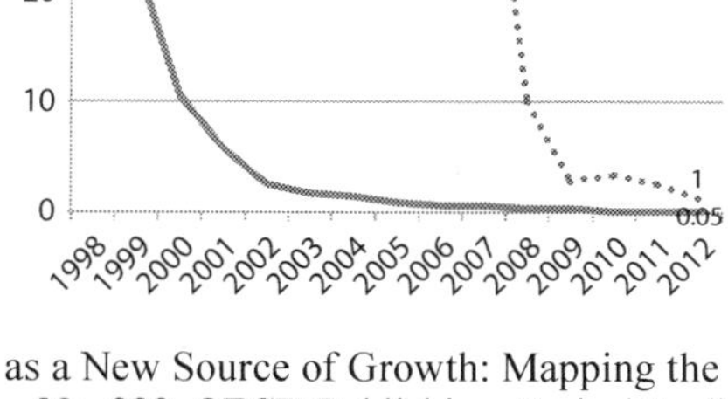

Source: OECD (2013), "Exploring Data-Driven Innovation as a New Source of Growth: Mapping the Policy Issues Raised by 'Big Data'", *OECD Digital Economy Papers*, No. 222, OECD Publishing, Paris, http://dx.doi.org/10.1787/5k47zw3fcp43-en.

Figure 4.11. **Data mining-related scientific articles, 1995-2014**

Per thousand articles

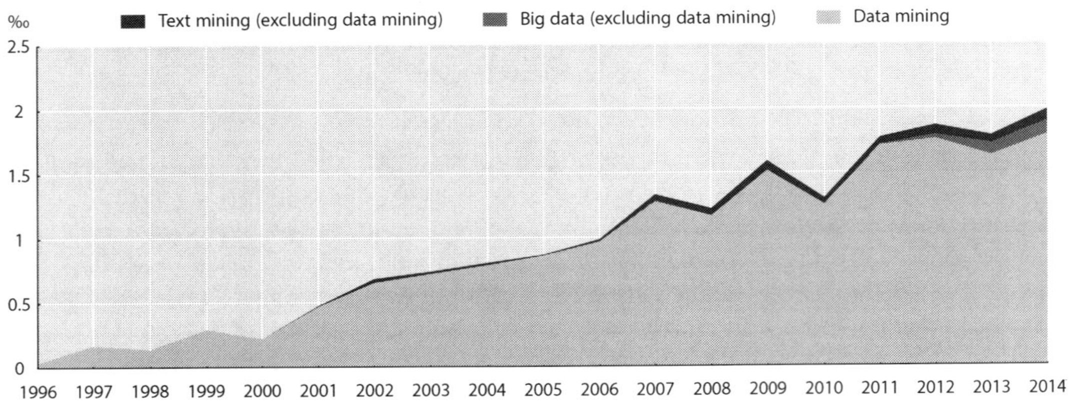

StatLink http://dx.doi.org/10.1787/888933147825

Source: OECD computations based on on Science Direct repository, www.sciencedirect.com, July 2014, in OECD (2014) *Measuring the Digital Economy: A New Perspective*, OECD Publishing, Paris, http://dx.doi.org/10.1787/9789264221796-en.

167. For example, in a 2011 report on big data, the McKinsey Global Institute estimated the value that could be created through the analysis and use of big data at USD 300 billion in the health sector in the United States and at EUR 250 billion in the general government sector in Europe. The same report estimates that use of big data could generate a total consumer surplus of USD 600 billion. Big data has substantial application in targeting government aid and services as well. It has been used, for example, to monitor refugee movements following natural disasters, in order to ensure that health risks could be accurately predicted and aid could be well targeted (World Economic Forum, 2012).

168. The McKinsey Global Institute Report notes five broad ways in which leveraging big data can create value for businesses:

i. Creating transparency by making data more easily accessible in a timely manner to stakeholders with the capacity to use the data.

ii. Managing performance by enabling experimentation to analyse variability in performance and understand its root causes.

iii. Segmenting populations to customise products and services.

iv. Improve decision making by replacing or supporting human decision making with automated algorithms.

v. Improve the development of new business models, products, and services.

4.3.3. Network effects

169. Networks effects refer to the fact that decisions of users may have a direct impact on the benefit received by other users. A simple example of this is the introduction of the fax machine. While a single fax machine had no utility by itself, users choosing to purchase a fax machine received the benefit of the decisions of earlier users to purchase a fax machine, in the form of the ability to communicate through this new technology with an existing network of potential counterparties.

170. These network effects are an important feature of many businesses in the digital economy. Network effects are seen whenever compatibility with other users is important, even where the primary purpose of a particular technology may not be to interact with others. For example, a widely-adopted operating system will generally have a larger amount of software written for it, resulting in a better user experience. These effects are known as positive externalities, meaning situations in which the welfare of a person is improved by the actions of other persons, without explicit compensation. For example, when additional people join a social network, the welfare of the existing users is increased, even though there is no explicit agreement compensation among the users for this improvement. Externalities can also be negative. For example, as an increasing number of persons use a communications network at the same time, congestion may decrease the value to each user of the network, with no compensation among the affected parties (Easley and Kleinberg, 2010).

171. Some network effects come from users' marginal utility to each other: the more users there are, the higher the value created is. A simple example is a media sharing site, in which all content is generated by users, and the experience of users is enhanced as additional users join and share content. Where a business model encourages interactivity among users, it tends to encourage these network effects. For example, in certain business models, network effects come from a competitive advantage gained from the critical mass of buyers and sellers. A retail site may develop an architecture that encourages users to review and tag products. These user reviews enhance the ability of users to make informed choices, while product tagging improves their ability to find products relevant to their interests.

172. Other network effects derive from vertical integration, relying on synergies between different layers or different applications to create added value and consolidate market position. This is particularly illustrated by the trend toward the "Internet of Things", in which companies deploy software in many devices and objects, and leverage this web of infrastructure to sell goods or services either to the owners of those devices or to advertisers. In this model, hardware and software infrastructure becomes a privileged channel to get in touch with end users and to create value by monetising their attention (advertising-based business models), the data that flows from them, or the externalities generated through network effects, or through selling them goods or services.

4.3.4. Multi-sided business models

173. A multi-sided business model is one that is based on a market in which multiple distinct groups of persons interact through an intermediary or platform, and the decisions of each group of persons affects the outcome for the other groups of persons through a positive or negative externality. In a multi-sided business model, the prices charged to the members of each group reflect the effects of these externalities. If the activities of one side create a positive externality for another side (for example more clicks by users on links sponsored by advertisers), then the prices to that other side can be increased.

174. An example of a multi-sided business model involving positive externalities for different sides of the market is a payment card system, which will be more valuable to merchants if more consumers use the card, and more valuable to consumers if more merchants accept the card. Similarly, an operating system is more valuable to end users if more developers write software for it, and more valuable to software developers if more potential software purchasers use the operating system.

175. A negative externality from one side for another side (e.g. displays of intrusive and unattractive advertising banners) can be offset by a lower price, or even no charge or a

reward for the users. The classic case in which one side experiences negative externalities from the other side's participation is found in the media industry. In that case, a company attracts users by providing content (television or radio programming, a magazine, a trade publication, a phonebook, or a newspaper) for free or at a cost less than the cost of production. The media company displays advertisements to its readers/listeners/viewers and earns revenue from advertisers whose ads it displays. Alternatively, it might earn revenue from selling information about its readers/listeners/viewers to interested parties.

176. The rise of the digital economy made multi-sided business models more prevalent in a cross-border context. In this regard, two key characteristics of multi-sided business models in the digital economy should be noted:

- **Flexibility:** The nature of digital information and the infrastructure of the Internet greatly expand the facility to design and implement multi-sided business models. Resources such as content, user data, or executable code can be stored to create value long after they have been produced. This specific nature of digital resources makes them an asset in business models where the different sides of the market can be created then dynamically adapted based on evolving technology, the latest expression of consumer demand, and a firm's position on the market. In addition, as discussed below, digital technology has enhanced the ability to collect, analyse and manipulate user and market data, which has allowed platforms to enhance the value to one side of a market of the participation of the other side of the market.
- **Reach:** The digital economy also makes it easier to locate the different sides of the same business model in different countries. Whereas many traditional multi-sided business models such as broadcasting paid for by advertising, or shopping malls were confined to a limited perimeter due to physical constraints or to regulations, over-the-top businesses in the digital economy can more easily connect two sides that are located far from one another to maximise value on each side. For instance, resources designed to collect data can be located near individual users, whereas the infrastructure necessary to sell this data to paying customers can be located elsewhere.

177. The digital economy features two prominent categories of multi-sided business models. First, a business can operate several applications that provide complementary services. This creates two types of synergy: on the one hand, the various activities pool their resources such as executable code, content, or user data; on the other hand, the activities may be put into a package that is more attractive for users. Second, vertical platform models are used to make resources available for third-party developers so as to attract their creativity as part of open innovation strategies. A platform is often the result of the large-scale development of an application that gets commoditised. For example, a company may develop a social networking service, using internally produced applications to attract consumers and funding operations through the sale of advertising. The company may also choose to open an application programming interface (API) which allows developers to easily implement applications using the platform. Access to the API minimises the developers' initial investment and facilitates their access to the market of consumers that use the platform. The participation of the developers, in turn, enhances the user experience, thereby further strengthening the company's position in the marketplace.

4.3.5. Tendency toward monopoly or oligopoly

178. In some markets, particularly where a company is the first actor to gain traction on an immature market, network effects combined with low incremental costs may enable the company to achieve a dominant position in a very short time. This ability to gain traction can be enhanced where a patent or other intellectual property right grants one competitor the exclusive power to exploit a particular innovation in a particular market. The impact of these network effects tend to lead to this result, for example, where companies provide a platform or market in which users on one side of the market prefer to use only a single provider, so that value to those users is enhanced when a single standard is chosen, and the price that can be charged to the other side is enhanced because the platform becomes the only means of access to those users. Ease of adoption of a new platform means that some players, as a result of customer choices compounded by network effects, have been able to rise to a dominant market position extremely quickly. In some cases, despite the volatility outlined below, companies have been able to leverage that market position to secure dominance. In markets that feature this tendency, network effects are magnified. It should be noted, however, that in the digital economy, many networks operate simultaneously, with the result that in many cases competition in a monopolised market may be influenced by other markets, which combined with the reduced entry barriers, can moderate monopoly power in the first market.

4.3.6. Volatility

179. Technological progress has led to progress in miniaturisation and a downward trend in the cost of computing power. In addition, neither an Internet end user nor in many cases the service provider are required to pay a marginal price for using the network. These factors, combined with increased performance and capital expenditure have markedly reduced barriers to entry for new Internet-based businesses. These factors have combined to foster innovation and the constant development of new business models. As a result, in short periods of time, companies that appeared to control a substantial part of the market and enjoyed a dominant position for a short period of time have found themselves rapidly losing market share to challengers that built their businesses on more powerful technology, a more attractive value proposal, or a more sustainable business model. Due to the fast pace of innovation, the few companies that have managed long-term success typically have done so by investing substantial resources in research and development and in acquiring start-ups with innovative ideas, launching new features and new products, and continually evaluating and modifying business models in order to leverage their market position and maintain dominance in the market.

Notes

1. E-commerce includes orders made over the Internet, through an extranet (a network where outside business partners, supplier or customers can have limited access to a portion of enterprise intranet/network), or through an electronic data interchange (EDI – a proprietary electronic system used for exchanging business data over networks).

2. Cloud computing is defined in the report of the US National Institute of Standards and Technology (NIST) as "a model for enabling ubiquitous, convenient, on-demand network access to a shared

pool of configurable computing resources (e.g. networks, servers, storage, applications, and services) that can be rapidly provisioned and released with minimal management effort or service provider interaction."

According to NIST, the cloud model is composed of five essential characteristics:

- **On-demand self-service**: A user can unilaterally act without requiring human interaction with each service's provider.
- **Broad network access**: Capabilities are available over the network and accessed through standard mechanisms that promote use by heterogeneous client platforms (e.g. mobile phones, laptops, and PDAs).
- **Resource pooling**: The provider's computing resources (e.g. storage, processing, memory, network bandwidth, and virtual machines) are pooled to serve multiple users using a multi-tenant model.
- **Rapid elasticity**: Capabilities can be rapidly and elastically provisioned.
- **Measured service**: resources use can be monitored, controlled, and reported providing transparency for both the provider and consumer of the utilised service.

3. The ICT Top 250 list is a well-established list compiled by the OECD since 2002. The sources used to identify the top ICT firms include Business Week's Information Technology 100, Software Magazine's Top 50, Forbes 2000, Washington Post 200, Forbes Largest Private Firms, Top 100 Outsourcing, World Top 25 Semiconductors. The list relies on financial reports available publicly. The OECD defines ICT activities as production of goods or services "primarily…intended to fulfil or enable the function of information processing and communication by electronic means, including transmission and display" and therefore ICT firms are those that produce the equipment, software and services that enable those activities. Each of the top 250 firms is classified by ICT industry sector: *(i)* communication equipment and systems; *(ii)* electronics; *(iii)* semiconductors; *(iv)* IT equipment and systems; *(v)* IT services; *(vi)* software; *(vii)* Internet; and *(viii)* telecommunication services. Note that these figures describe total revenue earned, rather than net profits.

Bibliography

DDMI (Data Driven Marketing Institute) (2013), "The Value of Data: Consequences for Insight, Innovation, and Efficiency in the U.S. Economy", DMA.

Emarketer.com (2014), "Worldwide Ecommerce Sales to Increase Nearly 20% in 2014", www.emarketer.com/Article/Worldwide-Ecommerce-Sales-Increase-Nearly-20-2014/1011039 (accessed on 02 June 2015).

Easley. D, Kleinberg. J (2010), *Networks, Clouds and Markets: Reasoning about a Highly Connected World*, Cambridge University Press, United Kingdom.

Gartner, Inc. (2013), "Gartner says Mobile App Stores Will See Annual Downloads Reach 102 Billion in 2013", www.gartner.com/newsroom/id/2592315 (accessed on 15 May 2014).

OECD (2015), OECD Digital Economy Outlook 2015, OECD Publishing Paris, http://dx.doi.org/10.1787/9789264232440-en.

OECD (2014), *Measuring the Digital Economy: A New Perspective*, OECD Publishing, Paris, http://dx.doi.org/10.1787/9789264221796-en.

OECD (2013), *OECD Science, Technology and Industry Scoreboard 2013: Innovation for Growth*, OECD Publishing, Paris. http://dx.doi.org/10.1787/sti_scoreboard-2013-en.

OECD (2013), "Exploring Data-Driven Innovation as a New Source of Growth: Mapping the Policy Issues Raised by "Big Data"", *OECD Digital Economy Papers*, No. 222, OECD Publishing, Paris, http://dx.doi.org/10.1787/5k47zw3fcp43-en.

OECD (2012), *OECD Internet Economy Outlook 2012*, OECD Publishing, Paris, http://dx.doi.org/10.1787/9789264086463-en.

OECD (2011), *OECD Guide to Measuring the Information Society 2011*, OECD Publishing, Paris, http://dx.doi.org/10.1787/9789264113541-en.

PricewaterhouseCoopers. (2015), *Global Entertainment and Media Outlook: 2015-2019.*

Vidyasekar, Archana Devi (2014) Future of B2B Online Retailing, www.frost.com, Accessed 14/09/2015, Frost and Sullivan.

World Trade Organisation (2013), *E-Commerce in Developing Countries: Opportunities and Challenges for Small and Medium-Sized Enterprises*, World Trade Organisation, Geneva.

Chapter 5

Identifying opportunities for BEPS in the digital economy

This chapter provides a general discussion of the common features of tax planning structures that raise base erosion and profit shifting (BEPS) concerns. It then provides a detailed description of the core elements of BEPS strategies with respect to both direct and indirect taxation.

5.1. Common features of tax planning structures raising BEPS concerns

180. As noted in the BEPS Action Plan (OECD, 2013), BEPS concerns are raised by situations in which taxable income can be artificially segregated from the activities that generate it, or in the case of value added tax (VAT), situations in which no or an inappropriately low amount of tax is collected on remote digital supplies to exempt businesses or multi-location enterprises (MLEs) that are engaged in exempt activities. These situations undermine the integrity of the tax system and potentially increase the difficulty of reaching revenue goals. In addition, when certain taxpayers are able to shift taxable income away from the jurisdiction in which income producing activities are conducted, other taxpayers may ultimately bear a greater share of the burden. BEPS activities also distort competition, as corporations operating only in domestic markets or refraining from BEPS activities may face a competitive disadvantage relative to multinational enterprises (MNEs) that are able to avoid or reduce tax by shifting their profits across borders.[1]

181. The Task Force on the Digital Economy (TFDE) discussed a number of tax and legal structures that can be used to implement business models in the digital economy. These structures are outlined in Annex B and show existing opportunities to achieve BEPS. In many cases, the nature of the strategies used to achieve BEPS in digital businesses is similar to the nature of strategies used to achieve BEPS in more traditional businesses. Some of the key characteristics of the digital economy may, however, exacerbate risks of BEPS in some circumstances, in the context of both direct and indirect taxation. Therefore, it is necessary to examine closely not only how business models may have evolved in the digital economy, but also how overall business models can be implemented in an integrated manner on an international scale from a legal and tax structuring perspective.

182. The following paragraphs consider in more detail how BEPS strategies manifest in the digital economy. The discussion below is intended to help identify the key elements of BEPS strategies in the context of direct taxation, and how those strategies take advantage of the key features of the digital economy. In addition, in the context of VAT, while there is considerable diversity in the structure of VAT systems and in how they operate in practice, the discussion below broadly illustrates ways in which the digital economy places pressure on VAT systems.

5.2. BEPS in the context of direct taxation

183. The February 2013 Report *Addressing Base Erosion and Profit Shifting* (OECD, 2013b) identifies a number of co-ordinated strategies associated with BEPS in the context of direct taxation, which can often be broken down into four elements:

- Minimisation of taxation in the market country by avoiding a taxable presence, or in the case of a taxable presence, either by shifting gross profits via trading structures or by reducing net profit by maximising deductions at the level of the payer.
- Low or no withholding tax at source.
- Low or no taxation at the level of the recipient (which can be achieved via low-tax jurisdictions, preferential regimes, or hybrid mismatch arrangements) with entitlement to substantial non-routine profits often built-up via intra-group arrangements.
- No current taxation of the low-tax profits at the level of the ultimate parent.

Figure 5.1. **BEPS planning in the context of income tax**

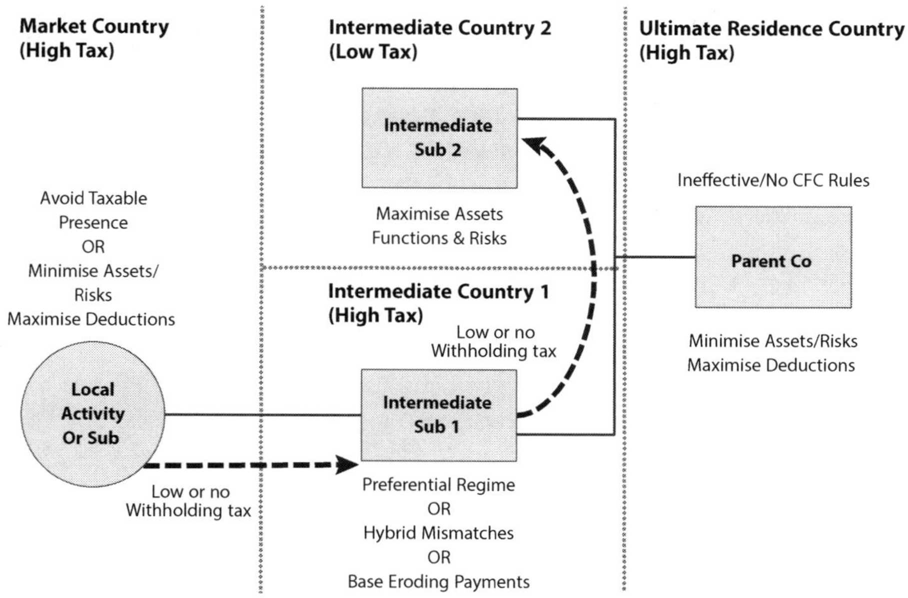

5.2.1. Eliminating or reducing tax in the market country

5.2.1.1. Avoiding a taxable presence

184. In many digital economy business models, a non-resident company may interact with customers in a country remotely through a website or other digital means (e.g. an application on a mobile device) without maintaining a physical presence in the country. Increasing reliance on automated processes may further decrease reliance on local physical presence. The domestic laws of most countries require some degree of physical presence before business profits are subject to taxation. In addition, under Articles 5 and 7 of the OECD Model Tax Convention, a company is subject to tax on its business profits in a country of which it is a non-resident only if it has a permanent establishment (PE) in that country. Accordingly, such non-resident company may not be subject to tax in the country in which it has customers.

185. Companies in many industries have customers in a country without a PE in that country, communicating with those customers via phone, mail, and fax and through independent agents. That ability to maintain some level of business connection within a country without being subject to tax on business profits earned from sources within that country is the result of particular policy choices reflected in domestic laws and relevant double tax treaties, and is not in and of itself a BEPS issue. However, while the ability of a company to earn revenue from customers in a country without having a PE in that country is not unique to digital businesses, it is available at a greater scale in the digital economy than was previously the case. Where this ability, coupled with strategies that eliminate taxation in the State of residence, results in such revenue not being taxed anywhere, BEPS concerns are raised. In addition, under some circumstances, tax in a market jurisdiction can be artificially avoided by fragmenting operations among multiple group entities in order to qualify for the exceptions to PE status for preparatory and auxiliary activities, or by otherwise ensuring that each location through which business is conducted falls below the PE threshold. Structures of this type raise BEPS concerns.

5.2.1.2. Minimising the income allocable to functions, assets and risks in market jurisdictions

186. In many cases, an MNE group does maintain a degree of presence in countries that represent significant markets for its products. In the context of the digital economy, an enterprise may establish a local subsidiary or a PE, with the local activities structured in a way that generates little taxable profit. Where these structures accurately reflect the functions performed in each jurisdiction, the mere fact that business functions needed to conduct business in a particular country may be more limited in one type of business than in another does not raise BEPS issues in and of itself. This is true even if tax rates are among the factors taken into account when deciding to centralise business operations in a particular location. The ability to allocate functions, assets and risks in a way that minimises taxation does, however, create incentives to, for example, contractually allocate them in a way that does not fully reflect the actual conduct of the parties, and that would not be chosen in the absence of tax considerations. For example, assets, in particular intangibles, and risks related to the activities carried out at the local level may be allocated via contractual arrangements to other group members operating in a low-tax environment in a way that minimises the overall tax burden of the MNE group.

187. Under these structures, there is an incentive for the affiliate in the low-tax environment to undervalue (typically at the time of the transfer) the transferred intangibles or other hard-to-value income-producing assets, while claiming that it is entitled to have large portions of the MNE group's income allocated to it on the basis of its legal ownership of the undervalued intangibles, as well as on the basis of the risks assumed and the financing it provides. Operations in higher tax jurisdictions can be contractually stripped of risk, and can avoid claiming ownership of intangibles or other valuable assets or holding the capital that funds the core profit making activities of the group. Economic returns are thus reduced and income is shifted into low-tax environments.

188. Examples of digital economy structures that can be used to minimise the tax burden in market jurisdictions through contractual allocation of assets and risks include using a subsidiary or PE to perform marketing or technical support, or to maintain a mirrored server to enable faster customer access to the digital products sold by the group, with a principal company contractually bearing the risks and claiming ownership of intangibles generated by these activities. A company may, for example, limit risk at the local company level by limiting capitalisation of that entity so that it is financially unable to bear risk. In the case of businesses selling tangible products online, a local subsidiary or PE may maintain a warehouse and assist in the fulfilment of orders. These subsidiaries or PEs will be taxable in their jurisdiction on the profits attributable to services they provide, but the amount they earn may be limited. Alternatively, functions allocated to local staff under contractual arrangements may not correspond with the substantive functions performed by the staff. For example, staff may not have formal authority to conclude contracts on behalf of a non-resident enterprise, but may perform functions that indicate effective authority to conclude those contracts. If the allocations of functions, assets, and risks do not correspond to actual allocations, or if less-than-arm's length compensation is provided for intangibles of a principal company, these structures may present BEPS concerns.

5.2.1.3. Maximising deductions in market jurisdictions

189. Once a taxable presence in the market country has been established, another common technique to reduce taxable income is to maximise the use of deductions for payments made to other group companies in the form of interest, royalties, service fees, etc. In many cases,

MNEs engaging in BEPS practices attempt to reduce taxable income in a source country by maximising the amount of deductible payments made to affiliates in other jurisdictions. For example, an affiliate in a low-tax jurisdiction may, due to a favourable credit rating, be able to borrow money at a low rate. It may then lend money to its subsidiaries in high-tax jurisdictions at a higher rate, thereby reducing the income of those subsidiaries by the amount of the deductible interest payments. Alternatively, an affiliate may use hybrid instruments to create deductible payments for a subsidiary in a source country that result in no inclusion in the country of residence of the affiliate. Payments (including underpayments) for the use of intangibles held by low-tax group companies or for services rendered by other group companies can also be used to reduce taxable income in the market country. These techniques can be used to reduce the taxable income from the local operations to extremely low amounts.

5.2.2. Avoiding withholding tax

190. A company may be subject to withholding tax in a country in which it is not a resident if it receives certain payments, including interest or royalties, from payers in that country. If allowed under a treaty between the jurisdictions of the payer and recipient, however, a company in the digital economy may be entitled to reduced withholding or exemption from withholding on payments of profits to a lower-tax jurisdiction in the form of royalties or interest. Structures that involve treaty shopping by interposing shell companies located in countries with favourable treaty networks that contain insufficient protections against treaty abuse raise BEPS concerns.

5.2.3. Eliminating or reducing tax in the intermediate country

191. Eliminating or reducing tax in an intermediate country can be accomplished through the application of preferential domestic tax regimes, the use of hybrid mismatch arrangements, or through excessive deductible payments made to related entities in low or no-tax jurisdictions.

192. Companies may locate functions, assets, or risks in low-tax jurisdictions or countries with preferential regimes, and thereby allocate income to those locations. While functions are often located in a particular jurisdiction for non-tax reasons such as access to skilled labour or necessary resources, as business functions grow increasingly mobile, taxpayers may increasingly be able to locate functions in a way that takes advantage of favourable tax regimes.

193. In the context of the digital economy, for example, the rights in intangibles and their related returns can be assigned and transferred among associated enterprises, and may be transferred, sometimes for a less-than-arm's length price,[2] to an affiliate in a jurisdiction where income subsequently earned from those intangibles is subject to unduly low or no-tax due to the application of a preferential regime. This creates tax planning opportunities for MNEs and presents substantial risks of base erosion. Heavy reliance in the digital economy on intangibles as a source of value may exacerbate the ability to concentrate value-creating intangibles in this way.

194. Companies may also reduce tax in an intermediate country by generating excessive deductible payments to related entities that are themselves located in low or no-tax jurisdictions or otherwise entitled to a low rate of taxation on the income from those payments. For example, an operating company located in an intermediate jurisdiction may use intangibles held by another affiliate in a low-tax jurisdiction. The royalties for the use of these intangibles may be used to effectively eliminate taxable profits in the intermediate jurisdiction. Alternatively,

an entity in an intermediate jurisdiction may make substantial payments to a holding company located in a low or no-tax jurisdiction for management fees or head office expenses. Companies may also avoid taxes in an intermediate country by using hybrid mismatch arrangements to generate deductible payments with no corresponding inclusion in the country of the payee. Companies may also use arbitrage between the residence rules of the intermediate country and the ultimate residence country to create stateless income. In addition, companies may assert that the functions performed, assets used, and risks assumed in the intermediate country are limited.

5.2.4. Eliminating or reducing tax in the country of residence of the ultimate parent

195. Broadly speaking, the same techniques that are used to reduce taxation in the market country can also be used to reduce taxation in the country of the ultimate parent company of the group or where the headquarters are located. This can involve contractually allocating risk and legal ownership of mobile assets like intangibles to group entities in low-tax jurisdictions, while group members in the jurisdiction of the headquarters are undercompensated for the important functions relating to these risks and intangibles that continue to be performed in the jurisdiction of the headquarters. In this situation it can be claimed that a marginal remuneration for the important functions is arm's length and that all the remaining profits should be attributed to the legal owner of movable assets or to the party that is contractually bearing the risk.

196. In addition, companies may avoid tax in the residence country of their ultimate parent if that country has an exemption or deferral system for foreign-source income and either does not have a controlled foreign company (CFC) regime that applies to income earned by controlled foreign corporations of the parent, or has a regime with inadequate coverage of certain categories of passive or highly mobile income, including in particular certain income with respect to intangibles. For example, the parent company may transfer hard-to-value intangibles to a subsidiary in a low or no-tax jurisdiction, thereby causing income earned with respect to those intangibles to be allocated to that jurisdiction without appropriate compensation to the parent company. In some cases, a CFC regime might permit the residence jurisdiction to tax income from these intangibles. Many jurisdictions, however, either do not have a CFC regime, have a regime that fails to apply to certain categories of income that are highly mobile, or have a regime that can be easily avoided using hybrid mismatch arrangements.

5.3. Opportunities for BEPS with respect to VAT

197. To the extent that Guidelines 2 and 4 of the OECD's "Guidelines on place of taxation for B2B supplies of services and intangibles" (see Chapter 6 and Annex D below) are not implemented, under certain conditions opportunities for tax planning by businesses and corresponding BEPS concerns for governments in relation to VAT may arise with respect to *(i)* remote digital supplies to exempt businesses and *(ii)* remote digital supplies acquired by enterprises that have establishments (branches) in more than one jurisdiction (MLE) that are engaged in exempt activities.

5.3.1. Remote digital supplies to exempt businesses

198. VAT is generally not designed to be a tax on businesses as businesses are generally able to recover any tax they pay on their inputs. Many VAT jurisdictions using the destination principle for business-to-business (B2B) digital supplies will generally require a business customer in their jurisdiction to self-assess VAT on acquisitions of remotely delivered services and intangibles and then allow the business to claim a credit for this self-assessed VAT. The vast number of cross-border supplies made between businesses (other than businesses engaged in exempt activities) do not therefore, generally create BEPS concerns. BEPS concerns in a VAT context could arise however, with respect to offshore digital supplies made to exempt businesses (e.g. the financial services industry). Where a business is engaged in VAT-exempt activities, no VAT is levied on the exempt supplies made by the business, while VAT incurred by the business on the associated inputs is not deductible.

199. For example, a business acquiring a data processing service from a non-resident supplier would be required to self-assess VAT according to the rules of the jurisdiction in which it is located and could claim an off-setting credit for this self-assessed VAT (some jurisdictions may not require the business to self-assess tax as it is entitled to an offsetting credit). If the business customer is an exempt business, it is still required to self-assess VAT in these jurisdictions but would not be able to claim a credit for the self-assessed tax. The exempt business is then "input taxed" in its residence jurisdiction, where it is assumed to use the service for making exempt supplies.

200. However, some jurisdictions currently do not require the exempt business to self-assess VAT on the services and intangibles acquired from abroad. In such case, no VAT is levied on the transaction. BEPS concerns also arise if the data processing services would be subject to VAT in the jurisdiction where the supplier is resident (established, located). The VAT would then accrue to the jurisdiction in which the supplier is situated and not the jurisdiction of the exempt business. This is likely to raise concerns particularly where this jurisdiction has no VAT or a VAT rate lower than the rate in the jurisdiction of the exempt business customer. In these cases, the exempt business customer would pay no VAT or an inappropriately low amount of VAT. The above cases illustrate how an exempt business could pay no or an inappropriately low amount of VAT when acquiring digital supplies from suppliers abroad. They also illustrate how domestic suppliers of competing services could face potential competitive pressures from non-resident suppliers. Domestic suppliers are required to collect and remit VAT on their supplies of services to domestic businesses while non-resident suppliers could structure their affairs so that they collect no or an inappropriately low amount of VAT.

5.3.2. Remote digital supplies to a multi-location enterprise

201. BEPS concerns could also arise in cases where a digital supply is acquired by an MLE. It is common practice for multinational businesses to arrange for a wide scope of services to be acquired centrally to realise economies of scale. Typically, the cost of acquiring such a service or intangible is initially borne by the establishment that has acquired it and, in line with normal business practice, is subsequently recharged to the establishments using the service or intangible. The establishments are charged for their share of the service or intangible on the basis of the internal recharge arrangements, in accordance with corporate tax, accounting and other regulatory requirements. However, many VAT jurisdictions do not currently apply VAT to transactions that occur between establishments of one single legal entity.

202. This means that where an establishment of an MLE acquires a service, for instance data processing services, for use by other establishments in other jurisdictions, no additional

VAT would apply on any internal cost allocations or recharges made within the MLE for the use of these services by other establishments. On the other hand, the establishment that acquired the service will be generally entitled to recover any input VAT on the acquisition of these services if it is a taxable business. In other words, the other establishments using the data processing services are able to acquire their portion of these services without incurring any VAT. This is generally not a great concern from a VAT perspective if all of the establishments of the MLE using the service are taxable businesses. This is because in this case they have a right to recover any input VAT. However, where the establishments using the data processing services are exempt businesses, they are not normally entitled to recover VAT paid on their inputs.

203. Take for example processing of data relating to banking transactions: if an establishment of a multinational bank would acquire such services directly from a local supplier, it would generally incur input VAT on these services; it would not be able to deduct this input VAT as it relates to VAT-exempt activities. Alternatively, this establishment of a multinational bank could acquire these processing services though another establishment of the same bank in another country and then reimburse this other establishment for the cost of acquiring these services on its behalf. This would allow the establishment of this bank to acquire the processing services without incurring any VAT in the jurisdiction where it is located, as no VAT is levied on the dealings between establishments of the same legal entity. If the acquiring establishment would be located in a country without a VAT, the multinational bank could acquire these services for all its establishments around the world without incurring any input VAT at all by channelling its acquisitions through its establishment in a no VAT jurisdiction. VAT-exempt businesses can make substantial VAT savings by using such channelling structures.

Notes

1. Such competitive disadvantages may also arise when competing enterprises are subject to different levels of taxation in their home jurisdictions, although that is beyond the concerns raised by BEPS.
2. Even when the country from which the Internet Protocol (IP) is transferred requires that transfers be made at arm's length, taxpayers may take aggressive positions that in fact result in less than an arm's length amount being recorded for tax purposes with respect to the transfer.

Bibliography

OECD (2013a), *Action Plan on Base Erosion and Profit Shifting*, OECD Publishing, Paris, http://dx.doi.org/10.1787/9789264202719-en.

OECD (2013b), *Addressing Base Erosion and Profit Shifting*, OECD Publishing, Paris, http://dx.doi.org/10.1787/9789264192744-en.

Chapter 6

Tackling BEPS in the digital economy

This chapter discusses how work on the actions of the base erosion and profit shifting (BEPS) Action Plan and in the area of indirect taxation is expected to address BEPS issues exacerbated by the key features of the digital economy, highlighting how these features were taken into account to ensure that the measures developed effectively address BEPS in the digital economy.

6.1. Introduction

204. Many of the key features of the digital economy, particularly those related to mobility, generate BEPS concerns in relation to both direct and indirect taxes. For example, the importance of intangibles in the context of the digital economy, combined with the mobility of intangibles for tax purposes under existing tax rules, generates substantial BEPS opportunities in the area of direct taxes. The mobility of users creates substantial challenges and risks in the context of the imposition of value added tax (VAT). The ability to centralise infrastructure at a distance from a market jurisdiction and conduct substantial sales into that market from a remote location, combined with increasing ability to conduct substantial activity with minimal use of personnel, generates potential opportunities to achieve BEPS by fragmenting physical operations to avoid taxation.

205. Work on the actions of the BEPS Action Plan (OECD, 2013) has taken into account these key features in order to ensure that the proposed solutions fully address BEPS in the digital economy. The following sections describe how the outputs of the BEPS Project, as well as the work on consumption taxes, are expected to address these BEPS concerns once implemented.

6.2. Restoring taxation on stateless income

206. Structures aimed at artificially shifting profits to locations where they are taxed at more favourable rates, or not taxed at all, will be addressed by the work carried out in the context of the BEPS Project. At the same time, the work on BEPS will increase transparency between taxpayers and tax administrations and among tax administrations themselves. Risk assessment processes at the level of the competent tax administration will be enhanced by measures such as the mandatory disclosure of aggressive tax planning arrangements and uniform transfer pricing documentation requirements, coupled with a template for country-by-country (CBC) reporting. There are already indications of the impact of such increased transparency measures and other forthcoming outputs of the BEPS Project on the tax planning and structuring decisions of multinational enterprise (MNE) groups.

207. The comprehensiveness of the BEPS Action Plan will ensure that, once the different measures have been implemented in a co-ordinated manner, taxation is more aligned with the location in which economic activities take place. This will address BEPS issues at the level of both the market jurisdiction and the jurisdiction of the ultimate parent company, with the aim of putting an end to the phenomenon of so-called stateless income. BEPS issues in the market jurisdiction should be addressed by preventing treaty abuse (Action 6) and preventing the artificial avoidance of permanent establishment (PE) status (Action 7). BEPS issues in the ultimate residence jurisdiction should be addressed by strengthening controlled foreign company (CFC) rules (Action 3). Both market and residence BEPS issues should be addressed by neutralising the effects of hybrid mismatch arrangements (Action 2), by limiting the base erosion via interest deductions and other financial payments (Action 4), by countering harmful tax practices more effectively (Action 5), and by ensuring that transfer pricing outcomes are in line with value creation (Actions 8-10). In the context of VAT, under certain conditions opportunities for tax planning by businesses and corresponding BEPS concerns for governments may arise to the extent that the OECD's Guidelines on place of taxation (see Annex D) for business-to-business (B2B) supplies of services and intangibles are not implemented.

208. Although all of the elements of the BEPS Action Plan will have an impact on BEPS in the digital economy, Actions 3 (strengthen CFC rules), 7 (prevent the artificial avoidance

of PE status), and 8-10 (assure that transfer pricing outcomes are in line with value creation) were identified as particularly relevant to the digital economy.

209. In the work on Action 3, it was noted that income from digital goods and services may be particularly mobile due to the importance of intangibles in the provision of such goods and services.

210. In the context of Action 7, it was noted that the work should consider whether certain activities that were previously considered preparatory or auxiliary for the purposes of these exceptions may be increasingly significant components of businesses in the digital economy, and if so, under what circumstances such activities may be considered core activities, and whether a reasonable, administrable rule to this effect can be developed. The work would also consider whether and how the definition of PE may need to be modified to address circumstances in which artificial arrangements relating to the sales of goods or services of one company in a multinational group effectively result in the conclusion of contracts, such that the sales should be treated as if they had been made by that company.

211. Finally, in the context of the work on Actions 8-10, it was noted that companies in the digital economy rely heavily on intangibles in creating value and producing income, and that many BEPS structures adopted by participants in the digital economy involve the transfer of intangibles or rights in intangibles to tax-advantaged locations, coupled with the position that these contractual allocations, together with legal ownership of intangibles, justify large allocations of income to the entity allocated the risk even if it performs little or no business activity. It was concluded that the BEPS work in the area of transfer pricing should take these issues in account and should also devote attention to the implications of the increased integration of MNEs and the spread of global value chains in which various stages of production are spread across multiple countries, including whether it was possible to provide simpler and clearer guidance on the application of transfer pricing methods, including profit splits in the context of global value chains.

6.2.1. Measures that will address BEPS issues in the market jurisdiction

212. A number of measures of the BEPS Action Plan will have the primary effect of restoring source taxation, in particular with respect to treaty abuse (Action 6) and artificial avoidance of PE status (Action 7).

6.2.1.1. Prevent treaty abuse (Action 6)

213. The Report *Preventing the Granting of Treaty Benefits in Inappropriate Circumstances* (OECD, 2015a) provides model rules to tackle the abuse of tax treaties. These rules provide for a minimum standard to address treaty shopping arrangements through which companies are set up in a country in order to take advantage of the treaty network of that country rather than for carrying on business activities in that country. They also prevent the use of structures involving the use of dual resident companies that claim to be resident of a particular treaty country to achieve double non-taxation. Further, the rules address unintended cases of non-taxation that result from tax treaties, in particular where countries eliminate double taxation through the exemption method. The report reflects the further work that has been done with respect to the precise contents of the model provisions and related Commentary and the implementation of the minimum standard.

214. The denial of treaty benefits in cases that could otherwise inappropriately result in double non-taxation will ensure that the market country will be able to apply its domestic law unconstrained by treaty rules aimed at preventing double taxation. This is of relevance

both in cases where the foreign company has claimed not to have a taxable presence in that country in the form of a PE or when there is indeed a taxable presence in the form of a PE or a group company, but the relevant taxable income is reduced by deductible payments. In cases where such deductible payments would be subject to a withholding tax under domestic law, the market country will be able to apply such a withholding tax without any treaty limitation.

6.2.1.2. Prevent the artificial avoidance of PE status (Action 7)

215. The treaty definition of PE may limit the application of domestic law rules applicable to the taxation of the business profits of non-resident companies derived from sources in the market country. The work done with respect to Action 7 was aimed at preventing the artificial avoidance of the treaty threshold below which the market country may not tax. This work was identified by the Task Force on the Digital Economy (TFDE) as a key area of focus in order to ensure that BEPS risks in the digital economy could be addressed. The work therefore took into account the key features of the digital economy in developing changes to the definition of PE to ensure that artificial arrangements cannot be used to circumvent the threshold for exercising taxing rights.

216. The work involved modifying the definition of PE to address circumstances in which artificial arrangements relating to the sales of goods or services of one company in a multinational group effectively result in the conclusion of contracts, such that the sales should be treated as if they had been made by that company. For example, where the sales force of a local subsidiary of an online seller of tangible products or an online provider of advertising services habitually plays the principal role in the conclusion of contracts with prospective large clients for those products or services, and these contracts are routinely concluded without material modification by the parent company, it will result in a PE for the parent company even though the subsidiary does not formally conclude those contracts, and even though the contracts may be standard form contracts. As a result, once the outcome of this work is implemented, such strategies will no longer be effective.

217. The work also ensures that where essential business activities of an enterprise are carried on at a given location in a country, the enterprise cannot benefit from the list of exceptions usually found in the definition of PE. It was therefore agreed to modify Article 5 (4) of the OECD Model Tax Convention to ensure that each of the exceptions included therein is restricted to activities that are otherwise of a "preparatory or auxiliary" character. In addition to broader tax challenges (see Chapter 7), this raises BEPS issues when the lack of taxation in the market country is coupled with techniques that reduce or eliminate tax in the country of the recipient or of the ultimate parent. In addition, a new anti-fragmentation rule was introduced to ensure that it is not possible to benefit from these exceptions through the fragmentation of business activities among closely related enterprises. As a result, where certain activities that were previously granted the benefit of these exceptions have become increasingly significant components of businesses in the digital economy, such that they are not preparatory or auxiliary in character, those activities will no longer be entitled to an exception from PE status. For example, the maintenance of a very large local warehouse in which a significant number of employees work for purposes of storing and delivering goods sold online to customers by an online seller of physical products (whose business model relies on the proximity to customers and the need for quick delivery to clients) would constitute a PE for that seller. Some countries, however, consider that there is no need to modify Art. 5(4) and that the list of exceptions in subparagraphs a) to d) of paragraph 4 should not be subject to the condition that the activities referred to in these subparagraphs be of a preparatory or auxiliary character. These countries may adopt a different version of Art. 5(4) as long as they include the anti-fragmentation rule referred to above.

6.2.2. Measures that will address BEPS issues in both market and ultimate parent jurisdictions

218. A number of measures in the BEPS Action Plan will contribute to address BEPS issues both at the level of the market jurisdiction and at the level of the parent company jurisdiction. These include the measures developed in the course of the work on Action 2 (neutralise the effects of hybrid mismatch arrangements), Action 4 (limit base erosion via interest deductions and other financial payments), Action 5 (counter harmful tax practices more effectively), and Actions 8-10 (assure that transfer pricing outcomes are in line with value creation).

6.2.2.1. Neutralise the effects of hybrid mismatch arrangements (Action 2)

219. The BEPS Action Plan notes that hybrid mismatch arrangements can be used to achieve unintended double non-taxation or long-term tax deferral by, for example, creating two deductions for a single expense, generating deductions in one jurisdiction without corresponding income inclusions in another, or misusing foreign tax credit or participation exemption regimes. In common with other MNEs, digital economy businesses take advantage of hybrid mismatch arrangements to achieve BEPS by stripping income from a market or intermediate jurisdiction or by avoiding application of CFC rules or other anti-abuse regimes. The 2015 Report on *Neutralising the Effects of Hybrid Mismatch Arrangements* (OECD, 2015b) sets out recommendations regarding the design of domestic rules and the development of model treaty provisions to neutralise the effect of hybrid instruments and entities, and includes detailed commentary explaining how the recommendations are intended to operate in practice.

6.2.2.2. Limit base erosion via interest deductions and other financial payments (Action 4)

220. The innovation that is essential to success in the digital economy must be financed. Many large and well-established digital economy players are cash rich and they often finance new ventures, the acquisition of start-ups, or other assets with intra-group debt. It is often the case that taxpayers will establish and capitalise entities in low-tax environments that are then able to engage in transactions with associated enterprises that have the effect of eroding the tax base. For example, an affiliate in a low-tax environment might be established to lend to high-tax operating entities. Interest deductions on loans from such low-tax entities can present BEPS concerns in countries where business operations actually take place. Where the capital contributed to the low-tax entity to fund these activities is borrowed from third-party lenders, the base erosion effect of these arrangements may be exacerbated.

221. In other words, existing rules may allow affiliate entities in a low-tax environment to fund the profit-generating activities of the group with intercompany debt, even though the MNE group as a whole may be much less heavily leveraged. This ultimately reduces tax at the level of the market jurisdiction and at the level of the parent company jurisdiction, with the interest often going untaxed anywhere for a number of reasons (such as the availability of preferential regimes, the use of hybrid instruments, and the availability of generous deductions). Existing tax planning arrangements within the integrated global businesses that also characterise the digital economy take advantage of this type of structuring to achieve BEPS.

222. The work done with respect to Action 4 provides an agreed framework for best practices in the design of domestic rules, in order to reduce opportunities for BEPS via

interest and other deductible financial payments. This work addresses BEPS in respect of interest paid to both related parties and third parties and addresses both inbound and outbound investment scenarios. The framework is based on a fixed ratio rule that limits an entity's net deductions for interest (and payments economically equivalent to interest) to a specified percentage of its earnings before interest, taxes, depreciation and amortisation (EBITDA). To ensure that countries apply a fixed ratio that is low enough to tackle BEPS, while recognising that not all countries are in the same position, the recommended approach includes a corridor of possible ratios of between 10 and 30% along with factors that countries should take into account in setting their fixed ratio within this corridor. Recognising that some groups are highly leveraged with third party debt for non-tax reasons, the recommended approach allows the fixed ratio rule to be supplemented by a group ratio rule that allows an entity with net interest expense above a country's fixed ratio to deduct interest up to the level of the net interest/EBITDA ratio of its worldwide group. Alternatively the fixed ratio rule based on net interest/EBITDA can be supplemented by an "equity test", whereby the fixed ratio rule does not apply if an entity can show that its equity/total assets ratio is equal to or exceeds that of its group (within a small tolerance). The framework also recommends that countries introduce targeted rules to address specific risks.

6.2.2.3. Counter harmful tax practices more effectively (Action 5)

223. Digital economy companies heavily rely on intangibles to create value and produce income. Intangibles, and income arising from the exploitation of intangibles, are by definition geographically mobile. Over the last decade, a number of OECD and non-OECD countries have introduced regimes which provide for a preferential tax treatment for certain income arising from the exploitation of intellectual property (IP), generally through a 50% to 80 % deduction or exemption of qualified IP income.

224. The work undertaken under Action 5 has therefore included an examination of intangible regimes of the type described to determine whether they constitute harmful preferential tax regimes within the meaning of the OECD's 1998 Report "Harmful Tax Competition: An Emerging Global Issue". Action 5 of the BEPS Action Plan also requires there to be substantial activity for any preferential regime and as a result the existing substance factor has been elaborated and elevated in importance. In the context of IP regimes, agreement was reached on the "nexus approach" which uses expenditures as a proxy for substantial activity, ensuring that taxpayers can only benefit from IP regimes where they engaged in research and development and incurred actual expenditures on such activities. In the context of other preferential regimes, the same principle can be applied, so that such regimes would be found to meet the substantial activities requirement where the taxpayer undertook the core income generating activities required to produce the type of business income covered by the preferential regime. Sixteen IP regimes were evaluated as part of this work.

6.2.2.4. Assure that transfer pricing outcomes are in line with value creation (Actions 8-10)

225. The BEPS work on transfer pricing addresses BEPS issues that commonly arise among companies active in the digital economy as well as other taxpayers. Taken together, the overall objective of the transfer pricing actions is to bring the allocation of income within a multinational group of companies more directly in line with the location of the economic activity that gives rise to that income (*Aligning Transfer Pricing Outcomes with Value Creation*, OECD, 2015c). This objective is pursued by focusing on key transfer pricing

issues including issues related to *(i) the transfer and use of* intangibles including hard-to-value intangibles, and cost contribution arrangements, *(ii)* delineating the actual transaction and business risks, and *(iii)* global value chains and transactional profit split methods.

i. Intangibles, including hard-to-value intangibles, and cost contribution arrangements

226. A key feature of many BEPS structures adopted by participants in the digital economy involves the transfer of intangibles or rights in intangibles to tax advantaged locations. Digital economy companies rely heavily on intangibles in creating value and producing income. Depending on the local law, transfers of intangibles and rights in intangibles at non-arm's length prices can occur in connection with licensing arrangements, cost contribution arrangements or tax structures that separate deductions relevant to the development of the intangible from the income associated with it. Transfers of intangibles at non-arm's length prices can occur *(i)* because of difficulties in valuing transferred intangibles at the time they are transferred; *(ii)* because of unequal access to information relating to value between taxpayers and tax administrations; and *(iii)* because some arrangements result in the transfer of hidden or unidentified intangibles without payment.

227. The BEPS work on intangibles addresses these issues by taking several steps. First, the work provides a broad but clear definition of intangibles for transfer pricing purposes, and makes clear that that any intangible item for which unrelated parties would provide compensation upon transfer must be compensated in transfers between associated enterprises. This will help ensure that transfers of hidden intangibles are not used to shift income. Second, the work ensures that entities within an MNE group that contribute value to intangibles either by performing or managing development functions or by bearing and controlling risks are appropriately rewarded for doing so. Specifically, the revised guidance ensures that legal ownership alone does not entitle the owner to premium profits, but that the group companies performing the important functions, contributing assets or assuming risks related to the development, enhancement, maintenance, protection and exploitation of intangibles will receive an appropriate return.

228. The work also makes clear that valuation techniques can be used to determine arm's length transfer prices when comparable transfers of intangibles cannot be identified. In situations where hard-to-value intangibles are transferred, the work ensures that post-transfer profitability of an intangible can be taken into account in the valuation in specified circumstances in order to balance the availability of information between taxpayers and tax administrations.

229. Revised guidance on cost contribution agreements (CCA) ensures that such arrangements are appropriately analysed and produce outcomes that are consistent with how and where value is created. Specifically, it ensures that the same guidance for valuing and pricing intangibles, including hard-to-value intangibles, is applicable to CCA as to other kinds of contractual arrangement. It ensures also that contributions made to CCA, with specific focus on intangibles, should not be measured at cost where this is unlikely to provide a reliable basis for determining the value of the relative contributions of participants, since this may lead to non-arm's length results.

ii. Delineating the actual transaction and allocating business risks

230. BEPS structures aimed at shifting income into low-tax environments often feature a contractual allocation of business risk into a low-tax affiliate. It then may be argued that these contractual risk allocations, justify large allocations of income to the entity allocated the risk. The argument entails the assertion that other entities in the group are contractually insulated from risk so that a low-tax affiliate is entitled to substantial amounts of income after compensating other low risk group members for their functions. The revised guidance challenges such assertions by determining that risks contractually assumed by a party that cannot in fact exercise meaningful and specifically defined control over the risks, and does not have the financial capacity to assume the risks, will be allocated to the party that does exercise such control and have the financial capacity to assume the risk. This revision is part of the requirement to accurately delineate the actual transaction between the associated enterprises by supplementing, where necessary, the terms of any contract with the evidence of the actual conduct of the parties. In combination with the proper application of transfer pricing methods in a way that prevents the allocation of profits to locations where no contributions are made to these profits, this revised guidance will lead to the allocation of an appropriate return to group companies performing the important functions, contributing important assets and controlling economically significant risks, as determined through the accurate delineation of the actual transaction.

iii. Global value chains and transactional profit split methods

231. When the arm's length principle was initially devised, it was common that each country in which an MNE group did business had its own subsidiary with full functionality and carrying out a broad range of activities reflecting the group's business as a whole. This structure was dictated by a number of factors, including slow communications, currency exchange rules, customs duties, and relatively high transportation costs that made integrated global supply chains difficult to operate. With the advent of improvements in information and communication technology (ICT), reductions in many currency and custom barriers, and the move to digital products and a service based economy, these barriers to integration broke down and MNE groups began to operate much more as single global firms.

232. Developments in ICT have thus accelerated and changed the spread of global value chains in which corporate legal structures and individual legal entities become less important and MNE groups move closer to the economist's conception of a single firm operating in a co-ordinated fashion to maximise opportunities in a global economy. Attention will therefore be devoted to the implications of this increased integration in MNEs and will evaluate the need for greater reliance on value chain analyses and transactional profit split methods.

233. The consultation process on the transactional profit split method in the course of the BEPS Project confirmed that this method can be useful when properly applied to align profits with value creation in certain circumstances. The further work on the transactional profit split method will therefore examine their application to highly integrated business operations and develop profit splitting factors that show strong correlation with value creation. This work should also address situations where comparables are not available because of the structures designed by taxpayers and could include revised guidance on the use of profit methods. This work will be carried out in 2016 and 2017 and may be relevant for highly integrated MNE groups in the digital economy.

6.2.3. Measures that will address BEPS issues in the jurisdiction of the ultimate parent

234. The work on designing effective CFC rules may also contribute to restoring taxation in the jurisdiction of the ultimate parent company. As noted in the BEPS Action Plan, one source of BEPS concerns is the possibility of creating affiliated non-resident taxpayers and routing income of resident enterprises through that non-resident affiliate. Although CFC rules have been introduced in many countries to address this, there remain many jurisdictions that lack CFC rules. Where CFC rules do exist, they do not always address BEPS in a comprehensive manner. However, effective CFC rules can reduce the incentive to shift profits from a source country into a low-tax jurisdiction. The report on Action 3, *Designing Effective Controlled Foreign Company Rules* (OECD, 2015d) provides recommendations in the form of six building blocks, including a definition of CFC income which sets out a non-exhaustive list of approaches or combination of approaches that CFC rules could use for such a definition. These approaches include categorical, substance, and excess profits analyses which could be applied on their own or combined with each other. The recommendations are designed to ensure that jurisdictions that choose to implement them will have effective CFC rules.

235. To address BEPS issues within the digital economy, CFC rules must effectively address the taxation of mobile income typically earned in the digital economy. Although CFC rules vary significantly from jurisdiction to jurisdiction, income from digital goods and services provided remotely is frequently not subject to current taxation under CFC rules. Accordingly, a MNE in a digital business can earn income in a CFC in a low-tax jurisdiction by locating key intangibles there and using those intangibles to sell digital goods and services without that income being subject to current tax, even without the CFC itself performing significant activities in its jurisdiction. As a result, a digital economy company may pay little or no tax in the CFC jurisdiction while also avoiding tax in the source country and the country of ultimate residence.

236. To address this situation, consideration was given to a number of approaches for CFC rules that could target income typically earned in the digital economy, such as IP income and income earned from the remote sale of digital goods and services. Such income may be particularly mobile due to the importance of intangibles in the provision of such goods and services and the relatively few people required to carry out online sales activities. Countries can implement these approaches to design CFC rules that would subject income that is typically earned in the digital economy to taxation in the jurisdiction of the ultimate parent company. For instance countries could use the categorical analyses to define CFC income to include types of revenue typically generated in digital economy transactions such as license fees and certain types of income from sales of digital goods and services. If countries adopted the excess profits approach this could characterise any "excess profits" generated in low tax jurisdictions, which may include profits attributable to IP-related assets, as CFC income. This approach could potentially limit the use of offshore deferral structures popular with digital economy MNEs that indefinitely defer foreign income from taxation in the residence jurisdiction. Both approaches may be combined with a substance analysis aimed at verifying whether the CFC is engaged in substantial activities in order to accurately identify and quantify shifted income.

6.3. Addressing BEPS issues in the area of consumption taxes

237. The digitisation of the economy has greatly facilitated the ability of businesses to acquire a wide range of services and intangibles from suppliers in other jurisdictions around the world and to structure their operations in a truly global manner. These developments

have allowed exempt businesses to avoid and minimise the amount of unrecoverable VAT they pay on their inputs. Section 5.3 of Chapter 5 outlined the BEPS concerns that may arise from the opportunity for businesses to structure their affairs in such a way that no or an inappropriately low amount of VAT is borne by exempt businesses on remotely delivered services and intangibles.

238. The implementation of Guidelines 2 and 4 of the OECD's International VAT/GST Guidelines on place of taxation for business-to-business (B2B) supplies of services and intangibles (see Annex D) will minimise BEPS opportunities for supplies of remotely delivered services and intangibles made to exempt businesses, including exempt entities that operate through establishments (branches) in multiple jurisdictions (multiple location entities (MLEs)).

239. Guideline 2 recommends that the taxing rights on cross-border supplies of services and intangibles between businesses be allocated to the jurisdiction where the customer has located its business establishment and that business customers be required to self-assess VAT on remotely delivered services or intangibles acquired from offshore suppliers according to the rules of the jurisdiction in which they are located.

240. Guideline 4 provides that when a supply is made to a business that is established in more than one jurisdiction, taxation should accrue to the jurisdiction where the customer's establishment (branch) using the service or intangible is located. These Guidelines set out the possible mechanisms for tax authorities to achieve the desired result in practice, which is allocation of the right to levy VAT on B2B services and intangibles to the jurisdiction where these services are used for business purposes irrespective of how the supply and acquisition of these services and intangibles were structured.

6.4. Preliminary conclusions

241. As described in Chapter 5, while no unique BEPS issues are presented by the digital economy, many of the key features of the digital economy, particularly those related to mobility, exacerbate BEPS concerns. These key features have been taken into account in the work under the BEPS Action Plan to address BEPS in the context of direct taxes, including in particular the work on CFC rules (Action 3), addressing the artificial avoidance of PE status (Action 7) and transfer pricing (Actions 8-10). As a result, it is expected that the implementation of these measures, as well as the other measures developed in the BEPS Project, will substantially address the BEPS issues exacerbated by the digital economy.

242. To ensure that BEPS can be addressed, implementation must occur quickly. In this regard, certain measures, such as the revisions to the Transfer Pricing Guidelines will be immediately applicable, while other measures, such as those relating to CFC rules and interest deductibility, will require domestic law changes. Several actions, including Action 2 (neutralise the effects of hybrid mismatch arrangements), 6 (prevent treaty abuse), 7 (prevent the artificial avoidance of PE status) and 14 (make dispute resolution mechanisms more effective) will result in modifications to the OECD Model Tax Convention. To avoid the need to engage in a series of time-consuming and costly bilateral negotiations in order to update the global network of more than 3 500 bilateral tax treaties to reflect these changes, 88 countries have begun negotiating a multilateral instrument to implement the treaty-related BEPS measures and modify bilateral tax treaties in a synchronised and efficient manner. Development of this multilateral instrument is expected to be concluded by the end of 2016.

Bibliography

OECD (2015a), *Preventing the Granting of Treaty Benefits in Inappropriate Circumstances, Action 6 – 2015 Final Report*, OECD/G20 Base Erosion and Profit Shifting Project, OECD Publishing, Paris, http://dx.doi.org/10.1787/9789264241695-en.

OECD (2015b), *Neutralising the Effects of Hybrid Mismatch Arrangements, Action 2 – 2015 Final Report*, OECD/G20 Base Erosion and Profit Shifting Project, OECD Publishing, Paris, http://dx.doi.org/10.1787/9789264241138-en.

OECD (2015c), *Aligning Transfer Pricing Outcomes with Value Creation, Actions 8-10 – 2015 Final Reports*, OECD/G20 Base Erosion and Profit Shifting Project, OECD Publishing, Paris, http://dx.doi.org/10.1787/9789264241244-en.

OECD (2015d), *Designing Effective Controlled Foreign Company Rules, Action 3 – 2015 Final Report*, OECD/G20 Base Erosion and Profit Shifting Project, OECD Publishing, Paris, http://dx.doi.org/10.1787/9789264241152-en.

OECD (2013), *Action Plan on Base Erosion and Profit Shifting*, OECD Publishing, Paris, http://dx.doi.org/10.1787/9789264202719-en.

OECD (1998), Report "Harmful Tax Competition: An Emerging Global Issue", www.oecd.org/tax/transparency/44430243.pdf.

Chapter 7

Broader direct tax challenges raised by the digital economy and the options to address them

This chapter discusses the challenges that the digital economy raises for direct taxation, with respect to nexus, the tax treatment of data, and characterisation of payments made under new business models, as well as certain administrative challenges faced by tax administrations in applying the current rules. The chapter then provides an overview of potential options that have been discussed by the Task Force on the Digital Economy to address these challenges.

7.1. The digital economy and the challenges for policy makers

243. The spread of the digital economy brings about many benefits, for example in terms of growth, employment and well-being more generally. At the same time it gives rise to a number of challenges for policy makers. These challenges extend well beyond domestic and international tax policy and touch upon areas such as international privacy law and data protection, as well as accounting and regulation.

244. From a strategic tax policy perspective, the uptake of digital technologies may potentially constrain the options available to policymakers in relation to the overall tax mix. For decades, companies have contributed to public expenses via a broad range of taxes in addition to corporate income tax. These taxes include employment taxes, environmental taxes, property and land taxes. The development of digital technologies has the potential to enable economic actors to operate in ways that avoid, remove, or significantly reduce, their tax liability within these bases. This may increase the pressure on a smaller number of taxpayers to compensate for the related loss of revenues. It also highlights the importance of designing corporate income and consumption tax systems that promote growth and investment, while reducing inequality and establishing a level playing field among economic actors.

245. The following sections examine a number of the tax challenges raised by the digital economy in relation to corporate income tax.

7.2. An overview of the tax challenges raised by the digital economy

246. The evolution of business models in general, and the growth of the digital economy in particular, have resulted in non-resident companies operating in a market jurisdiction in a fundamentally different manner today than at the time international tax rules were designed. For example, while a non-resident company has always been able to sell into a jurisdiction without a physical presence there, advances in information and communication technology (ICT) have dramatically expanded the scale at which such activity is now possible. In addition, traditionally for companies to expand opportunities in a market jurisdiction, a local physical presence in the form of manufacturing, marketing, and distribution was very often required. These in-country operations would have engaged operations such as procurement, inventory management, local marketing, branding and other activities that earned a local return subject to tax in the market country. Advances in business practices, coupled with advances in ICT and liberalisation of trade policy, have allowed businesses to centrally manage many functions that previously required local presence, rendering the traditional model of doing business in market economies obsolete. The fact that existing thresholds for taxation rely on physical presence is partly due to the need in many traditional businesses for a local physical presence in order to conduct substantial sales of goods and services into a market jurisdiction. It is also due in part to the need to ensure that the source country has the administrative capability of enforcing its taxing rights over a non-resident enterprise. The fact that less physical presence is required in market economies in typical business structures today – an effect that can be amplified in certain types of businesses in the ICT sector – therefore raises challenges for international taxation.

247. Other elements of the digital economy have also raised challenges for policy makers. As noted above, growing reliance in certain new business models on data may raise tax challenges both in terms of characterisation of and attribution of value from data, and in terms of the changing ways in which users and customers interact with businesses. Further, new revenue streams adopted in particular due to the spread of multi-sided business models or the use of massive computing power and broadband connection

trigger questions regarding the appropriate characterisation of certain transactions and payments for tax purposes. Finally, digital technologies make it easier to do business across jurisdictions, as well as enabling consumers to access products and services from anywhere in the world, generating challenges in terms of collecting the appropriate amounts of consumption tax.

248. In general terms, in the area of direct taxation, the main policy challenges raised by the digital economy fall into three broad categories:

- **Nexus**: The continual increase in the potential of digital technologies and the reduced need in many cases for extensive physical presence in order to carry on business, combined with the increasing role of network effects generated by customer interactions, can raise questions as to whether the current rules to determine nexus with a jurisdiction for tax purposes are appropriate.
- **Data**: The growth in sophistication of information technologies has permitted companies in the digital economy to gather and use information across borders to an unprecedented degree. This raises the issues of how to attribute value created from the generation of data through digital products and services, and of how to characterise for tax purposes a person or entity's supply of data in a transaction, for example, as a free supply of a good, as a barter transaction, or some other way.
- **Characterisation:** The development of new digital products or means of delivering services creates uncertainties in relation to the proper characterisation of payments made in the context of new business models, particularly in relation to cloud computing.

249. These challenges raise questions as to whether the current international tax framework continues to be appropriate to deal with the changes brought about by the digital economy and the business models that it makes possible, and also relate to the allocation of taxing rights between source and residence jurisdictions. These challenges also raise questions regarding the paradigm used to determine where economic activities are carried out and value is created for tax purposes, which is based on an analysis of the functions performed, assets used and risks assumed. At the same time, when these challenges create opportunities for achieving double non-taxation, for example due to the lack of nexus in the market country under current rules coupled with lack of taxation in the jurisdiction of the income recipient and of that of the ultimate parent company, they also generate BEPS issues.

250. Although the challenges related to corporate income tax (nexus, data and character) are distinct in nature, they may overlap with each other. For example, the characterisation of payments may trigger taxation in the jurisdiction where the payor is resident or established and hence overlap with the issue of nexus. Similarly, the collection of data from users located in a jurisdiction may trigger questions regarding whether it should give rise to nexus with that jurisdiction, and if so, whether and how the income generated from the use of these data should be attributed to that nexus. It also raises questions regarding how income from transactions involving data should be characterised for tax purposes.

251. The digital economy also creates challenges for value added tax (VAT) systems, particularly where goods, services and intangibles are acquired by private consumers from suppliers abroad. This is partly due to the absence of an effective international framework to ensure VAT collection in the jurisdiction of consumption. For economic actors, and in particular small and medium enterprises (SMEs), the absence of an international standard for charging, collecting and remitting the tax to a potentially large number of tax authorities, creates difficulties and high compliance costs. From a government viewpoint,

there is a risk of loss of revenue and trade distortion, as well as the challenge of managing tax liabilities generated by a high volume of low value transactions, which can create a significant administrative burden but marginal revenues.

252. In addition to these policy challenges, which are further discussed below, the Task Force on the Digital Economy (TFDE) has also identified a number of administrative issues raised by the digital economy. These latter issues are outlined in the box at the end of this chapter.

7.3. Nexus and the ability to have a significant presence without being liable to tax

253. Advances in digital technology have not changed the fundamental nature of the core activities that businesses carry out as part of a business model to generate profits. To generate income, businesses still need to source and acquire inputs, create or add value, and sell to customers. To support their sales activities, businesses have always needed to carry out activities such as market research, marketing and advertising, and customer support. Digital technology has, however, had significant impact on how these activities are carried out, for example by enhancing the ability to carry out activities remotely, increasing the speed at which information can be processed, analysed and utilised, and, because distance forms less of a barrier to trade, expanding the number of potential customers that can be targeted and reached. Digital infrastructure and the investments that support it can be leveraged today in many businesses to access far more customers than before. As a result, certain processes previously carried out by local personnel can now be performed cross-border by automated equipment, changing the nature and scope of activities to be performed by staff. Thus, the growth of a customer base in a country does not always need the level of local infrastructure and personnel that would have been needed in a "pre-digital" age.

254. This increases the flexibility of businesses to choose where substantial business activities take place, or to move existing functions to a new location, even if those locations may be removed both from the ultimate market jurisdiction and from the jurisdictions in which other related business functions may take place. As a result, it is increasingly possible for a business's personnel, IT infrastructure (e.g. servers), and customers each to be spread among multiple jurisdictions, away from the market jurisdiction. Advances in computing power have also meant that certain functions, including decision-making capabilities, can now be carried out by increasingly sophisticated software programmes and algorithms. For example, contracts can in some cases be automatically accepted by software programmes, so that no intervention of local staff is necessary. As discussed below, this is also true in relation to functions such as data collection, which can be done automatically, without direct intervention of the employees of the enterprise.

255. Despite this increased flexibility, in many cases large multinational enterprises (MNEs) will indeed have a taxable presence in the country where their customers are located. As noted in Chapter 4, there are often compelling reasons for businesses to ensure that core resources are placed as close as possible to key markets. This may be because the enterprise wants to ensure a high quality of service and have a direct relationship with key clients. It may also be because minimising latency is essential in certain types of business, or because in certain industries regulatory constraints limit choices about where to locate key infrastructure, capital, and personnel. It is therefore important not to overstate the issue of nexus. Nevertheless, the fact that it is possible to generate a large quantity of sales without a taxable presence should not be understated either and it raises questions about whether the current rules continue to be appropriate in the digital economy.

256. These questions relate in particular to the definition of permanent establishment (PE) for treaty purposes, and the related profit attribution rules. It had already been recognised in the past that the concept of PE referred not only to a substantial physical presence in the country concerned, but also to situations where the non-resident carried on business in the country concerned via a dependent agent (hence the rules contained in paragraphs 5 and 6 of Article 5 of the OECD Model Tax Convention). As nowadays it is possible to be heavily involved in the economic life of another country without having a fixed place of business or a dependent agent therein, concerns are raised regarding whether the existing definition of PE remains consistent with the underlying principles on which it was based. For example, the ability to conclude contracts remotely through technological means, with no involvement of individual employees or dependent agents, raises questions about whether the focus of the existing rules on conclusion of contracts by persons other than agents of an independent status remains appropriate in all cases.

257. These concerns are exacerbated in some instances by the fact that in certain business models, customers are more frequently entering into ongoing relationships with providers of services that extend beyond the point of sale. This ongoing interaction with customers generates network effects that can increase the value of a particular business to other potential customers. For example, in the case of a retail business operated via a website that provides a platform for customers to review and tag products, the interactions of those customers with the website can increase the value of the website to other customers, by enabling them to make more informed choices about products and to find products more relevant to their interests.

258. Similarly, users of a participative networked platform contribute user-created content, with the result that the value of the platform to existing users is enhanced as new users join and contribute. In most cases, the users are not directly remunerated for the content they contribute, although the business may monetise that content via advertising revenues (as described in relation to multi-sided business models below), subscription sales, or licensing of content to third parties. Alternatively, the value generated by user contributions may be reflected in the value of business itself, which is monetised via the sale price when the business is sold by its owners. Concerns that the changing nature of customer and user interaction allows greater participation in the economic life of countries without physical presence are further exacerbated in markets in which customer choices compounded by network effects have resulted in a monopoly or oligopoly.

259. These various developments must be understood in light of their relationship to more traditional ways of doing business. For example, while having a market in a country is clearly valuable to a seller, this condition by itself has not created a taxing right in the area of direct taxation to this point. It is also true that data about markets and about customers has always been a source of value for businesses as illustrated by phenomena such as frequent flyer programmes, loyalty programmes, the creation and sale of customer lists, and marketing surveys (in which customers participate for no remuneration), to name a few. The traditional economy also benefited from "network" effects in ways that are perhaps less obvious than the network effect present in social networks. Sellers of fax machines, for example, were dependent on a sufficiently broad supplier of purchasers in order to ensure that their product had value. The digital economy has, however, enabled access to markets with less reliance on physical presence than in the past. In addition, the digital economy has enabled collection and analysis of data at unprecedented levels, and has enhanced the impact of customer and user participation in the market, as well as the degree of network effects. It has been suggested that the lower marginal costs in digital businesses coupled with increased network effects generated by higher levels of user participation may justify

a change in tax policy. See, e.g. Crémer (2015); Pistone and Hongler (2015). In considering policy changes to reflect customer interactions to the imposition of income tax, however, potential impact on traditional ways of doing business must be taken into account in order to maintain coherence in cross border tax policy. In addition, consideration should be given both to solutions based on income tax and to solutions focused on indirect taxes.

260. Another specific issue raised by the changing ways in which businesses are conducted is whether certain activities that were previously considered preparatory or auxiliary (and hence benefit from the exceptions to the definition of PE) may be increasingly significant components of businesses in the digital economy. For example, as indicated in Chapter 6, if proximity to customers and the need for quick delivery to clients are key components of the business model of an online seller of physical products, the maintenance of a local warehouse could constitute a core activity of that seller. Similarly, where the success of a high-frequency trading company depends so heavily on the ability to be faster than competitors that the server must be located close to the relevant exchange, questions may be raised regarding whether the automated processes carried out by that server can be considered mere preparatory or auxiliary activities.

261. Although it is true that tax treaties do not permit the taxation of business profits of a non-resident enterprise in the absence of a PE to which these profits are attributable, the issue of nexus goes beyond questions of PE under tax treaties. In fact, even in the absence of the limitations imposed by tax treaties, it appears that many jurisdictions would not in any case consider this nexus to exist under their domestic laws. For example, many jurisdictions would not tax income derived by a non-resident enterprise from remote sales to customers located in that jurisdiction unless the enterprise maintained some degree of physical presence in that jurisdiction. As a result, the issue of nexus also relates to the domestic rules for the taxation of non-resident enterprises.

7.4. Data and the attribution of value created from the generation of marketable location-relevant data through the use of digital products and services

262. Digital technologies enable the collection, storage and use of data, and also enable data to be gathered remotely and from a greater distance from the market than previously. Data can be gathered directly from users, consumers or other sources of information, or indirectly via third parties. Data can also be gathered through a range of transactional relationships with users, or based on other explicit or implicit forms of agreement with users. Companies collect data through different methods. These can be proactive, requesting or requiring users to provide data and using data analytics, or primarily reactive, with the quantity and nature of the information provided largely within the control of users e.g. social networking and cloud computing. As set out in Chapter 3, data gathered from various sources is often a primary input into the process of value creation in the digital economy. Leveraging data can create value for businesses in a variety of ways, including by allowing businesses to segment populations in order to tailor offerings, to improve the development of products and services, to better understand variability in performance, and to improve decision making. The expanding role of data raises questions about whether current nexus rules continue to be appropriate or whether any profits attributable to the remote gathering of data by an enterprise should be taxable in the State from which the data is gathered, as well as questions about whether data is being appropriately characterised and valued for tax purposes. As noted above, the issue of data collection is not new, although the ability to collect and categorise data has increased exponentially in large part due to computing power

and the growth of the internet. As a result, addressing the growing role of data would require consideration of potential impact on more traditional business models as well.

263. While it is clear that many businesses have developed ways to collect, analyse, and ultimately monetise data, it may be challenging for purposes of an analysis of functions, assets, and risks, to assign an objective value to the raw data itself, as distinct from the processes used to collect, analyse, and use that data. For accounting purposes, the value of data collected by a business, like other self-created intangibles, would generally not appear on the balance sheet of the business, and would therefore not generally be relevant for determining profits for tax purposes. Although data purchased from another related or unrelated business would be treated as an asset in the hands of the buyer (and its subsequent sale would generate tax consequences), outright sale of data is only one of many ways in which collection and analysis of data can be monetised. For example, as with other user contributions, the value of data may be reflected in the value of the business itself, and may be monetised when the business is sold. Even where data itself is sold, the value of that data may vary widely depending on the capacity of the purchaser to analyse and make use of that data. The issue of valuing data as an asset is further complicated by existing legal questions about the ownership of personal data, and the ability of users to control whether businesses can access and utilise user data by using digital services anonymously, or by deleting data stored in local caches. Many jurisdictions have passed data protection and privacy legislation to ensure that the personal data of consumers is closely protected. Under most such legislation, this information is considered to be the property of the individual from which it is derived, rather than an asset owned by a company or a public good. Economic literature analysing intangibles, in contrast, has tended to embrace modern business realities and value also assets whose ownership may not be protected by legal rules (Corrado et al., 2012).

264. The value of data, and the difficulties associated with determining that value, is also relevant for tax purposes in the cross-border context and triggers questions regarding whether the remote collection of data should give rise to nexus for tax purposes even in the absence of a physical presence, and if so (or in the case of an existing taxable presence) what impact this would have on the application of transfer pricing and profit attribution principles, which in turn require an analysis of the functions performed, assets used and risks assumed. The fact that the value of data can impact tax results places pressure on the valuation of data. Further, the fact that the value of data can impact tax results if attributable to a PE or if held by a local subsidiary and sold to a foreign enterprise, but not if collected directly by a foreign enterprise with no PE, places pressure on the nexus issues and raises questions regarding the location of data collection. This distinction between the taxation of those with a PE and those without a PE was, of course, present in the traditional economy as well.

265. In addition, data, including location-specific data, may be collected from customers or devices in one country using technology developed in a second country. It may then be processed in the second country and used to improve product offerings or target advertisements to customers in the first country. Determining whether profit is attributable to each of these functions and the appropriate allocation of that profit between the first country and the second country raises tax challenges. These challenges may be exacerbated by the fact that in practice a range of data may be gathered from different sources and for different purposes by businesses and combined in various ways to create value, making tracing the source of data challenging. This data may be stored and processed using cloud computing, making the determination of the location where the processing takes place similarly challenging.

266. Additional challenges are presented by the increasing prominence in the digital economy of multi-sided business models. A key feature of two-sided business models is that the ability of a company to attract one group of customers often depends on the company's ability to attract a second group of customers or users. For example, a company may develop valuable services, which it offers to companies and individuals for free or at a price below the cost of providing the service, in order to build a user base and to collect data from those companies and individuals. This data can then be used by the business to generate revenues by selling services to a second group of customers interested in the data itself or in access to the first group. For example, in the context of internet advertising data collected from a group of users or customers can be used to offer a second group of customers the opportunity to tailor advertisements based on those data. Where the two groups of customers are spread among multiple countries, challenges arise regarding the issue of nexus mentioned above and in determining the appropriate allocation of profits among those countries. Questions may also arise about the appropriate characterisation of transactions involving data, including assessing the extent to which data and transactions based on data exchange can be considered free goods or barter transactions, and how they should be treated for tax and accounting purposes. However, as discussed more generally above, the location of advertising customers and the location of users are frequently aligned in practice, such that the value of the user data is reflected in the advertising revenue generated in a country. The scale of this challenge may, in addition, be mitigated by the fact that advertising will frequently require a local presence to attract advertisers.

267. The changing relationship of businesses with users/customers in the digital economy may raise other challenges as well. The current tax rules for allocating income among different parts of the same MNE require an analysis of functions performed, assets used, and risks assumed. This raises questions in relation to some digital economy business models where part of the value creation may lie in the contributions of users or customers in a jurisdiction. As noted above, the increased importance of users/customers therefore relates to the core question of how to determine where economic activities are carried out and value is created for income tax purposes.

7.5. Characterisation of income derived from new business models

268. Products and services can be provided to customers in new ways through digital technology. The digital economy has enabled monetisation in new ways, as discussed in Chapters 3 and 4, and this raises questions regarding both the rationale behind existing categorisations of income and consistency of treatment of similar types of transactions.

269. Prior work by the Treaty Characterisation Technical Advisory Group (TAG), discussed further in Annex A examined many characterisation issues related to e-commerce. Although this work remains relevant, new business models raise new questions about how to characterise certain transactions and payments for domestic and tax treaty law purposes.[1] For example, although the TAG considered the treatment of application hosting, cloud computing has developed significantly since that work, and the character of payments for cloud computing is not specifically addressed in the existing Commentary to the OECD Model Tax Convention. The question for tax treaty purposes is often whether such payments should be treated as royalties (particularly under treaties in which the definition of royalties includes payments for rentals of commercial, industrial, or scientific equipment), fees for technical services (under treaties that contain specific provisions in that respect), or business profits. More specifically, questions arise regarding whether infrastructure-as-a-service transactions should be treated as services (and hence payments characterised as business profits for treaty

purposes), as rentals of space on the cloud service provider's servers by others (and hence be characterised as royalties for purposes of treaties that include in the definition of royalties payments for rentals of commercial, industrial, or scientific equipment), or as the provision of technical services. The same questions arise regarding payments for software-as-a-service or platform-as-a-service transactions.

270. In the future, development and increasing use of 3D printing may also raise character questions. For example, if direct manufacturing for delivery evolves into a license of designs for remote printing directly by purchasers, questions may arise as to whether

Box 7.1. **Administrative challenges in the digital economy**

There is a pressing need to consider how investment in skills, technologies and data management can help tax administrations keep up with the ways in which technology is transforming business operations. The borderless nature of digital economy produces specific administrative issues around identification of businesses, determination of the extent of activities, information collection and verification, and identification of customers. These issues are outlined below, while possible ways to address them are outlined in the later sections of this chapter. Further, operational work is underway within the Forum on Tax Administration to develop a strong voluntary compliance culture and expand the use of modern technology for self-service delivery purposes (OECD, 2014).

- **Identification:** While global business structures in the digital economy involve traditional identification challenges, these challenges are magnified in the digital economy. For example, the market jurisdiction may not require registration or other identification when overseas businesses sell remotely to customers in the jurisdiction, or may have issues with implementing registration requirements, as it is often difficult for tax authorities to know that activities are taking place, to identify remote sellers and to ensure compliance with domestic rules. Difficulties in identifying remote sellers may also make ultimate collection of tax difficult.
- **Determining the extent of activities:** Even if the identity and role of the parties involved can be determined, it may be impossible to ascertain the extent of sales or other activities without information from the offshore seller, as there may be no sales or other accounting records held in the local jurisdiction or otherwise accessible by the local revenue authority. It may be possible to obtain this information from third parties such as the customers or payment intermediaries, but this may be dependent on privacy or financial regulation laws.
- **Information collection and verification:** To verify local activity, the market jurisdiction's tax administration may need to seek information from parties that have no operations in the jurisdiction and are not subject to regulation therein. While exchange of information can be a very useful tool where the proper legal basis is in place, this is predicated on knowledge of where the offshore entity is tax resident and information retained or accessible by the reciprocating tax authority. This can create challenges for a market jurisdiction revenue authority seeking to independently verify any information provided by the offshore entity.
- **Identification of customers:** There are in principle a number of ways in which a business can identify the country of residence of its client and/or the country in which consumption occurs. These could include freight forwarders or other customs documentation or tracking of Internet Protocol (IP) and card billing addresses. However, this could be burdensome for the business and would not work where customers are able to disguise their location.

and under what circumstances payments by purchasers may be classified as royalties rather than as business profits, or may be treated as fees for technical services.

271. Under most tax treaties, business profits would be taxable in a country only if attributable to a PE located therein. In contrast, certain other types of income, such as royalties, may be subject to withholding tax in the country of the payer, depending on the terms of any applicable treaty. Whether a transaction is characterised as business profits or as another type of income, therefore, can result in a different treatment for tax treaty purposes. There is therefore a need to clarify the application of existing rules to some new business models.

272. At the same time, when considering questions regarding the characterisation of income derived from new business models it may be necessary to examine the rationale behind existing rules, in order to determine whether those rules produce appropriate results in the digital economy and whether differences in treatment of substantially similar transactions are justified in policy terms. In this respect, further clarity may be needed regarding the tax treaty characterisation of certain payments under new business models, especially cloud computing payments (including payments for infrastructure-as-a-service, software-as-a-service, and platform-as-a-service transactions). In addition, issues of characterisation have broader implications for the allocation of taxing rights for direct tax purposes. For example, if a new type of business is able to interact extensively with customers in a market jurisdiction and generate business profits without physical presence that would rise to the level of a PE, and it were determined that the market jurisdiction should be able to tax such income on a net basis, modifying the PE threshold and associated profit attribution rules could permit such taxation. Source taxation could also be ensured by creating a new category of income that is subject to withholding tax. As a result, the issue of characterisation has significant implications for the issue of nexus.

7.6. Developing options to address the broader direct tax challenges of the digital economy

273. In the context of its work, the TFDE received and discussed several proposals for potential options to address the broader direct tax challenges raised by the digital economy, including novel work carried out by academics (Bloch, 2015; Bourreau, 2015; Brauner, 2015; Crémer, 2015; Hongler, 2015). As there is a substantial overlap between the challenges related to nexus, data, and characterisation, it was considered that rather than attempting to individually target them, any potential option should instead focus more generally on the ability of businesses in the digital economy to *(i)* derive sales income from a country without a physical presence, and *(ii)* use the contributions of users in the value chain (including through collection and monitoring of data), and monetise these contributions by selling the data to third parties, by selling targeted ads, by selling the business itself, or in any other way.

274. The options analysed by the TFDE in 2014 included modifications to the exceptions from PE status, alternatives to the existing PE threshold, the imposition of a withholding tax on certain types of digital transactions, and the introduction of a tax on bandwidth use.

275. With respect to the exceptions from PE status, work in the context of Action 7 of the BEPS Project (preventing the artificial avoidance of PE status) analysed whether activities that may previously have been preparatory or auxiliary should continue to benefit from exceptions (contained in Article 5(4) of the OECD Model Tax Convention) to the permanent establishment definition where they have become core components of a

business. As a result of this work, these exceptions have been modified to ensure that they are available only for activities that are of a preparatory or auxiliary nature.

276. The technical details of the other three options have been developed further and are presented below. Like the challenges they are intended to address, the impact of these options overlaps in a number of respects. They have therefore been conceived in a way that allows them to be either combined into a single option or chosen individually. More specifically, elements of the three potential options could be combined into a new concept of nexus for net-basis taxation (a "significant economic presence"), with the intent to reflect situations where an enterprise leverages digital technology to participate in the economic life of a country in a regular and sustained manner without having a physical presence in that country. In this context, the application of a withholding tax on digital transactions could be considered as a tool to enforce compliance with net taxation based on this potential new nexus, while an equalisation levy could be considered as an alternative to overcome the difficulties raised by the attribution of income to the new nexus.

7.6.1. A new nexus based on the concept of significant economic presence

277. This option would create a taxable presence in a country when a non-resident enterprise has a significant economic presence in a country on the basis of factors that evidence a purposeful and sustained interaction with the economy of that country via technology and other automated tools. These factors would be combined with a factor based on the revenue derived from remote transactions into the country, in order to ensure that only cases of significant economic presence are covered, limit compliance costs of the taxpayers, and provide certainty for cross-border activities. The following sections describe the details of such an option, together with potential approaches for attributing income to the new nexus.

7.6.1.1. Revenue-based factor

278. As a general matter, revenue that is generated on a sustained basis from a country could be considered to be one of the clearest potential indicators of the existence of a significant economic presence. This is based on the assumption that even in multi-sided business models, and particularly those dependent on network effects, the two markets are likely to be strongly interrelated, and as a result are likely to besituated in the same country. To the extent that the country of the users and country of the paying customers are aligned, the value of an enterprise's users and user data would generally be reflected in the enterprise's revenue in a country. In other words, because user data serves to enhance the value of the services an enterprise offers, a strong user network (and the attendant user data) is likely to result in enterprises either selling more or enterprises charging more for its core products/services, or both. Under such circumstances, the revenues earned from customers in a country are a potential factor for establishing nexus in the form of a significant economic presence in the country concerned. Revenues will not be sufficient in isolation to establish nexus but they could be considered a basic factor that, when combined with other factors, could potentially be used to establish nexus in the form of a significant economic presence in the country concerned. In addition, the use of revenue as a basic factor could limit the compliance costs of taxpayers and provides a high degree of tax certainty for cross-border activities. In developing a revenue factor, consideration was given to the following technical issues:

- ***Transactions covered.*** One approach that could be considered in defining a basic revenue factor is to include only revenues generated from digital transactions concluded with in-country customers through an enterprise's digital platform.

Specifically, these transactions would involve the conclusion of a contract for the sale (or exchange) of goods and services between two or more parties effectuated through a digital platform where the contract conclusion primarily relies on automated systems. Such an approach could however create incentives for particular ways of doing business with remote customers. For example, such an approach would treat remote digital transactions differently from mail-order transactions (e.g. catalogue shopping) and telephone transactions (e.g. sale through call centres). Although in practice the latter transactions are less likely to enable a business to generate a significant amount of revenue, all three ways of transacting enable businesses to engage in sales transactions without physical presence in the country of the customer. In addition, businesses may leverage digital technology to reach a broader range of customers in another country without entering into digital transactions (e.g. website displaying the products but routing the customers to a call centre to perform the final purchase). Accordingly, to ensure that taxpayers in similar situations carrying out similar transactions will be subject to similar levels of taxation, it may be preferable to define the factor so as to include all revenue generated by transactions concluded by the non-resident enterprise remotely with in-country customers. Potential adverse effects associated with such a broad scope would in any case be addressed by the application of the other factors (see further below at 7.6.1.4).

- ***Level of the threshold.*** The core element of the revenue factor could be the gross revenues generated from remote transactions concluded with customers in the country concerned. This amount should be framed in absolute terms and in local currency, in order to minimise the risk of manipulation. A key objective in setting the level of threshold would be to set it at a high enough level to minimise the administrative burden for tax administrations as well as the compliance burden on and level of uncertainty for the taxpayer, while ensuring that nexus is less likely to be created in cases in which minimal tax revenue would be collected. The size of the country's market might also be a relevant factor in setting the level of the revenue threshold. Given the relative mobility and flexibility in choosing the location of automated functions related to revenue-generating activities in the digital economy, the factor could be applied on a related-group basis rather than on a separate-entity basis to prevent any risk of artificial fragmentation of distance selling activities with customers of the same country among a variety of foreign affiliated entities. This aggregation rule could be introduced as a rebuttable presumption, with the taxpayer being able to demonstrate that it did not artificially fragment the distance selling activities in order to manipulate the revenue threshold.
- ***Administration of the threshold.*** An accurate application of the revenue threshold would depend on the ability of the country to identify and measure remote sales activities of the non-resident enterprise. One possible approach to address this challenge could be to introduce a mandatory registration system for enterprises that meet the factors giving rise to a significant economic presence. On the other hand, it could be difficult for tax authorities to know when activities are taking place and at what scale, to identify remote sellers, and ultimately to ensure compliance. Similarly, in the case of transactions concluded and fulfilled entirely online, it may be difficult for enterprises to identify with certainty the country of residence of clients. In this respect, regimes introduced to ensure compliance with VAT/GST rules by non-resident suppliers could prove extremely useful (see also Chapter 8 for additional details).

7.6.1.2. Digital factors

279. In the case of "brick and mortar" businesses, the ability to reach significant numbers of customers in a country generally depends on a variety of factors, including a store's location, local marketing and promotion, payment options, and sales and customer service employees. In the digital economy, the ability to establish and maintain a purposeful and sustained interaction with users or customers in a specific country via an online presence depends on analogous factors. A range of digital factors based on the current development of the digital economy could be used as part of a test for significant economic presence, including the following:

- ***A local domain name***. A non-resident enterprise targeting customers or users in a country will generally obtain the digital equivalent of a local "address" where the non-resident enterprise establishes its store front, typically taking the form of a localised or specialised domain name. For example, while an enterprise's "home" domain name might be ".com", the enterprise's site targeting one country would likely use a domain name reflecting that, in order to make it more likely that a local user would find the local site. This is reinforced by the need of enterprises to protect their trademarks by purchasing related domain names, including a local country domain name. In summary, while it is possible for an enterprise to do business in a country without a local domain name, the choice to do so carries reputational risk from potential domain "squatting" and trademark infringement from not protecting the enterprise's business name, trademarks and trade names across various domains. Accordingly, MNEs doing substantial cross-border business would very likely operate in a country via a local domain name. Whether local domain names will remain the predominant method for accessing markets, however, is uncertain. In the near future, merchants selling camera equipment globally may, for example, use a generic ".camera" domain name, thus reducing the relevance of country specific domain name.

- ***A local digital platform***. Non-resident enterprises frequently establish "local" websites or other digital platforms in order to present the goods or services being offered in the light that most appeals to the local users or customers, taking into account language and cultural norms in particular. Local websites or digital platforms could include features intended to facilitate interaction by local users and customers with the site's content, services and functions. Such features include language, local marketing such as targeted discounts and promotions, and local terms of service for users and customers that reflect the commercial and legal context of the local environment. Although some enterprises may elect to only operate only in one language and not attempt to undertake local marketing or promotional efforts, establishing a local platform is often critical to attracting meaningful numbers of local users and customers. Note, however, that local platforms do not necessarily correspond to political boundary lines.

- ***Local payment options***. A non-resident enterprise that maintains a purposeful and sustained interaction with the economy of a country will frequently ensure that local customers have a seamless purchasing experience with prices reflected in local currency, taxes, duties and fees already calculated, with the option of using a local form of payment to complete the purchase. Integration of local forms of payment into a site's commercial features is a complicated technical, commercial, and legal exercise requiring substantial resources, and an enterprise would normally not undertake such an investment unless it purposefully participates in the country's economic life. While this factor may be less relevant in countries that share a common currency, it generally is a critical commercial requirement in countries that have stringent banking regulations, currency controls, or low penetration of international credit cards.

7.6.1.3. User-based factors

280. Given the importance of network effects in the digital economy, the user base and the associated data input may also be important indicators of a purposeful and sustained interaction with the economy of that another country. A range of factors based on users could be used to reflect the level of participation in the economic life of a country, namely:

- ***Monthly active users (MAU).*** One factor reflecting the level of penetration in a country's economy is the number of "monthly active users" (MAU) on the digital platform that are habitually resident in a given country in a taxable year. The term MAU refers to registered user who logged in and visited a company's digital platform in the 30-day period ending on the date of measurement. A factor based on MAU presents the advantage of measuring the customer/user base in a given country both in terms of size and level of engagement. Given that little material is publicly available on the process of defining and identifying MAU, more detailed metrics would need to be developed in consultation with businesses and IT experts for the purpose of using this factor, such as how to identify a unique "user" or what level of engagement is required for a user to be considered "active". Reliability and veracity of the information would also need to be ensured, to address fraudulent accounts, multiple accounts, false information volunteered by users, and "bot"-produced data, to name a few.
- ***Online contract conclusion.*** Another factor indicating the level of participation of an enterprise in the economic life of a country is the regular conclusion of contracts. This is the focus of the existing "dependent agent" PE test contained in Article 5 of the OECD Model which, in broad terms, requires that this contract conclusion be carried out in the country by a person acting on behalf of the non-resident enterprise. In the digital economy, contracts can frequently be concluded with customers via a digital platform without the need for the intervention of local personnel or dependent agents. For example, online platforms providing free services to their users often specify on their websites that by accessing or using the products and services of the company the user agrees to the "Terms of Service" and each use of the platform results in the conclusion of a legally binding agreement. The number of contracts concluded through a digital platform with customers or users that are habitually resident in the country in any taxable year could therefore be considered an important factor.
- ***Data collected.*** Another factor which could be considered to reflect an enterprise's level of participation in the economic life of a country is the volume of digital content collected through a digital platform from users and customers habitually resident in that country in a taxable year. The focus would be on the origin of the data collected, irrespective of where that data is subsequently stored and processed (e.g. data warehouse). The range of data captured by the threshold would not be confined to personal data, but would cover also, e.g. user created content, product reviews, and search histories. This core element could be coupled with proportionality tests, such as whether the volume of digital content collected exceeds a percentage of the enterprise's overall stored digital content. Information on data collected is increasingly available, reliable and up-to-date, especially if the factor is focusing on data collected that is effectively stored by the non-resident

enterprise on a server. At the same time, businesses may not necessarily maintain separate and comprehensive track records of the volume of data collected and stored on a country-by-country basis. In addition, the volume of data collected (and stored) from users in a country may not necessarily reflect an effective contribution to the profits generated by the non-resident enterprise, as the value of raw data is rather uncertain and particularly volatile.

7.6.1.4. Possible combinations of the revenue factor with the other factors

281. For purposes of this potential option, total revenue in excess of the revenue threshold would be an indicator of the existence of a significant economic presence.

282. Total revenue, however, may not by itself suffice to evidence a non-resident enterprise's regular and sustained participation in the economic life of a country. To be an appropriate measure of participation in the economic life of a country, the revenue factor could be combined with other factors, such as the digital and/or user-based factors that indicate a purposeful and sustained interaction with the economy of the country concerned. In other words, a link would have to be created between the revenue-generating activity of the non-resident enterprise and its significant economic presence in the country. The choice of which factors should be combined with the revenue factor to ascertain whether a significant economic presence should be deemed to exist is likely to be driven by the unique features and economic attributes of each market (e.g. size, local language, currency restrictions, banking system).

283. This concept may be illustrated by an example. If a non-resident enterprise generates gross revenues above the threshold from transactions with in-country customers concluded electronically through a localised digital platform where the customer is required to create a personalised account and utilise the local payment options offered on the site to execute the purchase, it could be considered that there is a link between the revenue generated from that country and the digital and/or user-based factors evidencing a significant economic presence in that country. In contrast, it would be more difficult to find such a link where a non-resident enterprise generates gross revenues above the threshold from transactions with in-country customers through in-person negotiation taking place outside of the market jurisdiction, if the enterprise only maintains a passive website that provides product information with no functionalities permitting transactions or intensive interaction with users (including data collection).

7.6.2. Determining the income attributable to the significant economic presence

284. Attribution of profits is a key consideration in developing a nexus based on significant economic presence. The option outlined in 7.6.1 above would establish nexus for taxation in cases where an enterprise has no physical presence in the country concerned. Consideration must therefore be given to what changes to profit attribution rules would need to be made if the significant economic presence option were adopted, while ensuring parity to the extent possible between enterprises that are subject to tax due to physical presence in the market country (i.e. local subsidiary or traditional PE) and those that are taxable only due to the application of the option.

7.6.2.1. Existing rules and principles

285. A significant economic presence associated with little or no physical presence in terms of tangible assets and/or personnel in the other country is not likely to involve the carrying on of any functions of the enterprise in the traditional sense. Unless significant

adjustments are made to the existing rules, therefore, it would not be possible to allocate any meaningful income to the new nexus.

286. Several adjustments to existing principles were considered during the course of the work, including allocating business functions handled remotely through automated systems to the significant economic presence, as well as treating customers and users as performing certain functions on behalf of an enterprise under certain circumstances. Other substantial departures from existing rules, such as replacing a functional analysis with an analysis based on game theory that would allocate profits by analogy with a bargaining process within a joint venture, were also considered (see Pellefigue, 2015). All such potential adjustments, however, would require substantial departures from existing standards for allocating profits within a MNE operating in multiple jurisdictions, which are currently based on an analysis of the functions, assets and risks of the enterprises concerned. It was concluded, therefore, that, unless there is a substantial rewrite of the rules for the attribution of profits, alternative methods would need to be considered.

7.6.2.2. Methods based on fractional apportionment

287. Another approach considered would be to apportion the profits of the whole enterprise to the digital presence either on the basis of a predetermined formula, or on the basis of variable allocation factors determined on a case-by-case basis. In the context of a significant economic presence, the implementation of a method based on fractional apportionment would require the performance of three successive steps: *(1)* the definition of the tax base to be divided, *(2)* the determination of the allocation keys to divide that tax base, and *(3)* the weighting of these allocation keys.

288. It is important to note that the domestic laws of most countries use profit attribution methods based on the separate accounts of the PE, rather than fractional apportionment. In addition, fractional apportionment methods would be a departure from current international standards. Furthermore, pursuing such an approach in the case of application of the new nexus would produce very different tax results depending on whether business was conducted through a "traditional" permanent establishment, a separate subsidiary or the new nexus. Given those constraints, fractional apportionment methods were not pursued further.

7.6.2.3. Modified deemed profit methods

289. The use of empirical presumption methods such as "deemed profit" systems is sometimes a way to avoid profit computations based on the taxpayer's accounts in situations where a high proportion of expenses associated with revenues are incurred overseas, making it difficult from a practical perspective to audit locally. Deemed profits methods have been used, for example, in the insurance industry, by applying a coefficient based on the ratio of profit to gross premiums of resident insurance companies to gross premiums received from policy holders in the source country.

290. In the context of a nexus based on significant economic presence, one possible approach would thus be to regard the presence to be equivalent to a physical presence from which the non-resident enterprise is operating a commercial business and determine the deemed net income by applying a ratio of presumed expenses to the non-resident enterprise's revenue derived from transactions concluded with in-country customers, hence aligning it to one of the key factors of the option as described above. Determining an appropriate ratio would depend on a number of factors, including the industry concerned, the degree of integration of the particular enterprise, and the type of product and service provided. One

possible approach would thus be to classify taxpayers by industry and apply an industry-specific profit percentage. A more refined approach would be to divide taxpayers within a given industry into additional classes based on relevant factors (e.g. capital equipment, turnover, employees), with a specific profit percentage within each band. The determination of the latter percentage would require an extensive analysis of actual profit margins of domestic taxpayers operating in the same specific class of industry or type of business.

291. Deemed profit methods are generally perceived as relatively easy to administer and raise revenue. However, for large MNE groups with complex structures operating in many lines of business, applying multiple industry-specific presumptive profit margins to the same significant economic presence presents several practical challenges. Another challenge relates to the comparability of digital and traditional business models when considering the applicability of such deemed profit margins. Many digital business models have a different cost structure than traditional business models, such that adjustments to margins found in this context are very likely to be required. In addition, application of deemed profit methods in this context may be considered as a substantial departure from current international standards, resulting in a tax liability even where there are no actual profits generated through the significant economic presence. One possible way to mitigate this negative impact would be to create a rebuttable presumption limited to situations where the foreign taxpayer is able to demonstrate that its overall activity (or specific line of business related to the activity of the significant economic presence if it can be ring-fenced from other business activities of the enterprise) is in a loss-making position at the end of the fiscal year.

7.6.3. A withholding tax on digital transactions

292. A withholding tax on payments by residents (and local PEs) of a country for goods and services purchased online from non-resident providers has also been considered. This withholding tax could in theory be imposed as a standalone gross-basis final withholding tax on certain payments made to non-resident providers of goods and services ordered online or, alternatively, as a primary collection mechanism and enforcement tool to support the application of the nexus option described above, i.e. net-basis taxation. Both approaches raise similar technical issues with respect to the scope of transactions covered and the collection of the ensuing tax liability. In addition, the application of a standalone final withholding tax raises specific challenges regarding trade obligations and EU law.

7.6.3.1. Scope of transactions covered

293. The scope of transactions covered by the tax must be clearly defined, so that taxpayers and withholding agents will know when the tax applies, and to ensure that tax administrations will be able to ensure compliance. The scope should also be defined as simply as possible in order to avoid unnecessary complexity and classification disputes. The need for clarity and simplicity, however, must be balanced against a need to ensure that similar types of transactions will be taxed similarly, in order to avoid creating incentives for or against particular ways of structuring them.

294. For this purpose, although listing specific types of transactions covered would provide a degree of clarity, it would also likely result in disputes over the character of transactions, particularly as technology continues to advance. Such an approach also could lead to differences in treatment for tax purposes between economically equivalent transactions depending on their form. For this reason, a more general definition of covered transactions appears more appropriate. The tax could be applied, for example, to transactions for goods or services ordered online (i.e. digital sales transactions), or to all sales operations concluded

remotely with non-residents. The latter would have the advantage of flexibility, and would ensure tax neutrality between similar ways of doing business, and may reduce disputes over characterisation. In addition, if withholding is used as a tool to support net-basis taxation, a broad scope covering all distance selling would be more consistent with the sales threshold discussed above in the context of a nexus based on significant economic presence.

7.6.3.2. Collection of the tax

295. In practice, the liability to pay a withholding tax on outbound payments is often shifted from the non-resident enterprise to a local collecting agent, such as the customer or a third-party payment processing intermediary. For such a mechanism to function efficiently, the agent responsible for withholding must have access to information about the covered transactions sufficient to know when the tax will apply, and must be reasonably expected to comply with its obligation to withhold.

296. In the case of B2B transactions, businesses resident in the source country may reasonably be expected to comply with the withholding obligation. In the case of B2C transactions, however, requiring withholding from the payor would be more challenging as private consumers have little experience nor incentive to declare and pay the tax due. Moreover, enforcing the collection of small amounts of withholding from large numbers of private consumers would involve considerable costs and administrative challenges.

297. One possible solution would be to require intermediaries processing the payment to withhold on the payment in a B2C context. As a practical matter, however, this presents several technical issues. For example, an intermediary would generally not have access to transaction-identifying information enabling it to determine its character and hence the amount of tax due. In practice, it would only see a value without any description of the underlying transaction, in which case it would not be able to determine with sufficient certainty when it was required to withhold. The task of the intermediary could be facilitated if the collection regime is supplemented by a mandatory registration system for non-resident enterprises whereby all remote sellers of goods and services must designate a dedicated bank account for all payments received from local customers. In the latter situation, intermediaries may be required to withhold the tax only for payments made to these specific bank accounts. However, the application of this approach may pose challenges in imposing compliance obligations on intermediaries that are situated in third-countries with no connection to the jurisdiction of the customer, thereby creating opportunities for tax avoidance strategies.

7.6.3.3. Negative impact of gross-basis taxation and relationship with trade and other obligations

298. The initial development and hosting of the technology required to provide products and services online typically requires substantial up-front investment of resources, including labour and capital. After initial creation of the technology, however, providing products and services online frequently requires only limited marginal costs for businesses. Where this is the case, it has been argued that payments made in consideration for digital goods or services share common features with royalties and fees for technical services, i.e. that gross revenue is a reliable proxy for net income. In many businesses, however, providing products and services online will require ongoing expenditures for continued product development (including maintenance of products and addition of new features), marketing, and ongoing customer support due to rapid product cycles as technology and competition evolve. Where this is the case, imposition of withholding tax on gross revenues

will be an imperfect proxy for tax on net income. One potential way to reduce the negative impact of gross-basis taxation would be to fix the rate at a relatively low amount that would reflect typical profit margins. Such margins could be determined, for example, on the basis of a statistical analysis of actual profit margins of local domestic taxpayers operating in the same specific class of industry or type of business.

299. Assuming that domestic suppliers of similar products are subject to net-basis taxation, the imposition of a standalone gross-basis final withholding tax on foreign suppliers for remote sales of goods and services is likely to raise substantial conflicts with trade obligations and EU law. Trade obligations may differ substantially depending on whether a particular digital transaction is treated as involving a product, in which case the General Agreement on Tariffs and Trade (GATT) would apply, or a service, in which case the General Agreement on Trade in Services (GATS) would apply. Both agreements generally require foreign suppliers of goods (in the case of GATT) and services (in the case of GATS) to be taxed no less favourably than domestic suppliers. However, GATS provides broad exceptions for the application of provisions of tax treaties and for the imposition of direct tax provisions aimed at ensuring the equitable or effective imposition of direct taxes. In contrast, GATT contains no exceptions to national treatment obligations, and simply prohibits parties from subjecting imported products to taxes in excess of those that would apply to similar products produced domestically. Thus, at least to the extent GATT applies (i.e. to goods delivered physically, and to digital products considered "goods" for trade purposes), consideration would need to be given to ways to preserve national treatment.

300. In addition, for some countries EU law imposes comparable obligations – i.e. non-discrimination between resident and non-resident businesses – that would not permit the application to non-resident suppliers of a gross-basis final withholding tax, even if the rate is fixed at a very low amount.

301. Given the above issues, a more viable approach could be to use this mechanism as a back-up mechanism to enforce net-basis taxation on the basis of a significant economic presence nexus, rather than as a standalone option. Whether the withholding tax is used as a gross basis payments tax or a collection mechanism for net basis income tax, remittance of the tax by local businesses would both ensure compliance and facilitate identification of the covered remote sales. One approach in this regard would be to establish a registration system for taxpayers that agree to file tax returns and pay tax on their net income, coupled with a credit system enabling taxpayers to pay any tax due on net income in addition to the tax withheld, or for taxpayers that are in a loss position on a net basis at the end of the fiscal year to claim a tax refund. However, such a system would need to take into account that taxpayers may have an incentive not to file a return where their net tax liability would be greater than the amount of withholding tax payable.

7.6.4. Introducing an "equalisation levy"

302. To avoid some of the difficulties arising from creating new profit attribution rules for purposes of a nexus based on significant economic presence, an "equalisation levy" could be considered as an alternative way to address the broader direct tax challenges of the digital economy. This approach has been used by some countries in order to ensure equal treatment of foreign and domestic suppliers. For example, in the area of insurance, some countries have adopted equalisation levies in the form of excise taxes based on the amount of gross premiums paid to offshore suppliers. Such taxes are intended to address a disparity in tax treatment between domestic corporations engaged in insurance activities and wholly taxable on the related profits, and foreign corporations that are able to sell insurance without

being subject to income tax on those profits, neither in the state from where the premiums are collected nor in state of residence. As discussed below, an equalisation levy could be structured in a variety of ways depending on its ultimate policy objective. In general, an equalisation levy would be intended to serve as a way to tax a non-resident enterprise's significant economic presence in a country. In order to provide clarity, certainty and equity to all stakeholders, and to avoid undue burden on small and medium-sized businesses, therefore, the equalisation levy would be applied only in cases where it is determined that a non-resident enterprise has a significant economic presence.

7.6.4.1. Scope of the levy

303. If the policy priority is to tax remote sales transactions with customers in a market jurisdiction, one possibility is to apply the levy to all transactions concluded remotely with in-country customers. To target the scope of the levy more closely to the situation in which a business establishes and maintains a purposeful and sustained interaction with users or customers in a specific country via an online presence, the levy would be applied only where the business maintains a significant economic presence as described above.

304. An alternative would be to limit the scope to transactions involving the conclusion through automated systems of a contract for the sale (or exchange) of goods and services between two or more parties effectuated through a digital platform. Although this would create an incentive to choose non-digital means of conducting transactions, it would also focus more closely on the specific types of transactions that have generated concern. There is no rule, however, that prevents a broader scope of application. Indeed, focusing too narrowly on specific types of transactions may limit the flexibility of the levy to accommodate future developments, which would limit its ultimate effectiveness in addressing the tax disparity between foreign and domestic suppliers of products through an online presence. The levy would be imposed on the gross value of the goods or services provided to in-country customers and users, paid by in-country customers and users, and collected by the foreign enterprise via a simplified registration regime, or collected by a local intermediary.

305. Alternatively, if the policy priority is to tax the value considered to be directly contributed by customers and users, then a levy could be imposed on data and other contributions gathered from in-country customers and users. For that purpose, a number of options could be available. One option would be to impose a charge based on the average number of MAU in the country. As noted above, however, measuring MAU accurately may prove to be challenging. Moreover, the number of MAU of a foreign enterprise may not be directly related to in-country revenue generated by a foreign enterprise. Setting an appropriate rate for a levy measured by active users would also be challenging, as the average value of each user to a non-resident enterprise may vary widely. Another option would be to base the levy on the volume of data collected from in-country customers and users. Similar to MAU, however, data may also vary widely in value depending on its content and the purpose for which it was gathered, and it would be challenging to identify a reliable direct connection between the in-country revenue and the data collected from in-country customers and users.

7.6.4.2. Potential trade and other issues

306. As is the case with the imposition of a gross-basis final withholding tax, a levy that applied only to non-resident enterprises would be likely to raise substantial questions both with respect to trade agreements and with respect to EU law. In order to address these questions, potential solutions that would ensure equal treatment of domestic and non-resident enterprises would need to be explored, as discussed above in section 7.6.3.3.

Depending on the structure of the levy, one option that could be considered would be to impose the tax on both domestic and foreign entities. If this approach were to be taken, however, presumably consideration would also need to be given to ways to mitigate the potential impact of applying both the corporate income tax and the levy to domestic entities and foreign entities taxable under existing corporate income tax rules.

7.6.4.3. Relationship with corporate income tax

307. Imposing an equalisation levy raises risks that the same income would be subject to both corporate income tax and the levy. This could arise either in the situation in which a foreign entity is subject to the levy at source and to corporate income tax in its country of residence or in the situation in which an entity is subject to both corporate income tax and the levy in the country of source. In the case of a foreign entity, for example, if the income is subject to corporate income tax in the country of residence of the enterprise, the levy would be unlikely to be creditable against that tax. To address these potential concerns, it would be necessary to structure the levy to apply only to situations in which the income would otherwise be untaxed or subject only to a very low rate of tax.

308. Another approach could be to allow a taxpayer subject to both CIT and the levy to credit the levy against its domestic corporate income tax. Such an approach would ensure that foreign entities with no nexus for corporate income tax purposes would be subject only to the levy in the source country, while the tax burden of entities subject to corporate tax would effectively be limited to the greater of the corporate income tax or the levy.

Note

1. In addition, the conclusions drawn by the TAG have not been accepted by all countries participating in the BEPS Project.

Bibliography

Bacache M. (2015) "Tax competition, tax coordination and e-commerce", in *Taxation and the digital economy: A survey of theoretical models*, France Stratégie, Paris.

Bloch, F. and Demange G. (2015), "Taxation and Privacy Protection on Internet Platforms", in *Taxation and the digital economy: A survey of theoretical models*, France Stratégie, Paris.

Bourreau M. et al. (2015), "Digital Platforms, Advertising and Taxation", in *Taxation and the digital economy: A survey of theoretical models*, France Stratégie, Paris.

Brauner Y. and Baez A. (2015), *Withholding Taxes in the Service of BEPS Action 1: Address the Tax Challenges of the Digital Economy*, IBFD White Papers, Amsterdam.

Corrado C. et al. (2012), "Intangible capital and growth in advanced economies: measurement and comparative results", IZA Discussion Paper No. 6733.

Crémer J. (2015), "Taxing network externalities", in *Taxation and the digital economy: A survey of theoretical models*, France Stratégie.

Gauthier S. (2015), "Optimal Discrimination Ban", in *Taxation and the digital economy: A survey of theoretical models*, France Stratégie.

Hongler P. and P. Pistone (2015), *Blueprints for a New PE Nexus to Tax Business Income in the Era of the Digital Economy*, IBFD White Papers, Amsterdam.

OECD (2014), *Increasing Taxpayers' Use of Self-service Channels*, OECD Publishing, Paris, http://dx.doi.org/10.1787/9789264223288-en.

Pellefigue J. (2015), "Transfer Pricing Economics for the Digital Economy", in *International Transfer Pricing Journal*, Vol. 22, Issue 2.

Chapter 8

Broader indirect tax challenges raised by the digital economy and the options to address them

This chapter discusses the challenges that the digital economy raises for indirect taxation, with respect to exemptions for imports of low-valued goods, and remote digital supplies to consumers. It then describes options to address these challenges.

8.1. Collection of VAT in the digital economy

309. Cross-border trade in goods, services and intangibles (which include for VAT purposes digital downloads) creates challenges for VAT systems, particularly where such products are acquired by private consumers from suppliers abroad. The digital economy magnifies these challenges, as the evolution of technology has dramatically increased the capability of private consumers to shop online and the capability of businesses to sell to consumers around the world without the need to be present physically or otherwise in the consumer's country. This often results in no or an inappropriately low amount of VAT being levied on these flows, with adverse effects on countries' VAT revenues and on the level playing field between resident and non-resident vendors. The main tax challenges related to VAT in the digital economy relate to *(i)* imports of low value parcels from online sales which are treated as VAT-exempt in many jurisdictions, and *(ii)* the strong growth in the trade of services and intangibles, particularly sales to private consumers, on which often no or an inappropriately low amount of VAT is levied due to the complexity of enforcing VAT-payment on such supplies.

8.1.1. Exemptions for imports of low valued goods

310. The first challenge regarding collection of VAT arises from the growth that has occurred in e-commerce and in particular, online purchases of physical goods made by consumers from suppliers in another jurisdiction. Countries with a VAT collect tax on imports of goods from the importer at the time the goods are imported using customs collection mechanisms. Many VAT jurisdictions apply an exemption from VAT for imports of low value goods as the administrative costs associated with collecting the VAT on the goods is likely to outweigh the VAT that would be paid on those goods. The value at which the exemption threshold is set varies considerably from country to country but regardless of the threshold value, many VAT countries have seen a significant growth in the volume of low value imports on which VAT is not collected.

311. Challenges arise from the ability of businesses to deliberately structure their affairs to take advantage of a country's low value thresholds and sell goods to consumers without the payment of VAT. For example, a domestic business selling low value goods online to consumers in its jurisdiction would be required to collect and remit that jurisdiction's VAT on its sales. The business could restructure its affairs so that the low value goods are instead shipped to its consumers from an offshore jurisdiction and therefore qualify under that VAT jurisdiction's exemption for low value importations. Similarly, a business starting up could structure its operations to deliberately take advantage of the low value exemption and locate offshore rather than in the jurisdiction in which its customers are located.

312. The exemption for low value imports results in decreased VAT revenues and the possibility of unfair competitive pressures on domestic retailers who are generally required, depending for instance on their size, to charge VAT on their sales to domestic consumers. As a consequence, the concern is not only this immediate loss of revenue and competitive pressures on domestic suppliers, but also the incentive that is created for domestic suppliers to locate or relocate to an offshore jurisdiction in order to sell their low value goods free of VAT. It should also be noted that such relocations by domestic businesses would have added negative impacts on domestic employment and direct tax revenues.

313. The exemptions for low value imports have therefore become increasingly controversial in the context of the growing digital economy. The difficulty lies in finding the balance between the need for appropriate revenue protection and avoidance of distortions of competition, which tend to favour a lower threshold and the need to keep the cost of collection proportionate to the relatively small level of VAT collected, which favours a

higher threshold. At the time when most current low value import reliefs were introduced, internet shopping did not exist and the level of imports benefitting from the relief was relatively small. Over recent years, many VAT countries have seen a significant and rapid growth in the volume of low value imports of physical goods on which VAT is not collected resulting in decreased VAT revenues and growing unfair competitive pressures on domestic retailers who are required to charge VAT on their sales to domestic consumers.

8.1.2. Remote digital supplies to consumers

314. The second challenge regarding collection of VAT arises from the strong growth in cross-border business-to-consumer (B2C) supplies of remotely delivered services and intangibles. The digital economy has increasingly allowed the delivery of such products by businesses from a remote location to consumers around the world without any direct or indirect physical presence of the supplier in the consumer's jurisdiction. Such remote supplies of services and intangibles present challenges to VAT systems, as they often result in no or an inappropriately low amount of VAT being collected and create potential competitive pressures on domestic suppliers.

315. Consider an example of an online supplier of streaming digital content such as movies and television shows. The supplies are made mainly to consumers who can access the digital content through their computers, mobile devices and televisions that are connected to the Internet. If the supplier is resident in the same jurisdiction as its customers, it would be required to collect and remit that jurisdiction's VAT on the supplies. However, if the supplier is a non-resident in the consumer's jurisdiction, issues may arise.

316. As noted in Chapter 2, broadly two approaches are used by countries for applying VAT to such cross-border supplies of services or intangibles: the first approach allocates the taxing rights to the jurisdiction where the supplier is resident whereas the second approach allocates the taxing rights to the jurisdiction where the customer is resident. If the first approach is applied to the supply of digital content in the example, then this supply will be subject to VAT in the supplier's jurisdiction at the rate that is applicable in that jurisdiction. If the jurisdiction of the supplier of the digital content in the example applies no VAT or a VAT with a lower rate than that of the consumer's jurisdiction, then no or an inappropriately low amount of VAT would be collected on this supply and none of the VAT revenue would accrue to the jurisdiction where the final consumption takes place.

317. The approach that allocates the taxing rights to the jurisdiction where the customer is resident would, in principle, result in taxation in the jurisdiction of consumption. However, under this approach, it is challenging for the private consumers' jurisdictions to ensure an effective collection of the VAT on services and intangibles acquired by such consumers abroad. One option is to require the private consumer to remit, or "self-assess", the VAT in its jurisdiction at the rate applicable in this jurisdiction. However, such consumer self-assessment mechanism has proven to be largely ineffective and as result, it is highly likely that no VAT would be paid by the consumer in this scenario. The OECD's E-commerce Guidelines (OECD, 2003) therefore recommend a mechanism that requires the non-resident supplier to register, collect and remit VAT according to the rules of the jurisdiction in which the consumer is resident. This results in the correct amount of VAT being paid in the jurisdiction of consumption. This approach, however, is dependent on the non-resident supplier complying with the requirement to register, collect and remit the VAT. In other words, if taxing rights are allocated to the jurisdiction of consumer residence without implementing a suitable mechanism to collect the tax in this jurisdiction, it is unlikely that VAT would be paid.[1]

318. The example above illustrates how domestic suppliers of competing services could face potential competitive pressures from non-resident suppliers. Domestic suppliers are required to collect and remit VAT on their supplies of services and intangibles to their domestic consumers while the non-resident supplier, depending on the scenario, could structure its affairs so that it collects and remits no or an inappropriately low amount of tax. The example also illustrates how an incentive could arise for domestic suppliers to restructure their affairs so that their supplies of services and intangibles are made from an offshore location, which could allow them to make the supplies with no or an inappropriately low amount of VAT. This incentive could arise as a response to competition from non-resident suppliers who are collecting no or an inappropriately low amount of VAT or as part of a strategy to gain a potential competitive advantage over domestic suppliers who are charging VAT. Such relocations by domestic businesses are likely to have a negative impact on domestic employment and direct tax revenues.

319. Against this background, jurisdictions are increasingly looking at ways to ensure the effective collection of VAT on services and intangibles acquired by resident consumers from suppliers abroad through a digital platform, in line with the destination principle, relying primarily on a requirement for non-resident suppliers to register and collect and remit the tax. Compliance with these requirements is essentially voluntary as the consumers' jurisdictions have limited means to enforce compliance by non-resident non-established suppliers. The experience in countries that have implemented such an approach suggests that a significant number of suppliers comply by either registering in the VAT jurisdiction and collecting and remitting tax on their remotely delivered services, or by choosing to establish a physical presence in the jurisdiction and effectively becoming a "domestic" supplier. It has been suggested that particularly the high-profile operators, which occupy a considerable part of the market, wish to be seen to be tax-compliant notably for reputational reasons. In the absence of a system that makes it easy for non-resident businesses to comply and without having well-functioning means of international co-operation between tax authorities, however, many non-resident suppliers are likely to fail to register and remit the VAT in the consumer's jurisdiction, without any real possibility for tax authorities to audit and sanction them. As a result, there is a loss of VAT revenue to these jurisdictions and potentially unfair competitive pressures on domestic suppliers.

320. It should also be noted that some VAT regimes that allocate taxing rights to the jurisdiction of the residence or the actual location of the consumer, have not implemented a mechanism for collecting the VAT on services acquired by private consumers from non-resident suppliers. This has notably been based on the consideration that it would be overly burdensome on tax administrations to operate such a collection mechanism. As a result, no VAT is paid on digital supplies imported in these jurisdictions by private consumers. The strong growth of the digital economy, particularly the growing scale of B2C trade in digital products, may render this approach increasingly unsustainable.

8.2. Addressing the broader indirect tax challenges of the digital economy

321. The collection of VAT on cross-border transactions concluded through digital media was identified by the Task Force on the Digital Economy (TFDE) as a key issue that must be addressed urgently to level the playing field between foreign and domestic suppliers and to protect countries' VAT revenues. The TFDE called for work on these issues by Working Party No 9 (WP9) of the OECD Committee on Fiscal Affairs (CFA), to be completed by the end of 2015 with the Associates in the BEPS Project participating on an equal footing with the OECD countries.

8.2.1. The collection of VAT on imports of low value goods

322. When they implemented the VAT exemption thresholds for imports of low value goods, jurisdictions generally attempted to find the appropriate balance between the administrative and compliance costs of taxing low value imports and the revenue loss and potential competitive distortions that the exemptions may create. However, these exemption thresholds were generally established before the advent and growth of the digital economy and a review may therefore be required to ensure that they are still appropriate.

323. If the efficiency of processing imports of low value goods and of collecting the VAT on such imports could be improved, governments may be in a position to lower these VAT exemption thresholds and address the issues associated with their operation. Against this background, WP 9 of the OECD CFA, with the Associates in the BEPS Project participating on an equal footing with the OECD countries, carried out work on possible options for a more efficient collection of VAT on imports of low value goods. A report was prepared on the basis of the outcome of this work outlining and assessing the main available approaches for improving the efficiency of collecting the VAT on such imports, which could allow governments to reduce or remove the exemption thresholds should they wish to do so (the Low Value Imports Report, reproduced in Annex C). This report does not set forth recommendations or guidelines but rather provides an analysis of possible approaches for improving the efficiency of the VAT collection on imports of low value goods. It assesses the available options or combinations of options for governments to consider depending on their domestic situation and their exposure to imports of low value goods.

324. The Low Value Imports Report focuses only on the collection of VAT on imports of low value goods, not on the collection of customs duties. Both the import VAT and the customs duties are generally collected by customs authorities and most countries also operate a *de minimis* threshold for customs duties, which is often higher than the VAT exemption threshold.[2] Against this background, the report explores models for collecting import VAT that would limit or remove the need for customs authorities to intervene in the VAT collection for imports that are not subject to customs duties. This is expected to lower the cost of collection of VAT on low value imports significantly. VAT on imports of goods above the customs threshold could (continue to) be collected together with customs duties and taxes under normal customs procedures. It is however recognised that customs authorities will keep an important role to play, notably for ensuring the safety and security of the value chain (e.g. detection and prevention of the unlawful movement of illicit and counterfeited goods).

325. The Low Value Imports Report identifies four broad models for collecting VAT on low value imports and it assesses their likely performance. These models are: *(1)* the traditional collection model; *(2)* the purchaser collection model; *(3)* the vendor collection model; and *(4)* the intermediary collection model. The distinction between these collection models is essentially based on the person liable to account for the VAT. The traditional collection model is the model that is generally applied currently for the collection of duties and taxes at importation, and that is often combined with a VAT exemption for imports of low value goods. The other three models present possible alternative approaches for a more efficient collection of VAT on the importation of low value goods. The operation of these models and their likely performance are summarised in the following paragraphs.

8.2.1.1. The traditional collection model

326. The traditional collection model, where VAT is assessed at the border for each imported low value good individually, is generally found not to be an efficient model for

collecting the VAT on imports of low value goods. This is certainly the case in the absence of electronic data transmission systems to replace the existing paper based and manual processes.

327. The efficiency of the traditional collection model may improve over time, as and when electronic systems for pre-arrival declaration and electronic tax assessment and payment are implemented worldwide to replace paper based and manual verification processes. These new electronic processes are already prevalent in the express carrier environment where they have resulted in considerable efficiency gains. The consistent use of such electronic systems would improve the efficiency of the traditional collection model for both tax administrations and vendors. Their worldwide implementation might allow the removal of the current VAT exemption thresholds. The Low Value Import Report notes, however, that these systems are not yet available to process the import of the considerable numbers of low value goods that are moved by postal services. These electronic processes for the postal environment are still under development and may only be available in the medium term.

8.2.1.2. The purchaser collection model

328. A model relying on the purchaser to self-assess and pay the VAT on its imports of low value goods is not likely to provide a sufficiently robust solution for an efficient collection of the tax. Although the purchaser collection model is likely to involve only limited compliance burden for vendors, the level of compliance by purchasers is expected to be low and this model would be highly complex and costly for customs and tax administrations to implement and operate.

8.2.1.3. The vendor collection model

329. A model requiring the non-resident vendors to charge, collect and remit the VAT in the country of importation could improve the efficiency of the collection of VAT on low value imports and thus create opportunities for governments to remove or reduce import exemption thresholds if they wish to do so. While a vendor collection model would create additional burden for non-resident vendors, these can be mitigated by complementing this model with a simplified VAT registration and compliance regime similar to the one suggested in the context of the OECD International VAT/GST Guidelines on B2C supplies of services and intangibles (B2C Guidelines). When a vendor supplies both goods and services into a particular jurisdiction, the registration system applied under the B2C Guidelines could be used for both kinds of supplies. This would reduce the administrative and compliance costs of the vendor registration. Going further, possible fast-track processing could be made available in customs for low value goods that are imported under this model. The Low Value Imports Report points out that the implementation of such a model is likely to involve considerable changes to existing customs and tax collection processes and systems, and that enhanced international and inter-agency (tax and customs administrations) co-operation would be required to help ensure compliance by non-resident vendors under this model.

8.2.1.4. The intermediary collection model

330. A model where VAT on imports of low value goods would be collected and remitted by intermediaries on behalf of non-resident vendors could improve the efficiency of the collection of VAT on such imports and thus create opportunities for governments to remove or reduce import exemption thresholds, assuming that such intermediaries would have the required information to assess and remit the right amount of taxes in the country of importation. The VAT collection by intermediaries would involve minimal compliance

burdens on vendors. It may, however, come at an additional cost that may be passed on to the purchaser. This model may be particularly effective when the VAT is collected by intermediaries that have a presence in the country of importation (e.g. express carriers, postal operators and locally implemented e-commerce platforms). The intermediaries' understanding of local tax and customs rules and procedures could provide benefits to both vendors and tax administrations. Four main types of intermediaries are identified:

- Postal operators: in the postal operators environment, information is limited and is mostly collected and transmitted on paper forms. Most postal operators do not have the appropriate systems in place to manage the assessment and collection of VAT on importation of low value goods. Electronic collection and transmission processes are being developed but the postal system would still require substantial adjustment to operate an efficient VAT collection model.
- Express carriers: in the express carriers environment, electronic data collection and transmission systems that enable an efficient collection and remittance of import VAT are most often already in place and such VAT collection and remittance to the authorities by express carriers is already common practice. A model whereby non-resident vendors could rely on express carriers to collect and remit the VAT on imports of low value goods could provide an efficient and effective solution, provided it is combined with sufficiently simple compliance regimes and with fast-track processing.
- Transparent e-commerce platforms: transparent e-commerce platforms are platforms that provide a trading framework for vendors but that are not parties to the commercial transaction between the vendor and the purchaser. These platforms generally have access to the key information that is needed for assessing the VAT due in the country of importation of low value goods. Some of the leading marketplaces already provide tax compliance services to their vendors. A model where VAT on imports of low value goods would be collected and remitted by such transparent e-commerce platforms on behalf of non-resident vendors could provide an efficient and effective solution, provided it is combined with sufficiently simple compliance regimes and with fast-track processing. It is recognised, however, that these e-commerce platforms may often still need to implement systems changes to ensure a sufficiently efficient and effective VAT collection and remittance process. When e-commerce platforms do not have a presence in the country of importation, enhanced international and inter-agency (tax and customs administrations) co-operation would be required to help ensure compliance by these platforms.
- Financial intermediaries: they do not collect the necessary information for the assessment and payment of the VAT on low value imports and the development of a model relying on these intermediaries to collect and remit the import VAT would involve deep changes in the data collection processes. It is therefore considered unlikely that financial intermediaries could play a role in a more efficient collection of VAT on imports of low value goods.

8.2.1.5. Overall conclusion

331. The assessment of the models outlined above suggests that a range of possible approaches are available for increasing the efficiency of the collection of VAT on low-value imports for countries to choose from, depending on national policy decisions and specific circumstances.

332. Jurisdictions could opt for a combination of models. For instance, an optional vendor collection model could be combined with an intermediary collection model (which may notably allow small and medium size businesses to comply more easily), whereby the vendor as well as the intermediary would benefit from a simplified VAT registration and compliance regime designed and operated in conformity with the system applied under the B2C Guidelines. Both models could be combined with further simplification arrangements, such as fast-track processing in customs. To increase compliance, these models could be combined with a fall-back rule whereby VAT would be collected under the traditional collection model (possibly from the final consumer), e.g. if VAT has not been paid either under the vendor or intermediary collection models. Risks of undervaluation or mis-description by foreign vendors of imported goods should be considered for the assessment of the models or combination of models.

333. The implementation of these models or a combination of them allow jurisdictions to remove or lower the VAT exemption thresholds, should they wish to do so.

334. It is recognised that any reform to improve the efficiency of the collection of VAT on low value imports will need to be complemented with appropriate risk assessment and enhanced international administrative co-operation between tax authorities to enforce compliance.

8.2.2. The collection of VAT on cross-border business-to-consumer supplies of services and intangibles

335. Recommended approaches for addressing the key challenge of collecting the VAT on the sales of digital products to private consumers by non-resident suppliers were developed by the OECD and G20 in the context of work on the International VAT/GST Guidelines (the "Guidelines"). These Guidelines were developed as a future global standard to address issues of double taxation and unintended non-taxation resulting from inconsistencies in the application of VAT to international trade. Their scope is not limited to the trade of digital products and covers trade in services and intangibles more generally. The Guidelines present a separate solution for business-to-business trade (B2B) and business-to-consumer (B2C) trade, recognising that VAT systems often employ different mechanisms to collect the tax for these categories of transactions. The recommended approach for addressing the challenge of collecting the VAT on the sales of digital products to private consumers by non-resident suppliers is included in the Guidelines that deal specifically with B2C (see Annex D).

336. The B2C Guidelines present a set of standards for determining the place of taxation for B2C supplies of services and intangibles, in accordance with the destination principle. They provide that the jurisdiction in which the customer has its usual residence has the right to collect VAT on remote supplies of services and intangibles, including digital supplies by offshore suppliers. This standard allows suppliers and tax administrations to predict with reasonable accuracy the place where the services or intangibles are likely to be consumed while taking into account practical constraints. The implementation of these standards aims at ensuring that VAT on such supplies in the market jurisdiction applies at the same rate as for domestic supplies. This ensures the even playing field between domestic and offshore suppliers, so that there is no tax advantage for foreign companies based in low or no tax jurisdictions selling to final consumers relative to domestic companies.

337. Regarding the key issue of the collection of VAT in the destination country, the B2C Guidelines indicate that, at the present time, the most effective and efficient approach to ensure the appropriate collection of VAT on cross-border B2C supplies is to require the non-resident supplier to register and account for VAT in the jurisdiction of taxation. The B2C Guidelines recommend that jurisdictions consider establishing a simplified registration and compliance regime to facilitate compliance for non-resident suppliers, the main features of which are

outlined in Table 8.1. The highest feasible levels of compliance by non-resident suppliers are likely to be achieved if compliance obligations in the jurisdiction of taxation are limited to what is strictly necessary for the effective collection of the tax. Appropriate simplification is particularly important to facilitate compliance for businesses faced with obligations in multiple jurisdictions. At the same time, in considering simplified registration for VAT purposes, it is important to underline that registration for VAT purposes is independent from the determination of whether there is a permanent establishment (PE) for income tax purposes. Recognising that a proper balance needs to be struck between simplification and the need of governments to safeguard the revenue, the B2C Guidelines indicate that it is necessary that jurisdictions take appropriate steps to strengthen international administrative co-operation, which is a key means to achieve the proper collection and remittance of the tax on cross-border supplies of services and intangibles by non-resident suppliers.

Table 8.1. **Main features of a simplified registration and compliance regime for non-resident suppliers**

Registration procedure	• The information requested could be limited to necessary details, which could include: - Name of business, including the trading name - Name of contact person responsible for dealing with tax administrations - Postal and/or registered address of the business and its contact person - Telephone number of contact person - Electronic address of contact person - Web sites URL of non-resident suppliers through which business is conducted in the taxing jurisdiction - National tax identification number, if such a number is issued to the supplier in the supplier's jurisdiction to conduct business in that jurisdiction. • The simplest way to engage with tax administrations from a remote location is by electronic processes. An on-line registration application could be made accessible on the home page of the tax administration's web site, preferably available in the languages of the jurisdiction's major trading partners.
Input tax recovery refunds	• Taxing jurisdictions could limit the scope of a simplified registration and compliance regime to the collection of VAT on B2C supplies of services and intangibles by non-resident suppliers without making the recovery of input tax available under the simplified regime. • Input tax recovery could remain available for non-resident suppliers under the normal VAT refund or registration and compliance procedure.
Return procedure	• As requirements differ widely among jurisdictions, satisfying obligations to file tax returns in multiple jurisdictions is a complex process that often results in considerable compliance burdens for non-resident suppliers. • Tax administrations could consider authorising non-resident businesses to file simplified returns, which would be less detailed than returns required for local businesses that are entitled to input tax credits. In establishing the requirements for information under such a simplified approach, it is desirable to strike a balance between the businesses' need for simplicity and the tax administrations' need to verify whether tax obligations have been correctly fulfilled. This information could be confined to: - Supplier's registration identification number - Tax period - Currency and, where relevant, exchange rate used - Taxable amount at the standard rate - Taxable amount at reduced rate(s), if any - Total tax amount payable. • The option to file electronically in a simple and commonly used format is essential to facilitating compliance.

Table 8.1. **Main features of a simplified registration and compliance regime for non-resident suppliers** *(continued)*

Payments	• Use of electronic payment methods is recommended, allowing non-resident suppliers to remit the tax due electronically. • Jurisdictions could consider accepting payments in the currencies of their main trading partners.
Record keeping	• Jurisdictions are encouraged to allow the use of electronic record keeping systems. • Jurisdictions could limit the data to be recorded to what is required to satisfy themselves that the tax for each supply has been charged and accounted for correctly and relying as much as possible on information that is available to suppliers in the course of their normal business activity. • This could include the type of supply, the date of the supply, the VAT payable and the information used to determine the place where the customer has its usual residence. • Taxing jurisdictions could require these records to be made available on request within a reasonable delay.
Invoicing	• Jurisdictions could consider eliminating invoicing requirements for business-to-consumer supplies that are covered by the simplified registration and compliance regime, in light of the fact that the customers involved generally will not be entitled to deduct the input VAT paid on these supplies. • If invoices are required, jurisdictions could consider allowing invoices to be issued in accordance with the rules of the supplier's jurisdiction or accepting commercial documentation that is issued for purposes other than VAT (e.g. electronic receipts). • It is recommended that information on the invoice remain limited to the data required to administer the VAT regime (such as the identification of the customer, type and date of the supply(ies), the taxable amount and VAT amount per VAT rate and the total taxable amount). Jurisdictions could consider allowing this invoice to be submitted in the language of their main trading partners
Availability of information	• Jurisdictions are encouraged to make available on-line all information necessary to register and comply with the simplified registration and compliance regime, preferably in the languages of their major trading partners. • Jurisdictions are also encouraged to make accessible via the Internet the relevant and up-to-date information that non-resident businesses are likely to need in making their tax determinations. In particular, this would include information on tax rates and product classification.
Use of third-party service providers	• Compliance for non-resident suppliers could be further facilitated by allowing such suppliers to appoint a third-party service provider to act on their behalf in carrying out certain procedures, such as submitting returns. • This could be especially helpful for small and medium enterprises and businesses that are faced with multi-jurisdictional obligations.

338. Consider an example of online suppliers of streaming digital content such as movies and television shows. The supplies are made mainly to consumers who can access the digital content through their computers, mobile devices and televisions that are connected to the Internet. Suppliers that are established in the same jurisdiction as their customers are required to collect and remit that jurisdiction's VAT on the supplies. If the supplier is a non-resident in the market jurisdiction, issues may arise in the absence of the standards as set forth in the B2C Guidelines. If taxing rights on the streaming services were allocated to the supplier's jurisdiction at the rate applicable in that jurisdiction, then domestic suppliers of competing services in the market jurisdiction could face potential competitive pressures if the supplier of the digital content is established in a jurisdiction that applies no VAT or a VAT with a lower rate than that of the market jurisdiction. In that case, no VAT or an inappropriately low amount of VAT would be collected and none of the VAT revenue would accrue to the jurisdiction where the final consumption takes place. On the other hand if taxing rights were to be allocated to the jurisdiction where the customer is resident but with no suitable mechanism available to collect the VAT in this jurisdiction, no VAT will actually be paid.

339. Under the B2C Guidelines, it is recommended that *(i)* the jurisdiction of the usual residence of the customer will have the right to levy VAT on the supply of the digital content, *(ii)* the foreign seller will be required to register for VAT in that market jurisdiction under a simplified registration and compliance regime, and *(iii)* the foreign seller will be required to charge and collect the VAT in that jurisdiction at the same rate as for domestic supplies. These Guidelines recognise explicitly that it is necessary to reinforce taxing authorities' enforcement capacity through enhanced international co-operation in tax administration in the field of indirect taxes. They recommend that such co-operation be enhanced through the development of a common standard for the exchange of information that is simple, minimises the costs for tax administrations and businesses by limiting the amount of data that is exchanged, and which can be implemented in a short timeframe.

Notes

1. While the example deals with streaming movies and TV shows, the same issues arise with most, if not all supplies of remotely delivered services to consumers, such as cloud computing, gaming, software downloads.

2. Most countries operate a de minimis threshold for customs duties, which is essentially regulated by the World Customs Organization's (WCO) Revised Kyoto Convention (RKC). It provides for a mandatory de minimis customs duties and taxes relief for small consignments. While this rule is obligatory for Contracting Parties to the RKC, the RKC does not prescribe the amount of such a threshold nor does it impose a minimum standard.

Bibliography

Corrado, C. et al. (2012), "Intangible capital and growth in advanced economies: Measurement and comparative results", IZA Discussion Paper No. 6733.

Lamensch, M. (2012), "Are 'reverse charging' and the 'one shop scheme' efficient ways to collect VAT on digital supplies?" *World Journal of VAT Law*, Vol. 1, Issue 1.

OECD (2013), *OECD Communications Outlook 2013*, OECD Publishing, Paris, http://dx.doi.org/10.1787/comms_outlook-2013-en.

OECD (2003), *Electronic Commerce-Commentary on Place of Consumption for Business to Business Supplies (Business Presence)*, OECD, Paris.

OECD (1998), "Electronic Commerce: Taxation Framework Conditions", a report by the Committee on Fiscal Affairs, page 4, www.oecd.org/tax/consumption/1923256.pdf.

Chapter 9

Evaluation of the broader direct and indirect tax challenges raised by the digital economy and of the options to address them

This chapter contains an evaluation of the options identified to address the broader tax challenges raised by the digital economy. The evaluation takes into account not only the impact on BEPS issues of the measures developed in the course of the BEPS Project, but also the economic incidence of the different options to tackle these broader tax challenges.

9.1. Broader tax challenges and options to address them

340. The digital economy triggers systemic questions about the ability of the current domestic and international tax systems to deal with the changes brought about by advances in information and communication technology (ICT). These tax policy issues have implications for the overall design of tax systems. These challenges may therefore have broader implications than BEPS and the countermeasures developed in the course of the Project. These include issues related to the allocation of taxing rights among countries as well as to the tax policy considerations that should be taken into account when weighing the relative costs and benefits of the various tax solutions. With respect to direct taxes, the broader tax challenges raised by the digital economy go beyond the question of how to put an end to double non-taxation, and chiefly relate to the question of how taxing rights on income generated from cross-border activities in the digital age should be allocated among countries. With respect to indirect taxes, the challenges chiefly relate to how to ensure that effective and efficient collection mechanisms are in place.

341. As the potential of digital technologies grows, features such as the heavy reliance on intangibles, the constant mobility of people, the use of machines and automation, the ability to reach customers globally without the need for extensive physical presence, and the changing role of customers in the digital age are continually increasing. These features raise questions about the paradigm used to determine where economic activities are carried out and value is generated for direct tax purposes, which is currently based on an analysis of the functions, assets and risks of the enterprises involved.

342. Several proposals for potential options to address the broader direct tax challenges were considered by the Task Force on the Digital Economy (TFDE) in 2014, including:

- modifications to the exceptions from permanent establishment (PE) status;
- alternatives to the existing PE threshold;
- the imposition of a withholding tax on certain types of digital transactions; and
- the introduction of an excise tax or other levy.

343. One of the initial conclusions of the TFDE was that modifications to the exceptions from the PE status contained in paragraph 4 of Article 5 of the OECD Model Tax Convention should be considered in the context of Action 7 of the BEPS Project, whether the application of the exception raised BEPS issues or broader tax challenges. This was due to the fact that some activities that were previously preparatory or auxiliary in the context of conventional business models may have become core functions of certain businesses in the digital economy. In addition to broader tax challenges, this raises BEPS issues when the lack of taxation in the market country is coupled with techniques that reduce or eliminate tax in the country of the recipient or of the ultimate parent.

344. As a result of the Action 7 work, it was agreed to modify Article 5(4) of the OECD Model Tax Convention to ensure that the availability of the exceptions to PE status is subject to the condition that the character of the activity conducted be merely preparatory or auxiliary in nature, rather than one of the core activities of the enterprise in question. For example, if proximity to customers and the need for quick delivery to clients are key components of the business model of an online seller of physical products, the maintenance of a very large local warehouse in which a significant number of employees work for purposes of storing and delivering goods sold online to customers would no longer be entitled to an exception from PE status. This treaty-related measure is expected to be implemented across the existing tax treaty network in a synchronised and efficient manner via the conclusion of a multilateral instrument that modifies bilateral tax treaties.

345. The technical details of the other three options were developed over 2015 in a way that allows them to be applied individually (i.e. a new "significant economic presence" nexus for net-basis taxation based with deemed profit attribution methods, the application of a withholding tax, or an equalisation levy) or combined. The application of these options would generally allow countries to impose a tax in situations where a foreign enterprise derives considerable sales income from the country without a physical presence therein, and/or uses the contributions of in-country users in its value chain, including through collection and monitoring of data.

346. In relation to indirect taxes, issues arise regarding the ability of VAT systems to deal with cross-border remote sales transactions between private consumers and foreign suppliers. In fact, the difficulty of ensuring compliance and collection of VAT on remote digital supplies of services and intangibles to final consumers is magnified where the supplier is not present physically or otherwise in the consumer's country. Similarly, countries applying an exemption from VAT for imports of low value goods have seen a significant growth in the volume of such imports on which VAT is not collected, thereby generating loss of tax revenue and potential competitive pressures on domestic suppliers. The work carried out by Working Party No. 9 (WP 9) of the OECD's Committee on Fiscal Affairs (CFA), which is encapsulated in the Guidelines on value added tax/goods and services tax (VAT/GST Guidelines) and described in Chapter 8, has resulted in general agreement on global standards on the allocation of VAT/GST taxing rights on cross-border transactions as well as in the identification of possible mechanisms supporting the implementation of these standards in an efficient manner.

347. Once implemented, the new VAT/GST Guidelines will facilitate cross-border digital transactions being subject to tax in the market country, hence helping level the playing field between non-resident enterprises and domestic enterprises. Consider the case of online sellers of streaming digital content such as movies and television shows to consumers who can access the digital content through their computers, mobile devices and televisions that are connected to the Internet. Without implementation of the B2C Guidelines, the market country generally has no nexus or may be unable to require the foreign seller to apply and remit VAT on such transaction. The result is a gap between the obligation on domestic enterprises to charge VAT on sales to local customers and that of foreign suppliers. Under the new B2C Guidelines, the country of the usual residence of the customer generally has the right, and is provided with mechanisms, to levy VAT on the sale of the digital content from abroad.

348. To summarise, like the challenges they are intended to address, the impact of the various options described above overlaps in a number of respects. For instance, both the new VAT/GST Guidelines and the "significant economic presence" option would generally provide the country where the customers are located the right to levy tax. Also, cognisant of the fact that there are different proposals as to how to approach the broader tax challenges, and given that many of the options proposed could actually be implemented in multiple ways, it was agreed that a full evaluation of the relevance, urgency, and scope of the broader direct tax challenges and of the potential options to address them would benefit from an analysis of the expected economic incidence of the three options outlined above.

9.2. Economic incidence of the options to address the broader direct tax challenges

349. The analysis focused on the ultimate resting point of the initial change in tax liabilities under each proposal after taxpayers have responded to the tax changes. Specifically, the expected economic incidence on consumers, capital owners (including shareholders) and

labour (workers) of the options was analysed in relation to the provision of digital goods and services by foreign suppliers without a taxable presence in the country of the customer under current rules. The conclusion is that all three of the tax options would be expected to have similar economic incidence:[1]

- *In the case of a perfectly competitive market for digital goods and services*, the incidence of the various options (and associated tax increase) is likely to be borne in part by labour, depending on the labour market conditions in the various countries in which foreign suppliers are located, and in part by consumers in market countries, assuming that the affected suppliers account for a significant share of worldwide market output, and depending on the availability of replacement suppliers with similar pre-tax costs and the availability of substitutes for the affected digital goods and services.
- *If the market is imperfectly competitive*, however, the various options (and associated tax increase) are likely to be borne by the equity owners of the affected foreign suppliers to a greater or lesser extent, depending on the degree to which firms are price-setters.

350. The details of the economic incidence analysis, including the associated conclusions, are included in Annex E.

9.3. Framework to evaluate the options

351. For purposes of evaluating the potential options, the TFDE agreed on a framework starting from the basic tax principles of neutrality, efficiency, certainty and simplicity, effectiveness and fairness, flexibility and sustainability, and in light of the overall proportionality of the changes in relation to the tax challenges they are intended to address. In evaluating potential options, no single principle can be given greater priority than any other. Instead, the assessment under the framework shall be based on an overall consideration of the individual factors that are part of it, and namely:

- ***Neutrality:*** taxpayers in similar situations carrying out similar transactions should be subject to similar levels of taxation, in order to avoid introducing distortions to the market. In other words, the same principles of taxation should apply to all forms of business, while taking into account specific features that may otherwise undermine an equal and neutral application of those principles.
- ***Efficiency:*** the benefits of any reform should outweigh the costs of its adoption, including transitional and implementation costs. Evaluation of the efficiency of potential options relative to the existing framework should therefore also take into account whether the administrative considerations underlying the existing rules are still applicable, or whether advances in technology may have made those practical constraints less important.
- ***Certainty and simplicity:*** tax rules that are easily understood make it easier for taxpayers to anticipate the tax consequences of transactions, and for administrators to evaluate compliance. A simple tax system is also likely to involve lower compliance costs, resulting in a more efficient taxation system.
- ***Effectiveness and fairness:*** as recognised in the Ottawa framework conditions, taxes imposed should produce the right amount of tax at the right time. In assessing the fairness of any proposed options, it is important to consider who may bear the ultimate tax burden and in what proportion. Effectiveness is important because a

tax system that is difficult to enforce is unlikely to be either equitable or neutral, and may undermine the public perceptions of the fairness of the whole system in the long term.

- ***Flexibility and sustainability:*** options should be evaluated based not only on whether they address the tax challenges in the current environment, but, to the extent possible given the difficulty of predicting future developments, on whether they can be expected to be flexible and dynamic enough to adapt to future commercial and technological developments.
- ***Proportionality:*** it is important to evaluate not only whether the proposed options address those tax challenges, but also what broader impact those options may have. Potential options shall be tailored to the scope of the particular challenges they are intended to address.

9.4. Impact of BEPS countermeasures

352. The broader tax challenges raised by the digital economy intersect with several other BEPS action items.

353. In the direct tax context, BEPS concerns are raised by situations in which taxable income can be artificially separated from the activities that generate it, resulting in the ability to reduce or eliminate tax across a whole supply chain, including both market and residence countries. The work to address the tax challenges of the digital economy has made clear that while no unique BEPS issues are presented by the digital economy, the key features of the digital economy do exacerbate BEPS concerns. As outlined in Chapter 6, the key features of the digital economy have been taken into account in the work under the BEPS Action Plan to address BEPS in the context of direct taxes, including in particular the work on CFC rules (Action 3), addressing the artificial avoidance of PE status (Action 7) and transfer pricing (Actions 8-10). As a result, it is expected that the implementation of these measures will substantially address the BEPS issues previously identified with respect to the digital economy. The effectiveness of the measures adopted in the context of the BEPS Project as well as the impact on both compliance by taxpayers and proper implementation by tax administrations will be monitored through a targeted mechanism.

354. Although the work to address BEPS is targeted at situations in which tax is reduced or eliminated in jurisdictions across the whole supply chain, its impact may go beyond BEPS in certain situations, such as in the case of the work under Action 7 to modify the exceptions to PE status. These changes will address BEPS structures in which a lack of PE in a market country is coupled with lack of taxation in the country of the recipient or ultimate parent, but at the same time the rules produced by this work will also apply more broadly where activities that were previously considered preparatory or auxiliary have now become core activities in certain business models.

355. Addressing BEPS in the digital economy may also indirectly affect the scope of the broader tax challenges raised by the digital economy, and hence the evaluation of the options to address them. For example, concerns about nexus for direct tax purposes relate to the ability of a non-resident enterprise to derive substantial amounts of income from a country without a physical presence therein. As noted in Chapter 4, however, there can be compelling reasons for businesses to have a degree of physical presence in a market, in order to ensure that core resources are placed as close as possible to key markets. Under the current tax system, however, it is very often possible to use artificial structures to

ensure that this physical presence either does not create a taxable presence or does not attract significant profits so that the bulk of the profits can then be shifted to a no or low-tax jurisdiction. Implementation of the BEPS measures is expected to have a substantial impact on this BEPS risk, so that the location of taxable profits will be better aligned with economic activity and value creation. At the same time, BEPS measures such as the modification of Article 5(4) of the OECD Model Tax Convention are expected to also mitigate some aspects of the broader tax challenges. As a result, the expected impact of the BEPS measures needs to be taken into account when evaluating the extent of the broader tax challenges and the options to address them.

9.5. Evaluation

356. As noted above, the TFDE considered several options to address the broader tax challenges raised by the digital economy, including modifications to the exceptions from PE status, alternatives to the existing PE threshold, the imposition of a withholding tax on certain types of digital transactions and the introduction of an equalisation levy, as well as the principles and mechanisms developed by WP 9 of the CFA to ensure that VAT is collected by the country where the customer is located. To evaluate these options, the TFDE agreed on a framework based on neutrality, efficiency, certainty and simplicity, effectiveness and fairness, flexibility and sustainability, and proportionality. It also analysed the economic incidence of the three options aimed at taxing income from the sales of digital goods and services by foreign suppliers without a PE under current rules, namely the new nexus in the form of a significant economic presence, the withholding tax on certain types of digital transactions and the equalisation levy.

357. As regards the different options analysed, the TFDE has concluded that:

- **The option to modify the exceptions to PE status in order to ensure that they are available only for activities that are in fact preparatory or auxiliary in nature has been considered by the TFDE and adopted as part of the work on Action 7 of the BEPS Project.** In order to ensure that profits derived from core activities performed in a country can be taxed in that country, Article 5(4) is modified to ensure that each of the exceptions included therein is restricted to activities that are otherwise of a "preparatory or auxiliary" character. In addition, a new anti-fragmentation rule was introduced to ensure that it is not possible to benefit from these exceptions through the fragmentation of business activities among closely related enterprises. These changes to the definition of PE of the OECD Model Tax Convention are included in the Report *Preventing the Artificial Avoidance of PE Status* (OECD, 2015) and are now expected to be implemented across the existing tax treaty network in a synchronised and efficient manner via the conclusion of the multilateral instrument that modifies bilateral tax treaties under Action 15.[2]
- **The collection of VAT/GST on cross-border transactions, particularly those between businesses and consumers, is an important issue**. In this regard, countries are recommended to apply the principles of the International VAT/GST Guidelines and consider the introduction of the collection mechanisms included therein. Implementation packages will be developed to ensure that countries can implement the International VAT/GST Guidelines in a co-ordinated manner. Work in this area will be carried out by the WP9, with the Associates in the BEPS Project participating on an equal footing.

- **Some aspects of the broader direct tax challenges currently raised by the digital economy are expected to be mitigated once the BEPS measures are implemented**. This is because once implemented, the BEPS measures are expected to better align the location of taxable profits with the location of economic activity and value creation. This will address BEPS and restore both source and residence taxation in a number of cases where cross-border income would otherwise go untaxed or would be taxed at very low rates. In addition, even in the modern digital economy many businesses often still require a local physical presence in order to be present in a market and maintain a purposeful and sustained interaction with the economy of that country. In this context, BEPS measures such as the modification of Article 5(4) of the OECD Model Tax Convention, are expected to also mitigate some aspects of the broader tax challenges. As a consequence, a quick implementation of the BEPS measures is needed, together with mechanisms to monitor their impact over time.

- **None of the other options analysed by the TFDE were recommended at this stage.** This is because, among other reasons, it is expected that the measures developed in the BEPS Project will have a substantial impact on BEPS issues previously identified in the digital economy, that certain BEPS measures will mitigate some aspects of the broader tax challenges, and that consumption taxes will be levied effectively in the market country. The options analysed by the TFDE to address the broader direct tax challenges, namely the new nexus in the form of a significant economic presence, the withholding tax on certain types of digital transactions and the equalisation levy, would require substantial changes to key international tax standards and would require further work. In the changing international tax environment a number of countries have expressed a concern about how international standards on which bilateral tax treaties are based allocate taxing rights between source and residence States. At this stage, it is however unclear whether these changes are warranted to deal with the changes brought about by advances in ICT. Taking the above into account, and in the absence of data on the actual scope of these broader direct tax challenges, the TFDE did not recommend any of the three options as internationally agreed standards.

- **Countries could, however, introduce any of the options in their domestic laws as additional safeguards against BEPS, provided they respect existing treaty obligations, or in their bilateral tax treaties.** The adoption of the options as domestic law measures could be considered, for example, if a country concludes that BEPS issues exacerbated by the digital economy are not fully addressed, or to account for the time lag between agreement on the measures to tackle BEPS at the international level and their actual implementation and application. The options may provide broad safeguards against BEPS and ensure that a domestic taxing right is available for remote transactions involving digital goods and services, which is currently not the case under most countries' domestic laws. Countries could take this approach with the intent to address their concerns about BEPS issues in the short term and gain practical experience with the application of the options over time, fostering co-ordinated domestic law approaches and informing possible future discussions. In addition, countries could bilaterally agree to include any of the options in their tax treaties.

- **Adoption as domestic law measures would require further calibration of the options in order to provide additional clarity about the details, as well as some adaptation to ensure consistency with existing international legal commitments**. Consistency with bilateral tax treaty obligations would have to be ensured, for example by applying the options solely with respect to residents of non-treaty countries, or in situations in which benefits of the treaty may be denied due to the application of anti-abuse rules that are in conformity with tax treaty obligations.

9.6. Next steps

358. **These conclusions may evolve as the digital economy continues to develop, in particular regarding robotics, the internet of things, 3D printing and the sharing economy.** As technology continues to advance, developments in advanced robotics will make it increasingly possible to perform complex tasks and take decisions with limited human intervention. As more devices are connected to the internet, the ability to collect, share, process, and act on data has been predicted to generate between nearly USD 4 trillion to USD 11 trillion in economic benefits globally in the year 2025, in the form of profits to device-makers, efficiencies, new businesses and savings to consumers from better-run products (McKinsey Global Institute, 2015). Possibilities arising from the ability to monitor and control things in the physical world electronically are important and require a thorough understanding of where value is created in the digital economy. Advances in the peer-to-peer sharing economy have reduced transaction costs, increased availability of information, and provided greater reliability and security, increasingly providing decentralised alternatives to more traditional business models. Finally, if current trends regarding the internet of things and 3D printing continue, flexibility about where business functions take place will continue to increase.

359. **It is therefore important to continue working on these issues and to monitor developments in the digital economy over time.** Monitoring will focus primarily on the following three areas. First, developments in ICT and new business models that have an impact on international tax policy. Second, the impact of implementation of the BEPS measures on the tax challenges exacerbated by the digital economy, as part of the wider post-BEPS monitoring process. Third, any actions taken by countries in the implementation of the options as domestic law measures or in their bilateral tax treaties, and their impact over time. Moreover, other relevant developments will be taken into account, notably in the field of VAT/GST, leveraging on the respective work carried out by WP 9.

360. **As part of this future work, it will also be important to review and analyse data that will become available over time.** This will provide a sound basis to ascertain the concrete extent of the broader direct tax challenges, in particular in relation to nexus. For example, data collected from remote sellers through simplified VAT/GST regimes, and statistical analyses of data from the Country-by-Country reporting template will provide a better indication of the ability of businesses in the digital economy to be able to participate in the economic life of a country without a taxable presence there. On the basis of the future monitoring work, a determination will also be made as to whether further work on the three options discussed and analysed by the TFDE should be carried out. This determination should be based on a broad look at the ability of existing international tax standards to deal with the tax challenges raised by developments in the digital economy, taking into account not just direct taxes, but also indirect taxes, administrative issues, countries' differing levels of development, as well as the impact of any potential change on cross-border trade and investment.

361. **To these aims, the work will continue following the completion of the other follow-up work on the BEPS Project.** This future work will be done in consultation with a broad range of stakeholders and on the basis of a detailed mandate to be developed during 2016 in the context of designing an inclusive post-BEPS monitoring process. A report reflecting the outcome of the continued work in relation to the digital economy should be produced by 2020.

Notes

1 The incidence analysis depends on the specific details of each policy option, including whether they are applicable to all or only a subset of sellers of digital goods.

2. Some countries consider that there is no need to modify Art. 5(4) and that the list of exceptions in subparagraphs a) to d) of paragraph 4 should not be subject to the condition that the activities referred to in these subparagraphs be of a preparatory or auxiliary character. These countries may adopt a different version of Art. 5(4) as long as they include the anti-fragmentation rule referred to above..

Bibliography

OECD (2015), *Preventing the Artificial Avoidance of Permanent Establishment Status, Action 7 – 2015 Final Report*, OECD/G20 Base Erosion and Profit Shifting Project, OECD Publishing, Paris, http://dx.doi.org/10.1787/9789264241220-en.

Chapter 10

Summary of the conclusions and next steps

This chapter summarises the conclusions reached with respect to the business models and key features of the digital economy, BEPS issues in the digital economy, and the broader tax policy challenges raised by the digital economy. It then describes the next steps to be undertaken.

362. **Action 1 of the base erosion and profit shifting (BEPS) Action Plan deals with the tax challenges of the Digital Economy**. Political leaders, media outlets, and civil society around the world have expressed growing concern about tax planning by multinational enterprises (MNEs) that makes use of gaps in the interaction of different tax systems to artificially reduce taxable income or shift profits to low-tax jurisdictions in which little or no economic activity is performed. In response to this concern, and at the request of the G20, the Organisation for Economic Co-operation and Development (OECD) published an *Action Plan on Base Erosion and Profit Shifting* (BEPS Action Plan, OECD, 2013) in July 2013. Action 1 of the BEPS Action Plan calls for work to address the tax challenges of the digital economy. The Task Force on the Digital Economy (TFDE), a subsidiary body of the Committee on Fiscal Affairs (CFA) in which non-OECD G20 countries participate as Associates on an equal footing with OECD countries, was established in September 2013 to develop a report identifying issues raised by the digital economy and detailed options to address them by September 2014. The TFDE consulted extensively with stakeholders and analysed written input submitted by business, civil society, academics, and developing countries. It issued an interim report in September 2014 and continued its work in 2015. The conclusions regarding the digital economy, the BEPS issues and the broader tax challenges it raises, and the recommended next steps are contained in this final report.

10.1. The digital economy, its business models, and its key features

363. **The digital economy is the result of a transformative process brought by information and communication technology (ICT).** The ICT revolution has made technologies cheaper, more powerful, and widely standardised, improving business processes and bolstering innovation across all sectors of the economy. For example, *retailers* allow customers to place online orders and are able to gather and analyse customer data to provide personalised service and advertising; the *logistics* sector has been transformed by the ability to track vehicles and cargo across continents; *financial services* providers increasingly enable customers to manage their finances, conduct transactions and access new products on line; in *manufacturing*, the digital economy has enhanced the ability to remotely monitor production processes and to control and use robots; in the *education* sector, universities, tutoring services and other education service providers are able to provide courses remotely, which enables them to tap into global demand; in the *healthcare* sector, the digital economy is enabling remote diagnosis and the use of health records to enhance system efficiencies and patient experience. The *broadcasting and media industry* have been revolutionised, expanding the role in news media of non-traditional news sources, and expanding user participation in media through user-generated content and social networking.

364. **Because the digital economy is increasingly becoming the economy itself, it would be difficult, if not impossible, to ring-fence the digital economy from the rest of the economy for tax purposes**. Attempting to isolate the digital economy as a separate sector would inevitably require arbitrary lines to be drawn between what is digital and what is not. As a result, the tax challenges and BEPS concerns raised by the digital economy are better identified and addressed by analysing existing structures adopted by MNEs together with new business models and by focusing on the key features of the digital economy and determining which of those features raise or exacerbate tax challenges or BEPS concerns. Although many digital economy business models have parallels in traditional business, modern advances in ICT have made it possible to conduct many types of business at substantially greater scale and over longer distances than was previously possible. These

include several varieties of e-commerce, online payment services, app stores, online advertising, cloud computing, participative networked platforms, and high-speed trading.

365. **The digital economy is in a continuous state of evolution and developments need to be monitored to evaluate their impact on tax systems**. The rapid technological progress that has characterised the digital economy has led to a number of emerging trends and potential developments. Although this rapid change makes it difficult to predict future developments with any degree of reliability, these potential developments should be monitored closely as they may generate additional challenges for tax policy makers in the near future. These developments include the *Internet of Things*, referring to the dramatic increase in networked devices; *virtual currencies*, including bitcoin; developments in *advanced robotics and 3D printing*, which have the potential to bring manufacturing closer to consumers, altering where and how value is created within manufacturing supply chains, as well as the characterisation of business income; the *sharing economy* which allows peer-to-peer sharing of goods and services, and *collaborative production* which allows crowdsourcing and crowdfunding; increased *access to government data*, which has the potential to improve accountability and performance, and to allow participation of third parties in government business; and *reinforced protection of personal data*, which is more widely available in the digital economy.

366. **The digital economy and its business models present some key features which are potentially relevant from a tax perspective**. These features include *mobility*, with respect to *(i)* the intangibles on which the digital economy relies heavily, *(ii)* users, and *(iii)* business functions; *reliance on data*, the massive use of which has been facilitated by an increase in computing power and storage capacity and a decrease in data storage cost; *network effects*, which refer to the fact that decisions of users may have a direct impact on the benefit received by other users; *the spread of multi-sided business models*, in which multiple distinct groups of persons interact through an intermediary or platform, and the decisions of each group of persons affect the outcome for the other groups of persons through a positive or negative externality; *tendency toward monopoly or oligopoly* in certain business models relying heavily on network effects; and *volatility* due to lower barriers to entry into markets and rapidly evolving technology, as well as the speed with which customers can choose to adopt new products and services at the expense of older ones.

367. **The digital economy has also accelerated and changed the spread of global value chains in which MNEs integrate their worldwide operations**. In the past, it was common for an MNE group to establish a subsidiary in each country in which it did business to manage the group's business in that country. This structure was dictated by a number of factors, including slow communications, currency exchange rules, customs duties, and relatively high transportation costs that made integrated global supply chains difficult to operate. Advances in ICT, reductions in many currency and custom barriers, and the move to digital products and a service-based economy, however, combined to break down barriers to integration, allowing MNE groups to operate much more as global firms. This integration has made it easier for business to adopt global business models that centralise functions at a regional or global level, rather than at a country-by-country level. Even for small and medium enterprises (SMEs), it has now become possible to be "micro-multinationals" that operate and have personnel in multiple countries and continents. ICT technologies have been instrumental in this major trend, which was further exacerbated by the fact that many of the major digital companies are young and were designed from the beginning to operate on an integrated basis at a global scale.

10.2. BEPS issues in the digital economy and how to address them

368. **While the digital economy does not generate unique BEPS issues, some of its key features exacerbate BEPS risks.** The TFDE discussed a number of tax and legal structures that can be used to implement business models in the digital economy. These structures highlight existing opportunities to achieve BEPS to reduce or eliminate tax in jurisdictions across the whole supply chain, including both market and residence countries. For example, the importance of intangibles in the context of the digital economy, combined with the mobility of intangibles for tax purposes under existing tax rules, generates substantial BEPS opportunities in the area of direct taxes. Further, the ability to centralise infrastructure at a distance from a market jurisdiction and conduct substantial sales of goods and services into that market from a remote location, combined with increasing ability to conduct substantial activity with minimal use of personnel, generates potential opportunities to achieve BEPS by fragmenting physical operations to avoid taxation. Some of the key characteristics of the digital economy also exacerbate risks of BEPS in the context of indirect taxation, in particular in relation to businesses that perform value added tax (VAT) exempt activities (exempt businesses).

369. **These BEPS risks have been discussed in the context of the BEPS Project, whose outputs are expected to align taxation with economic activities and value creation, and are expected to have a substantial impact on the BEPS issues previously identified in the digital economy.** Structures aimed at artificially shifting profits to locations where they are taxed at more favourable rates, or not taxed at all, are expected to be addressed by the different measures developed in the context of the BEPS Project. This will help address BEPS issues and restore taxing rights at the level of both the market jurisdiction and the jurisdiction of the ultimate parent company. BEPS issues in the market jurisdiction are expected to be addressed by preventing treaty abuse (Action 6) and by preventing the artificial avoidance of PE status (Action 7). BEPS issues in the ultimate residence jurisdiction are expected to be addressed by strengthening controlled foreign company (CFC) rules (Action 3). BEPS issues in both market and residence jurisdictions are expected to be addressed by neutralising the effects of hybrid mismatch arrangements (Action 2), by limiting the base erosion via interest deductions and other financial payments (Action 4), by countering harmful tax practices more effectively (Action 5), and by assuring that transfer pricing outcomes are in line with value creation (Actions 8-10). In addition, risk assessment processes at the level of the competent tax administration will be enhanced by measures such as the mandatory disclosure of aggressive tax planning arrangements (Action 12) and standardised transfer pricing documentation requirements coupled with a template for country-by-country reporting (Action 13). In the context of VAT, opportunities for tax planning by businesses and corresponding BEPS concerns for governments can be addressed to the extent that the OECD's Guidelines on place of taxation (see Annex D) for business-to-business (B2B) supplies of services and intangibles are implemented.

370. **Work on the BEPS Project has also examined a number of issues specifically relevant to the digital economy, its business models and its key features**. The TFDE identified certain specific issues generated by the key features of the digital economy that warrant attention from a tax perspective. Work on the relevant actions of the BEPS Action Plan was informed by these findings and took these issues into account to ensure that the proposed solutions fully address BEPS in the digital economy. Specifically, the BEPS issues raised by the digital economy include ensuring that core activities in the digital economy cannot inappropriately benefit from the exception from permanent establishment (PE) status, and that artificial arrangements relating to sales of goods and services cannot be used to avoid PE status.

371. The work on Action 7 (preventing the artificial avoidance of PE Status) concluded that activities previously considered to be merely preparatory or auxiliary in nature for the purposes of the exceptions usually found in the definition of PE may nowadays correspond to core business activities of an enterprise, particularly in the digital economy. It was therefore agreed to modify the list of exceptions contained in Article 5 (4) of the OECD Model Tax Convention to ensure that each of the exceptions included therein is restricted to activities that are otherwise of a "preparatory or auxiliary" character, and a new anti-fragmentation rule was introduced to ensure that it is not possible to benefit from these exceptions through the fragmentation of business activities among closely related enterprises. For example, the maintenance of a very large local warehouse in which a significant number of employees work for purposes of storing and delivering goods sold online to customers by an online seller of physical products (whose business model relies on the proximity to customers and the need for quick delivery to clients) would constitute a PE for that seller.

372. In addition, it was agreed to modify the definition of PE contained in Article 5(5) and 5(6) of the OECD Model Tax Convention to address circumstances in which artificial arrangements relating to the sales of goods or services of one company in a multinational group effectively result in the conclusion of contracts, such that the sales should be treated as if they had been made by that company. For example, where the sales force of a local subsidiary of an online seller of tangible products or an online provider of advertising services habitually plays the principal role in the conclusion of contracts with prospective large clients for those products or services, and these contracts are routinely concluded without material modification by the parent company, this activity would result in a permanent establishment for the parent company.

10.2.1. The importance of intangibles, the use of data, and the spread of global value chains, and their impact on transfer pricing rules

373. Companies in the digital economy rely heavily on intangibles in creating value and producing income. A key feature of many BEPS structures adopted by participants in the digital economy involves the transfer of intangibles or rights in intangibles to tax-advantaged locations. Further, it is then often argued that these contractual allocations, together with legal ownership of intangibles, justify large allocations of income to the entity allocated the risk even if it performs little or no business activity. Often this is accomplished by arguing that other entities in the group are contractually insulated from risk so that a low-tax affiliate is entitled to all residual income after compensating other low risk group members for their functions even if this affiliate has no capacity to control the risk. The BEPS work in the area of transfer pricing took these issues in account and revised the guidance for intangibles to clarify that legal ownership alone does not necessarily generate a right to all (or indeed any) of the return that is generated by the exploitation of the intangible. The group companies performing the important functions, contributing important assets and controlling economically significant risks, as determined through the accurate delineation of the actual transaction, will be entitled to an appropriate return. Under this guidance, members of the MNE group are to be compensated based on the value they create through functions performed, assets used and risks assumed in the development, enhancement, maintenance, protection and exploitation of intangibles. Specific guidance will also ensure that the analysis is not weakened by information asymmetries between the tax administration and the taxpayer in relation to hard-to-value intangibles, or by using special contractual relationships, such as a cost contribution arrangement.

374. In addition, the scope of the work to be done on the practical application of transactional profit split methods has been agreed. This work will take into account the

conclusions of this report and may be relevant for highly integrated MNEs in the digital economy. In this context, the work should also address situations where the availability of comparables is limited, for example due to the specific features of the controlled transactions.

10.2.2. The possible need to adapt CFC rules to the digital economy

375. Although CFC rules vary significantly from jurisdiction to jurisdiction, income from digital goods and services provided remotely is frequently not subject to current taxation under CFC rules. Such income may be particularly mobile due to the importance of intangibles in the provision of such goods and services and the relatively few people required to carry out online sales activities. The work on Action 3 resulted in recommendations in the form of six building blocks, including a definition of CFC income which sets out a non-exhaustive list of approaches or combination of approaches that CFC rules could use for such a definition. Countries can implement these approaches to design CFC rules that would subject income that is typically earned in the digital economy to taxation in the jurisdiction of the ultimate parent company. For instance, countries could use the categorical analyses to define CFC income to include types of revenue typically generated in digital economy transactions such as license fees and certain types of income from sales of digital goods and services. If countries adopted the excess profits approach this could characterise any "excess profits" generated in low tax jurisdictions, which may include profits attributable to IP-related assets, as CFC income. This approach could potentially limit the use of offshore deferral structures popular with digital economy MNEs that indefinitely defer foreign income from taxation in the residence jurisdiction. Both approaches may be combined with a substance analysis aimed at verifying whether the CFC is engaged in substantial activities in order to accurately identify and quantify shifted income.

10.3. Broader tax policy challenges raised by the digital economy

376. **The digital economy also raises broader tax challenges for policy makers.** These challenges relate in particular to nexus, data, and characterisation for direct tax purposes. These challenges trigger more systemic questions about the ability of the current international tax framework to deal with the changes brought about by the digital economy and the business models that it makes possible and hence to ensure that profits are taxed in the jurisdiction where economic activities occur and where value is generated. They therefore have a broad impact and relate primarily to the allocation of taxing rights among different jurisdictions. These challenges also raise questions regarding the paradigm used to determine where economic activities are carried out and value is generated for tax purposes, which is based on an analysis of the functions, assets and risks of the enterprise involved. At the same time, when these challenges create opportunities for achieving double non-taxation, for example due to the lack of nexus in the market country under current rules coupled with lack of taxation in the jurisdiction of the income recipient and of that of the ultimate parent company, they also generate BEPS issues in the form of stateless income. In addition, in the area of indirect taxes, the digital economy raises policy challenges regarding the collection of VAT.

377. **The challenges related to nexus, data and characterisation overlap with each other to a certain extent.** Although the challenges related to direct tax are distinct in nature, they often overlap with each other. For example, the collection of data from users located in a jurisdiction may trigger questions regarding whether that activity should give rise to nexus with that jurisdiction and regarding how data should be treated for tax purposes.

378. **Evolving ways of carrying on business raise questions about whether current nexus rules continue to be appropriate.** The continual increase in the potential of digital technologies and the reduced need in many cases for extensive physical presence in order to carry on business in a jurisdiction, combined with the increasing role of network effects generated by customer interactions, raise questions as to whether rules that rely on physical presence continue to be appropriate. The number of firms carrying out business transactions over the Internet has increased dramatically over the last decade. In 2014, B2C e-commerce sales were estimated to exceed USD 1.4 trillion, an increase of nearly 20% from 2013. According to estimates, the size of total worldwide e-commerce, when global B2B and consumer transactions are added together, equalled USD 16 trillion in 2013.

379. **Increasing reliance on data collection and analysis, and the growing importance of multi-sided business models raise questions about valuation of data, nexus, and profit attribution, as well as characterisation**. The appropriate allocation of taxable income among locations in which economic activities take place and value is created may not always be clear in the digital economy, particularly in cases where users and customers become an important component of the value chain, for example in relation to multi-sided business models and the sharing economy. The growth in sophistication of information technologies has permitted companies in the digital economy to gather and use information to an unprecedented degree. This raises the issues of how to attribute value created from the generation of data through digital products and services, whether remote collection of data should give rise to nexus for tax purposes, and of ownership and how to characterise for tax purposes a person or entity's supply of data in a transaction, for example, as a free supply of a good, as a barter transaction, or some other way.

380. **The development of new business models raises questions regarding characterisation of income.** The development of new digital products or means of delivering services creates uncertainties in relation to the proper characterisation under current rules of payments made in the context of new business models, particularly in relation to cloud computing. Further, to the extent that 3D printing becomes increasingly prevalent, it may raise characterisation questions as well, as direct manufacturing for delivery could effectively evolve into licensing of designs for remote printing directly by consumers.

381. **Cross-border trade in goods, services and intangibles creates challenges for VAT collection, particularly where such products are acquired by private consumers from suppliers abroad**. This is partly due to the absence of an effective international framework to ensure VAT collection in the market jurisdiction. For economic actors, and in particular SMEs, the absence of an international standard for charging, collecting and remitting the tax to a potentially large number of tax authorities creates large revenue risks and high compliance costs. For governments, there is a risk of loss of revenue and trade distortion, and the challenge of managing tax liabilities generated by a high volume of low value transactions, which can create a significant administrative burden but marginal revenues.

382. **The TFDE considered several options to address the broader tax challenges raised by the digital economy,** including modifications to the exceptions from PE status, alternatives to the existing PE threshold, the imposition of a withholding tax on certain types of digital transactions and the introduction of an "equalisation levy", as well as the principles and mechanisms developed by WP9 of the CFA to ensure that VAT is collected by the country where the customer is located. To evaluate these options, the TFDE agreed on a framework based on neutrality, efficiency, certainty and simplicity, effectiveness and fairness, flexibility and sustainability, and proportionality. It also analysed the economic incidence of the three options aimed at taxing income from the sales of digital goods and

services by foreign suppliers without a PE under current rules, namely the new nexus in the form of a significant economic presence, the withholding tax on certain types of digital transactions and the equalisation levy.

383. **As regards the different options analysed, the TFDE concluded that:**

- **The option to modify the exceptions to PE status in order to ensure that they are available only for activities that are in fact preparatory or auxiliary in nature has been considered by the TFDE and adopted as part of the work on Action 7 of the BEPS Project.[1] It is now expected to be implemented across the existing tax treaty network in a synchronised and efficient manner via the conclusion of the multilateral instrument that modifies bilateral tax treaties under Action 15.**
- **The collection of VAT/GST on cross-border transactions, particularly those between businesses and consumers, is an important issue. In this regard, countries are recommended to apply the principles of the International VAT/GST Guidelines for the collection of VAT on cross-border B2C supplies of services and intangibles and consider the introduction of the collection mechanisms included therein. Moreover, a range of possible approaches for a more efficient collection of VAT on the importation of low value goods is available to countries that wish to remove or lower the VAT exemption thresholds.**
- **Some aspects of the broader direct tax challenges currently raised by the digital economy are expected to be mitigated once the BEPS measures are implemented. A quick implementation of the BEPS measures is needed, together with mechanisms to monitor their impact over time.**
- **None of the other three options analysed by the TFDE were recommended at this stage. This is because, among other reasons, it is expected that the measures developed in the BEPS Project will have a substantial impact on BEPS issues previously identified in the digital economy, that certain BEPS measures will mitigate some aspects of the broader tax challenges, and that consumption taxes will be levied effectively in the market country.**
- **Countries could, however, introduce any of the options in their domestic laws as additional safeguards against BEPS, provided they respect existing treaty obligations, or in their bilateral tax treaties. Adoption as domestic law measures would require further calibration of the options in order to provide additional clarity about the details, as well as some adaptation to ensure consistency with existing international legal commitments.**

384. These conclusions may evolve as the digital economy continues to develop, in particular regarding robotics, the internet of things, 3D printing and the sharing economy and will depend on the actual impact of other measures on BEPS issues. It is therefore important to continue working on these issues and to monitor developments in the digital economy over time. As part of this future work, it will also be important to review and analyse data that will become available over time. This will provide a sound basis to ascertain the concrete extent of the broader direct tax challenges, in particular in relation to nexus. On the basis of the future monitoring work, a determination will also be made as to whether further work on the three options discussed and analysed by the TFDE should be carried out. This determination should be based on a broad look at the ability of existing international tax standards to deal with the tax challenges raised by developments in the digital economy, taking into account not just direct taxes, but also indirect taxes, administrative issues, countries' differing levels of development, as well as the impact of any potential change on cross-border trade and investment.

10.4. Next steps

385. On this basis, **agreement was reached that**:

- The work will continue following the completion of the other follow-up work on the BEPS Project. This future work will be done in consultation with a broad range of stakeholders, and on the basis of a detailed mandate to be developed during 2016 in the context of designing an inclusive post-BEPS monitoring process. A report reflecting the outcome of the continued work in relation to the digital economy should be produced by 2020.
- WP 1 of the CFA shall clarify the characterisation under current tax treaty rules of certain payments under new business models, especially cloud computing payments (including payments for infrastructure-as-a-service, software-as-a-service, and platform-as-a-service transactions,) with the Associates in the BEPS Project participating on an equal footing with the OECD countries.
- Implementation packages will be developed to ensure that countries can implement the International VAT/GST Guidelines in a co-ordinated manner. Work in this area will be carried out by the WP 9, with the Associates in the BEPS Project participating on an equal footing.

Note

1. Some countries consider that there is no need to modify Art. 5(4) and that the list of exceptions in subparagraphs a) to d) of paragraph 4 should not be subject to the condition that the activities referred to in these subparagraphs be of a preparatory or auxiliary character. These countries may adopt a different version of Art. 5(4) as long as they include the anti-fragmentation rule referred to above.

Bibliography

OECD (2013), *Action Plan on Base Erosion and Profit Shifting*, OECD Publishing, Paris, http://dx.doi.org/10.1787/9789264202719-en.

Annex A

Prior work on the digital economy

This annex summarises the content and output of the previous work on electronic commerce. Specifically, it presents the work that led to the 1998 Ministerial Conference on Electronic Commerce in Ottawa (Ottawa Conference) and its main outcomes. It then describes the follow-up work carried out in relation to tax treaty issues and to consumption tax issues.

A.1. 1996-98: Work leading to the Ottawa Ministerial Conference on Electronic Commerce

1. At its June 1996 meeting, the Committee on Fiscal Affairs (CFA) discussed the tax implications of the development of communications technologies. After a conference on electronic commerce organised by the Organisation for Economic Co-operation and Development (OECD) and the government of Finland in co-operation with the European Community (EC) Commission, the government of Japan and the Business and Industry Advisory Committee to the OECD (BIAC) in Turku in November 1997, the CFA adopted a series of proposals for the preparation of a Ministerial meeting on electronic commerce to be organised in Ottawa in October 1998. In preparation for that meeting, the CFA adopted the report: "Electronic Commerce: Taxation Framework Conditions" (OECD, 2001a), which drew the following main conclusions:

- The widely accepted general tax principles that guide governments in relation to conventional commerce should also guide them in relation to electronic commerce.
- Existing taxation rules can implement these principles.
- This approach does not preclude new administrative or legislative measures, or changes to existing measures, relating to electronic commerce, provided that those measures are intended to assist in the application of the existing taxation principles, and are not intended to impose a discriminatory tax treatment of electronic commerce transactions.
- The application of these principles to electronic commerce should be structured to maintain the fiscal sovereignty of countries, to achieve a fair sharing of the tax base from electronic commerce between countries and to avoid double and unintentional non-taxation.
- The process of implementing these principles should involve an intensified dialogue with business and with non-member economies.

Box A.1. **Ottawa taxation framework conditions – Principles**

Neutrality: Taxation should seek to be neutral and equitable between forms of electronic commerce and between conventional and electronic forms of commerce. Business decisions should be motivated by economic rather than tax considerations. Taxpayers in similar situations carrying out similar transactions should be subject to similar levels of taxation.

Efficiency: Compliance costs for taxpayers and administrative costs for the tax authorities should be minimised as far as possible.

Certainty and Simplicity: The tax rules should be clear and simple to understand so that taxpayers can anticipate the tax consequences in advance of a transaction, including knowing when, where and how the tax is to be accounted.

Effectiveness and Fairness: Taxation should produce the right amount of tax at the right time. The potential for tax evasion and avoidance should be minimised while keeping counteracting measures proportionate to the risks involved.

Flexibility: The systems for taxation should be flexible and dynamic to ensure that they keep pace with technological and commercial developments.

A.2. 1998: The Ottawa Ministerial Conference on Electronic Commerce

2. At the Ottawa Ministerial Conference on Electronic Commerce, leaders from governments (29 member countries and 11 non-member countries), heads of major international organisations, industry leaders, and representatives of consumer, labour and social interests discussed plans to promote the development of global electronic commerce. Ministers welcomed the 1998 CFA Report "Electronic Commerce: Taxation Framework Conditions" (OECD, 2001a), and endorsed a set of taxation principles (listed in Box A.1) which should apply to electronic commerce.

A.3. Post-Ottawa: CFA work and technical advisory groups

3. At its January 1999 meeting, the CFA decided that the work programme on electronic commerce would be taken forward by the Committee's existing subsidiary bodies, in their respective areas of responsibility. It also endorsed the establishment of the following "technical advisory groups" (TAGs), comprising representatives from OECD governments, non-OECD governments, business and science, thus comprising a broad range of interests and expertise:

- A **consumption tax TAG,** to advise on the practical implementation of the Ottawa principle of taxation in the place of consumption.
- A **technology TAG,** to provide expert technological input to the other TAGs.
- A **professional data assessment TAG,** to advise the feasibility and practicality of developing internationally compatible information and record-keeping requirements and tax collection arrangements.
- A **business profits (BP) TAG**, to advise on how the current tax treaty rules for the taxation of business profits apply in the context of electronic commerce and to examine proposals for alternative rules.
- A **treaty characterisation TAG,** to advise on the characterisation of various types of electronic commerce payments under tax treaties with a view to providing necessary clarifications in the Commentary.

4. Given the relevance for the current work on the tax challenges of the digital economy, the sections below describe the main output of the work conducted by the BP TAG and by the Treaty Characterisation TAG.

A.3.1. The work of the business profits TAG

5. The work of the BP TAG produced discussion drafts on "Attribution of Profit to a Permanent Establishment Involved in Electronic Commerce Transactions" (OECD, 2001b), released in February 2001, and "Place of Effective Management Concept: Suggestions for Changes to the OECD Model Tax Convention" (OECD, 2003a), released in May 2003.

6. The TAG also produced a report, "Treaty Rules and E-Commerce: Taxing Business Profits in the New Economy" (OECD, 2005), which was released in 2005. In that report, the BP TAG recognised that some aspects of existing international tax rules presented concerns. The report first examined a number of relatively restricted approaches to address those concerns in a manner that would not require fundamental changes to international tax rules, and made recommendations with respect to those alternatives. The report also discussed more fundamental changes. After summarising the existing treaty rules for

taxing business profits (liability to tax, permanent establishment (PE) concept, computation of profits, allocation of the tax base between countries), the report presented a critical evaluation of these rules against a number of specific criteria, which were derived from the Ottawa framework conditions. In assessing the current principles for taxing business profits against these criteria, the report highlighted a number of pros and cons of the current rules. For example, with respect to the important question where business profits originate ("the source issue") the report concluded that business profits should be viewed as originating from the location of the factors that allow the enterprise to realise business profits. The report therefore rejected the suggestion that the mere fact that a country provides the market where an enterprise's goods and services are supplied should allow that country to consider that a share of the profits of the enterprise is derived therefrom.

7. The BP TAG could, however, not agree on the related issue whether a supplier which is not physically present in a country may be considered to be using that country's legal and economic infrastructure and, if that is the case, whether and to what extent, such use of a country's legal and economic infrastructure should be considered to be one factor which would allow that country to claim source taxing rights on a share of the enterprise's profits. In addition, since the most "traditional" of business enterprises continue to incorporate electronic commerce business models, it was found not to be appropriate, nor possible, to design one set of nexus rules for "electronic commerce" companies, and another for non-electronic commerce companies. The final report also gave an overview of the various alternatives to the current treaty rules for taxing business profits that were discussed. These alternatives ranged from relatively minor changes to the existing rules to the adoption of complete new ones.

8. The following alternatives were found to entail relatively minor changes:

- *Modification of the PE definition to exclude activities that do not involve human intervention by personnel, including dependent agents*: This option would modify the PE definition to expressly exclude the maintenance of a fixed place of business used solely for the carrying on of activities that do not involve human intervention by personnel, including dependent agents.

- *Modification of the PE definition to provide that a server cannot, in itself, constitute a PE*: According to this alternative, the PE definition would not cover situations where a fixed place of business is used merely to carry on automated functions through equipment, data and software such as a server and website.

- *Modification of the PE definition/interpretation to exclude functions attributable to software*: paragraph 4 of Article 5 of the OECD Model Tax Convention provides a list of functions that are specifically excluded from the definition of a PE (the Article 5, paragraph 4 exceptions). This option would indirectly expand this list by excluding functions attributable to software when applying the Article 5, paragraph 4 exceptions.

- *Elimination of the existing exceptions in paragraph 4 of Article 5 or making these exceptions subject to the overall condition that they be preparatory or auxiliary*: One option would be to eliminate all the exceptions included in paragraph 4 of the definition of PE. A less radical option would be to make all the activities referred to in the existing exceptions subject to the overall limitation that they be of a preparatory or auxiliary nature.

- *Elimination of the exceptions for storage, display or delivery in paragraph 4 of Article 5*: This option suggested that paragraph 4 of Article 5 be amended so that the use of facilities solely for purpose of storage, display or delivery should no longer be considered not to constitute a PE.

- *Modification of the existing rules to add a force-of-attraction rule dealing with electronic commerce*: According to this alternative, paragraph 1 of Article 7 of the OECD Model Tax Convention would be amended to include a so-called "force-of-attraction" rule which would deal with electronic commerce operations. The aim would be to ensure that a country may tax profits derived from selling in that country, through an enterprise's website, products similar to those sold through a PE that the enterprise has in the country.
- *Adopting supplementary nexus rules for purposes of taxing profits arising from the provision of services*: The option would be to modify the OECD Model to include a provision, similar to that already found in the UN Model, that would allow for the taxation of income from services if the enterprise that provides such services is present in the other country for that purpose during a certain period of time. The rationale for the proposal was that service providers are very mobile and that the income-producing functions take place in foreign countries without the need to set up a physical facility or use a fixed base of operations.

9. After having examined these alternatives in light of the comments received, the report reached the following conclusions:

- The option to *modify the PE definition to exclude activities that do not involve human intervention by personnel, including dependent agents* would be unlikely to be adopted and did not need further consideration.
- As regards the options to *modify the PE definition to provide that a server cannot, in itself, constitute a PE* or to *exclude functions attributable to software when applying the preparatory or auxiliary exception*, the BP TAG concluded that while these options should not be pursued at that time, the application of the current rules to functions performed with the use of servers and software should be monitored to determine whether it raises practical difficulties or concerns, which could lead to further study of these alternatives or combinations or variants thereof.
- With respect to the option to *eliminate all the existing exceptions in paragraph 4 of Article 5*, the BP TAG concluded that this option should not be pursued.
- As regards the options to *make all the existing exceptions in paragraph 4 of Article 5 subject to the overall condition that they be preparatory or auxiliary* and to *eliminate the exceptions for storage, display and delivery in paragraph 4 of Article 5*, the BP TAG concluded the application of these exceptions should continue to be monitored to determine whether practical difficulties or concerns warrant any such changes.
- With respect to the option to *modify the existing rules to add a force-of-attraction rule dealing with electronic commerce*, the BP TAG concluded that it should not be pursued.
- As regards the option to *adopt supplementary nexus rules for purposes of taxing profits arising from the provision of services*, the BP TAG noted that this option would be examined in the context of the work that the OECD was to undertake on the application of tax treaties to services.

10. The following alternatives were found to require a fundamental modification of the existing rules:

- *Adopting rules similar to those concerning taxation of passive income to allow source taxation of payments related to some forms of electronic commerce (so as to subject them to source withholding tax)*: This alternative encompassed various approaches under which a withholding tax would be applied on all or certain cross-border payments related to electronic commerce. The discussion in the BP TAG focused on a general option under which a final withholding tax would be applied to electronic commerce payments made from a country, whether or not the recipient has personnel or electronic equipment in that country.

- *A new nexus: base eroding payments arising in a country*: This option contained a nexus rule that focuses only on whether the foreign enterprise is receiving a payment from an in-country payor that the payor may deduct for domestic tax purposes rather than on where the activities giving rise to the product or service are located. Under this nexus rule, the source state would be entitled to impose a withholding tax on all such cross-border payments.
- *Replacing separate entity accounting and arm's length by formulary apportionment of profits of a common group*: According to this alternative, the separate entity and arm's length principles would be replaced by a system based on formulary apportionment as the international method of allocating and measuring business profits that countries may tax. Under such formulary apportionment system, a formula would be used to divide the net profits of a company, or a group of related companies, doing business in more than one country among the countries where the corporation (or group) operates.
- *Adding a new nexus of "electronic (virtual) PE"*: This concept of "virtual PE" was a suggestion of an alternative nexus that would apply to electronic commerce operations. This could be done in various ways, such as extending the definition to cover so-called "virtual fixed places of business", "virtual agencies" or "on-site business presences." All of them would require a modification of the PE definition (or the addition of a new nexus rule in treaties).

11. The report concluded that it would not be appropriate to embark on any such changes at that time. Electronic commerce and other business models resulting from new communication technologies were not perceived by the BP TAG to justify, by themselves, a dramatic departure from the current rules. There did not seem to be actual evidence that the communications efficiencies of the Internet had caused any significant decrease to the tax revenues of capital importing countries. Also, it was considered that fundamental changes should only be undertaken if there was a broad agreement that a particular alternative was clearly superior to the existing rules and none of the alternatives that had been suggested appeared to meet that condition. It was recognised, however, that there was a need to continue to monitor how direct tax revenues are affected by changes to business models resulting from new communication technologies and that some aspects of the existing international rules for taxing business profits raised concerns. More generally, the report noted that the effect of many of these alternatives would extend far beyond electronic commerce it would therefore be important to take account of their impact on all types of business activities when considering them.

A.3.2. CFA work in the area of tax treaties

12. In addition to the work of the TAGs, the CFA directed its Working Parties to discuss and propose solutions with respect to the issues that had been raised by the TAGs. This led to some changes to the OECD Model Tax Convention and its Commentary which were incorporated in the 2003 update. The changes related to the definition of PE and to the characterisation of payments in particular under the definition of royalties contained in the Model Tax Convention.

A.3.2.1. Treaty rules for taxing business profits

13. The main content of the changes to the Commentary on Article 5 was to provide that the definition of PE, which is typically defined as a "fixed place of business through which business is conducted," could, under certain conditions, cover servers. In contrast, the changes to the Commentary rejected the view that a website could be regarded as a PE. Paragraphs (shown in Box A.2) were added to the OECD Commentary on Article 5 of the OECD Model Tax Convention in 2003 and are also included in the Commentary to the UN Model Tax Convention (see paragraphs 36-37 of the Commentary on Article 5 of the UN Model Tax Convention).

Box A.2. **Commentary on Article 5 of the OECD Model Tax Convention**

"42.1 There has been some discussion as to whether the mere use in electronic commerce operations of computer equipment in a country could constitute a permanent establishment. That question raises a number of issues in relation to the provisions of the Article.

42.2 While a location where automated equipment is operated by an enterprise may constitute a permanent establishment in the country where it is situated (see below), a distinction needs to be made between computer equipment, which may be set up at a location so as to constitute a permanent establishment under certain circumstances, and the data and software which is used by, or stored on, that equipment. For instance, an Internet website, which is a combination of software and electronic data, does not in itself constitute tangible property. It therefore does not have a location that can constitute a "place of business" as there is no "facility such as premises or, in certain instances, machinery or equipment" (see paragraph 2 above) as far as the software and data constituting that website is concerned. On the other hand, the server on which the website is stored and through which it is accessible is a piece of equipment having a physical location and such location may thus constitute a "fixed place of business" of the enterprise that operates that server.

42.3 The distinction between a website and the server on which the website is stored and used is important since the enterprise that operates the server may be different from the enterprise that carries on business through the website. For example, it is common for the website through which an enterprise carries on its business to be hosted on the server of an Internet Service Provider (ISP). Although the fees paid to the ISP under such arrangements may be based on the amount of disk space used to store the software and data required by the website, these contracts typically do not result in the server and its location being at the disposal of the enterprise (see paragraph 4 above), even if the enterprise has been able to determine that its website should be hosted on a particular server at a particular location. In such a case, the enterprise does not even have a physical presence at that location since the website is not tangible. In these cases, the enterprise cannot be considered to have acquired a place of business by virtue of that hosting arrangement. However, if the enterprise carrying on business through a website has the server at its own disposal, for example it owns (or leases) and operates the server on which the website is stored and used, the place where that server is located could constitute a permanent establishment of the enterprise if the other requirements of the Article are met.

42.4 Computer equipment at a given location may only constitute a permanent establishment if it meets the requirement of being fixed. In the case of a server, what is relevant is not the possibility of the server being moved, but whether it is in fact moved. In order to constitute a fixed place of business, a server will need to be located at a certain place for a sufficient period of time so as to become fixed within the meaning of paragraph 1.

Box A.2. **Commentary on Article 5 of the OECD Model Tax Convention** *(continued)*

42.5 Another issue is whether the business of an enterprise may be said to be wholly or partly carried on at a location where the enterprise has equipment such as a server at its disposal. The question of whether the business of an enterprise is wholly or partly carried on through such equipment needs to be examined on a case-by-case basis, having regard to whether it can be said that, because of such equipment, the enterprise has facilities at its disposal where business functions of the enterprise are performed.

42.6 Where an enterprise operates computer equipment at a particular location, a permanent establishment may exist even though no personnel of that enterprise is required at that location for the operation of the equipment. The presence of personnel is not necessary to consider that an enterprise wholly or partly carries on its business at a location when no personnel are in fact required to carry on business activities at that location. This conclusion applies to electronic commerce to the same extent that it applies with respect to other activities in which equipment operates automatically, e.g. automatic pumping equipment used in the exploitation of natural resources.

42.7 Another issue relates to the fact that no permanent establishment may be considered to exist where the electronic commerce operations carried on through computer equipment at a given location in a country are restricted to the preparatory or auxiliary activities covered by paragraph 4. The question of whether particular activities performed at such a location fall within paragraph 4 needs to be examined on a case-by-case basis having regard to the various functions performed by the enterprise through that equipment. Examples of activities which would generally be regarded as preparatory or auxiliary include:

– providing a communications link – much like a telephone line – between suppliers and customers;

– advertising of goods or services;

– relaying information through a mirror server for security and efficiency purposes;

– gathering market data for the enterprise;

– supplying information.

42.8 Where, however, such functions form in themselves an essential and significant part of the business activity of the enterprise as a whole, or where other core functions of the enterprise are carried on through the computer equipment, these would go beyond the activities covered by paragraph 4 and if the equipment constituted a fixed place of business of the enterprise (as discussed in paragraphs 42.2 to 42.6 above), there would be a permanent establishment.

42.9 What constitutes core functions for a particular enterprise clearly depends on the nature of the business carried on by that enterprise. For instance, some ISPs are in the business of operating their own servers for the purpose of hosting websites or other applications for other enterprises. For these ISPs, the operation of their servers in order to provide services to customers is an essential part of their commercial activity and cannot be considered preparatory or auxiliary. A different example is that of an enterprise (sometimes referred to as an "e-tailer") that carries on the business of selling products through the Internet. In that case, the enterprise is not in the business of operating servers and the mere fact that it may do so at a given location is not enough to conclude that activities performed at that location are more than preparatory and auxiliary. What needs to be done in such a case is to examine the nature of the activities performed at that location in light of the business carried on by the enterprise. If these activities are merely preparatory or auxiliary to the business of

Box A.2. **Commentary on Article 5 of the OECD Model Tax Convention** *(continued)*

selling products on the Internet (for example, the location is used to operate a server that hosts a website which, as is often the case, is used exclusively for advertising, displaying a catalogue of products or providing information to potential customers), paragraph 4 will apply and the location will not constitute a permanent establishment. If, however, the typical functions related to a sale are performed at that location (for example, the conclusion of the contract with the customer, the processing of the payment and the delivery of the products are performed automatically through the equipment located there), these activities cannot be considered to be merely preparatory or auxiliary.

42.10 A last issue is whether paragraph 5 may apply to deem an ISP to constitute a permanent establishment. As already noted, it is common for ISPs to provide the service of hosting the websites of other enterprises on their own servers. The issue may then arise as to whether paragraph 5 may apply to deem such ISPs to constitute permanent establishments of the enterprises that carry on electronic commerce through websites operated through the servers owned and operated by these ISPs. While this could be the case in very unusual circumstances, paragraph 5 will generally not be applicable because the ISPs will not constitute an agent of the enterprises to which the websites belong, because they will not have authority to conclude contracts in the name of these enterprises and will not regularly conclude such contracts or because they will constitute independent agents acting in the ordinary course of their business, as evidenced by the fact that they host the websites of many different enterprises. It is also clear that since the website through which an enterprise carries on its business is not itself a "person" as defined in Article 3, paragraph 5 cannot apply to deem a permanent establishment to exist by virtue of the website being an agent of the enterprise for purposes of that paragraph."

A.3.2.2. Treaty characterisation issues

14. Amendments to the Commentary on Article 12 of the OECD Model Tax Convention were also made to clarify the delimitation between the application of Articles 12 and 7 in the context of new business models in electronic commerce. These clarifications were included in the 2013 update and deal with *(i)* payment for the use of, or the right to use, a copyright, *(ii)* payments for know-how, *(iii)* mixed payments. These paragraphs are also included in the UN Model Tax Convention (see paragraphs 12-16 of the Commentary on Article 12 of the UN Model Tax Convention), although it was noted that some members disagreed with the conclusions reached regarding the character of several types of payment.

Box A.3. **Commentary on Article 12 – Payment for the use of, or the right to use, a copyright**

The following paragraphs 17.1 to 17.4 are included immediately after paragraph 17 of the Commentary on Article 12:

"17.1 The principles expressed above as regards software payments are also applicable as regards transactions concerning other types of digital products such as images, sounds or text. The development of electronic commerce has multiplied the number of such transactions. In deciding whether or not payments arising in these transactions constitute royalties, the main question to be addressed is the identification of that for which the payment is essentially made.

Box A.3. Commentary on Article 12 – Payment for the use of, or the right to use, a copyright *(continued)*

17.2 Under the relevant legislation of some countries, transactions which permit the customer to electronically download digital products may give rise to use of copyright by the customer, e.g. because a right to make one or more copies of the digital content is granted under the contract. Where the consideration is essentially for something other than for the use of, or right to use, rights in the copyright (such as to acquire other types of contractual rights, data or services), and the use of copyright is limited to such rights as are required to enable downloading, storage and operation on the customer's computer, network or other storage, performance or display device, such use of copyright should not affect the analysis of the character of the payment for purposes of applying the definition of "royalties".

*17.3 This is the case for transactions that permit the customer (which may be an enterprise) to electronically download digital products (such as software, images, sounds or text) for that customer's own use or enjoyment. In these transactions, the payment is essentially for the acquisition of data transmitted in the form of a digital signal and therefore does not constitute royalties but falls within Article 7 or Article 13, as the case may be. To the extent that the act of copying the digital signal onto the customer's hard disk or other non-temporary media involves the use of a copyright by the customer under the relevant law and contractual arrangements, such copying is merely the means by which the digital signal is captured and stored. This use of copyright is not important for classification purposes because it does not correspond to what the payment is essentially in consideration for (*i.e. *to acquire data transmitted in the form of a digital signal), which is the determining factor for the purposes of the definition of royalties. There also would be no basis to classify such transactions as "royalties" if, under the relevant law and contractual arrangements, the creation of a copy is regarded as a use of copyright by the provider rather than by the customer.*

17.4 By contrast, transactions where the essential consideration for the payment is the granting of the right to use a copyright in a digital product that is electronically downloaded for that purpose will give rise to royalties. This would be the case, for example, of a book publisher who would pay to acquire the right to reproduce a copyrighted picture that it would electronically download for the purposes of including it on the cover of a book that it is producing. In this transaction, the essential consideration for the payment is the acquisition of rights to use the copyright in the digital product, i.e. *the right to reproduce and distribute the picture, and not merely for the acquisition of the digital content."*

Box A.4. Change to the Commentary on Article 12 – Payments for know-how

Paragraph 11 of the Commentary on Article 12 was replaced by the following paragraphs 11 to 11.5 (additions to the existing text of paragraph 11 appear ***in bold italics***):

"11. In classifying as royalties payments received as consideration for information concerning industrial, commercial or scientific experience, paragraph 2 alludes to the concept of 'know-how'. Various specialist bodies and authors have formulated definitions of know-how which do not differ intrinsically. One such definition, given by the 'Association des Bureaux pour la Protection de la Propriété Industrielle' (ANBPPI), states that 'know-how is all the undivulged technical information, whether capable of being patented or not, that is necessary for the industrial reproduction of a product or process, directly and under the same conditions; inasmuch as it is derived from experience, know-how represents what a manufacturer cannot know from mere examination of the product and mere knowledge of the progress of technique'.

Box A.4. **Change to the Commentary on Article 12 – Payments for know-how** *(continued)*

11.1 In the know-how contract, one of the parties agrees to impart to the other, so that he can use them for his own account, his special knowledge and experience which remain unrevealed to the public. It is recognised that the grantor is not required to play any part himself in the application of the formulas granted to the licensee and that he does not guarantee the result thereof.

11.2 This type of contract thus differs from contracts for the provision of services, in which one of the parties undertakes to use the customary skills of his calling to execute work himself for the other party. ***Payments made under the latter contracts generally fall under Article 7.***

11.3 The need to distinguish these two types of payments, i.e. ***payments for the supply of know-how and payments for the provision of services, sometimes gives rise to practical difficulties. The following criteria are relevant for the purpose of making that distinction:***

– Contracts for the supply of know-how concern information of the kind described in paragraph 11 that already exists or concern the supply of that type of information after its development or creation and include specific provisions concerning the confidentiality of that information.

– In the case of contracts for the provision of services, the supplier undertakes to perform services which may require the use, by that supplier, of special knowledge, skill and expertise but not the transfer of such special knowledge, skill or expertise to the other party.

– In most cases involving the supply of know-how, there would generally be very little more which needs to be done by the supplier under the contract other than to supply existing information or reproduce existing material. On the other hand, a contract for the performance of services would, in the majority of cases, involve a very much greater level of expenditure by the supplier in order to perform his contractual obligations. For instance, the supplier, depending on the nature of the services to be rendered, may have to incur salaries and wages for employees engaged in researching, designing, testing, drawing and other associated activities or payments to subcontractors for the performance of similar services.

11.4 Examples of payments which should therefore not be considered to be received as consideration for the provision of know-how but, rather, for the provision of services, include:

– payments obtained as consideration for after-sales service,

– payments for services rendered by a seller to the purchaser under a guarantee,

– payments for pure technical assistance,

– payments for an opinion given by an engineer, an advocate or an accountant, and

– payments for advice provided electronically, for electronic communications with technicians or for accessing, through computer networks, a trouble-shooting database such as a database that provides users of software with non-confidential information in response to frequently asked questions or common problems that arise frequently.

11.5 In the particular case of a contract involving the provision, by the supplier, of information concerning computer programming, as a general rule the payment will only be considered to be made in consideration for the provision of such information so as to constitute know-how where it is made to acquire information constituting ideas and principles underlying the programme, such as logic, algorithms or programming languages or techniques, where this information is provided under the condition that the customer not disclose it without authorisation and where it is subject to any available trade secret protection.

Box A.4. **Change to the Commentary on Article 12 – Payments for know-how** *(continued)*

11.6 *In business practice, contracts are encountered which cover both know-how and the provision of technical assistance. One example, amongst others, of contracts of this kind is that of franchising, where the franchisor imparts his knowledge and experience to the franchisee and, in addition, provides him with varied technical assistance, which, in certain cases, is backed up with financial assistance and the supply of goods. The appropriate course to take with a mixed contract is, in principle, to break down, on the basis of the information contained in the contract or by means of a reasonable apportionment, the whole amount of the stipulated consideration according to the various parts of what is being provided under the contract, and then to apply to each part of it so determined the taxation treatment proper thereto. If, however, one part of what is being provided constitutes by far the principal purpose of the contract and the other parts stipulated therein are only of an ancillary and largely unimportant character, then it seems possible to apply to the whole amount of the consideration the treatment applicable to the principal part."* [*paragraph 45 below includes suggested changes to this last sentence*]

Box A.5. **Commentary on Article 12 – Mixed payments**

The last sentence of paragraph 11 of the Commentary on Article 12 was replaced by the following (deletions appear in ~~strikethrough~~ and additions in ***bold italics***):

"If, however, one part of what is being provided constitutes by far the principal purpose of the contract and the other parts stipulated therein are only of an ancillary and largely unimportant character, ***then the treatment applicable to the principal part should generally be applied to the whole amount of the consideration.*** ~~*then it seems possible to apply to the whole amount of the consideration the treatment applicable to the principal part.*~~*"*

A.3.3. CFA work in the area of consumption taxes

15. This section first looks at the elements of the 1998 Ottawa Taxation Framework Conditions (OECD, 2001a) specifically related to consumption taxes and discusses the E-commerce Guidelines (OECD, 2003b) and the Consumption tax guidance papers (OECD 2003c-d-e) that were developed to implement these conditions.

16. The need for an international co-ordination of the application of domestic value added tax (VAT) systems to international trade first became apparent following the emergence and strong growth of e-commerce. In the field of consumption taxes, the core elements of the *Taxation Framework Conditions* (OECD, 2001a) can be summarised as follows:

- Rules for the consumption taxation of cross-border trade should result in taxation in the jurisdiction where consumption takes place and an international consensus should be sought on the circumstances under which supplies are held to be consumed in a jurisdiction.
- For the purpose of consumption taxes, the supply of digitised products should not be treated as a supply of goods.
- Where business and other organisations within a country acquire services and intangibles from suppliers outside the country, countries should examine the use of

reverse charge, self-assessment or other equivalent mechanisms where this would give immediate protection of their revenue base and of the competitiveness of domestic suppliers.

17. These framework conditions were broad statements of general principle which required further elaboration to facilitate their practical application. As a follow-up to this work, in 2003 the CFA released its E-commerce Guidelines (2003b). The CFA also released the Consumption Tax Guidance Series (OECD 2003c-e-f) along with these Guidelines, consisting of three papers providing guidance on the implementation of the Guidelines in practice. These Guidelines and Guidance papers are summarised in the following sections.

A.3.3.1. The E-commerce Guidelines

18. Destination based taxation of cross-border e-business was the governing principle of the E-commerce Guidelines (2003b). Under the destination principle, tax is ultimately levied only on the final consumption within the jurisdiction where such consumption is deemed to occur. Exports are not subject to tax with refund of input taxes (that is, "free of VAT" or "zero-rated"), and imports are taxed on the same basis and at the same rates as domestic supplies. The E-commerce Guidelines (2003b)provide that:

- *For business-to-business transactions*, the place of consumption for cross-border supplies of services and intangibles that are capable of delivery from a remote location made to a non-resident business recipient should be the jurisdiction in which the recipient has located its business presence. This was referred to as the "main criterion". The Guidelines (2003b) indicated that countries may, in certain circumstances, use a different criterion to determine the actual place of consumption, where the application of the main criterion "would lead to a distortion of competition or avoidance of tax." This was referred to as the "override criterion".
- *For business-to-consumer transactions*, the place of consumption for cross-border supplies of services and intangibles that are capable of delivery from a remote location made to a non-resident private recipient should be the jurisdiction in which the recipient has its usual residence.

19. These Guidelines (2003b) were explicitly not applicable to *(i)* sub-national consumption taxes, *(ii)* suppliers who were registered or required to be registered in the customer's jurisdiction, *(iii)* services that are not capable of direct delivery from a remote location (such as hotel accommodation, transportation or vehicle rental), *(iv)* services for which the place of consumption could be readily identified, *(v)* services for which the place of consumption could be more appropriately determined by other criteria, *(vi)* specific types of services for which more specific approaches might be needed.

A.3.3.2. The consumption tax guidance papers

20. The CFA released three *Consumption Tax Guidance* (OECD, 2003c-d-e) papers along with the E-commerce Guidelines, to support their implementation in practice. These Guidance papers deal with: *(i)* Identifying place of taxation for business-to-business supplies by reference to the customer's business presence (OECD, 2003c); *(ii)* Simplified registration guidance (OECD, 2003d); and *(iii)* Verification of customer status and jurisdiction (OECD, 2003e). These papers are briefly summarised below:

- *Guidance paper on identifying place of taxation by reference to the customer's business presence:* the *Guidelines on the Definition of Place of Consumption*

(OECD, 2003c) described "business presence" as, "in principle, the establishment (for example, headquarters, registered office, or a branch of the business) of the recipient to which the supply is made." The Guidance paper on business presence underlined the importance of contracts in determining the business presence to which the supply is made. Normal commercial practices as evidenced in the terms of contracts (e.g. invoicing, terms of payment, use of intellectual property rights), should normally provide sufficient indicative evidence to assist both business and revenue administrations in determining the jurisdiction of consumption. The Guidance paper also discussed the "override criterion". It considered the case where a customer with branches in several jurisdictions that are not entitled to recover the input tax on a transaction, routed this transaction through branches in jurisdictions with no or a low VAT, "thus avoiding a significant amount of tax." The Guidance Paper suggested that a pure place of consumption override could be applied in such a case, according to which a country may require "a business presence" in its jurisdiction to account for tax to the extent that the supply is used in that jurisdiction. In addition, and in order to avoid double taxation, the country of the business presence that has acquired the supply may then choose to provide a correction proportionately equivalent to the tax collected by the other country under the application of this test.

- *Guidance paper on simplified registration systems* (OECD, 2003d): This guidance paper explored the possible implementation of a system for taxing e-commerce business-to-consumer (B2C) cross-border transactions in the customer's jurisdiction, based on vendor collection. It considered registration and declaration procedures and record-keeping requirements and recommended the use of simplified registration regimes and registration thresholds to minimise the potential compliance burden. It suggested that governments that implement simplified registration systems consider using electronic registration and declaration and encourages tax administrations to review and develop a legal basis to allow for the use of electronic record keeping systems.
- *Guidance paper on Verification of Customer Status and Jurisdiction* (OECD, 2003e): This Guidance Paper provided practical guidance on mechanisms that may be used to establish the status (business or private) and jurisdiction of customers, for low value electronic commerce transactions where vendors do not have an established relationship with the customer. It does not apply to high value B2B transactions where the vendor and the customer were assumed to have an established relationship. In these cases the supplier was assumed to be normally aware of the customer's status and jurisdiction and no additional verification process of the customer's declaration was considered necessary. The Paper concluded that the status and jurisdiction of a customer should be based on customer self-identification, supported by a range of other criteria including payment information, tracking and geo-location software, the nature of the supply and digital certificates.

Bibliography

OECD (2005), *Are the Current Treaty Rules for Taxing Business Profits Appropriate for E-commerce? Final Report*, OECD, Paris.

OECD (2003a), *Place of Effective Management Concept: Suggestions for Changes to the OECD Model Tax Convention*, OECD, Paris.

OECD (2003b), *Consumption Taxation of Cross Border Services and Intangible Property in the context of E-commerce, Guidelines on the Definition of Place of Consumption*, OECD, Paris.

OECD (2003c), *Commentary on Place of Consumption for Business-to-Business Supplies (Business Presence)*, OECD, Paris.

OECD (2003d), *Simplified Registration Guidance*, OECD, Paris.

OECD (2003e), Verification of customer status and jurisdiction, OECD, Paris.

OECD (2003f), *Model Tax Convention on Income and on Capital: Condensed Version 2003*, OECD Publishing, http://dx.doi.org/10.1787/mtc_cond-2003-en.

OECD (2001a), *Taxation and Electronic Commerce: Implementing the Ottawa Taxation Framework Conditions*, OECD Publishing, http://dx.doi.org/10.1787/9789264189799-en.

OECD (2001b), *Attribution of Profits to Permanent Establishments*, OECD Publishing, http://dx.doi.org/10.1787/9789264184527-en.

United Nations (2011), *United Nations Double Tax Convention between Developed and Developing Countries*, The United Nations, New York.

Annex B

Typical tax planning structures in integrated business models

The simplified examples below are based on what a number of tax administrations have observed. They are intended to provide an illustration of ways in which the implementation of business models through legal and tax structures may place pressure on the existing international tax framework. They are not exhaustive, and do not pretend to reflect the full scope of structures that may be used to achieve base erosion and profit shifting (BEPS).

B.1. Online retailer

1. RCo Group is a multinational enterprise (MNE) engaged in the online sale of physical goods and digital products. The websites of the Group display the products offered in the markets that they serve in local languages and allow customers to acquire these products on line through credit card payments. Physical products are delivered through independent courier services. Digital products are downloaded from one of RCo group's websites to the consumer's computer. RCo Group collects data on customer preferences on the basis of goods purchased, added to a list of "favorites", or browsed by customers. Using sophisticated proprietary software, RCo Group analyses the data it collects in order to make recommendations of goods to its potential customers and provide personalised advertising.

2. All intangibles used in operating the RCo Group websites and fulfilling orders are developed by employees of RCo, a company resident in State R. RCo also remotely co-ordinates the procurement and sale activities of the Group to minimise purchasing costs, maintain consistency among the various businesses and websites, improve efficiency of inventory management, and minimise overhead on the payment processing and back office functions. These co-ordination services are generally provided to regional operating lower-tier sales subsidiaries in return for a management service fee covering related expenses plus a markup.

3. Rights to existing and future intangibles used in operating the websites serving customers in a region that includes, among others, State T and State S (the State T/S region) are held by RCo Regional Holding, a subsidiary resident in State T. RCo Regional Holding acquired the rights through a cost-sharing arrangement in which it made a "buy in" payment to RCo equal to the value of the existing intangibles and agreed to share the cost of future development (to be performed exclusively by RCo personnel in State R) on the basis of the anticipated future benefit from the use of the technology in the State T/S region. RCo remains the legal owner of the intangibles from the MNE group and is responsible for functions pertaining to the registration and defence of Intellectual Property, RCo Regional Holdings' only acquires the rights to commercially exploit the Internet Protocol (IP) and not the legal ownership of the intangibles. In practice, RCo Regional Holding does not perform any supervision of the development activities carried out by RCo in State R. RCo Regional Holding acts as an IP manager for the T/S region and sublicenses the intangibles necessary for its various subsidiaries to operate their various country- or region-targeted websites. RCo Regional Holding also acts as a holding company for all subsidiaries in the State T/S region, although in practice, most co-ordination services continue to be performed at the level of RCo, and RCo Regional Holding's involvement with the subsidiaries is very limited. RCo Regional Holding has only one employee on its payroll, and the premises are limited to an "office hotel" where the company regularly rents different offices for the purpose of organising board meetings.

4. Orders from customers in State S, State T, and the rest of the State T/S region are handled by a subsidiary of RCo Regional Holding, RCo Regional OpCo, also resident in State T. RCo Regional OpCo is a hybrid entity that is treated as a company for tax purposes under the domestic law of State T, and as a transparent entity under the domestic law of State R. RCo Regional OpCo handles the sales, payment processing and settlement and has legal title to the physical and digital products sold on the websites serving customers in the State T/S region. Changes and updates to the websites are done from State T by employees of RCo Regional OpCo, who have overall responsibility for managing the various websites serving customers in the region. These functions are performed with minimal skilled

personnel. Other functions related to the online sale activity rely on automated processes conducted by sophisticated Internet-powered software applications regularly upgraded by employees of RCo in State R. Orders and sales are concluded electronically by customers in State T/S region on the basis of standardised contracts, the terms of which are set by RCo, and require no intervention from RCo Regional OpCo. Mirrors of the websites are hosted on servers in a number of countries in the region. RCo Regional OpCo staff very rarely have any contact with customers in the local market jurisdiction.

5. SCo, a subsidiary of RCo Regional OpCo resident in State S, provides services to RCo Regional OpCo in respect of logistics and after sales support with respect to orders from customers in State S. Orders for physical goods placed by customers in State S via the website managed by RCo Regional OpCo, are generally fulfilled from a warehouse located in State S owned and operated by SCo. Where products are not available in a State S warehouse, the order is generally fulfilled from the closest warehouse to the customer. After-sales support is handled by SCo through a call center. Orders for digital products placed by State S customers are generally downloaded from servers located in State S or in neighbouring countries, depending on network traffic at the time of the transaction. These servers are owned and operated by third parties through hosting arrangements with RCo Regional OpCo. SCo is remunerated on a cost-plus basis by RCo Regional OpCo.

6. The structure used by the RCo Group can be depicted as shown in Figure B.1.

Figure B.1. **Online retailer**

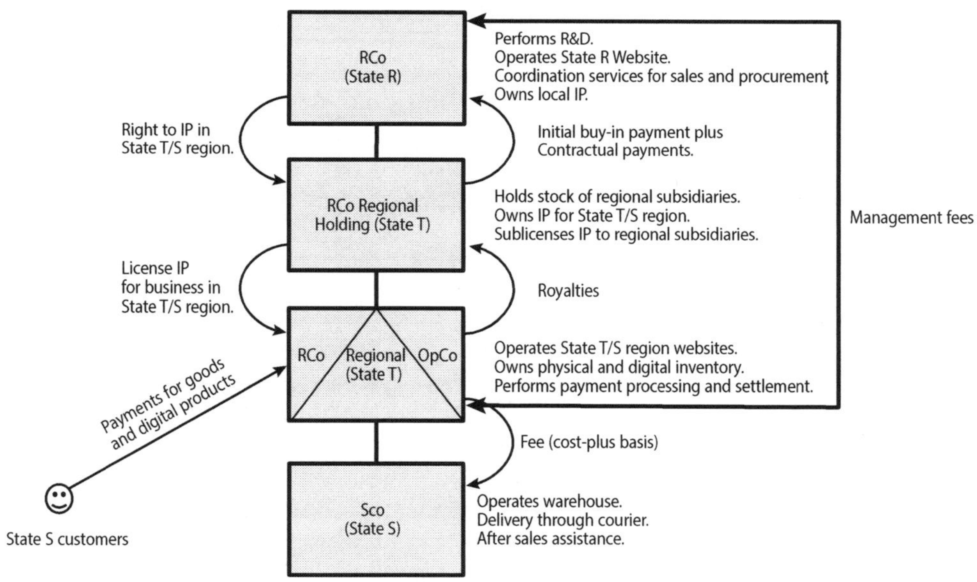

7. The manner in which RCo Group's business activity is structured as a legal matter has significant consequences for the Group's worldwide tax burden. Due to the contractual arrangements transferring and assigning the intangibles for the State T/S region (and related returns) to RCo Regional Holding and the lack of taxable presence of RCo Regional Holding in State S, most of the taxable income generated by the Group is concentrated in State T. More specifically, the following paragraphs describe the consequences that would arise in the different States concerned.

Direct tax consequences in state S

- SCo is allocated minimal taxable income, based on the position that SCo's risk and function profile is limited to routine services provided to RCo Regional OpCo.
- All revenues derived from the online sales of products to customers in State S are treated as income of RCo Regional OpCo, due to its role as the counterparty to the transactions. Because RCo Regional OpCo has no physical presence in State S, and SCo has no interaction with State S customers, State S does not tax the profits derived from these activities either because it has no right to do so under its domestic law or because the relevant double tax treaty prevents it from doing so in the absence of a permanent establishment (PE) of TCo in State S to which the income is attributable.

Direct tax consequences in state T

- State T imposes corporate tax on the profits earned by RCo Regional Holding. However, by virtue of a preferential regime available in State T for income derived from certain intangibles, RCo Regional Holding is entitled to a rate substantially less than the generally applicable corporate tax rate for the royalties included in its taxable profits.
- State T imposes corporate tax on the profits earned by RCo Regional OpCo from its online sale activities. RCo Regional OpCo's income, however, is almost entirely offset by the royalty payments made to RCo Regional Holding for the right to use the intangibles necessary to operate the regional websites, and the management fees paid to RCo for co-ordinating sales and procurement.
- The payments made by RCo Regional OpCo are not subject to any withholding since the royalty income is paid to RCo Regional Holding, a company resident in State T, and the management fee is paid to RCo, a non-resident company whose business profits may not be taxed in State T under the relevant tax treaty. No withholding is imposed under the relevant double tax treaty on the payments by RCo Regional Holding to RCo.

Direct tax consequences in state R

- State R imposes corporate income tax on the profits derived by RCo, including the buy-in payment received for the transfer of existing intangibles to RCo Regional Holding. However, because of the absence of a significant track record of RCo's performance at the time of the transaction, RCo may take the position that the value of those intangibles was very low, so that the actual amount of gain subject to corporate tax in State R would be very small.
- RCo also receives annual payments from RCo Regional Holding under the cost sharing arrangement, which may be at a rate much lower than the amount of royalties received by RCo Regional Holding. In addition, depending on the domestic law of State R, RCo may be entitled to R&D tax credits for a significant fraction of its expenditures, thereby significantly reducing its tax liability for corporate tax purposes.
- Under its controlled foreign company (CFC) rules, State R would under some circumstances treat royalties received by RCo Regional Holding as passive income subject to current taxation in the hands of RCo. However, because RCo Regional

OpCo is treated as a transparent entity for tax purposes in State R, the income of RCo Regional OpCo is treated as having been earned directly by RCo Regional Holding and is therefore treated as active income taxable in State R only when paid to RCo. This result would also be reached if State R imposed tax only on a territorial basis and did not have CFC rules.

VAT consequences

- With respect to value added tax (VAT), the treatment of the business-to-business (B2B) transactions is relatively straightforward, with the VAT levied either through the supplying business charging the tax or the recipient business self-assessing it. The input tax levied would generally be recoverable by the businesses through the input tax credit mechanism.
- The VAT treatment of the supplies to private consumers (business-to-consumer (B2C)) in State S will generally be different for supplies of physical products and supplies of digital products. Supplies by RCo Regional OpCo of physical goods stored in SCo's warehouse to consumers in State S would be subject to VAT in State S. State S may allow SCo to account for State S VAT on behalf of RCo Regional OpCo (e.g. as a fiscal representative). If the physical products would be shipped to consumers in State S from abroad, e.g. from State T, then these supplies would be zero rated in the exporting state and would be subject to VAT at the time of importation into State S. Depending on the value of the goods and the thresholds operated by State S, they may qualify for a VAT exemption under the relief for importations of low value goods. Also the supplies of digital products to final consumers in State S should in principle be subject to VAT in State S, in accordance with the destination principle. However, State S will have considerable difficulty enforcing the payment of the VAT on these supplies, as the supplier is not resident in State S and collecting the tax from the final consumers is ineffectual. While certain jurisdictions operate a mechanism requiring non-resident suppliers to register and remit the tax on supplies to resident private consumers, it is recognised that it is often challenging for tax authorities to enforce compliance with such requirements.

B.2. Internet advertising

8. The RCo Group provides a number of Internet services (e.g. search engines) to customers worldwide. Many of these online services are offered free of charge to consumers, whose use of the online services provides the RCo Group with a substantial amount of data, including location-based data, data based on online behaviour, and data based on personal information provided by users. Over the course of many years of data collection, refinement, processing, and analysis, the RCo Group has developed a sophisticated algorithm that targets advertisements to those users who are most likely to be interested in the products advertised. RCo Group derives substantially all of its revenues from the sale of advertising through its online platform, for a fee that is generally based on the number of users who click on each advertisement.

9. The technology used in providing the advertisement services, along with the various algorithms used to collect and process data in order to target potential buyers were developed by staff of RCo, the parent company of the Group situated in State R. The rights to exploit this technology in the T/S region are owned by a dual resident subsidiary of the group,

XCo. The latter company is incorporated in State T but effectively managed in State X. The technology rights for the T/S region were acquired by XCo under a cost-sharing arrangement whereby XCo agreed to make a "buy in" payment equal to the value of the existing technology and to share the cost of future enhancement of the transferred technology on the basis of the anticipated future benefit from the use of the technology in the T/S region. In practice, XCo does not actually perform any supervision of the development activities carried out by RCo in State R.

10. XCo licenses all of the rights in the technology used to operate the platform to a foreign subsidiary resident in State Y, YCo. The latter then sublicenses the technology to TCo, a company organised and resident in State T, earning a small "spread" between the royalties it receives and the royalties it pays on to XCo. YCo and TCo are hybrid entities that are treated as corporations for tax purposes in State Y and State T, but as transparent for tax purposes in State R. The physical presence of XCo in State X is minimal, both in terms of personnel and tangible assets (equipment, premises, etc.). In fact, neither XCo nor YCo has any employees on its payroll, and each company's activities are limited to board meetings taking place in an "office hotel" where the company regularly rents different offices.

11. TCo acts as the regional headquarters for the RCo group's operations in the T/S region, and employs a substantial number of people in managing the group's activities in that region. It operates the websites offering free online services to consumers in the T/S region, and serves as the legal counterparty for all sales of advertising in the T/S region. However the servers that host these websites may be placed throughout the region and/or located in State R and operated by RCo. Dependent on the time of the day, different members of the group may be responsible the maintenance of the website and fixing any network issues in the region.

12. Advertisement services contracts with TCo can be concluded electronically through TCo's websites on the basis of standard agreements, the terms of which are generally set by RCo. Advertisers located in the T/S region that wish to purchase advertising targeting users of RCo's products can thus do so directly through a website operated by TCo without having any interaction with the personnel located in State T. This advertising is available to local businesses in the T/S region, whether they are targeting customers in the T/S region or customers elsewhere.

13. For larger markets and in order to deal with key clients, the group has established a number of local subsidiaries. To promote the purchase of such advertising by businesses active in the T/S region, TCo has local affiliates, such as SCo, a company resident in State S, whose purpose is to promote the RCo family of products, including in particular the advertising services offered in the region. Local subsidiaries like SCo provide education and technical consulting to users and potential advertising clients, as well as marketing support in order to generate demand for the RCo advertising services. Local staff members have substantial and ongoing one-on-one interaction with local businesses, particularly the largest customers in the local market, many of which end up purchasing advertising. Compensation for the staff is partially based on the number of advertising contracts concluded between TCo and customers in State S and the income generated by TCo from the clients they support. In consideration for its promotion activities and technical support, TCo pays SCo a fee covering its expenses plus a mark-up. In general, customers supported by local affiliates such as SCo have no interaction with TCo staff.

14. The structure used by the RCo Group can be depicted as shown in Figure B.2.

Figure B.2. **Internet advertising**

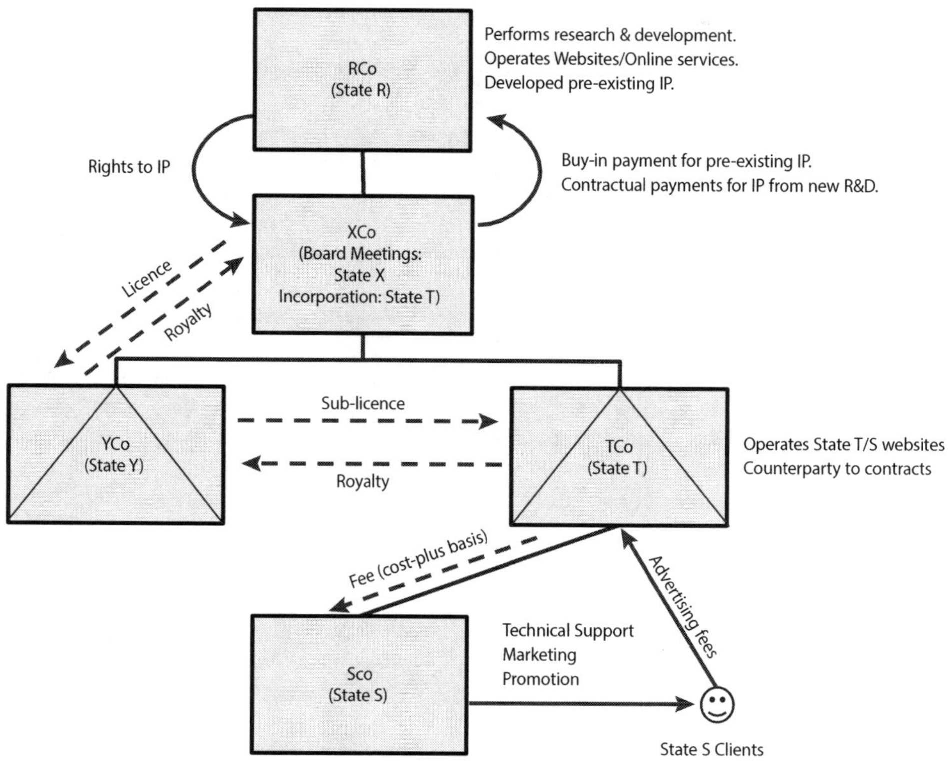

15. The manner in which RCo's business activity is structured has significant consequences from a tax perspective. Due to contractual arrangements among the different group companies, the bulk of the Group's income is allocated to State X, and only minimal taxable profits are allocated to State S, State R, and State T. More specifically, the following paragraphs describe the consequences that would arise in the different States concerned.

Direct tax consequences in state S

- SCo is allocated minimal taxable income, based on the position that SCo's functions are limited to those of a service provider.
- All revenues from sales of advertising in State S, including advertising purchased by State S residents and other regional customers, are treated as the revenues of TCo. The lack of authority for SCo staff to legally conclude contracts and the use of standardised contracts and on line contract acceptance by TCo result in TCo not being considered to have a PE in State S. As a result, State S does not tax the profits derived from these activities either because it has no right to do so under its domestic law or because the relevant double tax treaty prevents it from doing so in the absence of a PE of TCo in State S to which the income is attributable.

Direct tax consequences in state T

- State T imposes corporate tax on the profits earned by TCo from its various activities in the T/S region. TCo's income, however, is almost entirely offset by the royalty paid to YCo for its sublicense of the technology used by TCo to provide Internet services.
- This payment is not subject to withholding under the relevant double tax treaty.
- State T does not impose corporate income tax on XCo, due to it not being a resident under State T's domestic legislation.

Direct tax consequences in state Y

- State Y imposes corporate income tax on the profits of YCo, but those profits are limited to a small "spread" between the royalties received by YCo and the royalties paid by YCo to XCo.
- State Y does not impose any withholding on the payment of royalties under its domestic law.

Direct tax consequences in state X

- State X does not impose a corporate income tax.

Direct tax consequences in state R

- State R imposes corporate income tax on the profits derived by RCo, notably the buy-in payment received in consideration for the transfer of pre-existing technology to XCo and the annual payments received under the cost sharing arrangement. However, because of the absence of a significant track record of RCo's performance at the time of the transaction, RCo may take the position that the value of those intangibles was very low, so that the actual amount of gain subject to corporate tax in State R would be very small. Further, the annual payment – compensation for the costs supported by RCo for developing the intangibles without any markup – could potentially be at a rate much lower than the amount of royalties received by XCo. Finally, depending on the domestic law of State R, RCo may be entitled to R&D tax credits for a significant fraction of its expenditures, thereby further reducing its tax liability for corporate tax purposes.
- Under its controlled foreign company (CFC) rules, State R would under some circumstances treat royalties received by XCo as passive income subject to current taxation in the hands of RCo. However, because YCo and TCo are considered for tax purposes as transparent entities in State R, the latter's CFC rules would disregard the royalty transactions concluded between XCo, YCo and TCo. The income of YCo and TCo would be considered as having been earned directly by XCo, and would be treated as active income that would be taxable in State R only when paid to RCo.

VAT consequences

- With respect to VAT, the treatment of the B2B transactions is relatively straightforward with the VAT levied either through the supplying business charging the tax or the recipient business self-assessing it. The input tax levied would generally be recoverable by the businesses through the input tax credit mechanism. The exception would be where the business is engaged in making exempt supplies and therefore not entitled to recover the tax.
- The online services provided free of charge by TCo to consumers in the S/T region have in principle no VAT consequences, unless it is considered that TCo is providing consumers with Internet services for non-monetary consideration, in which case the customers' State may claim VAT on the fair market value of that consideration.

B.3. Cloud computing

16. The RCo Group is a developer of software (online games) which it operates on servers around the world and makes available to customers through various client interfaces in exchange for subscription fees.

17. The software itself, along with all technology associated with processing payment and maintaining security of customer data, was developed principally by engineers of RCo, a company resident in State R. In addition, RCo remotely co-ordinates marketing and selling activities in the various regions to minimise costs, maintain consistency among its various businesses and websites, and improve efficiency. Those co-ordination services are provided to regional operating lower-tier subsidiaries in return for a management service fee covering related expenses plus a markup.

18. RCo transferred the employees responsible for the management of the technology used in operating the client interfaces to PE Y, a foreign branch of RCo situated in State Y. RCo provides the rights to use the software and knowledge associated with the cloud computing services to various regional subsidiaries through licensing and sub-licensing arrangements.

19. TCo is a regional operating subsidiary of RCo resident in State T. Even though State T's market is small in relation to RCo's business, TCo employs a substantial number of people to operate the websites used to sell access to RCo's hosted software in the T/S region, which includes State S and other States. TCo has obtained under a public tender in State S all the licenses required to exercise certain regulated activities (online gaming). Contracts with customers in State S are concluded electronically through TCo's websites on the basis of standard agreements, the terms of which are set by RCo. TCo manages all payment processing and security associated with permitting access to the hosted software. Fees paid by the subscribers are collected through local bank accounts. In addition, TCo's personnel perform all required localisation of the software for use in markets in the State S. TCo operates a "server farm" located in State T, which is used as the primary datacentre to run the software, process customer transactions, and store customer data. Mirror servers owned by third parties (ISPs) are also regularly used in other locations around the world to ensure the most efficient possible access at all times by customers, as well as to decrease the risk of loss of data.

20. To promote demand for the use of RCo's hosted software in State S, a very significant market for RCo's business, TCo has a local subsidiary, SCo, whose stated purpose is to

promote the hosted software services in the region and offer online customer's care services. SCo does this both through local advertising and through direct interaction with prospective customers. SCo is compensated for its activities via a fee calculated on a cost-plus basis.

The structure used by the RCo Group can be depicted as shown in Figure B.3.

Figure B.3. **Cloud computing**

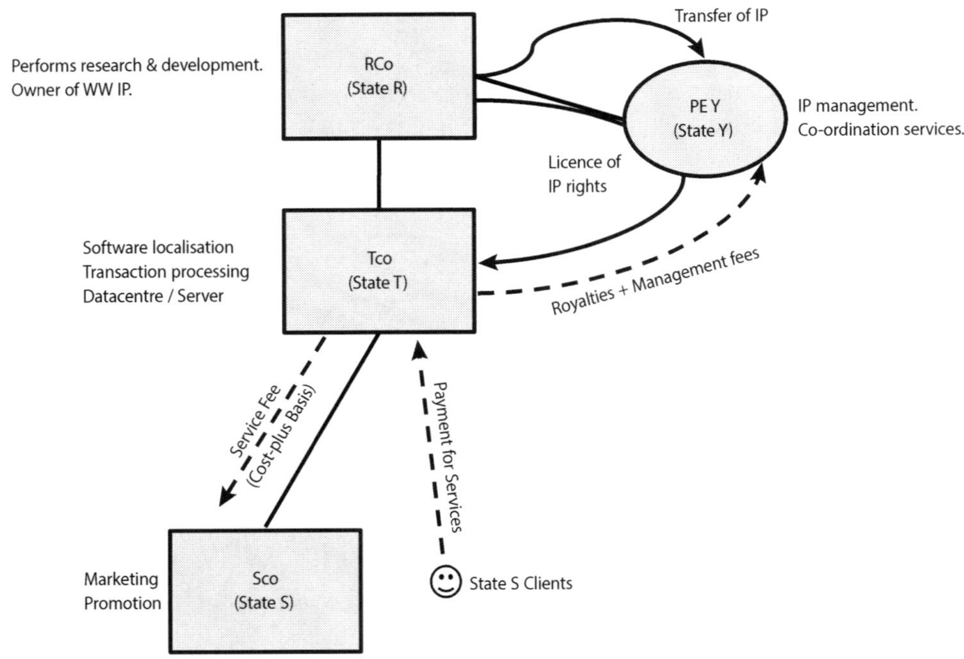

21. The manner in which RCo Group's business activity is structured as a legal matter has significant consequences for the Group's worldwide tax burden. Due to contractual arrangements and allocation of key functions most of the profits generated by the Group's business activity is allocated to State Y, thereby ensuring that minimal tax is being paid in States S T and R. More specifically, the following paragraphs describe the consequences that would arise in the different States concerned.

Direct tax consequences in state S

- SCo is allocated minimal taxable income, based on the position that its risk and function profile is limited to routine marketing and customer care services. All revenues from sales of cloud computing services in State S are treated as income of TCo, due to its role as the counterparty to the transactions with local customers and administrator of the websites. State S does not tax the profits derived from these activities because it has no right to do so under its domestic law or because the relevant double tax treaty prevents it from doing so in the absence of a PE of TCo in State S to which the income is attributable.

Direct tax consequences in state T

- State T imposes corporate income tax on the profits derived by TCo from its sales activities but TCo's income is largely offset by the royalty paid to RCo for its license of the technology used in providing the cloud computing services to customers, as well as by the management fees paid to RCo for its co-ordination services.
- Although the income from the royalties and fees paid by TCo is attributed to the PE in State Y, State T does not impose any withholding on those royalties and fees under the terms of the relevant tax treaty between State T and State R, as it considers the payment to be received by RCo, a resident of State R.

Direct tax consequences in state Y

- State Y imposes corporate income tax on the profits attributable to PE Y at a low rate. In addition, by virtue of a preferential regime available in State Y for income derived from certain intangibles, the income attributable to the PE Y is entitled to a rate substantially less than the generally applicable corporate tax rate for the royalties included in its taxable profits.

Direct tax consequences in state R

- State R imposes corporate tax on the profits derived by RCo on a territorial basis. As a result, and in accordance with the relevant double tax treaty, all the royalty income and management fees derived by RCo are treated as attributable to PE Y and, as such, excluded from RCo's corporate tax base in State R.The capital gain derived by RCo from the transfer of the existing technology to PE Yis not taxed in State R under the rules applicable to cross-border transfers of assets in the R/Y region. Further, RCo may be entitled to R&D tax credits for a significant fraction of its R&D expenditures, thereby reducing its tax liability in respect of the management fees.
- State R's domestic law does not provide for any CFC regime.

VAT consequences

- For VAT purposes, as in the previous examples, the VAT on the B2B transactions will be levied either through the supplying business charging the tax or the recipient business self-assessing it. The input tax levied would generally be recoverable by the businesses through the input tax credit mechanism. The exception would be where a business is engaged in making exempt supplies and therefore not entitled to recover the tax.
- In respect of B2C transactions, TCo's supplies to final consumers in State S should in principle be subject to VAT in there. However, States S will often have considerable difficulty in enforcing the collection of VAT on cloud services acquired from abroad by resident final consumers.

B.4. Internet app store

22. RCo Group is the creator of an operating system for mobile phones and other portable devices. It maintains a widely used Internet app store, through which users of RCo Group's phones and devices may pay to download applications (including both applications

developed and owned by RCo Group and by third-party developers) that enhance the function of their devices. In order to develop and sell applications through RCo Group's marketplace, third-party developers must use software provided by RCo Group in order to ensure compatibility with its operating system and consistency with standards set by RCo Group. Pricing for third-party applications is set by the third-party developers subject to guidelines set by RCo Group, with the developer receiving 75% of the revenues from sales through the app store, and RCo Group receiving 25%. Third-party developers may choose which markets their products will be sold in.

23. The development of the operating system and the Internet app store, as well as self-made applications sold through the app Store, was performed substantially by employees of RCo, a company resident in State R. The development of the third-party applications is performed around the world, depending on the location of the developers, most of which are individuals or small businesses.

24. Early in the life of the Group, RCo sold its rights to the technology used in developing and running its app Store, along with the developing tools and other software used to work with third-party developers around the world to a subsidiary, TCo, resident in State T, a very small market in relation to RCo Group's business. Simultaneously to the sale agreement, RCo concluded a service agreement whereby it continues to upgrade and develop the technology used in the app stores for the benefit of TCo in exchange for a fee covering its R&D expenses plus a markup. All the risks assumed related to the development of the technology were contractually allocated to TCo, which employs a substantial number of people to operate the various local versions of the application marketplace (tailored and developed by RCo) and steer the marketing strategy, but does not perform any supervision of the development activities carried out by RCo in State R. The app stores are hosted on servers located in State T and owned by TCo or, depending on network traffic at the time of the transaction, on third-party servers generally located in countries distinct from the country of the customer. TCo handles all transaction processing with customers and third party developers around the world (including State R). Contracts for purchase of applications are concluded electronically, through automated processes, on the basis of standardised terms set by TCo.

25. In larger markets, TCo has established local affiliates to assist the group with promoting the RCo operating system and the Internet app store to third-party developers, sellers and prospective purchasers of mobile devices. These local affiliates, such as SCo, a company established in State S, are never formally involved in the sales of specific applications and/or negotiation of agency agreements with third-party developers, though some face-to-face interactions may occur with local customers. The remuneration of these local affiliates is generally based on a fee covering their expenses plus a markup.

The structure used by the RCo Group can be depicted as shown in Figure B.4.

26. The manner in which RCo's business activity is structured as a legal matter has significant consequences for the Group's worldwide tax burden. RCo Group takes the position that due to contractual arrangements an affiliated company resident in State T, TCo, is entitled to all residual profits after compensating the other members of the group for their functions, thereby reducing the group's tax burden to a minimum in the other States involved. More specifically, the following paragraphs describe the consequences that would arise in the different States concerned.

Figure B.4. **Internet app store**

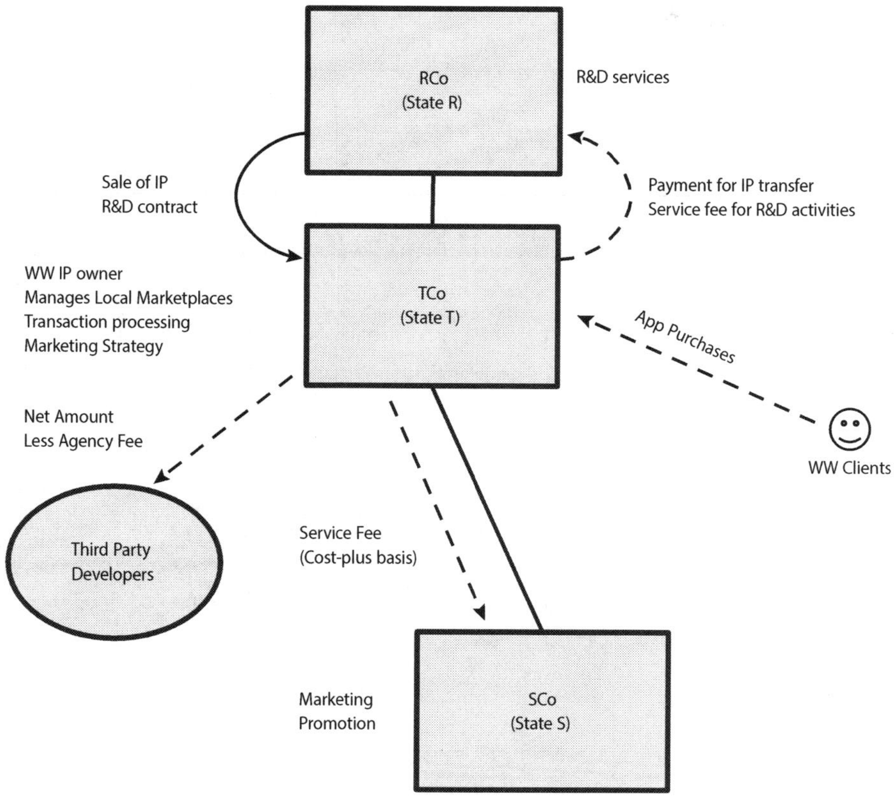

Direct tax consequences in state S

- SCo is allocated minimal taxable income, based on the position that the function profile of this local affiliate is limited to providing routine marketing and promotion services, with no direct selling activity to State S customers.
- All revenues from sales of applications in State S and State R are treated as income of TCo, due to its role as the counterparty to the transactions with local customers and administrator of local app stores. State S does not tax the profits derived from these activities either because it has no right to do so under its domestic law or because the relevant double tax treaty prevents it from doing so in the absence of a PE of TCo in State S to which the income is attributable.

Direct tax consequences in state T

- State T imposes corporate tax on the significant profits earned by TCo, but at a rate which is roughly 50% of the rates of State R and State S.
- No withholding is imposed on the various service fees paid by TCo to RCo and SCo under the relevant double tax treaty.

Direct tax consequences in state R

- State R imposes corporate income tax on the profits derived by RCo, notably the capital gain derived from the sale of the technology to TCo and the service fee received for its R&D activities. However, because of the absence of a significant track record of RCo's performance at the time of the transaction, RCo may take the position that the value of those intangibles was very low, so that the actual amount of gain subject to corporate tax in State R would be very small. In addition, depending on the domestic law of State R, RCo may be entitled to R&D tax credits in State R for a significant fraction of its expenditures, thereby reducing its tax liability for corporate tax purposes.
- State R imposes corporate tax on a territorial basis and does not have any CFC rules. As a result, RCo is exempt from tax both on income earned by TCo and on dividends received from TCo.

VAT consequences

- For VAT purposes, as in the previous examples, the VAT on the business-to-business transactions will be levied either through the supplying business charging the tax or the recipient business self-assessing it. The input tax levied would generally be recoverable by the businesses through the input tax credit mechanism. The exception would be where a business is engaged in making exempt supplies and therefore not entitled to recover the tax.
- In respect of B2C transactions, TCo will generally be considered as the supplier of the applications to the consumers for VAT purposes, rather than the third party developers of these applications. The transactions between TCo and the third party developers will then be treated as business-to-business supplies, although the turn-over of many third party developers may remain under the VAT-registration threshold, in which case these transactions may effectively not be subject to VAT.
- TCo would be required to collect and remit State T VAT on sales of any services to private consumers in State T. Supplies to consumers abroad will either be zero-rated in State T or will be subject to State T's (low) VAT rate. Supplies to such final consumers in other states should in principle be subject to VAT in these final consumers' state. These consumers' states, however, will often have considerable difficulty enforcing the collection of VAT on supplies of applications to consumers within their jurisdiction. This may result in consumers in these states being able to acquire the applications free of VAT or at a lower (foreign) VAT rate than if they had acquired the product domestically.

Annex C

The collection of VAT/GST on imports of low value goods

This annex contains the text of a report regarding possible approaches for a more efficient collection of VAT/GST on the import of low-value goods, which could allow governments to reduce or remove the VAT/GST exemption thresholds for such imports should they wish to do so.

C.1. Introduction

C.1.1. Addressing the tax challenges of the digital economy

1. BEPS[1] Action 1 on the tax challenges of the Digital Economy notably called for work on "how to ensure the effective collection of value added tax/goods and services tax (VAT/GST) with respect to the cross-border supply of digital goods and services". In response, the Report on *Addressing the Tax Challenges of the Digital Economy* (the Digital Economy Report, OECD, 2014) was developed by the Task Force on the Digital Economy (TFDE) and delivered to G20 Finance Ministers in September 2014. One of the main VAT/GST challenges that were identified relates to the growing volume of imports of low value parcels from online sales on which no VAT/GST is collected as a result of relief regimes for such low value imports that are operated in many jurisdictions. This leads to growing revenue losses and growing risks of competitive distortion.

2. The low value import VAT/GST relief regimes were mainly motivated by the consideration that the costs of collecting the VAT/GST on imported low value items were likely to outweigh the VAT/GST actually collected. At the time when most of these low value import reliefs were introduced, Internet shopping did not exist and the level of imports benefitting from the relief was relatively small. Over recent years, however, many countries have seen a significant and rapid growth in the volume of low value imports of physical goods on which VAT/GST is not collected. This has resulted in decreased VAT/GST revenues and the growing risk of unfair competitive pressures on domestic retailers who are required to charge VAT/GST on their sales to domestic consumers. It also creates an incentive for domestic suppliers to relocate to an offshore jurisdiction in order to sell their low value goods free of VAT/GST.

3. The Digital Economy Report concluded that governments could be in a position to remove or lower the exemption threshold for imports of low value goods, if tax authorities were able to improve the efficiency of processing such low value imports and of collecting the VAT/GST on such imports.

C.1.2. Scope and objective of this report

4. This report explores the possible approaches for a more efficient collection of VAT/GST on the import of low value goods, which may allow governments to reduce or remove the VAT/GST exemption thresholds, should they decide to do so. The objective of this report is not to set forth recommendations or guidelines but rather to provide an analysis of possible approaches for improving the efficiency of the VAT/GST collection. It assesses the available options or combinations of options for governments to consider depending on their domestic situation and their exposure to imports of low value goods.

5. This report focuses only on the collection of VAT/GST on imports of low value goods, not on the collection of import duties. Most countries operate a *de minimis* threshold for customs duties, which is essentially regulated by the World Customs Organization's (WCO) Revised Kyoto Convention (RKC – see Box C.1). It provides for a mandatory *de minimis* customs duties and taxes relief for small consignments.[2] While this rule is obligatory for Contracting Parties to the RKC, the RKC does not prescribe the amount of such a threshold nor does it impose a minimum standard.

6. Although both the customs duties and the import VAT/GST are generally collected by customs authorities, the customs duties relief threshold is often higher than the VAT/GST exemption threshold (e.g. EUR 150 for the customs duties relief in the European

Union against EUR 10-22 for the EU's VAT relief). Against this background, this report notably explores models for collecting import VAT/GST that would limit or remove the need for customs authorities to intervene in the VAT/GST collection for imports that are not subject to customs duties. This is expected to lower the cost of collection of VAT/GST on low value imports and could allow jurisdictions to remove or lower the VAT/GST exemption thresholds, should they wish to do so. VAT/GST on imports of goods above the customs threshold could (continue to) be collected together with customs duties and taxes under normal customs procedures.

7. This report first describes the main features of the typical supply chain for the sale, the customs clearance and the delivery of small packages and the role of the main stakeholders in this process (Section C.2). It then explores the potential options for the collection of VAT/GST on imports of such low value goods and provides an initial analysis of their advantages and disadvantages, their limits and the requirements for their application in practice (Section C.3). It also briefly describes the potential role of administrative co-operation on compliance (Section C.4) and summarises the outcome of the assessment of the likely performance of the options for the collection of VAT/GST on imports of low value goods (Section C.5). It finally draws an overall conclusion (Section C.6). This assessment is supported by "test cards" providing more detailed analysis of the options, appended to this report (Appendix C.A).

C.2. Main features of the supply chain for the sale, clearance and delivery of low value goods

C.2.1. Challenges

8. The supply chain for online sales of low value physical goods covers a broad spectrum of stakeholders starting with the vendor of the goods, an intermediary for making the secure payment to a vendor abroad through to a domestic transporter making the final delivery to the purchaser. It is different from the traditional model of importing, warehousing and then retailing goods. With developments in technology the potential marketplace has expanded to a truly global level and offers consumers an almost unending range of options to access the market and assess the value proposition of the goods that are for sale. Domestic vendors, governments and other traditional stakeholders have made strides to match these challenges but they are continuing to deal with a range of issues in the wake of the e-commerce revolution. E-commerce developments have, and still are, triggering deep changes in the size and the structure of the distance sales to private consumers.

9. Business models and supply chain arrangements are changing to meet the new challenges, remain cost-effective and to respond to growing demand. As customers are increasingly able to directly access foreign suppliers via the Internet, certain traditional intermediaries are becoming less prevalent (e.g. wholesalers) while new players emerge (such as e-commerce platforms and online payment providers) and others are adjusting (e.g. transporters). User-friendly shopping, buying and payment processes and speed of delivery through efficient distribution processes are crucial for online vendors. This requires a smooth interaction between the various stakeholders involved in this process and an increasingly significant amount of information exchanged between them.

10. These evolutions have also created increasing challenges for the existing tax systems. A key challenge is the collection of VAT/GST on online purchases of physical goods made by consumers from suppliers in another jurisdiction. Countries with a VAT/GST in principle

collect this tax on imports of goods from the importer at the time the goods are imported using customs collection mechanisms. Many jurisdictions apply an exemption from VAT/GST for the import of low value goods under a certain *de minimis* threshold, based on the consideration that the administrative costs associated with collecting the tax are likely to outweigh the VAT/GST actually collected. When most of these low value import reliefs were introduced, Internet shopping did not exist and the level of imports benefitting from the relief was relatively small. Over recent years, however, these exemptions have created growing pressure on tax revenues and risks of unfair competitive pressures on domestic retailers that are required to charge VAT/GST on sales to the domestic consumer. It also creates an incentive for domestic suppliers to relocate to an offshore jurisdiction in order to sell their low value goods free of VAT/GST. Such relocations may also have negative impacts on domestic employment and direct tax revenues.

11. The exemptions for low value imports have therefore become increasingly controversial in the context of the growing digital economy. The difficulty lies in finding the balance between the need for appropriate revenue protection, avoidance of distortions of competition, and the need to keep the cost of collection proportionate to the VAT/GST collected on imports of low value goods. As the VAT/GST exemption thresholds in many jurisdictions were established before the advent and growth of the digital economy, countries may need to review their policies on taxing e-commerce to ensure that they are still effective.

12. If customs and/or tax authorities were to make significant improvements to the efficiency of processing such low value imports and of collecting the VAT/GST on such imports, governments would be in a position to lower these thresholds and address the issues associated with its operation. Many jurisdictions are now looking for alternative and more efficient ways to collect the VAT/GST on imports of low value goods.

C.2.2. The role of the key stakeholders

13. This section provides an overview of the broad categories of key stakeholders and describes their respective roles and obligations in the traditional cross-border online sales and delivery process of low value physical goods. The impact of possible new options for taxing low value imports on the role of these stakeholders is considered under Section C.3. The following categories have been identified:

1. the purchasers;
2. the vendors;
3. the e-commerce platforms;
4. the transporters;
5. the financial intermediaries;
6. the customs/tax administrations.

14. These categories of stakeholders refer to their actual role in the supply chain rather than to their status or legal form. Their role is described against the background of the customs procedures for the importation of low value goods, which is outlined in Box C.1.

Box C.1. The customs procedures on importation of low value goods

Customs procedures are subject to a number of common standards such as the Revised Kyoto Convention[a] (RKC), the Immediate Release Guidelines[b] and the Harmonised System Nomenclature.[c] These standards include provisions for providing information to customs authorities, minimum data requirements, standardised classification of goods, risk-based approach simplified procedures, rules for the immediate release of specified consignments, etc.

These procedures do not aim solely at collecting taxes but also (and primarily) at facilitating trade and ensuring border security and protection against unlawful movements of prohibited, restricted or regulated goods.

Regarding the import of low value goods, the RKC provides for a mandatory *de minimis* customs duties and taxes relief for small consignments.[d] While this rule is obligatory for Contracting Parties to the RKC,[e] the RKC does not prescribe the amount of such a threshold nor does it impose a minimum standard. There could be limited exceptions where duties and taxes can apply irrespective of value, e.g. excisable goods.

Although they follow a number of common standards, each country has its own customs clearance procedures in place (a common Customs Code applies to the Member States of the European Union, which lays down common rules on customs procedures but also leaves them a certain scope for national rules).[f] These procedures generally follow similar patterns: when a low value good is imported, the person liable to pay the duties and taxes is the recipient of the goods mentioned on the customs declaration (the "importer of record" or the "declarant"). Under the RKC, the "declarant" is defined as any person who makes a goods declaration or in whose name such a declaration is made. This person can be the purchaser/consignee or the vendor/supplier of the goods, depending on the contract established between them. When the vendor is the importer of record or the declarant, he normally makes an onwards supply to the purchaser in the country of import and is thus registered for VAT/GST purposes in that country (this case does not fall within the scope of this report).

A third party can also be designated as a representative of the importer of record or the declarant for completing the customs procedures and pay the duties and taxes. In this case, the declaration can be in the name of the person being represented by the third party (direct representation) or in the third party's own name (indirect representation). In some countries when a third party acts under direct representation, the person he represents is held responsible; if the third party acts under indirect representation, it is held responsible. In some instances, the person and the third party will be considered severally and jointly liable for the payment of customs debt and the taxes due. In a number of countries, the third party is commonly registered as a "customs broker" in the country of import.

Notes

a. World Customs Organization's Revised International Convention on the Simplification and Harmonization of Customs Procedures – the 102 Member States are contracting parties to the RKC, which entered into force in 2006.

b. Guidelines for the Immediate Release of Consignments by Customs 2014.

c. Harmonized Commodity Description and Coding System generally referred to as "Harmonized System" or simply "HS" is a multipurpose international product nomenclature developed by the WCO.

d. According to Transitional Standard 4.13 of Chapter 4 of the General Annex of the RKC: "National legislation shall specify a minimum value and/or a minimum amount of duties and taxes below which no duties and taxes will be collected".

e. As of June 2015, the number of Contracting Parties to the RKC is 102.

f. The Customs Code (Council Regulation EEC/2913/92), to be replaced with the Union Customs Code on 1 May 2016 (Regulation EU/952/2013).

C.2.2.1. The purchasers

15. The role of purchasers is unique as they are present at the beginning and the end of the supply chain. They initiate the purchase, authorise the transfer of the funds to the vendor or to a designated intermediary and in most cases take receipt of the goods from the local transporter. The purchaser has full information on the product, its value and where it will be delivered.

16. Purchasers may not always be aware of their position with respect to import taxes and/or duties, which may result in situations where they face an unexpected claim for the payment of import taxes and/or duties at the moment of delivery. In such cases, this often leads to refusal to accept the delivery, creating uncertainties and costs for the vendor and the transporter who may face customs clearance procedures for the re-exportation of the returned goods and refunds of taxes and their re-importation in the origin country, if they are not simply abandoned.

17. Purchasers may be businesses (business-to-business (B2B) supplies) or private consumers (business-to-consumer (B2C) supplies). This report focuses on options for the collection of VAT/GST on imports of low value goods by private consumers. This is the area where domestic retailers, who are required to charge VAT/GST on their domestic sales, increasingly face the risk of unfair competition from online sales that are made free of VAT/GST under the import exemption threshold.[3] This issue does not normally arise in a B2B context, where business customers generally have a right to deduct the input tax.

C.2.2.2. The vendors

18. The role of the vendor is to provide the product to the purchaser. Identifying the vendor in an online sales transaction may not always be straightforward. From a commercial perspective, the online sale can be concluded *(1)* through the vendor's own website; *(2)* through a "transparent" third-party e-commerce platform, where the product is presented to the purchaser but the contract is still concluded between the original vendor and the purchaser, or *(3)* using a "non-transparent" third party e-commerce platform, where the purchaser contracts with the platform itself. The role of "transparent" and "non-transparent" platforms is described further in Section C.2.2.3 below.

19. Vendors typically collect sets of key data during the selling and delivery process, which may notably be useful (or necessary) to complete customs and tax obligations in the country of importation. These key data sets include details of the goods sold; the price paid for the goods; the place of delivery and the person to whom the goods are being consigned; the price paid for the transport; the payment details; the delivery mode and tracking data (including tracking number and carrier/postal operator); and possibly the amount of taxes due on importation and associated administrative costs when the price charged to the purchaser includes these costs. The status of the purchaser (business or final consumer) may also be known, depending on the contractual arrangements and circumstances.

20. Online vendors may potentially face customs and tax obligations and associated liability risks in all the countries where they make online sales of goods, which generally have each their own customs and tax procedures, rates and tax relief thresholds (note, however, that most of these procedures are harmonised for the 28 Member States of the European Union). This implies potentially high compliance costs, in particular for small and medium size enterprises (SMEs). This cost may be lower for imports of small value goods where simplified declarations are available, but the impact of entering a foreign

and unknown jurisdiction extends beyond the basic customs clearance issues and implies knowledge of local tax rates and thresholds, including the maintenance of this information.

21. Vendors may choose to rely on intermediaries to intervene in the customs and tax procedures, notably to expedite the delivery. This role is often played by transporters (see Section C.2.2.4 below) but can also be played by other third parties such as e-commerce platforms, and to a lesser extent in the trade of low value goods, by tax representatives. The intervention of such third parties in the customs clearance process inevitably comes with a cost, which can be relatively high per imported low value good, particularly when the turnover in the jurisdiction of destination is low.

22. The situation is simpler for vendors when the liability to pay the duties and taxes and to deal with the associated compliance obligations in the country of importation is on the purchaser. However, this may lead to suboptimal customer service and dissatisfied purchasers since duties and taxes and associated costs are generally collected from them at the time of delivery, i.e. after the sale has been concluded.

C.2.2.3. The e-commerce platforms

23. E-commerce platforms have developed over time from software that enables transactions via the Internet into comprehensive, online retail solutions that allow retailers to target, capture, engage and retain customers, through the traditional web store as well as via mobile and social media channels. Although their service offering and involvement in online sales processes may vary and will undoubtedly continue to evolve, this section describes some of the key services that e-commerce platforms typically provide.

24. E-commerce platforms typically operate the web store where products are displayed and where purchasers can make their orders. They provide software tools for vendors to upload their product catalogue to this website and to design shop pages. They operate a check-out module, which finalises the order, proposes a selection of payment and delivery methods to the purchaser and completes the necessary security checks to prevent fraud. Once the order is approved by the vendor, the purchaser is charged for the sale and the e-commerce platform remits the sales proceeds to the merchant and reports the transactions on the vendor's account pages. The platform may provide additional services to the vendor, for example advice on consumer protection, data privacy, and tax and customs rules. E-commerce platforms can also issue invoices on behalf of the vendor according to its instructions and handle purchasers' inquiries. Depending on the contract, the e-commerce platform may intervene in the return and refund process for rejected goods or leave this to be handled directly by the vendor. The platform charges a fee for its services to the vendor. The fee may be based on the value of the item sold and is usually withheld by the platform from the vendor's sales proceeds.

25. The e-commerce platforms typically collect and store considerable amounts of data, such as the vendor account information (incl. name, address, VAT registration details, bank details); the purchaser account information (this may include shipping and billing information and payment instrument details); each vendor's product catalogues; the record of each transaction (this may include the identification of the merchant and the purchaser, the products sold, the price per product and total price, and the payment method used). Depending on the contract with the vendor, the platform may keep a record of returned and refunded goods. This information is captured from data flows between the e-commerce platform and the vendor and to some extent from data flows between the e-commerce platform and the purchaser.

26. Most e-commerce platforms are "transparent platforms", i.e. they are normally not parties to the commercial transactions themselves. There is a contract for the provision of services between the e-commerce platform and the vendor. The contract for the sale itself is concluded between the vendor and the purchaser. There is no contract between the platform and the purchaser. The transparent e-commerce platform generally does not play any role in determining the price of the goods sold: this price (inclusive or exclusive of taxes, duties and costs) will normally be set by the vendor. The transparent e-commerce platforms do not intervene in the shipment process. In most cases, the goods will be shipped from the merchant to the customer by an express carrier or by a postal operator (see Section C.2.2.4 below).

27. For the purpose of this work "non-transparent platforms" are those that are deemed to buy and supply the products themselves. From a VAT/GST perspective, the sale from the original vendor to the platform and the subsequent resale by the platform to the purchaser are generally treated as two separate transactions, with each transaction triggering its own tax compliance obligations. Depending on the contractual arrangements, the non-transparent platform or the purchaser will face the customs and tax obligations and associated liability risks in the country of importation.

C.2.2.4. The transporters

28. This section describes the role of transporters in the e-commerce supply chain, their possible role in the assessment, collection and remittance of duties and taxes at importation and in the collection of data that can support this customs clearance process.

29. Unlike the trade in services and intangibles, the e-commerce sale of goods to final consumers generally implies the intervention of a transporter to bring the goods across borders to the purchaser. In the online trade of low value goods, this task is generally carried out by an express carrier or by a postal operator. Vendors of low value goods may also choose to organise the transportation themselves without using intermediaries (e.g. by renting spaces on flights or on boats), but that still requires them to deal with the customs clearance and to organise the delivery to the customer in the country of destination. This option is therefore very marginal in the context of e-commerce trade of low value goods and is not described in more details below.

C.2.2.4.1. The express carriers

30. Express carriers are specialist integrated service providers who ensure the transport door-to-door from the vendor to the purchaser, the information management process and, depending on the contract, the management of tax and customs procedures. They have control of goods throughout the exportation and importation process.

31. This section describes how the supply chain for express carriers is typically organised, recognising that this may vary depending on the organisation of individual businesses (see also Figure C.1). The vendor of the goods contracts with the carrier to transport the sold goods to their purchaser abroad. The vendor fulfills the order and requests the express carrier to pick up the goods. The express carrier collects the shipment from the vendor and the related data, which typically include the nature of the goods, their value and destination as declared by the vendor. The goods are taken to the express carrier's service station and processed to support their delivery. Data and scanned documents are transmitted in electronic format to the customs authorities in the country of export and in the country of destination for customs clearance. This system allows the customs authorities at destination to obtain

information prior to the arrival of a shipment in the country. The shipment is consolidated with other shipments and delivered to the outbound gateway at the port or airport. The express carrier performs the export customs clearance and the shipment is dispatched to the carrier's local hub. At this hub, shipments are separated and consolidated with other shipments for the destination gateway and the goods are transported to the destination. At the destination gateway, the shipment is cleared. Duties and taxes at importation are paid as appropriate. The goods are dispatched to the local station for delivery to the purchaser. The goods are delivered to the purchaser and if required, duties and taxes are collected from the purchaser.

Figure C.1. **The role of the express carriers**

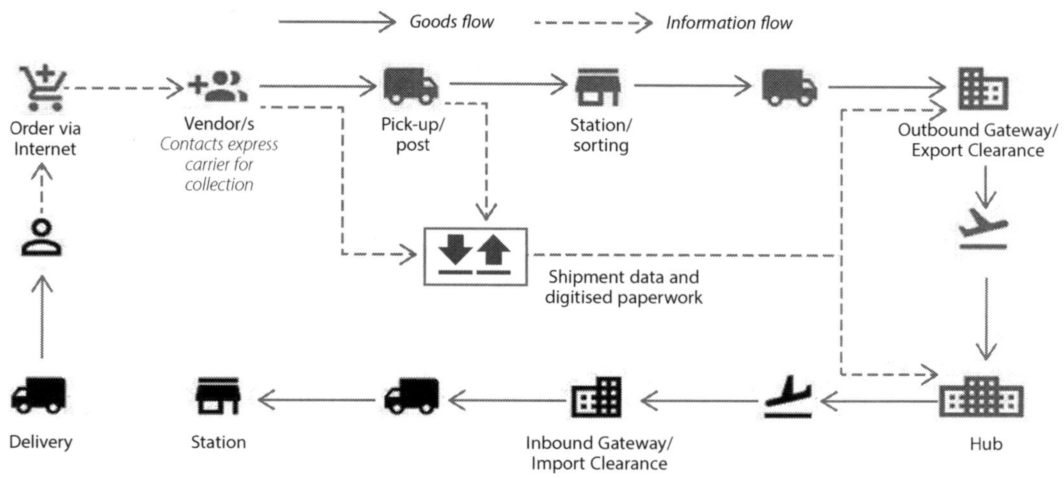

32. Express carriers are most often charged by vendors to complete the customs clearance procedures and pay the duties and taxes at importation. They have arrangements in place with customs authorities in most countries around the world allowing them to provide pre-arrival information and complete customs procedures electronically. As a declarant, they are responsible for the payment of duties and taxes to the authorities on importation (see Box C.1. above). Depending on the contract with the vendor, these duties and taxes may then be either forwarded to the vendor or charged to the purchaser at the time of delivery. In the latter case, this may lead to refusals to accept deliveries, creating uncertainties and costs for the vendor and the transporter (See Section C.2.2.1 above).

33. In some regions (e.g. Asia-Pacific and Middle-East), small vendors often consolidate their shipments using a "co-loader", who collects the goods and contracts with an express carrier to ship the goods to the customers. The co-loader also collects information and supporting documentation from the vendors and passes it to the express carrier. Following this intervention of the co-loader, the express carrier acts as described above and as illustrated in Figure C.1.

C.2.2.4.2. The postal operators

34. From a regulatory standpoint, postal operators are subject to Universal Postal Union[4] (UPU) regulations, which provide obligations regarding remittance of mail and consignments to the addressee and confidentiality of mail. Postal operators may be public or private companies.

35. The processes operated in the international mail environment generally differ from those operated by express carriers. This section describes the typical process operated by postal operators, recognising that these may vary depending on the countries and possible specific agreements between postal operators involved. The vendor remits the goods to his local post office and provides the necessary information using specific forms CN22 or CN23 depending on the value and/or weight of the package.[5] This information remains generally limited to the name and address of the consignee and the description of the contents of the package, their weight and their value. The postal operator relies on the sender for the correctness of this information and this may lead to concerns about the data quality, especially in cases of individual and occasional mailers. These paper forms are attached to the goods and are generally used by customs authorities as the bases for the customs clearance process. Although an electronic process is possible, few countries have the appropriate IT systems in place and the customs clearance process for postal package is therefore still very much paper based. In such case, there is no advance information sent to customs authorities in the country of destination allowing these authorities to obtain information prior to the arrival of a shipment in the country. When the paper form is used, the only way to assess the customs and tax status and liability of the package is through an intensive physical process of manually checking each good, in conjunction with the customs assessment for other risks. After having declared the goods for importation to the customs authorities, the postal operator in the destination country delivers them to the addressee.

36. Unlike express carriers, postal operators generally do not complete the tax and customs procedures. The addressee is liable for the duties and taxes and importation. The postal operator generally collects these duties and taxes from the addressee at the time of delivery. This may lead to the refusal to accept the delivery, creating uncertainties and costs for the postal operator (See Section C.2.2.1 above).

37. Discussions are currently taking place within the UPU and WCO on a possible transition from the existing paper-based process to an electronic exchange of information, to increase efficiency and allow the use of modern risk management tools (see Section C.2.2.6 below). However, the timing for the implementation of electronic procedures may vary between countries and there is presently no clear indication as to when this will become common practice.

C.2.2.5. The financial intermediaries

38. The traditional role of the financial intermediaries consists in the transfer of the payment from the purchaser to the vendor. In the e-commerce environment, where the purchaser may have very limited knowledge of the vendor and may fear identity theft and fraud, the security of the purchaser's bank data is a major concern. As a response, financial intermediaries have developed payment solutions that are only indirectly associated with the purchaser's bank account. These include secure debit cards, which avoid the risk involved with the vendor storing credit card information, and online payment systems provided by specialised online payment service providers. Typically, the vendor enters into an agreement with the payment service provider to facilitate payments from purchasers. Payment made by purchasers may be made directly to an "e-money" account with the payment service provider or directly to the vendors' bank account. The system is secured and generally the vendor does not receive the bank, credit or debit card data of the purchaser. The purchaser may not always be required to have an account with the payment service provider.

39. During the payment process, the financial intermediary collects and stores data such as the vendor and the purchaser account information (name, address, bank details). However, in most cases, the financial intermediary does not collect information about the nature of the goods being sold or the place where they are delivered.

C.2.2.6. Customs and tax administrations

40. Overall, the role of customs authorities is threefold: trade facilitation, border protection and the collection of duties and taxes at importation.

41. The trade facilitation role notably includes the collection of trade information for governments, traders and other interested parties and ensuring a fast and efficient processing of the customs clearance procedure.[6] The border protection role has increased in the last decades given the increasingly important role of customs authorities in supply chain safety and security. This border protection role notably includes the detection and prevention of the unlawful movement of a wide range of prohibited, restricted or regulated goods, such as illicit drugs, weapons, counterfeit goods and goods of consumer safety concern, terrorist material, illegal movement of money and products threatening the biosecurity. Although they still have an important tax collection role to play, the role of the customs authorities in the collection of import duties has become less prominent over time, as trade liberalisation has led to the progressive reduction of these duties. Notwithstanding this diminishing role in tax collection, and regardless of the models used for the collection of duties and taxes at importation, customs authorities will continue to play its crucial role in border protection and in the safety and security risk assessment. This role is designed and carried out independently from tax considerations and it remains further outside the scope of this report.

42. Customs authorities' role with regard to tax collection includes ensuring the correct assessment, reporting and payment of customs duties, excise, VAT/GST and other possible taxes payable on imported goods.

43. Unlike the border protection role, the efficiency of the tax collection activity is often measured by comparing the potential tax revenue with the cost of collection at the border. Most countries operate a *de minimis* threshold for customs duties, which is regulated by the WCO's Revised Kyoto Convention (RKC – see Box C.1. above). While this rule is obligatory for Contracting Parties to the RKC, no minimum standard is prescribed. The scope of this obligation will be examined by the WCO in light of e-commerce developments and the work being done by the OECD on alternate collection models. Although both the customs duties and the import VAT/GST are generally collected by customs authorities, the customs duties relief threshold is generally higher than the VAT/GST exemption threshold (e.g. EUR 150 for the customs duties relief in the European Union against EUR 10-22 for the EU's VAT relief – see also Appendix C.A to this report).

44. Taxes, excise and customs duties are most often collected by the customs authorities at the time of importation or of clearance of customs duties. Customs authorities collect the taxes on behalf of tax administrations and according to the tax rules in place. Appropriate assessment, collection and control require close co-operation between tax and customs authorities. The customs clearance procedures vary according to the value of the goods and the transporter (express carrier or postal operator) that is used to convey the consignments. These are summarised in Table C.1.

Table C.1. **Customs and VAT/GST clearance procedures (for goods not submitted to other specific duties such as excise)**

Value	VAT/GST	Customs declaration	
		Postal service (under the UPU)	Courier firms
Below VAT/GST and customs thresholds	• No VAT/GST • No customs duties	Declaration CN 22/CN23	Simplified declaration
Above VAT/GST threshold (if lower than customs threshold)	• VAT/GST payable • No customs duties	Declaration CN 22/CN23	Full or simplified declaration
Above customs and VAT/GST thresholds	• VAT/GST payable • Customs duties payable	Declaration CN22 or CN23 (depending on the value) or full/ simplified declaration (depending on the amount and the country considered)	Full or simplified declaration

Note: This table is partly based on data provided by the report prepared for the European Commission "Assessment of the application and the impact of the VAT exemption for importation of small consignment" http://ec.europa.eu/taxation_customs/taxation/vat/key_documents/reports_published/index_en.htm.

45. Over recent years, the electronic processing of imports in particular in the express carrier environment has increasingly helped streamline the customs processes in various jurisdictions so that these processes can be relatively fast. The transition towards electronic processing of imports is also high on the agenda within the postal environment. The UPU recently amended its Convention to allow and encourage countries to replace paper forms with electronic data provision,[7] preparing the ground for advanced electronic submission of data (see Section C.2.2.4.2.). Also The European Union has launched a multi-annual strategic plan (2016-2020) for the computerisation of customs[8] in the context of the implementation of the new Union Customs Code that will become applicable from 1 May 2016. The objective is to allow for the use of electronic declarations and the pre-arrival provision of information to customs authorities in order to streamline the customs process. Although these improvements primarily target the safety and security needs, customs and tax authorities may use this data collection process to streamline the collection of duties and taxes. It must be noted, however, that it will most likely take several years before the transition to electronic processing of imports will be completed worldwide.

C.2.3. The importance of information

46. The information flow between the stakeholders and its capture by the customs or tax authorities is of paramount importance for the efficient and effective collection and remittance of taxes at importation. When goods are sold in the e-commerce context, the vendor and purchaser are the only stakeholders with full knowledge of the description of the goods and the price paid for their acquisition. The transporter may have some or all the information, particularly where it processes the customs clearance in the country of destination. However, the transporter may not be aware of any possible undervaluation or mis-description of the goods by the vendor. Some information is also collected by e-commerce platforms, when they are used as an intermediary in the transaction. The payment intermediary collects some information of the sale, essentially the price paid, the identity of the payer and the payee, but not the description or physical movement of the goods. Table C.2 provides an overview of the minimum information that is typically available to each stakeholder in the supply chain of imports of low value goods. Stakeholders have generally developed sophisticated IT systems for collecting, processing and storing the necessary business information and any change in

the tax collection method would require adjustments to such systems, which would inevitably have a cost. The availability of the necessary data for the various stakeholders and its impact on the possible role of these stakeholders in collecting the import VAT/GST is considered in further detail in the assessment of the possible models for collecting VAT/GST on low value imports (see Section C.3 below).

Table C.2. **Minimum information available to each stakeholder in the supply chain**

Stakeholder	Nature of the goods	Value	Country of destination	Time of import/ delivery	Transportation data	Taxes and duties (incl. thresholds)
Purchaser	Yes	Yes	Yes	Yes	Maybe	Maybe
Vendor	Yes	Yes	Yes	Maybe	Yes	Maybe
Transparent e-commerce platform	Some	Yes	Maybe	Maybe	Maybe	Some/Maybe
Express carrier	Yes	Yes	Yes	Yes	Yes	Yes
Postal operator	Maybe	Maybe	Yes	Yes	Yes	Yes
Financial intermediary	No	Yes	Maybe	No	No	No

C.3. Key features and assessment of the options for collecting VAT/GST on imports of low value goods

C.3.1. Introduction

47. The taxation of imports of low value goods creates pressure points for all business stakeholders involved in the supply chain. Key pressure points include the collection and storage of timely and reliable data to be transmitted to the customs and tax authorities; the development and management of IT systems to verify and manage the information flows between the various stakeholders and its transmission to tax and customs authorities; and managing the liability for completing the correct tax and customs processes and for remitting the duties and taxes at importation. A key challenge for both administrations and stakeholders in relation to the imports of low value goods is the different process for the collection of duties and taxes on importation: whereas the VAT/GST on domestic sales is simply declared and remitted periodically on the basis of monthly or quarterly returns, the declaration and payment of such taxes on imports must often be done individually for each item imported. This places considerable pressures on all stakeholders involved in remitting and collecting such taxes on importation.

48. This section explores the main options that are currently available for collecting the VAT/GST on the import of low value goods and assesses the likely performance in light of a set of evaluation criteria (described in Section C.3.2 below).

49. Although this report does not look into the safety and security aspects, these will continue to play an important role and none of the options considered should imply a degradation of the important role customs authorities play in this area.

50. Based on the available know-how and expertise with respect to low value import relief regimes and the possible reform of such regimes, four broad models were identified for collecting VAT/GST on low value imports. The distinction between these collection

models is essentially based on the person liable to account for the VAT/GST. These models are:

1. the Traditional Collection model;
2. the Purchaser Collection model;
3. the Vendor Collection model; and
4. the Intermediary Collection model.

51. The Traditional Collection model is the model that is generally applied currently for the collection of duties and taxes at importation, and that is often combined with a VAT/GST exemption for imports of low value goods. The other three models present possible alternative approaches for a more efficient collection of VAT/GST on the importation on low value goods, which could allow countries to reduce or remove the VAT/GST exemption thresholds for the importation of these goods.

C.3.2. Method for assessing the likely performance of the VAT/GST collection models

52. The options (collection models) examined in this report are assessed according to an evaluation framework based on the Ottawa taxation framework.[9] Under this evaluation framework, the performance of the collection models was tested against the following criteria:

- **Neutrality**: Taxpayers in similar situations carrying out similar transactions should be subject to similar levels of taxation;
- **Efficiency of compliance and administration**: Compliance costs for taxpayers and administrative costs for tax authorities should be minimised as far as possible;
- **Certainty and simplicity**: The tax and duty rules should be clear and simple to understand, so that taxpayers can anticipate the tax/duty consequences in advance of the transaction, including knowing when, where and how the tax/duty is to be accounted for;
- **Effectiveness**: The reduction/removal of the exemption threshold so that the right amount of tax is collected in the right place (i.e. country of importation where the goods are consumed);
- **Fairness**: The potential for tax evasion and avoidance (e.g. undervaluation and mis-description) should be minimised (while keeping counteracting measures proportionate to the risks involved);
- **Flexibility**: The systems for the taxation should be flexible and dynamic to ensure that they keep pace with technological and commercial developments.

53. In addition to the assessment provided under Section C.3.3 below, "Test cards" were compiled, outlining the advantages and disadvantages for each of the collection models with a high, medium or low score for each of the evaluation criteria. These test cards are in the Appendix C.A to this report.

54. The description of each separate model under Section C.3.3 below does not suggest that models should be considered in isolation from each other. Such models can be combined to obtain the appropriate result. For instance, an optional Vendor Collection could be combined with an Intermediary Collection model (to reduce compliance costs for small and medium size businesses) and traditional customs clearance procedures as a fall-back rule.

C.3.3. Assessment of the collection models

C.3.3.1. The Traditional Collection model

55. Under the Traditional Collection model, the customs authorities generally determine the duties and taxes payable on each individual consignment of goods on the basis of the import customs declaration. In principle, the VAT/GST on imports is collected at the same time as the customs duties before the goods are released from customs control. Many countries however do not apply this model to imports of low value goods: they treat these imports as VAT/GST-exempt based on the consideration that the administrative costs of identifying and collecting revenue (including costs associated with risk screening) under this model are likely to outweigh the revenue gained with the revenue collected.

56. The operation of the Traditional Collection model is illustrated in Figure C.2. The import VAT/GST is generally charged on the basis of the customs value, to which certain elements may be added such as costs of transport and other ancillary costs, and duties (though duties will generally not be collected on imports of low value goods sold online, as these are generally below the dutiable threshold). The person designated as the declarant/consignee/importer of record on the import declaration is generally liable to account for the VAT/GST on the import to the customs authority. This traditional approach targets the first taxing point within the border control, as illustrated in the flow chart below.

Figure C.2. **Traditional Collection Model**

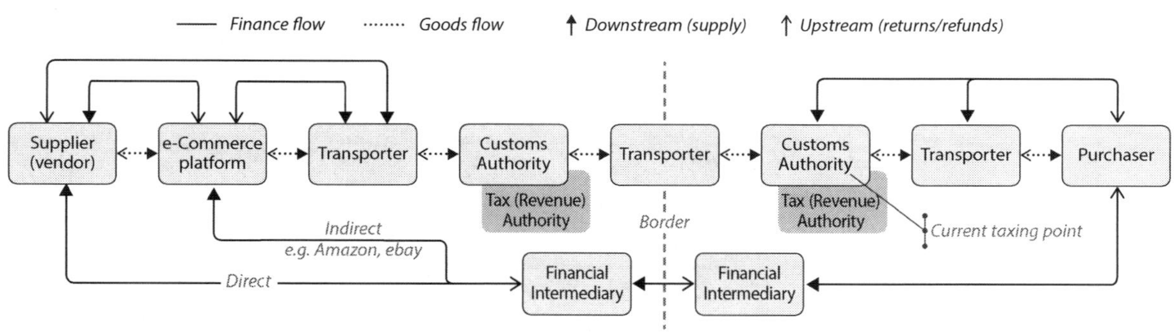

57. When goods are imported through express carriers, the relevant data and scanned documents are most often transmitted in electronic format to the customs authorities in the country of export and in the country of destination for customs clearance. This system allows the customs authorities at destination to obtain information prior to the arrival of a shipment in the country (see Section C.2.2.4.1 above). Thanks to the electronic processing, in particular pre-arrival processing and risk assessment implemented by many administrations, this advance cargo information complemented with advance payment of duties and taxes allows these to be cleared immediately on arrival without being stopped at the border for examination or assessment.

58. The situation is different in the postal environment. This process is still predominantly paper based and relies primarily on the sender in a third country to provide the correct data (see Section C.2.2.4.2 above). In the absence of electronic data transmission systems, the importation through postal operators typically requires that each individual consignment is stopped at the border so that the necessary information to assess the tax implications can be captured, liabilities can then be established and the appropriate process to ensure

the payment of duties and taxes be made. Processing and controlling these transactions is difficult and labour intensive, as relevant customs authorities need to handle each package manually. This is increasingly difficult to achieve in practice for each individual parcel that is imported through the postal chain, particularly now that the volume of such goods has increased massively as a result of the strong growth of Internet shopping.

59. Consignments, in many cases, are not released to the consignee until the liabilities of taxes and/or duties are discharged. Consignments for which established liabilities of taxes or duties have not been paid must generally be returned to the consignor. They may also be considered "abandoned" or even be destroyed in certain cases.

60. The burdens and the costs associated with paper and manual processing of imports of low value goods and the low revenue at stake were the main motivations for the introduction of VAT/GST relief regimes for such imports by countries around the world.

61. However, advances in technology have created opportunities for tax authorities and businesses to improve the efficiency of tax collection on imports of low value goods. Over recent years, electronic processing of imports in the express carriers environment has helped streamline the customs processes in various jurisdictions so that customs processes can be completed quicker at lower cost. In the international postal environment, electronic systems that are being developed for safety and security purposes could also be used in the future for tax purposes (see Section C.2.2.6 above). An increased take-up of electronic declarations and the pre-arrival provision of such information would produce cost savings and improve the efficiency of tax collection at the border, though ensuring the proper quality of data would remain a challenge.

62. Further VAT/GST rates and tariff simplifications for the declaration of goods could also be considered, subject to national legislation, to ease the tax assessment and control at the border and minimise the potential for disputes.

63. The assessment of the Traditional Collection model shows that this model, based on individual control of each consignment at the border with information provided on paper forms and tax liabilities established at the time of arrival in the country, is no longer adapted to the e-commerce environment.

64. On the other hand, new electronic processes developed in the express carriers' environment provide opportunities for substantial efficiency gains (see Section C.2.2.4.1). The consistent use of such electronic pre-arrival declaration and assessment systems would improve the efficiency of compliance and administration, certainty and simplicity for the vendors (although with an associated cost) and provide flexible, market-based solutions.

65. A wide application of those new electronic processes, including in the postal environment, might allow the reduction or removal of the current *de minimis* thresholds and provide greater neutrality to the system. However, it may take considerable time before such electronic processes be implemented in the postal environment globally.

C.3.3.2. The Purchaser Collection model

66. Under the Purchaser Collection model, the purchaser would be required to self-assess and pay the VAT/GST on its purchases of low value goods. Standard customs procedures would apply for goods above the *de minimis* customs value.

67. Three main options can be distinguished. The first two options are "pre-release" options whereas the third option is a "post-release" approach:

- Purchaser pre-registration, whereby the purchaser pre-registers its details with customs authorities and uses an identifier through the web store checkout process, with voluntary self-assessment and payment of tax at that point to authorities or at the point of importation when this could be reconciled to the item;
- Real-time purchaser self-assessment on delivery, whereby the purchaser is required to self-assess its own liability and pay to a delegated authority at the time of release of the goods;
- Post-release purchaser self-assessment, whereby the purchaser is required to periodically or annually account for the tax through a reporting mechanism such as a VAT/GST declaration or the income tax return.

68. This model targets the very end of the chain, i.e. the purchaser, as illustrated below.

Figure C.3. **Purchaser Collection Model**

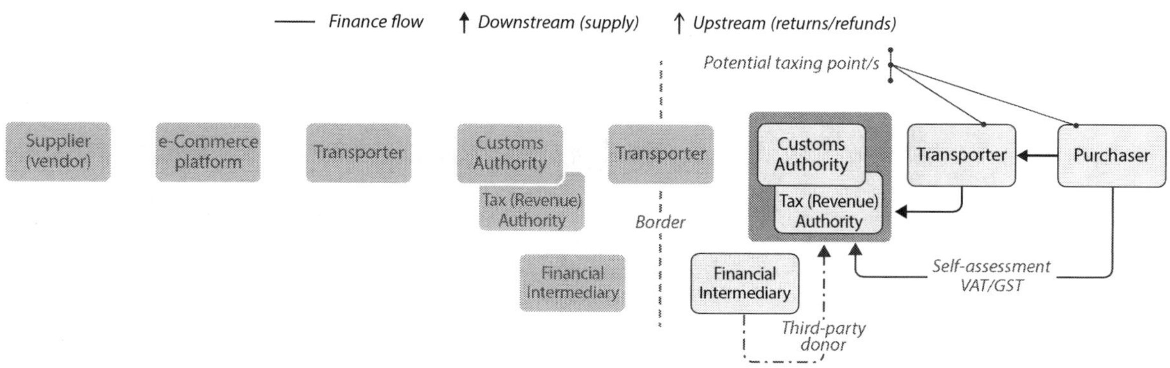

69. A major disadvantage of all the elements of this model is that they are based on self-compliance. The model notably relies on the purchaser to know the exact value for the calculation of the VAT/GST liability. There is a high likelihood that purchasers either under-report or not comply if there is no consequence visible to them for doing so. Additionally, this model requires that all the customers have complete information and knowledge about the applicable VAT/GST regime (tax base and rates), which may often not be the case.

70. From a customs and tax administration perspective, this approach would most likely require the development and implementation of an entirely new administrative process and information technology system. There may be some limited ability for customs or tax authorities to use third party data to risk-assess consignees against actual and projected liabilities through tax gap analysis. This model would increase the administrative burden considerably and may even be impossible to implement in practice without a *de minimis* threshold, as it would effectively require monitoring of almost anyone who can make a purchase online.

C.3.3.3. The Vendor Collection model

71. Under a Vendor Collection model, the obligation to collect and remit the VAT/GST relating to imports of low value goods would be on the non-resident vendor.[10] The non-resident vendors would be required to register for VAT/GST in the destination jurisdiction and remit the VAT/GST there (as a registered non-resident vendor).

72. Vendors can be assumed to know or to be able to know with reasonable certainty the information that is required for a proper collection and remittance of the VAT/GST on imports of low value goods, i.e. the description of the goods, the jurisdiction to which the goods are to be sent, the value of the goods including any transport and postal costs and, if any, customs duties where they are included in the VAT/GST base.

73. Figure C.4 illustrates the possible operation of this model. This figure shows that various options could be available with respect to the person remitting the tax on importation and with respect to the time when the tax is collected.

Figure C.4. **Vendor Collection Model**

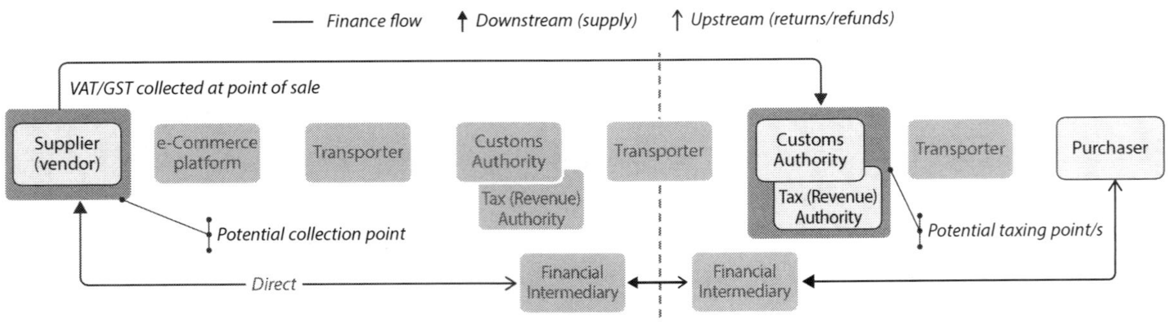

74. Under the Vendor Collection model, the vendor would be liable to account for the VAT/GST on the imported goods. The tax and customs regimes in the jurisdiction of import must be aligned to avoid multiple taxable events and double taxation or unintended non-taxation; and to ensure consistency regarding the time at which the VAT/GST is due. Appropriate synergies should also be ensured between vendors and intermediaries that may possibly intervene in the sales and delivery process (transparent e-commerce platform, transporter), to properly identify the party that is liable for the customs clearance and for the remittance of import VAT/GST and to identify the goods on which import VAT/GST has been paid.

75. The VAT/GST would be collected at the point of sale and these taxes would be included in the purchase price of the items sold. The remittance of VAT/GST to the tax authorities by the vendor could be at a time before, during or after the point of importation. To ease cost of compliance pressures on the vendor, consideration could be given to only require submission of periodic returns and remittance of the VAT/GST collected during the reference period. No VAT/GST would then need to be collected at the border for consignments that are identified as being sent by a registered non-resident vendor. In case of refunds of items, an additional simplification could be implemented to allow the vendor to make the associated adjustments of VAT/GST, so that the purchaser needs only deal with the vendor. There may be some minor differential approaches under VAT/GST between jurisdictions to achieve the legal framework for this outcome but the practical application could be largely indistinguishable for most transactions.

76. A Vendor Collection regime could allow jurisdictions to remove their VAT/GST relief regimes for low value imports, lower the exemption threshold or, if the supply is taxed rather than the importation, zero-rate the applicable import threshold. Alternatively, it could also allow them to replace a *de minimis* threshold that is calculated per imported item by a threshold that is calculated at the level of the vendor, although the jurisdictions of

importation may have to track and monitor whether or not foreign vendors have exceeded their threshold.

77. A key challenge of the Vendor Collection model is to ensure compliance by non-resident vendors. This model may increase the revenue risks for tax authorities given that it may move away from the traditional customs process of collecting the VAT/GST at the current point of entry, i.e. at the border.[11] To address this challenge, a two-pronged approach could be adopted whereby, on one hand, compliance is facilitated and encouraged by simplifying procedures and providing additional incentives for vendors to comply and, on the other hand, creating a deterrent for non-compliance through the implementation of a fall-back rule whereby goods for which no VAT/GST has been accounted for under the Vendor Collection model are stopped at the border and are processed under the Traditional Collection models. Rules could also be implemented to deter misreporting or underreporting. The enforcement of compliance under the Vendor Collection model would be further supported through enhanced international administrative co-operation (see Section C.4 below).

78. The following paragraphs look in some further detail at the possible options for facilitating and encouraging compliance by non-resident vendors. The VAT/GST simplified procedures proposed below do not apply to safety and security customs procedures, which will continue to apply in every circumstance.

C.3.3.3.1. Simplified VAT/GST registration and compliance regime

79. Jurisdictions should consider implementing a simplified VAT/GST registration and compliance regime to facilitate compliance for non-resident vendors under a Vendor Collection model. Simplification may be particularly important to facilitate compliance for vendors faced with obligations in multiple jurisdictions. Where compliance procedures are too complex, their application for non-resident vendors may lead to non-compliance or to certain suppliers declining to serve customers in certain jurisdictions.

80. Under such a simplified registration and compliance regime, the VAT/GST compliance obligations in the jurisdiction of importation could be limited to what is strictly necessary for the effective collection of the tax, without prejudice to the other customs obligations, in particular with regard to safety and security. It could be designed and operated along the same principles as the simplified compliance and registration regime that is suggested in the context of the OECD International VAT/GST Guidelines on business-to-consumer supplies of services and intangibles (B2C Guidelines). When a vendor supplies both goods and services into a particular jurisdiction, the registration system applied under the B2C Guidelines could be used for both kinds of supplies. This would reduce the administrative and compliance costs of the vendor registration.

81. The simplest way to engage with tax administrations from a remote location is most likely through electronic processes. Technology can be used to develop a range of electronic services to support compliance and administration processes, in particular those concerned with registration, tax returns and declarations and payment of the tax liabilities. Applied effectively, these technologies can deliver considerable benefits both to tax administrations and taxpayers (e.g. lower compliance and administrative costs and faster and more accessible services for taxpayers).

82. The simplified registration and compliance regime for low value imports could be operated separately from the traditional registration and compliance regime, without the same rights (e.g. input tax recovery) and obligations (e.g. full reporting) as a traditional

regime. The non-resident vendor could be required to remit the tax online when he receives payment from the customer or, more simply, to submit periodic online returns and remit the VAT/GST collected during the reference period. In order to avoid fraud, these vendors would not be allowed to claim input tax deductions on such VAT/GST returns, but only under the traditional refund mechanisms available to non-residents. Interaction with and impact on other systems operating in the customs environment would need to be considered and addressed.

83. Within regional organisations or customs unions, the registration of the vendor may be further facilitated by a registration in only one member country. Under such a "One Stop Shop" approach (OSS), non-resident vendors of low-value goods register in one member country and remit the tax there. This member country transfers the tax to the appropriate country (e.g. the country of final destination of the imported item). Such an OSS has been operated in the European Union since 2003 with respect to B2C supplies of e-services and telecommunication, radio and television broadcasting services supplied by non-EU suppliers.[12]

84. New technologies can be employed to facilitate the processing of the low value goods that are imported under the simplified registration and compliance regime at the border. Vendors, transporters, customs and revenue authorities may jointly identify how this can work best with existing reporting systems so that there is alignment with current business cross-border practice. Bar code identification, Unique Consignment Reference number (UCR) and Radio Frequency Identification (RFID) could be used to complement current systems in the identification of the registered vendors and to verify the proper collection of the import VAT/GST on these imports. Such electronic processes would reduce delays and costs along the supply chain, in particular if they are employed consistently across countries. They could notably support the implementation of a fast-track regime for processing the low value imports for which import VAT/GST is paid under the Vendor Collection model. These new technologies could also be used to improve and accelerate the safety and security controls made by the customs authorities and to reinforce international administrative co-operation.

C.3.3.3.2. Simplified VAT/GST registration and compliance regime with fast-track tax processing

85. One way to further limit risks of non-compliance under the Vendor Collection model is to present it as an option to non-resident vendors and to incentivise the use of this option by providing fast-track processing of goods to vendors who account for the VAT/GST under the Vendor Collection model in the country of importation. As speed of delivery is a crucial factor for online sales, such a fast-track procedure can provide an incentive for non-resident vendors to opt for the Vendor Collection model and to comply with it. Imports from vendors that do not register for VAT/GST or that do not comply with the Vendor Collection regime would be subject to the Traditional Collection model process. Depending on their cost and availability, a number of IT tools could be used by tax administrations to verify the appropriate use of the fast track by the vendors.

86. Such a fast-track process would require the implementation of alternative and secure methods for identification of the relevant goods (i.e. goods for which VAT/GST has already been accounted for by the vendor or that have been declared by the vendor in a periodic return). These methods may include, for instance the use of bar codes, stickers, RFID, a specific classification by the UPU (since the UPU identifies and codifies item attributes), WCO Unique Consignment Reference Number (UCR), etc.

C.3.3.3.3. Vendor collection under a bulk-shipper scheme

87. Under a bulk-shipper scheme, vendors would lodge only one import declaration for all low-value consignments that are shipped together instead of having to submit import declarations for each imported item. Under this model, the consignor would make one single taxable importation, which would be taxable even if, taken separately, the imported goods would be below a *de minimis* threshold. Processing charges by customs and intermediaries are minimised given that only one import declaration would be submitted as opposed to many declarations for each individual item (although information for each shipment may still be requested for safety and security purposes). A bulk-shipper scheme could operate separately from a direct VAT/GST registration and be exclusive of it. Any bulk shipper scheme should be consistent with other taxes and duties requirements, including for shipments consisting of products possibly subject to different VAT/GST rates.

C.3.3.3.4. Overall assessment of the Vendor Collection model

88. The application of a Vendor Collection model could improve the efficiency of the collection of VAT/GST on the import of low value goods and thus create opportunities for governments to remove or reduce import VAT/GST exemption thresholds if they wish to do so.[13] This model places additional administrative and compliance costs on tax authorities and vendors alike but these costs can be minimised through some form of simplified registration and compliance regimes (it should be noted that customs and security procedures will continue to apply). In addition to this, the application of fast track processing and "One Stop Shop" regimes at regional/national level could facilitate tax compliance obligations by non-resident vendors, including small and medium size vendors.

89. The application of a Vendor Collection model would require changes to the tax administration and customs procedures in order to ensure the proper registration and management of non-resident vendors, including the assessment and collection of the import VAT/GST. This would require robust and capable IT systems to be in place in order to capture and manage the tax collection. Consideration should also be given to introducing measures that will mitigate double taxation and unintended non-taxation that may arise from differences in tax and customs rules. Voluntary registration of non-resident vendors involves specific non-compliance risks that would need to be addressed by simplification measures but also with appropriate risk assessment and robust international administrative co-operation.

90. The Vendor Collection model could be made optional and could be combined with alternative models such as the Traditional Collection model (as a fall-back) and with the use of intermediaries (see Section C.3.3.4 below).

C.3.3.4. The Intermediary Collection model

91. Under this approach, the liability to remit the VAT/GST on the imported goods in the jurisdiction of importation is transferred from the non-resident vendor onto particular intermediaries[14] in the supply chain. Intermediaries may often be better placed to remit the tax on imports in the jurisdiction of importation. The intermediaries' understanding of local language and of tax rules and procedures could provide benefits to both tax authorities and vendors, particularly to small and medium enterprises. Under the Intermediary Collection model, consideration needs to be given to intermediaries' ability to collect and remit the tax prior to the importation, rather than at the time of importation (in which case their intervention may not increase the efficiency of the collection of import VAT/GST). Simplified registration and compliance regimes such as those possibly applicable to non-resident vendors

under the Vendor Collection model (see Section C.3.3.3 above) could also be considered under the Intermediary Collection model. Managing taxes may require changes in intermediaries' data collection process, both in terms of quantity and quality of data. There is also a risk element associated with potential tax liability and the respective responsibilities of the vendor and the intermediaries in this regard should be clearly established. Any proposed model that would imply a distinct VAT/GST collection system from the customs process should ensure consistency between both processes to avoid double or unintended non-taxation.

92. This approach may rely on different types of intermediaries: transporters, commercial agents such as transparent e-commerce platforms and financial intermediaries. Commercial agents can represent vendors and facilitate accurate VAT/GST collection at the point of sale.

93. Figure C.5 illustrates the possible operation of the Intermediary Collection model.

Figure C.5. **Intermediary Collection Model**

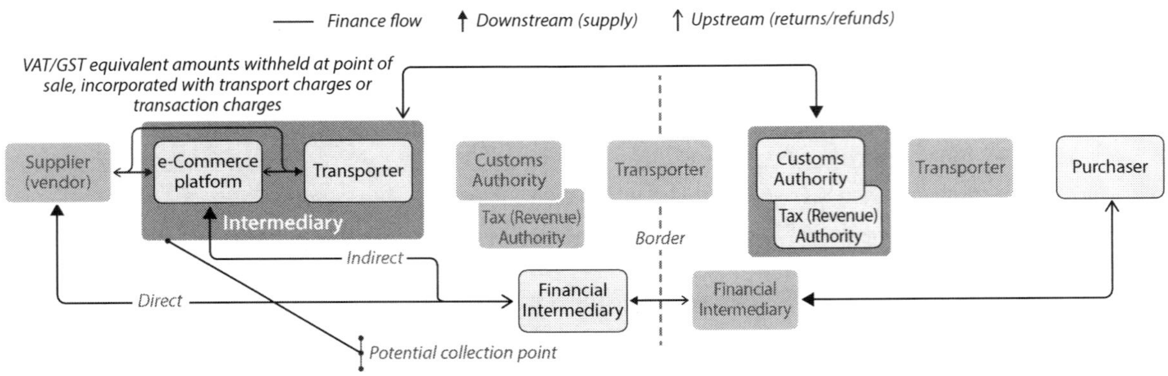

C.3.3.4.1. Collection by the postal operators

94. Postal operators may intervene as intermediaries both in the exporting and importing country, as the liability to account for the VAT/GST may be transferred from the postal operator in the exporting jurisdiction to the postal operator in the jurisdiction of importation. The postal operators already collect some information from the sender in the jurisdiction of origin of the goods and this information is passed on to the postal operator in the jurisdiction of destination. The information (sender, addressee, description of the goods, the value and whether they are gifts or commercial items) is currently transmitted on paper forms attached to the goods (see Section C.2.2.4.2 above).

95. The intervention of postal operators as intermediaries in the process of collecting VAT/GST on low-value imports would need to be supported by the use of electronic collection and transmission processes. This could be provided by the use of Electronic Postal Declarations (EPD). This is an electronic solution for the customs declaration (an "electronic CN 23") for goods moved by the postal services that is being developed by the UPU and the WCO based on already developed joint messaging standards. The UPU's Customs Declaration System (CDS) is already being implemented/piloted by some countries e.g. by Canada.[15] Also the EU is working on the introduction of a simplified declaration for postal items and on the use electronic data capture in this context. This is an important part of the delivery of upcoming changes in the European Union Customs Code.[16] This mechanism may notably facilitate the automatic calculation of tax liabilities and the collection of the tax at importation of electronically declared goods of any value. As a result, the administrative burdens of collecting

the tax for postal operators and governments would be minimised. This would place postal imports on an equal footing with express and freight goods where electronic procedures already exist. However, these electronic processes are still under development and may only be available in the medium term.

96. In the current situation, where information is mostly collected and transmitted on paper forms, the intervention of postal operators in the VAT/GST collection on imports of low value goods would not provide a reliable solution.

C.3.3.4.2. Collection by express carriers

97. Express carriers already play an important role in the assessment and collection of taxes and duties on the importation of low value goods (see Section C.2.2.4.1 above). They could therefore be eligible as intermediaries with a liability to account for VAT/GST at importation. They can generally be expected to know the information that is needed to support the collection of the VAT/GST (based on the information provided by the vendor) on the imports of low value goods in the jurisdiction of importation. Fast and easy tax and customs processes should be in place for compensating the additional burden of accounting for VAT/GST on low value goods.

98. The VAT/GST collection and remittance by express carriers is already common practice for goods above the VAT/GST relief threshold and for other taxes and duties. The difference between the current system and the possible new model to be applied to low value goods would be the development of a specific VAT/GST declaration and collection system for the payment of VAT/GST on the import of low value goods. This would allow for a separate VAT/GST treatment of such low value imports.

C.3.3.4.3. Collection by transparent e-commerce platforms and other commercial agents that provide a trading framework for vendors

99. Under this approach, transparent e-commerce platforms that provide a trading framework for vendors but that are not parties to the commercial transaction between the vendor and the purchaser (see Section C.2.2.3 above), would remit the VAT/GST on the low value imports in the jurisdiction of importation. Based on the contract with the vendor, such e-commerce platforms can perform a role similar to a tax representative that is liable to remit the VAT/GST to the jurisdiction of importation on behalf of the vendor. Those e-commerce platforms can have access to the information that is needed to support the collection of the VAT/GST (location of the vendor, of the purchaser, description of the goods and their value), based on the information provided by the vendor.

100. Some of the biggest marketplaces already provide such tax compliance services to their vendors. One of the market leaders provides a "global shipping programme", whereby it collects from the purchaser *(1)* the price of the item and remits it to the seller, and *(2)* the international shipping costs and any import VAT/GST and other duties and remits it to the international shipping provider (who presumably remits the tax to the tax authorities in the jurisdiction of importation). Marketplaces will generally offer such services against a fee.

101. For e-commerce platforms to play a role in the tax collection and compliance process, they would need to have appropriate business and IT processes in place. For example, the purchaser's address collected by the platform and transferred to the merchant for shipment should be verified as well as the applicable tax treatment in the country of destination. This also requires the transmission of data to the customs or tax authorities. Also the merchant's status in each destination country should be taken into account.

Finally, the platform will need to transmit the relevant information to the customs and/or tax authorities and administrative obligations should be completed for the correct assessment and payment of the tax. The development and maintenance of such appropriate business and IT system has obviously a cost for the e-commerce platform. Given the constant development of e-marketplaces, it may well be that such intermediaries may include such tax compliance services in their service offering to vendors.

102. The VAT/GST collection and remittance by transparent e-commerce platforms for imports of low value goods would provide greater neutrality to the system but may involve additional costs when IT systems and processes need to be adjusted. Appropriate systems should be in place to encourage compliance (similar to those offered to the vendors in the Vendor Collection model) and customs procedures should be adjusted accordingly. Just as for the Vendor Collection model, the risks for non-compliance by non-resident e-commerce platforms may be addressed by the implementation of a fall-back rule whereby goods for which no VAT/GST has been accounted for under the Intermediary Collection model are stopped at the border and are processed under the Traditional Collection model. Tax administrations' capacity to enforce compliance would need to be reinforced through enhanced international administrative cooperation (see Section C.4 below).

C.3.3.4.4. Collection by financial intermediaries

103. During the payment process, financial intermediaries collect and store data such as the vendor and the purchaser account information (name, address, bank details). Information collected by traditional financial institutions, such as retail banks and credit card companies, will generally be limited to what is necessary to validate the card's authenticity and/or confirm that sufficient funds are available on the purchaser's account to pay for the purchase. Information collected will generally not include the nature of the transaction (sale of goods or of services, other transfers), the nature of the goods being sold, the place where they are delivered or their tax treatment. Emerging new payment intermediaries may not collect more information, unless they are strongly connected to the vendor and have access to the sale data.

104. For the payment provider to assume the liability for remitting the VAT/GST on low value imports from online sales, a number of practical and legal conditions should be met: the payment provider should be able to collect from the vendor or from the purchaser the required information for collecting and remitting the appropriate amount of tax in the jurisdiction of importation and the legal arrangements should be in place to allow the communication of the information to the tax authorities. The cost of establishing and managing these embedded tax features in the payment system would have to be recovered from the vendor or from the purchaser. In addition, legislation, backed by appropriate regulation, would be required to ensure compliance.

105. The VAT/GST collection and remittance by financial intermediaries would need deep changes in the data collection and processing systems, since these intermediaries currently do not collect the relevant information for the assessment and payment of the VAT/GST and do not have systems in place to support the remittance of the tax in the jurisdictions of importation. It is therefore unlikely that financial intermediaries could play a role in a more efficient collection of VAT/GST on imports of low value goods.

C.4. Supporting enforcement through enhanced mutual administrative cooperation

106. It is recognised that any reform to improve the efficiency of the collection of VAT/GST on low value imports will need to be complemented with enhanced administrative co-operation between tax authorities to enforce compliance. This co-operation should include the exchange of information, which would notably be helpful for identifying vendors and purchasers, for monitoring the value of sales/imports and for assessing whether the proper amounts of VAT/GST have been collected from purchasers and remitted to the tax authorities in the jurisdiction of importation.

107. WP9 is developing work on the enhanced administrative co-operation and exchange of information in the context of its work on the International VAT/GST Guidelines. The outcome of this work will also be relevant for the operation of regimes for collecting VAT/GST on the importation of low value goods. It will notably consider how administrative co-operation and exchange of information arrangements in the customs area could support the enforcement of regimes for collecting the import VAT/GST on low-value goods. The WCO has developed a number of instruments and tools supporting exchange of information (e.g. the Nairobi Convention, the Model Bilateral Agreement on Mutual Assistance and the Globally Networked Customs (GNC)). Based on these instruments, customs administrations have entered into bilateral or multilateral agreements/arrangements for the exchange of information.

C.5. Summary assessment of the collection models

108. Section C.3 of this report presents four possible models for collecting the VAT/GST on imports of low value goods and discusses their advantages and disadvantages, their limits and the requirements for their successful application in practice. The initial analysis of these models is supported by "test cards" in the Appendix C.A to this report, which show the outcome of the assessment of likely performance of these models against a set of evaluation criteria based on the Ottawa framework principles.

109. The outcome of this assessment should be considered with caution since the performance of each model is likely to depend on its implementation in practice and on the specific economic, legal and administrative circumstances of the jurisdiction that implements the model. Moreover, it is most likely that the solution for a more efficient collection of VAT/GST on imports of low value goods lies in a combination of approaches rather than in the implementation of one single model. A detailed assessment should therefore look at the performance of various combinations of these models rather than at their performance in isolation. For example, a Vendor Collection model is likely to achieve proper compliance and administrative efficiency gains only if it is combined with a simplified registration and compliance regime. Models that provide for the assessment and payment of the VAT/GST prior to the customs declaration (such as the vendor or e-commerce platform models) would require the alignment of tax and customs rules to avoid double or unintended non-taxation. They would also require systems for ensuring the appropriate labelling of the taxed goods for the customs control and a fall-back rule for cases of non-compliance. Models relying on voluntary registration would also require appropriate risk assessment tools and international administrative co-operation to minimise the potential for evasion and avoidance.

110. The analysis presented in this report and in the Appendix C.A provides a high-level overview of the key potential strengths and weaknesses of the main available models for collecting the VAT/GST on the imports of low value goods. It is intended to assist governments and tax administrations in evaluating whether and to what extent the implementation of these

models could improve the efficiency of the collection of the VAT/GST on imports of low value goods to a level that is considered sufficient to reduce or remove the exemption threshold, should they wish to do so.

C.5.1. Traditional Collection model

111. The Traditional Collection model, where VAT/GST is assessed at the border for each imported low value good individually, is generally found not to be an efficient model for collecting the VAT/GST on imports of low value goods. This is certainly the case in the absence of electronic data transmission systems. The VAT/GST exemption thresholds for the import of low value goods, which are implemented as a consequence of the complexity of the Traditional Collection model, lead to growing VAT/GST revenue losses and increasing risks of unfair competition between domestic and non-resident vendors. These relief regimes are also increasingly vulnerable to fraud given the exponential growth of the volume of imports of low value goods and the practical impossibility of checking the value (above or below the exemption threshold) of each of the imported items. This results in a system where effectiveness is not ensured and where neutrality is challenged.

112. The efficiency of the Traditional Collection model may improve over time, as and when electronic pre-arrival declaration and tax assessment and payment systems are implemented worldwide to replace paper based and manual verification processes. These new electronic processes are already used in the express carriers' environment where they have resulted in considerable efficiency gains. The consistent use of such electronic systems would improve the efficiency of compliance and administration, certainty and simplicity for the vendors and provide flexible, market-based solutions. Their worldwide implementation might allow the removal of the current VAT/GST exemption thresholds and provide greater neutrality to the system. However, these systems are not yet available to process the import of the considerable numbers of low value goods that are moved by postal services. These electronic processes for the postal environment are still under development and may only be available in the medium term.

C.5.2. Purchaser Collection model

113. A model relying on the purchaser to self-assess and pay the VAT/GST on its imports of low value goods is not likely to provide a sufficiently robust solution for a more efficient collection of VAT/GST on the imports of low value goods. Although it could simplify the compliance process for vendors and could create a more neutral environment in theory, compliance levels are expected to be low while compliance burden for purchasers would be high and the administrative cost and complexity for customs and tax administrations would be considerable.

C.5.3. Vendor Collection model

114. A model requiring the non-resident vendors of low value goods to charge, collect and remit the VAT/GST on the imports of low value goods in the country of importation could improve the efficiency of the collection process and thus create opportunities for governments to remove or reduce import VAT/GST exemption thresholds. A Vendor Collection model would create additional burden for non-resident vendors, which can be mitigated by complementing it with simplified VAT/GST registration and compliance regimes and possible fast-track tax processing and bulk shipper schemes to support compliance. In addition, the implementation of this model would involve considerable systems changes and adjustment of

customs and tax processes to avoid double or unintended non-taxation. The implementation of appropriate risk assessment methods and the enhanced international and inter-agency (tax and customs administrations) co-operation would be required to support the compliance by non-resident vendors under this model.

C.5.4. The Intermediary Collection odel

115. A model where VAT/GST on imports of low value goods would be collected and remitted by intermediaries on behalf of non-resident vendors could improve the efficiency of the collection of VAT/GST on low value imports and thus create opportunities for governments to remove or reduce import VAT/GST exemption thresholds, assuming that such intermediaries would have the required information to assess and remit the right amount of taxes in the country of importation. The VAT/GST collection by intermediaries would involve minimal compliance burdens on vendors but would come at an additional cost that may be passed on to the purchaser. This model may be particularly effective when the VAT/GST is collected by intermediaries that have a presence in the country of importation (e.g. express carriers, postal operators and locally implemented e-commerce platforms). The intermediaries' understanding of local tax and customs rules and procedures could provide benefits to both vendors and tax administrations.

116. The following paragraphs look more specifically at the possible role of the main types of intermediaries that could intervene in the collection of VAT/GST on the imports of low value goods: the postal operators, the express carriers, the e-commerce platforms and the financial intermediaries.

117. In the postal environment, information is mostly collected and transmitted on paper forms and minimal data is collected from the other stakeholders. Against this background, most postal operators do not have the appropriate systems in place to manage the assessment and collection of VAT/GST on importation of low value goods. Electronic collection and transmission processes are being developed but the postal system would still require substantial adjustment to operate an efficient, effective and fair VAT/GST collection model.

118. In the express carriers environment, electronic data collection and transmission systems are most often already in place and VAT/GST collection and remittance to the tax authorities is also already common practice. A model whereby non-resident vendors rely on express carriers to collect and remit the VAT/GST on imports of low value goods provides an efficient and effective solution, provided it is combined with sufficiently simple compliance regimes and with fast-track processing. Given the existing commercial relationships between the express carriers and the vendors, such a model would provide certainty and fairness. It must be noted, however, that express carriers must rely in practice on the correctness of the information provided by the vendors for the assessment of the tax liability and the associated compliance obligations.

119. Transparent e-commerce platforms already have most of the information that would be needed for assessing the VAT/GST due in the country of importation of low value goods. Some of the leading marketplaces already provide tax compliance services to their vendors. A model where VAT/GST on imports of low value goods would be collected and remitted by these e-commerce platforms on behalf of non-resident vendors could provide an efficient and effective solution and thus create opportunities for governments to remove or reduce import VAT/GST exemption thresholds. However, many transparent e-commerce platforms would still need to develop and implement considerable systems changes to ensure appropriate levels of efficiency, certainty and effectiveness. Just as for express carriers,

simplified tax and customs procedures would be needed to ensure an efficient and effective collection and remittance of VAT/GST on the imports of low value goods. E-commerce platforms would also have to rely on information provided by the vendors for the assessment of the tax liability and the associated compliance obligations. When e-commerce platforms do not have a presence in the country of importation, risk assessment and simplification measures similar as those mentioned for the Vendor Collection model should be considered.

120. Financial intermediaries do not collect the relevant information for the assessment and payment of the VAT/GST and the development of a model relying on the payment system would involve deep changes in the data collection processes. It is therefore unlikely that financial intermediaries could play a role in a more efficient collection of VAT/GST on imports of low value goods.

C.6. Overall conclusion

121. The assessment of the models suggest that a range of possible approaches are available for increasing the efficiency of the collection of VAT/GST on low-value imports for countries to choose from, depending on national policy decisions and specific circumstances.

122. Jurisdictions could opt for a combination of models. For instance, an optional Vendor Collection model with a simplified registration and compliance regime could be combined with an Intermediary Collection model (which may notably allow small and medium size businesses to comply more easily). Both models could be combined with further simplification arrangements, such as fast-track processing and/or a bulk-shipper scheme. To increase compliance, these models could be combined with a fall-back rule whereby VAT/GST would be collected under the Traditional Collection model (possibly from the final consumer) e.g. if VAT/GST has not been paid either under the Vendor or Intermediary Collection models. Risks of undervaluation or mis-description by foreign vendors of imported goods should be considered for the assessment of the models or combination of models.

123. The implementation of these models or a combination of them allow jurisdictions to remove or lower the VAT/GST exemption thresholds, should they wish to do so.

124. It is recognised that any reform to improve the efficiency of the collection of VAT/GST on low value imports will need to be complemented with appropriate risk assessment and enhanced international administrative co-operation between tax authorities to enforce compliance.

Appendix C.A

Test cards for the analysis of the VAT/GST collection models

The findings in these tables are sensitive to the opinions of a sample of tax officials and businesses. They do not cover every possible element that might be required in order to fully assess the models considered. Therefore, the information that they include and the initial assessments made are not presented as, or intended to be, definitive.

A. Traditional collection model

	Ranking	Comment	Advantages	Disadvantages	Challenges
Neutrality	Low	The Traditional Collection model is generally combined with a low-value goods VAT/GST relief, which creates risks of competitive distortions in the domestic market.	Neutrality is advanced when electronic declaration and assessment procedures are in place that allow for the removal of the VAT/GST relief regimes and for a reasonably efficient collection of the VAT/GST on these imports.	Electronic declaration and assessment procedures are not generally implemented. Notably the movement of low value goods via postal services is still entirely paper based. The Traditional Collection model is therefore generally combined with a low-value goods VAT/GST relief, which creates risks of competitive distortions between domestic and non-resident vendors.	The distortive effect resulting from current VAT/GST thresholds has increased with the exponential development of e-commerce. The development of electronic declaration and assessment procedures may allow the removal of the VAT/GST relief regimes, but these procedures are not common practice. Particularly in the postal environment, the transition from paper based to electronic procedures is expected to take several years.
Efficiency of compliance and administration	Low	Paper-based procedures and separate treatment of each individual consignment create significant administrative and compliance costs. The development of electronic procedures may significantly reduce the administrative and compliance costs and speed up customs processes.	The current development of electronic declaration and assessment systems, in particular in the express carrier environment, leads to reasonably efficient procedures in certain countries/business models (primarily those that rely on express couriers for transport/delivery of the low value goods).	In the absence of electronic data transmission systems, the importation procedure requires that each individual consignment is stopped at the border for manual control of tax liabilities, involving slow and expensive processes. The use of intermediaries for completing procedures and paying VAT/GST at the border has a cost for the vendor/the purchaser.	Process efficiencies could be leveraged from the current approach, especially for consignment imported through international post. In particular, the postal operators in some countries are working together to drive the take up of electronic declarations for postal items.
Certainty and simplicity	Medium	Vendors are facing a plethora of customs processes and VAT/GST relief thresholds that exist globally.	In the express carriers environment, compliance services already exist that help vendors to cope with the various tax and customs obligations.	Pre-arrival information about the goods is limited particularly in the international postal environment. Unexpected charges for the purchaser when taxes and duties must be paid on the delivery of the good generate refusals of the consignment and possible abandonment of the goods. The lack of harmonisation of customs rules and procedures in each jurisdiction creates uncertainties for the stakeholders.	The consistent development of electronic processes for improving the flow of information between the stakeholders would improve the certainty and simplicity of the customs processes.
Effectiveness	Medium	The VAT/GST exemption thresholds for imports of low-value goods may be reduced or removed if appropriate and consistent electronic processes are implemented.	If electronic declaration and assessment systems are consistently used and appropriate data flows are ensured, the capacity of the system to collect the right amount of taxes at the right place would be considerably improved.	In the absence of appropriate electronic processes, the cost efficiency of traditional customs procedures does not allow the removal of the VAT/GST relief thresholds.	Techniques regarding the capture and exchange of information between the stakeholders are evolving fast. Customs authorities and postal operators need to move towards greater and more consistent use of new technologies.

A. Traditional collection model *(continued)*

	Ranking	Comment	Advantages	Disadvantages	Challenges
Fairness	Low			The Traditional Collection model is generally combined with a low-value goods VAT/GST relief, which are vulnerable to fraud through under declaration or mis-declaration. It is recognised that such risks of under declaration or mis-declaration may also exist in the absence of such exemptions.	Cooperation between customs and tax authorities and between countries may reduce the risk of non-compliance.
Flexibility	Medium	Flexibility has improved in the express carriers environment while progress is still to be made in the postal environment.	The electronic systems developed by express carriers are providing flexible solutions.	The paper based processes, which are still often applied, do not provide flexibility.	Electronic procedures are currently being developed at the level of Universal Postal Union (UPU), the World Customs Organisation (WCO) and the European Union (EU).

B. Purchaser collection model

	Ranking	Comment	Advantages	Disadvantages	Challenges
Neutrality	Low	Theoretically neutral as domestic sales and imports would be subject to the same level of taxation in the country of consumption. In practice, however, non-compliance is likely to create distortion in the jurisdiction of importation. Foreign small businesses whose sales would become subject to VAT/GST in the jurisdiction of destination may be at a competitive disadvantage compared to domestic small businesses that remain under the domestic VAT/GST registration threshold and whose sales are VAT/GST exempt.	The vendor would have no VAT/GST obligations in the jurisdiction of importation.	May deter compliant purchasers from purchasing abroad (if they have for instance to file a VAT/GST form to account for the tax on each purchase). It may also affect domestic competitiveness as it may create an incentive for non-compliant customers to purchase abroad.	

B. **Purchaser collection model** *(continued)*

	Ranking	Comment	Advantages	Disadvantages	Challenges
Efficiency of compliance and administration	Low		Minimal compliance costs for non-resident vendors.	This option maximises the compliance challenges as theoretically the whole resident population is in scope of this approach. This provides the greatest number of touch-points of any of the proposals. Implementing this option would require significant investment in systems changes and new administrative processes in most countries. The compliance burden is shifted to the purchaser who is generally not properly prepared/equipped for this.	It would be very difficult if not impossible for the tax administration to police such a regime.
Certainty and simplicity	Low			Uncertainty about procedures and complexity to comply non-compliance is likely to cause non-compliance leading to lost tax revenues. Private consumers are unlikely to keep track of goods imported or to be aware of the rules.	
Effectiveness	Low			The likelihood that the purchaser would self-account the VAT/GST is very low. Tax likely to be applied inconsistently (if at all) as result of poor compliance. Compliance is difficult, if not impossible, to enforce as the entire population is potentially liable to account for the VAT/GST.	
Fairness	Low			Self-assessing the tax would create an administrative burden for the customer. The consumer can avoid tax easily through non-compliance.	
Flexibility	Low	It is difficult to foresee whether an electronic self-declaration system would allow consumers to comply with their tax obligations while ensuring an effective collection of VAT/GST.			

C. Vendor collection model

	Ranking	Comment	Advantages	Disadvantages	Challenges
Neutrality	**Medium**	Measures to facilitate compliance for small/micro businesses may have to be considered. Foreign small businesses that would have to account for VAT/GST in the jurisdiction of destination may be at a competitive disadvantage compared to domestic small businesses that remain under the domestic VAT/GST registration threshold.	May even the playing field between non-resident sellers and domestic sellers (above the VAT/GST registration threshold for small businesses).	Relies very much on self-compliance by the vendors. Should therefore be combined with a fall-back rule based on the Traditional Collection model: in case of non-compliance, import VAT/GST is collected according to the traditional process. This would require authorities to operate two methods in parallel (Vendor Collection + Traditional Collection model)	
Efficiency of compliance and administration	**Low** **Medium (simplified regime)**		Moves some of the tasks involving the collection of import VAT/GST from customs authorities onto non-resident vendors, who are increasingly looking for technology-facilitated solutions for a quick/efficient collection and remittance of such import VAT/GST. Under an optional Vendor Collection model with simplified registration and compliance procedure and fast-track processing, only the vendor who elects to do so would have to VAT/GST register in the country of importation. This creates an incentive for non-resident to opt for vendor collection and to comply. A bulk-shipper scheme would allow vendors to lodge only one import declaration for all low-value consignments shipped together (instead of for each imported item). All consignments would be taxed even if, taken separately, they would be below the threshold. The operation of "one stop shop" systems in groups of countries may reduce further the compliance costs.	May involve significant burdens for non-resident vendors of having to register and account for tax in every country to which export to, in the absence of simplified registration and compliance mechanism. This may create a disincentive for small operators to comply. Some suppliers may also decide not to supply to smaller markets. For tax authorities: significant increase in registrations and corresponding costs (especially if extended to payment of duties) and additional costs to change customs procedures to remove the exemption and, in case such regime would be implemented, to manage fast-tracking and receive electronic data in advance of importation.	Compliance burden should be reduced for suppliers of having to register for VAT/GST in every country to which they export. This can be achieved by implementing simplified registration and compliance regimes allowing the vendor to pay and declare VAT/GST online in the jurisdiction of importation. In practice, VAT/GST might have to be remitted at the time of the payment of the goods (and thus before goods are imported) or on a periodic return. Rules regarding the chargeable event of the VAT/GST might have to be amended and secure systems to identify packages coming from non-resident VAT/GST registered suppliers may have to be implemented. Customs controls for safety and security will remain applicable, even if VAT/GST simplified procedures apply.

C. Vendor collection model *(continued)*

	Ranking	Comment	Advantages	Disadvantages	Challenges
Certainty and simplicity	**Medium** **High (simplified regime)**		Fast-track processing would encourage vendor to register. Simplified registration and compliance mechanisms may reduce the compliance burden for the vendor. Under the bulk-shipper scheme, processing charges would be minimised.	Uncertainty around interaction with customs/excise duties and procedures, e.g. legal issues over defining who the importer is. A simplified compliance mechanism may involve considerable systems changes. Optional fast track: customs authorities may need to implement systems changes to distinguish goods subject to the fast track from the others.	The existence of simplified registration and compliance mechanisms/fast track will not remove the customs safety and security controls.
Effectiveness	**Low** **Medium (with fall-back rule and enhanced administrative co-operation)**			May not be attractive (not effective) for businesses without a fast-track process. This approach relies on self-compliance by the vendors. In the absence of a fall-back rule, non-compliance could significantly reduce revenues.	Ideally, tax authorities should receive electronically data of shipments in advance under the simplified registration and compliance regime. Effectiveness will notably be influenced by the frequency of remittance: instant/ transaction wise or consolidated/ monthly/bi-monthly?
Fairness	**Medium**		Potential for undervaluation and mis-description can be minimised.	Enforcing compliance from non-resident may remain a challenge in the absence of enhanced international administrative co-operation.	Since, this regime relies on self-compliance by the vendors, enforcement needs to be supported by robust mutual administrative co-operation and other control mechanisms.
Flexibility	**Medium**	A vendor collection system would necessarily rely on technological developments.			Flexibility can be improved if vendors have the possibility to choose between a range of alternative methods.

D. Intermediary collection model

	Ranking	Comment	Advantages	Disadvantages	Challenges
Neutrality	**Medium**		This approach would even the playing field between domestic and non-resident vendors (including SMEs) assuming that intermediaries have the required information to collect and remit the import VAT/GST.	The postal services environment is not ready to switch to this model to collect VAT/GST on imports of low value goods. A transition to electronic processing is under preparation but will only be implemented in the mid (or even long) term. Most financial intermediaries do not have relevant information to assess and collect VAT/GST.	Efficient electronic data transmission and verification should be in place for all intermediaries that would intervene in the VAT/GST assessment and collection process. Success is likely to depend on the availability of simplified compliance mechanisms and incentives such as *fast-track* processing.

D. Intermediary collection model *(continued)*

	Ranking	Comment	Advantages	Disadvantages	Challenges
Efficiency of compliance and administration	**Medium**	Some additional burden on transporters to operate a VAT/GST collection and remittance system, but most information systems already exist for express carriers.	Minimal administrative burdens for vendors as these are shifted onto intermediaries. As only a limited number of intermediaries are likely to be involved, this model is broadly efficient for the tax administration. Revenue is secured through known express carriers or designated postal operators. Simplified compliance mechanism may reduce the compliance costs for the intermediary and make the system more accessible to SMEs. Express carriers already use electronic procedures and could relatively easily switch to this model to collect VAT/GST on imports of low value goods.	The postal services environment is still very much paper based and reliant on (often very) limited information provided by the vendor. The postal environment is not ready to switch to this model to collect VAT/GST on imports of low value goods. A transition to electronic processing is under preparation but will only be implemented in the mid (or even long) term. Transparent e-commerce platforms would need to adjust their data collection and verification process. Most financial intermediaries do not have relevant information to assess and collect VAT/GST. Additional fees charged by the intermediaries for the collection and remittance of VAT/GST may increase the price of the low value imported goods. These fees are however expected to reduce over time as the industry develops. There may be a cost to the tax and customs authorities to adjust their systems, although administrations are likely to be able to leverage on the systems that are already in place to e-process packages imported through express carriers.	When e-commerce platforms do not have a presence in the country of importation, risk assessment and simplification measures similar as those mentioned for the Vendor Collection model should be considered.
Certainty and simplicity	**Medium** **High for express couriers** **Low for financial intermediaries**		Express carriers already have systems in place for declaring/paying import VAT/GST. Certain e-commerce platforms already operate tax compliance programmes.	Intermediaries have to rely on information provided by the vendors. The postal services environment is still reliant on (often very) limited information provided by the vendor. Financial intermediaries do not access to the necessary information on the nature and the destination of the goods to assess the applicable VAT/GST.	Not feasible for traditional financial intermediaries.

D. **Intermediary collection model** *(continued)*

	Ranking	Comment	Advantages	Disadvantages	Challenges
Effectiveness	**Medium** **High for express couriers** **Low for financial intermediaries**		Rules can be enforced on transporters (express couriers; postal operators) since tax administration in country of importation has jurisdiction over the transporter. Express carriers already use electronic procedures and could relatively easily switch to this model to collect VAT/GST on imports of low value goods. Electronic processes will support more effective audit strategies based on computer-assisted auditing using electronic records	Tax administration in country of importation do not have jurisdiction over the intermediary, although mutual assistance could offset this. Financial intermediaries do not have access to the necessary information on the nature and the destination of the goods to assess the applicable VAT/GST.	
Fairness	**Medium**		Potential for fraud through mis-description and undervaluation is reduced, if intermediaries have access to reliable information (which is not the case for financial intermediaries). Electronic processes will allow for computer-assisted auditing using electronic records, which reduces the risk of fraud and non-compliance.	The postal services environment is still reliant on (often very) limited information provided by the vendor, which is difficult if not impossible to verify due to the paper based and manual verification process. Financial intermediaries do not have the appropriate information on the nature and the destination of the goods to assess the applicable VAT/GST.	Intermediaries such as express carriers have to rely on information provided by the vendors.
Flexibility	**Medium**	An intermediary collection system would necessarily rely on technological developments.		The postal services environment is still very much paper based and reliant on (often very) limited information provided by the vendor. The postal environment is not ready to switch to this model to collect VAT/GST on imports of low value goods. A transition to electronic processing is under preparation but will only be implemented in the mid (or even long) term. Transparent e-commerce platforms would need to adjust their data collection and verification process. Most financial intermediaries do not have relevant information to assess and collect VAT/GST.	

Appendix C.B

Low value import relief – Exemption thresholds

VAT/GST exemption thresholds for low value imports

This table shows VAT/GST exemption thresholds for low value import items dispatched by a foreign supplier to a purchaser in a given country. It does not cover other import scenarios such as imports of goods exchanged between private individuals or imports of goods in the personal luggage of travellers.

Country	Currency [a]	Threshold [a]	Threshold in USD approx. [b]
Australia	AUD	1 000	861
Argentina	USD	25	25
Austria	EUR	22	28
Belgium	EUR	22	28
Brazil	BRL	0	0
Canada	CAD	20	18
Chile	CLP	0	0
Czech Republic	EUR	22	28
Costa Rica	CRC	0	0
Denmark	DKK	80	13
Estonia	EUR	22	28
Finland	EUR	22	28
France	EUR	0	0
German	EUR	22	28
Greece	EUR	22	28
Hungary	EUR	22	28
Iceland	ISK	2 000	16
Ireland	EUR	22	28
Israel	USD	75	75
Italy	EUR	22	28
Japan	JPY	10 000	87
Korea	KRW	150 000	138
Latvia	EUR	22	28
Luxembourg	EUR	22	28
Mexico	USD	300	300

Country	Currency[a]	Threshold[a]	Threshold in USD approx.[b]
Netherlands	EUR	22	28
New Zealand	NZD	400	309
Norway	NOK	200	29
Poland	EUR	0	0
Portugal	EUR	22	28
Russian Federation	RUB	0	0
Saudi Arabia	N/A	N/A	N/A
Singapore	SGD	400	310
Slovak Republic	EUR	22	28
Slovenia	EUR	22	28
South Africa	ZAR	100	9
Spain	EUR	22	28
Sweden	EUR	22	28
Switzerland	CHF	62.5 (goods taxed at standard rate) 200 (goods taxed at reduced rate)	65 (goods taxed at standard rate) 208 (goods taxed at reduced rate)
Turkey	TRY	0	0
United Kingdom	GBP	15	24
United States	N/A	N/A	N/A
Uruguay	USD	50 (non-express) 200 (express delivery)	50 (non-express) 200 (express delivery)

Notes: a. Amounts are shown in the currency in which they were provided by delegates (i.e. either in local currency, EUR or USD).

b. To facilitate cross-country comparison, the amounts have been converted into USD at market rates on 1 November 2014. Note that these conversion rates have not been adjusted for purchasing power parity.

The statistical data for Israel are supplied by and under the responsibility of the relevant Israeli authorities. The use of such data by the OECD is without prejudice to the status of the Golan Heights, East Jerusalem and Israeli settlements in the West Bank under the terms of international law.

Source: 2014 Low value imports questionnaire. For the countries that did not respond to the low value imports questionnaire, the information is based on the 2014 Consumption Tax Trends Publication. (Situation as at 1 January 2014).

Notes

1. The OECD/G20 Action Plan on Base Erosion and Profit Shifting (BEPS Action Plan) was launched in September 2013 by OECD and G20 countries working on an equal footing. The Project provides for 15 actions to be delivered by 2015, with a number of actions to be delivered in 2014.

2. According to Transitional Standard 4.13 of Chapter 4 of the General Annex of the RKC: "National legislation shall specify a minimum value and/or a minimum amount of duties and taxes below which no duties and taxes will be collected". There could be limited exceptions where duties and taxes can apply irrespective of value, e.g. excisable goods.

3. Foreign small businesses that would have to account for VAT/GST on their sales in the jurisdiction of destination could be at a competitive disadvantage compared to domestic small businesses that are exempt from the VAT/GST because of their size and that would only incur VAT/GST on their inputs. However, the focus of this report is on the efficiency in the collection of VAT/GST on imports only.

4. The Universal Postal Union (UPU) was established during the second half of the 19th Century. The UPU Convention and subsidiary regulations facilitate and govern the movement of post between member countries. The UPU became a specialised agency of the UN in 1948.

5. Forms CN22 and CN23 used by postal operators for customs clearance are not tax forms. They are primarily designed for postal customs declaration. However the information contained in these forms can be used for tax purposes by customs or tax authorities.

6. WTO Agreement on Trade Facilitation, General Council Decision of 28 November 2014, https://www.wto.org/english/thewto_e/minist_e/mc9_e/nov14dectradfac_e.htm.

7. Article 9 of the UPU Convention was amended to "*include the principle of complying with requirements for providing electronic advance data on postal items*".

8. The Electronic Customs Initiative, http://ec.europa.eu/taxation_customs/customs/policy_issues/electronic_customs_initiative/electronic_customs_legislation/index_en.htm.

9. OECD (1998), "Electronic Commerce: Taxation Framework Conditions", a report by the Committee on Fiscal Affairs, page 4, www.oecd.org/tax/consumption/1923256.pdf.

10. In this context, "vendor" includes non-transparent intermediaries where the sale from the original vendor to the intermediary and the subsequent resale to the purchaser are considered two separate transactions for VAT/GST purposes.

11. Within customs unions, once the goods are released into free circulation, it may be difficult to trace them. This would be particularly challenging for jurisdictions that operate a common external tariff and a common domestic market, such as Member States of the European Union.

12. In the EU, an OSS was established for B2C supplies of electronic, telecommunication, radio and television broadcasting services performed by non-EU suppliers. This system was introduced in 2003. Briefly, the system works as follows. A non-resident supplier chooses one EU Member State to register for VAT and to perform all related VAT compliance. When sales to other EU Member States are performed, the system automatically applies the VAT rate in the EU country of consumer. At the end of the reporting period, the non-resident supplier submits a declaration with all sales split per EU jurisdictions. The EU Member State of registration then distributes the appropriate VAT revenues to each EU Member State of consumption.

13. Foreign small businesses that would have to account for VAT/GST on their sales in the jurisdiction of destination could be at a competitive disadvantage compared to domestic small businesses that are exempt from the VAT/GST because of their size and that would only incur VAT/GST on their inputs. However, the focus of this report is on the efficiency in the collection of VAT/GST on imports only.

14. "Non-transparent" intermediaries as described in paragraph 27 above are not considered in this section.

15. https://www.canadapost.ca/cpotools/apps/cdc?execution=e3s1.

16. The Union Customs Code (UCC) was adopted on 9 October 2013 as Regulation (EU) No 952/2013 of the European Parliament and of the Council.

Bibliography

OECD (2014), *Addressing the Tax Challenges of the Digital Economy,* OECD/G20 Base Erosion and Profit Shifting Project, OECD Publishing, Paris, http://dx.doi.org/10.1787/9789264218789-en.

Annex D

OECD international VAT/GST guidelines

Chapter 3

Determining the place of taxation for cross-border supplies of services and intangibles

This annex contains the chapter of the International VAT/GST Guidelines which deals specifically with the application of VAT/GST to cross-border supplies of services and intangibles

A. The destination principle

3.1. VAT neutrality in international trade is generally achieved through the implementation of the "destination principle". The destination principle is designed to ensure that tax on cross-border supplies is ultimately levied only in the jurisdiction where the final consumption occurs, thereby maintaining neutrality within the VAT system as it applies to international trade. This principle is set out in Guideline 3.1.

> **Guideline 3.1**
>
> **For consumption tax purposes internationally traded services and intangibles should be taxed according to the rules of the jurisdiction of consumption.**

3.2. In order to apply the destination principle to internationally traded services and intangibles, VAT systems must have mechanisms for identifying the jurisdiction of consumption by connecting such supplies to the jurisdiction where the final consumption of the services or intangibles is expected to take place. VAT systems need place of taxation rules to implement the destination principle not only for business-to-consumer supplies, which involve final consumption, but also for business-to-business supplies, even though such supplies do not involve final consumption. Business-to-business supplies are taxed under the VAT's staged collection process, and, in this context, the place of taxation rules should facilitate the ultimate objective of the tax, which is to tax final consumption. These Guidelines set out the recommended approaches that reflect the destination principle for determining the place of taxation for business-to-consumer and business-to-business cross-border supplies of services and intangibles.

3.3. Place of taxation rules are needed for supplies of goods as well as for supplies of services and intangibles. Implementing the destination principle with respect to cross-border supplies of goods is facilitated by the existence of border controls or fiscal frontiers. Implementing the destination principle with respect to international trade in services and intangibles is more difficult, because the nature of services and intangibles is such that they cannot be subject to border controls in the same way as goods. The Guidelines in this chapter therefore concentrate on supplies of services and intangibles.[1] They set out recommended approaches that reflect the destination principle for determining the jurisdiction of taxation for international supplies of services and intangibles while ensuring that:

- international neutrality is maintained
- compliance by businesses involved in these supplies is kept as simple as possible
- clarity and certainty are provided for both business and tax administrations
- the costs involved in complying with the tax and administering it are minimal, and
- barriers to evasion and avoidance are sufficiently robust.

3.4. This chapter should not be read as requiring jurisdictions to literally incorporate the Guidelines on determining the place of taxation as legal rules in national legislation. These Guidelines seek to identify common objectives and suggest means for achieving them with a view to promoting a consistent implementation of the destination principle for determining the place of taxation for supplies of services and intangibles. It is recognised that a variety of models for structuring and designing place of taxation rules are operated by VAT systems around the world. Many systems operate on the basis of a categorisation approach, in which supplies are divided into categories with a place of taxation specified for each category. Other models favour an iterative approach, in which the principle underlying the place of taxation rule is described in more general terms and where a series of rules are applied consecutively to determine the appropriate place of taxation. These differences in legal drafting style are generally not absolute and elements of both approaches can be found in both models. The key common feature among the various VAT design models is that they generally aim to implement the destination principle, under which the place of taxation rules are intended to impose tax at the place of consumption. These Guidelines seek to ensure that these place of taxation rules are applied consistently by promoting an internationally accepted understanding of what is the place of taxation of internationally traded services and intangibles and by setting out consistent and effective approaches for determining this place of taxation with a view to minimising uncertainty, revenue risks, compliance costs and administrative burdens for tax authorities and businesses.

3.5. The approaches used by VAT systems to implement the destination principle for business-to-business supplies and the tax collection methods used for such supplies are often different from those used for business-to-consumer supplies. This distinction is attributable to the different objectives of taxing business-to-business and business-to-consumer supplies: taxation of business-to-consumer supplies involves the imposition of a final tax burden, while taxation of business-to-business supplies is merely a means of achieving the ultimate objective of the tax, which is to tax final consumption. Thus, the objective of place of taxation rules for business-to-business supplies is primarily to facilitate the imposition of a tax burden on the final consumer in the appropriate country while maintaining neutrality within the VAT system. The place of taxation rules for business-to-business supplies should therefore focus not only on where the business customer will use its purchases to create the goods, services or intangibles that final consumers will acquire, but also on facilitating the flow-through of the tax burden to the final consumer while maintaining neutrality within the VAT system. The overriding objective of place of taxation rules for business-to-consumer supplies, on the other hand, is to predict, subject to practical constraints, the place where the final consumer is likely to consume the services or intangibles supplied. In addition to the different objectives of the place of taxation rules for business-to-business and business-to-consumer supplies, VAT systems often employ different mechanisms to enforce and collect the tax for both categories of supplies. These different collection mechanisms often influence the design of place of taxation rules and of the compliance obligations for suppliers and customers involved in cross-border supplies. In light of these considerations, this chapter presents separate Guidelines for determining the place of taxation for business-to-business supplies and for business-to-consumer supplies. This should not be interpreted as a recommendation to jurisdictions to develop separate rules or implement different mechanisms for each type of supply in their national legislation.

3.6. In theory, place of taxation rules should aim to identify the actual place of business use for business-to-business supplies (on the assumption that this best facilitates implementation of the destination principle) and the actual place of final consumption for business-to-consumer supplies. However, these Guidelines recognise that place of taxation rules are in practice rarely aimed at identifying where business use or final consumption actually takes place. This is a consequence of the fact that VAT must in principle be charged at or before the time when the object of the supply is made available for business use or final consumption. In most cases, at that time the supplier will not know or be able to ascertain where such business use or final consumption will actually occur. VAT systems therefore generally use proxies for the place of business use or final consumption to determine the jurisdiction of taxation, based on features of the supply that are known or knowable at the time that the tax treatment of the supply must be determined. The Guidelines in this chapter identify such proxies for determining the place of taxation of supplies of services and intangibles, both for business-to-business supplies and for business-to-consumer supplies.

3.7. For the purposes of these Guidelines business-to-business supplies are assumed to be supplies where both the supplier and the customer are recognised as businesses, and business-to-consumer supplies are assumed to be supplies where the customer is not recognised as a business. Such recognition may include the treatment for VAT purposes specifically or in national law more generally (notably in jurisdictions that have not implemented a VAT).

3.8. Jurisdictions that implement different approaches for determining the place of taxation and/or different collection mechanisms for business-to-business supplies and for business-to-consumer supplies are encouraged to provide clear practical guidance on how suppliers can establish the status of their customer (business or non-business). Jurisdictions may consider adopting a requirement for suppliers to provide a customer's VAT registration number, business tax identification number, or other such indicia (e.g. information available in commercial registers) to establish their customer's status. Where a supplier, acting in good faith and having made reasonable efforts, is not able to obtain the appropriate documentation to establish the status of its customer, this could lead to a presumption that this is a non-business customer in which case the rules for business-to-consumer supplies would apply. To facilitate suppliers' identification and verification of their customers' status, jurisdictions are encouraged to consider implementing an easy-to-use process that would allow suppliers to verify the validity of their customers' VAT registration or tax identification numbers. Where, in respect of some or all types of services, jurisdictions do not distinguish between business-to-business and business-to-consumer supplies, such guidance might not be necessary.

B. Business-to-business supplies – The general rule

B.1. Defining the general rule

Guideline 3.2

For the application of Guideline 3.1, for business-to-business supplies, the jurisdiction in which the customer is located has the taxing rights over internationally traded services or intangibles.

3.9. By and large, when a business buys in services or intangibles from another jurisdiction, it does so for the purposes of its business operations. As such, the jurisdiction of the customer's location can stand as the appropriate proxy for the jurisdiction of business use, as it achieves the objective of neutrality by implementing the destination principle. This is the jurisdiction where the customer has located its permanent business presence.

3.10. This proxy is referred to in these Guidelines as the general rule for business-to-business supplies, as distinguished from specific rules that are covered by Guidelines 3.7 and 3.8. According to this general rule, the jurisdiction where the customer is located has the taxing rights over services or intangibles supplied across international borders. The supplier makes the supply free of VAT in its jurisdiction but retains the right to full input tax credit (subject to clearly legislated exceptions in that jurisdiction) on inputs related to making such international supplies. Only in exceptional and clearly specified circumstances should the place of taxation vary from this general rule.[2]

3.11. This section and the following sections provide further guidance on how the jurisdiction of a customer's location can be determined.

Guideline 3.3

For the application of Guideline 3.2, the identity of the customer is normally determined by reference to the business agreement.

3.12. Under Guideline 3.3, the identity of the customer is "normally determined by reference to the business agreement" as it is expected that business agreements reflect the underlying supply. The business agreement will assist the supplier, the customer and tax administrations in identifying the nature of the supply and the identity of the parties to the supply. When supplies are made between separate legal entities with only a single location, the location of the customer also will be known once the identity of the customer is determined.[3] It is appropriate to first describe "business agreement" for the purposes of these Guidelines and explain how tax administrations and businesses may approach the determination of the business agreement.

Box 3.1. **Business Agreement**

Business agreements consist of the elements that identify the parties to a supply and the rights and obligations with respect to that supply.[a] They are generally based on mutual understanding.[b]

Notes

a. Agreements that do not lead to supplies for tax purposes are not regarded on their own as "business agreements" for the purposes of these Guidelines.

b. It is recognised, however, that on occasion supplies may occur without a mutual understanding, e.g. a court order that imposes obligations on one or more parties. In such cases the "imposed" agreement should nevertheless be considered as a "business agreement".

3.13. The term "business agreement" has been adopted for the purpose of these Guidelines because it is a general concept, rather than a term with a technical meaning, and it is not specific to any individual jurisdiction. In particular, it is not restricted to a contract (whether written or in some other format) and is therefore wide in its application, as explained below.

3.14. In order to determine the place of taxation under the general rule, it is necessary to demonstrate the nature of the supply as well as the identity of the supplier and the customer.

3.15. In many cases, particularly those involving significant sums of money or complex matters beyond a straightforward supply, it is likely that the parties to a business agreement will draw up legally enforceable contracts. These contracts will normally specify the parties to the business agreement and set out their respective rights and obligations. However, contracts in themselves should not be seen as the only relevant elements of a business agreement.

3.16. Other relevant elements of the business agreement come in many forms and include, for example, general correspondence, purchase orders, invoices, payment instruments and receipts. Legislation and business practices in jurisdictions invariably differ and generally not for tax reasons. They may differ with respect to national laws concerning contract issues and other commercial requirements. They may also differ between different industry sectors. It is, therefore, neither possible nor desirable to draw up a prescriptive or exhaustive list of items that must be present in a business agreement. Rather, these Guidelines suggest sources of information that would help both tax administrations and business.

3.17. A business agreement need not be confined to written material. In certain sectors, relevant elements may be found in the form of audio recordings of telephone conversations leading to conclusions of agreements to supply or receive services and/or intangibles. Relevant elements of a business agreement may also be found in electronic form such as e-mails and on-line ordering records, payment and similar material and formats that are likely to emerge as new technologies develop.

3.18. It is recognised that business agreements are often not concluded in isolation. Consequently other agreements, including those not regarded as business agreements (e.g. agreements that do not involve a supply[4]), may provide the context of the supplies made under a particular business agreement. These other agreements may therefore form a part of the relevant elements of that business agreement.

3.19. In the light of the previous paragraphs, the business agreement in force at the time the supply is made is the agreement that governs the implementation of the general rule.

3.20. To ease burdens in practice for both tax administrations and business, it is recommended that jurisdictions take into account the application of Guidelines 3.2 and 3.3 in a way that is consistent with the previous paragraphs. Wherever possible, tax administrations are encouraged to communicate these approaches and relevant national laws as clearly and as widely as possible.

B.2. Applying the general rule – Supply of a service or intangible to a legal entity with single location ("single location entity" – "SLE")

3.21. In principle, applying the general rule for business-to-business supplies to legal entities[5] with a single location ("single location entities" – "SLEs") is relatively straightforward. The Commentary under Section B.4 provides further practical guidance.

B.3. Applying the general rule – Supply of a service or intangible to a legal entity with multiple locations ("multiple location entity" – "MLE")

3.22. When a supply is made to a legal entity that has establishments[6] in more than one jurisdiction (a "multiple location entity", "MLE"), an analysis is required to determine which of the jurisdictions where this MLE has establishments has taxing rights over the service or intangible acquired by the MLE.

3.23. In such a case, jurisdictions are encouraged to apply an approach that would ensure that taxation accrues to the jurisdiction where the customer's establishment using the service or intangible is located.

Guideline 3.4

For the application of Guideline 3.2, when the customer has establishments in more than one jurisdiction, the taxing rights accrue to the jurisdiction(s) where the establishment(s) using the service or intangible is (are) located.

3.24. "Use of a service or intangible"[7] in this context refers to the use of a service or intangible by a business for the purpose of its business operations. It is irrelevant whether this use is immediate, continuous, directly linked to an output transaction or supports the business operations in general.

3.25. A number of possible approaches are currently adopted by jurisdictions to identify which customer's establishment is regarded as using a service or intangible and where this establishment is located. The following broad categories of approaches can be distinguished:

- Direct use approach, which focuses directly on the establishment that uses the service or intangible.
- Direct delivery approach, which focuses on the establishment to which the service or intangible is delivered.
- Recharge method, which focuses on the establishment that uses the service or intangible as determined on the basis of internal recharge arrangements within the MLE, made in accordance with corporate tax, accounting or other regulatory requirements.

3.26. Each of the approaches described above seeks to ensure that taxation of the supply of a service or intangible to a MLE accrues to the jurisdiction where the customer's establishment that is regarded as using the service or intangibles is located. It is likely that each of these approaches will have its merits in particular circumstances. The principle behind any approach should be to achieve a sound balance between the interests of business (both suppliers and customers) and tax administrations.

B.3.1. Direct use

3.27. Under this approach, taxing rights for the supply of a service or intangible to a MLE are directly allocated to the jurisdiction of the customer's establishment that is regarded as using this service or intangible.

3.28. This approach may be particularly effective in circumstances where there is obvious use by an establishment of the customer MLE. It is then relatively straightforward for the supplier and customer to ensure that this is reflected properly in the business agreement. In these circumstances, both the supplier and the customer would have the necessary information to support a proper tax treatment at the time of the supply and the business agreement would provide an appropriate audit trail to the tax authorities.

3.29. This approach may be more difficult in circumstances where the supplier does not know, and perhaps cannot know, which customer establishment uses the supply or in circumstances where the actual use is not known with certainty at the time of the business agreement. This approach also may not deal adequately with cases where the service or intangible is used by different establishments in different jurisdictions ("multiple use"). In such cases this approach may create considerable compliance difficulties for suppliers and customers and may affect the efficiency of tax administration and collection.

B.3.2. Direct delivery

3.30. Under this approach, taxing rights for the supply of a service or intangible to a MLE are directly allocated to the jurisdiction of the customer's establishment to which the supplier delivers the service or intangible.

3.31. The "direct delivery" approach may provide an effective solution for supplies of services or intangibles that are likely to be used at the location of the establishment to which they are delivered ("physically supplied", such as catering or on-the-spot training). In such cases both the supplier and customer are likely to know the location of the establishment of direct delivery at the time of the supply and are likely to reflect this in the business agreement. The supplier and the customer would therefore have the necessary information to support a proper tax treatment at the time of the supply and the business agreement would provide an appropriate audit trail to the tax authorities.

B.3.3. Recharge method

3.32. This approach requires MLEs to internally recharge the cost of an externally acquired service or intangible to their establishments that use this service or intangible, as supported by internal recharge arrangements. Under the recharge method, these internal recharges are used as a basis for allocating the taxing rights over the external service or intangible to the jurisdiction where the MLE's establishment using this service or intangible is located. Further information and guidance on this approach is to be found in the Commentary under Section B.5 below.

3.33. This approach may be useful in cases where a service or intangible supplied by an external supplier to a MLE is acquired by one establishment of this MLE for use wholly or partially by other establishments located in different jurisdictions ("multiple use"). It is common practice for multinational businesses to arrange for a wide scope of services, such as administrative, technical, financial and commercial services, to be acquired centrally to realise economies of scale. Typically, the cost of acquiring such a service or intangible is then initially borne by the establishment that has acquired the service or intangible and, in line with normal business practice, is subsequently recharged to the establishments using the service or intangible. The establishments are charged for their share of the service or intangible on the basis of the internal recharge arrangements, in accordance with corporate tax, accounting and other regulatory requirements.

3.34. It may be difficult, if not impossible, for a supplier in such a multiple-use scenario to know which establishments of a MLE will actually use the service or intangible supplied to this MLE and to ensure a correct VAT treatment in accordance with the location of these establishments of use (see paragraph 3.29 above). Even if the supplier knew where the service or intangible supplied to a MLE were used, it could be challenging, particularly in a multiple-use scenario, to implement and administer a system whereby the supplier's taxing decision depends on the location of the establishments of use.

3.35. The recharge method could offer an effective solution for identifying the place of taxation of the supply of a service or intangible to a MLE, particularly in multiple-use scenarios. Under this approach, the supplier would rely on the business agreement with the MLE to support the proper VAT treatment of the supply to the MLE. It would be for the customer MLE to ensure the correct VAT treatment of this service or intangible, based on the internal allocation of the cost to its establishments using this service or intangible. This would build on existing business processes and information that will generally already be available for accounting, tax or other regulatory purposes, and would therefore not create undue compliance burdens. These processes and information should also facilitate the production of appropriate and reliable audit trails for tax authorities.

3.36. Jurisdictions that consider implementing the recharge method may need to address a number of potentially complex aspects of this method. These include questions regarding the scope of this method, acceptable methods for the proper allocation of taxable amounts to the establishment(s) of use and the timing of the recharges, the impact of internal recharges on the right to deduct input VAT and questions about documentation requirements and the process to account for any tax due on internal recharges. Jurisdictions may also need to take account of tax administration concerns such as the additional number of transactions that may have to be audited due to the internal recharges. Jurisdictions that consider implementing this recharge method are encouraged to take these concerns into careful consideration and to provide clear guidance on the operation of this method. The Commentary under Section B.5 below looks at a number of these aspects in further detail.

B.3.4. Conclusion

3.37. Each of the approaches described above seeks to ensure that taxation of the supply of a service or intangible to a MLE accrues to the jurisdiction where the customer's establishment(s) using the service or intangible is (are) located. These Guidelines do not aim to set out which approach should be preferred or to rule out alternatives: each approach is likely to have specific merits in particular circumstances. These approaches are not mutually exclusive and could be combined according to the information that is available to the supplier and the customer. It is for jurisdictions to adopt the approach or approaches that they consider appropriate, taking into account their legal and administrative framework and practices.

3.38. Any approach should, in principle:

- seek to ensure that taxation of the supply of a service or intangible to a MLE accrues to the jurisdiction(s) where the customer's establishment(s) regarded as using the service or intangible is (are) located; and
- achieve a sound balance between the interests of business (both suppliers and customers) and tax administrations.

3.39. Jurisdictions are encouraged to seek the right balance between the objectives of protecting tax revenue and of keeping compliance and administrative costs as low as possible, while minimising distortions of competition. Jurisdictions are also encouraged to provide clear, accessible and dependable information to increase certainty and to ensure the correct VAT treatment of the supply of a service or intangible to a MLE, both by the supplier and by the customer.

3.40. The key objective of these Guidelines is to help reduce uncertainty and risks of double taxation and unintended non-taxation resulting from inconsistencies in the application of VAT to international trade. Jurisdictions are therefore encouraged to adopt an approach that minimises the potential for double taxation or unintended non-taxation. The more jurisdictions adopt the same approach, the greater the reduction in complexity, uncertainty and risks of double taxation and unintended non-taxation.

B.4. Commentary on applying the general rule – Supply of a service or intangible to a legal entity with single location ("single location entity" – "SLE")

3.41. For the purposes of this section, the businesses to which the general rule applies are assumed to be separate legal entities, whether related by common ownership or not. These legal entities are located solely in their respective jurisdictions and have no business presence elsewhere.

3.42. Under the general rule for business-to-business supplies, the place of the customer's location serves as a proxy for the jurisdiction of business use. The result of applying this general rule is that the jurisdiction where the customer is located has the taxing rights over services and intangibles supplied across international borders.

3.43. In order to support a satisfactory application of the general rule to single location entities, this section considers its application from the perspectives of the supplier, customer and tax administrations. Examples 1 and 2 in the Annex 1 to this chapter provide relatively straightforward illustrations of how this general rule operates. Examples 3, 4 and 5 in the Annex 1 illustrate how this general rule is applied in more complex situations.

B.4.1. Supplies to single location entities – Supplier

3.44. In a business-to-business environment, it is reasonable to assume that suppliers will normally have developed a relationship with their customers. This will be particularly so in cases where supplies of services or intangibles are made on an on-going basis or in cases where one supply is made and the value of that supply is significant enough to warrant the development of business agreements such as contracts.

3.45. The principal effect of the general rule on suppliers is that they need to identify and be able to demonstrate who their customer is in order to make the supply free of VAT in their jurisdiction if the customer is located outside the supplier's jurisdiction. Once satisfied that the customer is a business and is located in another jurisdiction, the supplier makes that supply free of VAT in its jurisdiction as, under the general rule, the taxing rights over that supply are in the jurisdiction of the customer's location.

3.46. In many cases this will be straightforward and can be determined by reference to the business agreement. The nature of the service or intangible being supplied and the wording used in any supporting documentation may also contribute to verification of the international and business nature of the supply.

3.47. To avoid unnecessary burdens on suppliers, it is recommended that the customer be liable to account for any tax due. This can be achieved through the reverse charge mechanism (sometimes referred to as "tax shift" or "self-assessment") where that is consistent with the overall design of the national consumption tax system.[8] Accordingly, the supplier should then not be required to be identified for VAT or account for tax in the customer's jurisdiction.

3.48. The general rule applies in any situation where the supplier and customer are separate legal entities irrespective of whether they are related through any form of common ownership, management or control.

3.49. The application of the general rule will not be affected by the circumstance that the supplier *(i)* supplies a customer who supplies onwards the services or intangibles to a third party,[9] or *(ii)* directly provides the services or intangibles to a third party that is not the customer under the business agreement or *(iii)* is paid by a third party that is not the customer under the business agreement. This is explained in further detail in the following paragraphs.

B.4.1.1. The determination of the place of taxation is not affected by any onward supply

3.50. It is common for multinational businesses to centralise certain procurement activities in one jurisdiction in order to obtain the economic benefits of single large agreements as opposed to multiple lower value agreements. These are generally referred to as "global" agreements. The central procurement company then supplies onwards the supplies or parts of the supplies to the various related businesses around the world.

3.51. The onward supply of those services to related businesses will be covered by separate business agreements entered into between the central procurement company and each of the related businesses. If the related businesses are the customers under those business agreements, the taxing rights over these onward supplies will be in the jurisdictions where these related businesses are located, in accordance with the general rule. If these jurisdictions operate a reverse charge mechanism, these related businesses will be liable to account for any VAT at the rate applicable in their jurisdictions.

3.52. The procurement company may well supply a business located in the same jurisdiction as the original supplier (see Annex 1 to this chapter – Example 3). When one applies the general rule, the place of taxation should be decided for each supply individually so that the determination of the place of taxation of services or intangibles for VAT purposes will not be affected by any subsequent supply or lack of such supply. The supplier should accordingly determine the identity of the customer by reference to the relevant business agreement. Where the customer is located in another jurisdiction, the supplier is entitled to make the supply free of VAT. As long as there is no evasion or avoidance, the fact that the customer subsequently supplies the services or intangibles onwards to a third party business is not, in itself, relevant, even where the third party business is located in the jurisdiction of the supplier.

B.4.1.2. The determination of the place of taxation is not affected by the direct provision of the services or intangibles to a third party business other than the customer of the supply

3.53. The supplier may also be required under the terms of the business agreement to provide services or intangibles directly to a third party (see Annex 1 to this chapter – Example 3). As long as there is no evasion or avoidance, the customer remains the customer identified in the business agreement and it is this customer's location that determines the place of taxation. The mere direct provision of the supply to a third party business does not, in itself, affect that outcome. Accordingly, the general rule should be applied in such a way that the supplier makes a supply free of VAT to a foreign customer even if the third party business is located in the same jurisdiction as the supplier.

B.4.1.3. The determination of the place of taxation is not affected by the direction of the payment flows and the identity and location of the payer

3.54. Particular care may be required where payment flows differ from the flows of services or intangibles. Typically, a customer pays a supplier for services or intangibles supplied under a business agreement. However, there may be circumstances where another party may pay for that supply. For instance, it is common for multinational groups of businesses to reduce costs by appointing a company within a group to be the "paymaster"[10] responsible for payments under the relevant agreement to pay for services and intangibles acquired. In such cases, services or intangibles supplied by the supplier or the supplier's foreign subsidiaries to foreign customers may be paid for by the customer's parent business located in the supplier's jurisdiction, although the supplies may not be made to the parent business (See Annex 1 to this chapter – Example 5). When the general rule is applied, the place of taxation should be decided for each supply individually. The direction of the payment flows and the identity and location of the payer are not, in themselves, relevant. The payment flows are consideration for the supplies under the relevant business agreements but do not, in themselves, create additional supplies, alter the supplies, nor identify the customer or customer location. Accordingly, the supplier makes the supply to the customer identified in the relevant business agreement and the place of taxation is that customer's location. As long as there is no evasion or avoidance, the supplier is therefore entitled to make a supply free of VAT to a foreign customer even if that supply is paid by a third party business located in the same jurisdiction as the supplier.

B.4.2. Supplies to single location entities – Customer

3.55. It is recommended that the customer be liable to account for any tax due under the reverse charge mechanism where that is consistent with the overall design of the national consumption tax system. Under this procedure, the customer is typically required to declare the VAT due on the supply received from the foreign supplier as output tax on the relevant VAT return. The rate to be applied is the rate applicable in the customer's jurisdiction. The customer is then entitled to input tax deduction to the extent allowed under the rules of its jurisdiction.

3.56. If the customer is entitled to full input tax deduction on the relevant supply, it may be that local VAT legislation does not require declaration of the output tax under the reverse charge mechanism. This is an option provided in some jurisdictions and businesses in this position should ensure that they are aware of their jurisdiction's requirements in this respect. Similarly, some jurisdictions may employ a type of VAT that does not require application of a reverse charge as it would not suit the nature of the tax as applied. Businesses importing services and intangibles from a foreign supplier should ensure that they are familiar with their domestic legislation and administrative practices.

3.57. The customer is obliged to pay any tax due on the supply under the reverse charge mechanism where that is consistent with the overall design of the national consumption tax system. The customer is liable to pay even where *(i)* the customer supplies onwards the services or intangibles to a third party *(ii)* the services or intangibles are not directly provided to the customer or *(iii)* the customer does not pay for the supply. This is explained in further detail in the following paragraphs.

B.4.2.1. The determination of the place of taxation is not affected by any onward supply

3.58. As stated in paragraph 3.50, it may be that the customer supplies onwards the services or intangibles from the foreign supplier as separate supplies (e.g. within a "global" agreement). As long as there is no evasion or avoidance, the place of taxation for these supplies should be decided for each supply individually and the original international supply is not affected (see Annex 1 to this chapter – Example 3). The general rule continues to apply. It is likely that the customer when supplying onwards the supplies or parts of the supplies to related businesses will have entered into business agreements with those businesses. If the related businesses are the customers under those business agreements, the taxing rights over these onward supplies will be in the jurisdictions where these related businesses are located, in accordance with the general rule. If these jurisdictions operate a reverse charge mechanism, these related businesses will be liable to account for any VAT at the rate applicable in their jurisdictions.

B.4.2.2. The determination of the place of taxation is not affected by the direct provision of the services or intangibles to a third party business other than the customer of the supply

3.59. As described in paragraph 3.53, the customer may, under the terms of the relevant business agreement, require that the services or intangibles be provided directly to a third party. Even if that third party is located in a different jurisdiction from that of the customer identified in the business agreement, the place of taxation remains in the jurisdiction where the customer identified in the business agreement is located. If this jurisdiction operates a reverse charge mechanism, this customer identified in the business agreement will be liable to account for any VAT at the rate applicable in its jurisdiction (see Annex 1 to this chapter – Example 3).

B.4.2.3. The determination of the place of taxation is not affected by the direction of the payment flows and the identity and location of the payer

3.60. As described in paragraph 3.54, multinational business groups may appoint a group member to act as paymaster for services or intangibles supplied to the group (i.e. a "paymaster" agreement). Consequently, the customer is not the party who pays the supplier for the supply under the business agreement. In such situations the direction of the payment flows and the identity and location of the payer are not, in themselves, relevant. The supply is to the customer identified in the relevant business agreement and the place of taxation is that customer's location (see Annex 1 to this chapter – Example 5).

B.4.3. Supplies to single location entities – Tax administrations

3.61. The growth in international supplies of services and intangibles has led to increased complexity for tax administrations as well as for businesses. The intangible nature of many services is such that the comparative simplicity for goods (exports relieved, imports taxed) cannot be replicated with respect to services and intangibles. It is, therefore, important that tax administrations make it clear to both businesses and to staff responsible for carrying out compliance checks and audits what the rules are in their own jurisdiction and that they should be applied according to the facts of each individual supply.

3.62. Under the general rule supplies of services and intangibles are subject to tax according to the rules of the jurisdiction where the customer is located. This means that a supplier of international business-to-business services and intangibles makes such supplies free of VAT in its jurisdiction. The tax administration of the supplier may require the supplier to produce evidence that the customer is a business and that this business is located in another jurisdiction. To minimise compliance burdens on the supplier, tax administrations are encouraged to provide businesses with clear guidance on the evidence they require.

3.63. It is recommended that the customer be liable to account for any VAT due to its local tax administration under the reverse charge mechanism where that is consistent with the overall design of the national consumption tax system. Tax administrations are encouraged to make businesses aware of the need to account for any tax on "imported" services and intangibles from their suppliers in other jurisdictions. The normal domestic rate applicable to the nature of the services or intangibles involved should be applied. If the customer is entitled to full input tax credit in respect of this supply, it may be that local VAT legislation does not require the reverse charge to be declared on the local VAT return. In such cases tax administrations are encouraged to publicise this to business. Jurisdictions that require this declaration are likewise encouraged to make it clear that tax is required to be accounted for in this way.[11]

3.64. The reverse charge mechanism has a number of advantages. First, the tax authority in the jurisdiction of business use can verify and ensure compliance since that authority has personal jurisdiction over the customer. Second, the compliance burden is largely shifted from the supplier to the customer and is minimised since the customer has full access to the details of the supply. Third, the administrative costs for the tax authority are also lower because the supplier is not required to comply with tax obligations in the customer's jurisdiction (e.g. VAT identification, audits, which would otherwise have to be administered, and translation and language barriers). Finally, it reduces the revenue risks associated with the collection of tax by non-resident suppliers, whether or not that supplier's customers are entitled to deduct the input tax.

3.65. The determination of the place of taxation of services or intangibles for VAT purposes should be decided for each supply individually. As long as there is no evasion or avoidance, it will, therefore, not be affected by *(i)* any subsequent onward supply or lack of such supply, *(ii)* the direct provision of the services or intangibles to a third party business other than the customer or *(iii)* by the direction of the payment flows and the identity and location of the payer. This is explained in further detail in the following paragraphs.

B.4.3.1. The determination of the place of taxation is not affected by any onward supply

3.66. As stated in paragraphs 3.50 and 3.58, businesses with related separate legal entities in other jurisdictions may supply onwards the services or intangibles they have bought in within a "global" agreement from foreign to other related companies. These supplies should be subject to the normal VAT rules, including the general rule in respect of international services and intangibles (see Annex 1 to this chapter – Example 3). Accordingly, it is recommended that:

- the tax administration in the supplier's jurisdiction allow the supplier to make a supply free of VAT, providing the supplier can identify the customer and demonstrate that the customer is located abroad
- the tax administration in the customer's jurisdiction ensures that the customer accounts for any tax due on the supply from the foreign supplier, using the reverse charge mechanism where that is consistent with the overall design of the national consumption tax system.

B.4.3.2. The determination of the place of taxation is not affected by the direct provision of the services or intangibles to a third party business other than the customer of the supply

3.67. As stated in paragraphs 3.53 and 3.59, even if some or all of the services or intangibles are not directly provided in the jurisdiction of the customer but rather are directly provided in another jurisdiction such as, for instance, the jurisdiction of the supplier or of a third party business, the general rule continues to apply (see Annex 1 to this chapter – Example 3). The customer's jurisdiction remains the jurisdiction with the taxing rights. For example, an accountancy firm may have entered into a business agreement with a customer located in another jurisdiction but may perform much of the work in its own jurisdiction and also provide its services directly to a third party business. As long as there is no evasion or avoidance, this does not, in itself, prevent the place of taxation from being the customer's location. Accordingly it is recommended that:

- the tax administration in the supplier's jurisdiction does not seek tax from the supplier based entirely on the fact that the supplier is directly providing the services or intangibles there, but allows it to make a supply free of VAT to the foreign customer identified in the business agreement
- the tax administration in the customer's jurisdiction ensures that the customer accounts for any tax due on the supply from the foreign supplier, using the reverse charge mechanism, even if the services or intangibles were directly provided by a local third party business.

B.4.3.3. The determination of the place of taxation is not affected by the direction of the payment flows and the identity and location of the payer

3.68. Paragraphs 3.54 and 3.60 recognise that there may be situations where another party pays for the supply to the customer in the business agreement (see Annex 1 to this chapter – Example 5). That third party business is usually referred to in multinational groups as the group "paymaster" and may not be supplied with any services or intangibles itself. Regardless of where that third party business is located, the services or intangibles are supplied to the customer identified in the relevant business agreement and the taxing rights belong to the jurisdiction in which that customer is located. Accordingly it is recommended that:

- the tax administration in the supplier's jurisdiction does not seek tax from the supplier based entirely on the fact that the paymaster third party business is located there, but allows it to make the supply free of VAT to the foreign customer identified in the business agreement
- the tax administration in the customer's jurisdiction ensures that the customer accounts for any tax due on the supply from the foreign supplier, using the reverse charge mechanism, even if the supply is paid for by a third party business.

3.69. The foregoing approach leads to a logical result because supplies are subject to tax in the jurisdiction in which the services or intangibles are used by the business in accordance with the destination principle as implemented by the general rule and there is neither double taxation nor unintended non-taxation in any of the jurisdictions involved.

3.70. Annex 1 to this chapter provides examples of how the general rule on place of taxation for business-to-business supplies of services and intangibles to single location entities, can be applied in practice.

B.5. Commentary on applying the recharge method under the general rule – Supply of a service or intangible to a legal entity with multiple locations ("multiple location entity" – "MLE")

3.71. Guideline 3.4 recommends that taxing rights over a supply of a service or intangible to a MLE accrue to the jurisdiction(s) where the establishment(s) using the service or intangible is (are) located. It is recognised that a number of possible approaches could be used to identify which establishment of the customer MLE is regarded as using a service or intangible and where this establishment is located. The following broad categories of approaches can be distinguished:

- direct use approach, which focuses directly on the establishment that uses the service or intangible
- direct delivery approach, which focuses on the establishment to which the service or intangible is delivered
- recharge method, which focuses on the establishment that uses the service or intangible as determined on the basis of internal recharge arrangements within the MLE, made in accordance with corporate tax, accounting or other regulatory requirements.

3.72. Paragraphs 3.25 to 3.40 provide a broad description of these approaches and their possible use in practice. This Commentary looks in further detail at the recharge method, as tax administrations may be less familiar with the possible operation of this method than with other approaches.

3.73. The recharge method requires MLEs to internally recharge the costs of externally acquired services or intangibles to their establishments that use these services or intangibles, as supported by internal recharge arrangements. Under the recharge method, these internal recharges are used as a basis for allocating the taxing rights over such services or intangibles to the jurisdiction(s) where the establishment(s) using this service or intangible is (are) located.

3.74. This can be achieved by following a two-step approach:

- The first step follows the business agreement between the external supplier and the MLE. The taxing rights over the supply to the MLE are allocated to the jurisdiction of the customer establishment that represents the MLE in the business agreement with the supplier.
- The second step is required when the service or intangible is used wholly or partially by one or more other establishments than the establishment that has represented the MLE in the business agreement with the supplier. This second step follows the internal recharge made by the MLE for allocating the external cost of the service or intangible to the establishment, or establishments, using this service or intangible. This internal recharge is used as the basis for allocating the taxing rights over the service or intangible to the jurisdiction where these establishment(s) of use is (are) located, by treating this internal recharge of the externally acquired service or intangible as within the scope of VAT.

3.75. The following sections consider the application of the recharge method from the perspectives of the supplier, customer and tax administrations. Annex 2 to this chapter provides an example of how the recharge method could be applied in practice.

B.5.1. First step – Supply to the MLE

B.5.1.1. Supplier

3.76. As is the case for any supply, the supplier will need to identify and be able to demonstrate who the customer is and where this customer is located in order to determine where the taxing rights will accrue.

3.77. Under the first step of the recharge method, the taxing rights are allocated to the jurisdiction of the establishment that represents the MLE in the business agreement with the supplier. The various elements of the business agreement with the supplier should identify this establishment and where it is located. Once satisfied that this establishment is located in a jurisdiction other than the supplier's, the supplier will be entitled to make the supply free of VAT in its jurisdiction.

B.5.1.2. Customer

3.78. Where the customer's establishment that has represented the MLE in the business agreement is located in a jurisdiction other than the supplier's, it is recommended that this establishment be liable for any tax due on the transaction. This can be achieved through the reverse charge mechanism (also referred to as "tax shift" or "self-assessment") where this is consistent with the overall design of the national consumption tax system. Under this procedure, this customer's establishment will typically be required to declare the tax due on the supply received from the foreign supplier as output tax on the relevant VAT return. The rate to be applied will be the normal domestic rate applicable to the nature of the service or intangible in the jurisdiction of the customer's establishment. The customer's establishment that makes the recharge will deduct the related input tax in line with the normal rules that ensure VAT neutrality.

3.79. If the customer establishment that has represented the MLE in the business agreement is entitled to full input tax credit in respect of this supply, it may be that local VAT legislation does not require the reverse charge to be made.

B.5.1.3. Tax administrations

3.80. The tax administration in the jurisdiction of the supplier will need to know the nature of the supply as well as the identity of the customer and the jurisdiction in which the customer is located. Where the service or intangible is supplied to a business located in another jurisdiction, this supply will be made free of VAT in the jurisdiction of the supplier. The supplier will therefore need to hold all the relevant information that constitutes the business agreement to demonstrate the nature of the supply and the identity of the customer. Where this customer is a MLE, under the recharge method the business agreement will need to provide evidence of the identity of the establishment that represents the MLE in the business agreement and the location of this establishment. Tax administrations are encouraged to provide businesses with clear guidance on the evidence they require.

3.81. The customer's establishment that has represented the MLE in the business agreement with the supplier will account for any VAT due to its local tax administration under the reverse charge mechanism where that is consistent with the overall design of the national consumption tax system. Tax administrations are encouraged to make businesses aware of the need to account for any tax on "imported" services or intangibles from suppliers in other jurisdictions, including if these services or intangibles are acquired by an establishment of a MLE.

3.82. If the customer's establishment is entitled to full input tax credit in respect of this supply, it may be that local VAT legislation would not require the reverse charge to be made. In such cases tax administrations are also encouraged to publicise this.

B.5.2. Second step – Recharge to the establishment(s) of use

B.5.2.1. Supplier

3.83. The external supplier of the service or intangible to the MLE has no involvement in the recharge of the service or intangible to the customer's establishment of use. This is the sole responsibility of the customer MLE.

B.5.2.2. Customer

3.84. The customer's establishment that has entered into the business agreement with the external supplier will either have acquired the service or intangible for its own use or will have acquired it wholly or partially for use by other establishments of the customer MLE. In the latter case, the customer establishment that has represented the MLE in the business agreement with the external supplier is required to subsequently charge the other establishment(s) of the MLE using the service or intangible. Under the recharge method, this internal charge of the external service or intangible is treated as consideration for a supply within the scope of VAT.

3.85. There will be no recharge if the service or intangible was acquired by an establishment of the MLE for its own use.

3.86. Whether or not there will be a recharge for a service or intangible acquired by an establishment of a MLE for use wholly or partially by another establishment of this MLE in the same jurisdiction, will depend on the internal rules of this jurisdiction. This Commentary deals only with cross-border supplies of services and intangibles.

3.87. As for any other supply, the establishment of recharge will need to identify and be able to demonstrate which is the establishment of use and where this establishment is located.

3.88. Under the recharge method, MLEs will need to have internal arrangements in place to support and facilitate the internal charges between their different establishments. MLEs and tax administrations will rely on these internal arrangements to provide them with the information that would otherwise be covered by a business agreement. These internal arrangements are hereafter referred to as recharge arrangements for the purpose of the application of the recharge method.

3.89. The various elements of the recharge arrangement should facilitate the identification of the establishment of recharge and the establishment(s) of use to which an internal recharge is made and should provide sufficient information to evidence a consistent and correct VAT treatment of the recharge.

3.90. This may be straightforward in many cases, particularly where MLEs have adopted an arrangement where specific services or intangibles acquired externally are recharged as such to the establishment of use. This may for instance be the case for large expenses that can be isolated and charged to the establishment of use, for example in installing a new computer system or performing a major upgrade. Such arrangements are of great practical convenience, as they allow the service or intangible that is recharged as well as the basis for the recharge to be clearly identified. MLEs are encouraged to adopt such arrangements as much as possible for their internal recharges.

3.91. It is recognised however that it will not always be possible to adopt this approach in practice. This may be the case, for instance, where a service or intangible is acquired for use by multiple establishments and a separate recording of use by each of the establishments would be disproportionately burdensome. This may occur where legal services or marketing services are acquired centrally for several establishments of a MLE. A detailed analysis of these services and their use by each of the establishments may be difficult or overly burdensome in certain circumstances. In such cases, MLEs may find it necessary to use cost allocation or apportionment methods that include a certain degree of estimation or approximation of the actual use of the service by each establishment.

3.92. Tax administrations that implement the recharge method are encouraged to allow such cost allocation or apportionment methods where the straightforward recharge for specific services or intangibles would be disproportionately burdensome and to provide businesses with clear guidance on the allocation or apportionment approaches that they consider allowable.

3.93. Such cost allocation or apportionment methods (allocation keys) should be "fair and reasonable", in that they should produce recharges that are commensurate with the reasonably expected use by the establishments of use, follow sound accounting principles and contain safeguards against manipulation. Where possible, information that is already available for accounting and tax and other regulatory purposes should be used. There is no single solution that would be appropriate in all cases. What is "fair and reasonable" depends not only on the type of service but also on the size and structure of a company, the sector and the complexity of the business environment in which it operates. Whatever allocation key is used, it should be capable of being justified and applied consistently without creating undue compliance and administrative burden for businesses and tax administrations.

3.94. Commonly used allocation keys include: number of employees, square meters of office space, number of fleet cars, computer usage, advertising expenses, number of accounting entries, number of invoices processed, etc. A clear, directly measurable allocation key may not always be available, for example in relation to legal expenses, general systems maintenance, etc. In such cases, it is not uncommon for costs to be allocated on the basis of the respective size of the establishments.

3.95. It is important for the proper operation of the recharge method that the relationship between the initial supply of the service or intangible to the MLE (first step) and the onward recharge to the establishment(s) of use (second step) does not become obscured. The objective of the recharge method is to ensure that taxing rights over supplies to an MLE are effectively allocated to the jurisdiction where the establishment of use is located. The MLE will therefore be expected to ensure that tax administrations can reasonably establish the relationship between the initial supply and the recharge and that they can notably establish the link between the price of the initial supply and the amount of the recharge, without requiring a recharge on a transaction-by-transaction basis.

3.96. The establishment of recharge will be entitled to make the recharge free of VAT in its jurisdiction on the basis of the information available in the recharge arrangement, as the other establishment(s) will be located in other jurisdictions. The elements of the recharge arrangement should demonstrate which establishment(s) is (are) using the service and its (their) location in another jurisdiction. It is recommended that the establishment of recharge issue a document equivalent to an invoice for the recharge to the establishment(s) of use.

3.97. To ensure VAT neutrality for the establishment that makes the recharge, general input VAT deduction rules should apply for this establishment in respect of the input VAT on the service or intangible received and subsequently recharged. The application of the recharge method should not influence the MLE's right to input VAT deduction in respect of purchases other than the service or intangible to which the recharge method is applied.

3.98. It is recommended that the establishment of use be liable for any tax due on the recharge. This can be achieved through reverse charge mechanisms (also referred to as "tax shift" or "self-assessment") where this is consistent with the overall design of the national consumption tax system. It may be that local VAT legislation does not require the reverse charge to be made.

3.99. When a service or intangible is used wholly by an establishment other than the one that represented the MLE in the business agreement, the taxable amount would in principle be the amount of the recharge that corresponds to the purchase price of the service or intangible.

3.100. Where the service or intangible is used by several establishments, the taxable amount for each establishment would in principle be the part of the purchase price of the service or intangible that is recharged to this establishment on the basis of an acceptable apportionment or allocation approach.

3.101. The taxable amount should be evidenced by the recharge arrangement. The rate to be applied would in principle be the normal domestic rate applicable to the nature of the service or intangible in the jurisdiction of the customer's establishment of use. This customer's establishment would then be entitled to deduct input tax to the extent allowed under the rules of its jurisdiction.

3.102. Where the recharge of a service or intangible purchased from an external supplier is bundled with an internal cost charge (e.g. salary expense of internally supplied services), it is for the MLE to separate the cost of the externally purchased service or intangible from the other costs and to evidence the internal character of these other costs if this would be necessary to ensure that the recharge method is applied only on the cost of the externally purchased service or intangible.

B.5.2.3. Tax administrations

3.103. Tax administrations are encouraged to provide clear guidance to businesses on the operation of the recharge method, including its scope, the allocation or apportionment approaches that they consider acceptable and the documentation requirements to support this method, the input VAT deduction rules to ensure VAT neutrality for the establishment that makes the recharge, the time of taxation rules to be applied to the internal recharge and the process to account for any tax due on an internal recharge.

3.104. In line with normal audit policies, tax administrations will need an audit trail that enables them, when necessary, to review commercial documentation down to the transaction level in order to identify the nature of the individual service that is recharged and thus to determine whether the place of taxation, the taxable amount and the applicable rate of tax are correct.

3.105. This documentation may include a copy of the original invoice from the external supplier, the allocation method and allocation key used and any other documents or electronic records that show how the VAT was calculated (e.g. distinction between recharge of external costs and internal added value), the documentation from the establishment that makes the recharge requesting payment (i.e. document equivalent to an invoice), accounting entries and documentation supporting the payment by the establishment of use.

3.106. In cases where the separation of external costs from other costs within an internal recharge would be necessary to ensure that the recharge method is applied only on the cost of the externally purchased service or intangible, tax administrations may wish to allow methods that include a certain degree of approximation, notably if a detailed separation would be considered disproportionally burdensome (e.g. in view of the limited amounts involved).

3.107. In addition, it will in principle also be necessary for auditors at the tax administration in the jurisdiction of use to satisfy themselves that:

- Any cross-border recharge of external costs between establishments has been treated as within the scope of VAT.
- Establishments have accounted for VAT correctly on any such recharge, including where netting has taken place.[12]
- The establishment of use has accounted for VAT as if a recharge arrangement were in place, in cases where a service has been purchased by another establishment in a different jurisdiction and the establishment of use has not been recharged even though this recharge was required.

3.108. Where possible, tax administrations should use information that is already available for accounting or tax and other regulatory purposes, to avoid creation of new methodologies and processes purely for VAT purposes.

3.109. It is recommended that any tax due on the internal recharge of a service or intangible purchased from an external supplier be accounted for by the MLE's establishment of use. This can be achieved through reverse charge mechanisms where this is consistent with the overall design of the national consumption tax system. However, it is recognised that local VAT legislation may not require the reverse charge to be made if the establishment of use is entitled to full input tax credit in respect of this supply. In such cases, the tax administration is encouraged to publicise this. Jurisdictions that do require a reverse charge to be made are likewise recommended to make this clear.

C. Business-to-consumer supplies – The general rules

C.1. Introduction

3.110. It is theoretically more straightforward in the business-to-consumer[13] context than in the business-to-business context to implement the destination principle, as set out in Guideline 3.1, to ensure that tax on services and intangibles is ultimately levied only in the jurisdiction where the final consumption occurs. In the business-to-business context, the place of taxation rules should facilitate the ultimate goal of taxing business-to-consumer supplies in the jurisdiction where final consumption occurs, while at the same time ensuring that the burden of the tax does not rest on either business, unless intentionally provided by legislation (see Guideline 2.1 on VAT neutrality in international trade; Chapter 2 of the International VAT/GST Guidelines). In the business-to-consumer context, the objective is simply to tax the final consumption in the jurisdiction where it occurs with the tax burden resting on the final consumer. Accordingly, the primary objective for place of taxation rules in the business-to-consumer context is to predict with reasonable accuracy the place where the services or intangibles are likely to be consumed while taking into account practical constraints, and ideally such place of taxation rules should be simple and practical for taxpayers to apply, for customers to understand and for tax administrations to administer.

3.111. Achieving this objective for business-to-consumer supplies of services was reasonably easy in the past, when consumers typically purchased services from local suppliers and those supplies generally involved services that could be expected to be consumed in the jurisdiction where they were performed.[14] Consequently, some jurisdictions chose to implement VAT systems that determined the place of taxation for such services primarily by reference to the supplier's location, on the assumption that this was where these services were normally performed and where final consumers were actually located when consuming the service. A place of taxation rule based on the supplier's location was often supplemented by a place of taxation rule based on place of performance or other proxies, for cases in which the supplier's location was a less reliable indicator of the location where services were likely to be consumed (e.g. entertainment or sporting events). Over time, a range of services developed for which the supplier's location or the place of performance was used less often to determine the place of taxation and as a consequence the applicability of other rules increased, notably referring to the customer's location. At the same time, VAT systems were implemented in certain jurisdictions that determined the place of taxation using an iterative application of multiple proxies, and such jurisdictions often favoured the customer's location as the key proxy for determining the place of taxation for both business-to-business and business-to-consumer supplies. Still other jurisdictions used a very broad place of effective consumption rule to determine the place of taxation. As a result of these different approaches, there was a lack of consistency and clarity about which jurisdiction should have the right to tax particular supplies of services and intangibles.

3.112. The emergence of the global economy, with its growing reliance on digital supplies, created further challenges for these traditional approaches to determining the place of taxation for business-to-consumer supplies of services and intangibles. Advances in technology and trade liberalisation increasingly enabled businesses to supply services and intangibles to customers around the world, leading to a strong growth in international business-to-consumer trade in remotely supplied services and intangibles. These developments created challenges for VAT systems that used a proxy based on the supplier's location or the place of performance to determine the place of taxation. Where services or intangibles can be supplied remotely to customers who may be located anywhere in the world when they consume the service or intangible, the supplier's location and the place of performance are less likely to accurately predict the likely place of consumption. Place of taxation rules based on those proxies are thus unlikely to lead to an appropriate result. Moreover, often the actual place of performance might be unclear. For example, a technician in one country might take control of a computer in another country to resolve an issue using key strokes performed thousands of kilometres from the computer, using information and communication infrastructure located in a number of different jurisdictions. In such a case, it could be difficult to reach a consistent conclusion on whether the place of performance is where the technician is, where the computer is or somewhere in between.

3.113. For supplies of services and intangibles whose consumption bears no necessary relationship to the location in which the supply is performed and in which the person performing the supply is located, a rule based on the customer's usual residence is the most appropriate approach for determining the place of taxation in a business-to-consumer context. The place in which customers have their usual residence is used by VAT systems around the world as a proxy for predicting the place of consumption of many types of services and intangibles supplied to final consumers. This approach reflects the presumption that final consumers ordinarily consume services and intangibles in the jurisdiction where they have their usual residence and it provides a clear connection to a readily identifiable place. It ensures that the services and intangibles acquired by final consumers from foreign suppliers are taxed on the same basis and at the same rate as domestic supplies, in accordance with Guideline 2.4 on VAT neutrality in international trade (see Chapter 2 of the International VAT/GST Guidelines). There is therefore no tax advantage for final consumers in buying from low or no tax jurisdictions. A place of taxation rule based on the customer's usual residence is also reasonably practical for suppliers to apply, provided that a simplified registration and compliance regime is available (see Sections C.3.2 and C.3.3). It is also reasonably practical for tax administrations to administer, provided that it is supported by effective international co-operation in tax administration and enforcement (see Section C.3.4).

3.114. Against this background, two general rules are recommended for determining the place of taxation for business-to-consumer supplies of services and intangibles:

- for supplies that are physically performed at a readily identifiable place and that are ordinarily consumed at the same time and place where they are physically performed in the presence of both the person performing the supply and the person consuming it ("on-the-spot supplies"), Guideline 3.5 recommends a place of taxation rule based on the place of performance
- for supplies that are not covered by Guideline 3.5, Guideline 3.6 recommends a place of taxation rule based on the customer's usual residence.[15]

3.115. These general rules effectively result in the allocation of the taxing rights over business-to-consumer supplies of services and intangibles to the jurisdiction where it can reasonably be assumed that the final consumer is actually located when consuming the supply. This is the place where the final consumer consumes the on-the-spot supply, or the final consumer's usual residence where he or she is presumed to consume a remotely supplied service or intangible.

C.2. Business-to-consumer supplies – On-the-spot supplies

3.116. The place of physical performance of the supply is the appropriate proxy to determine the place of consumption for on-the-spot supplies of services and intangibles to final consumers. For the purposes of these Guidelines, on-the-spot supplies are services and intangibles that are normally physically performed at a readily identifiable place and are ordinarily consumed at the same time and place where they are physically performed, and that ordinarily require the presence of both the person performing the supply and the person consuming it. As well as providing a reasonably accurate indication of the place of consumption, a place of taxation rule based on the place of physical performance is simple and practical for suppliers to apply and for tax administrations to administer.

Guideline 3.5

For the application of Guideline 3.1, the jurisdiction in which the supply is physically performed has the taxing rights over business-to-consumer supplies of services and intangibles that

- **are physically performed at a readily identifiable place, and**
- **are ordinarily consumed at the same time as and at the same place where they are physically performed, and**
- **ordinarily require the physical presence of the person performing the supply and the person consuming the service or intangible at the same time and place where the supply of such a service or intangible is physically performed.**

3.117. Guideline 3.5 is aimed primarily at supplies that are typically consumed at an identifiable place where they are performed, rather than supplies that can be provided remotely or that can be consumed at a time and place other than the place of performance. Examples include services physically performed on the person (e.g. hairdressing, massage, beauty therapy, physiotherapy); accommodation; restaurant and catering services; entry to cinema, theatre performances, trade fairs, museums, exhibitions, and parks; attendance at sports competitions.[16]

3.118. The final consumption of these supplies ordinarily requires the physical presence of both the person performing the supply, who is usually the supplier, and the person consuming it. The application of Guideline 3.5 thus results in the allocation of the taxing rights to the jurisdiction where the final consumer is located when consuming the supply and where the person performing the supply is located at the time of final consumption.

3.119. On-the-spot supplies can be acquired by businesses as well as by private consumers. Jurisdictions could therefore adopt the approach that is recommended by Guideline 3.5 for business-to-consumer supplies, as a specific rule in the business-to-business context (see paragraphs 3.165-3.166). Such an approach would relieve suppliers of on-the-spot supplies, which are often small or medium businesses, of the compliance burden of having to distinguish between final consumers and businesses when making their taxing decision.[17]

C.3. Business-to-consumer supplies – Supplies of services and intangibles other than those covered by Guideline 3.5

3.120. For supplies of services and intangibles that lack an obvious connection with a readily identifiable place of physical performance and that are not ordinarily consumed at the place where they are physically performed in the presence of the person performing the supply and of the person consuming it, the place of physical performance generally does not provide a good indication of the likely place of consumption. This includes, for example, supplies of services and intangibles that are likely to be consumed at some time other than the time of performance, or for which the consumption and/or performance are likely to be ongoing, as well as services and intangibles that can easily be provided and consumed remotely.

3.121. For such business-to-consumer supplies of services and intangibles, the place of usual residence of the customer is a more appropriate proxy for the jurisdiction of consumption, as it can be assumed that these types of services and intangibles will ordinarily be consumed in the jurisdiction where the customer has his or her usual residence.

Guideline 3.6

For the application of Guideline 3.1, the jurisdiction in which the customer has its usual residence has the taxing rights over business-to-consumer supplies of services and intangibles other than those covered by Guideline 3.5.

3.122. Examples of supplies of services and intangibles that are not covered by Guideline 3.5 could include: consultancy, accountancy and legal services; financial and insurance services; telecommunication and broadcasting services; online supplies of software and software maintenance; online supplies of digital content (movies, TV shows, music, etc.); digital data storage; and online gaming.

C.3.1. Determining the jurisdiction of the usual residence of the customer

3.123. The jurisdiction in which the customer of a business-to-consumer supply has its usual residence is generally where the customer regularly lives or has established a home. Such customers are not considered to have their usual residence in a jurisdiction where they are only temporary, transitory visitors (e.g. as a tourist or as a participant to a training course or a conference).

3.124. Suppliers should be able to rely on information that is known or that can reasonably be known at the time when the tax treatment of the supply must be determined, thereby taking into account the different types of supplies and the circumstances in which such supplies are typically delivered.

3.125. The evidence available to suppliers about the jurisdiction in which the customer has its usual residence is likely to depend on the business model, the type and value of the supplies and on the suppliers' delivery model. Particularly in e-commerce, where activities often involve high volume, low-value supplies that rely on minimal interaction and communication between the supplier and its customer, it will often be difficult to determine the customer's place of usual residence from an agreement. Jurisdictions should provide clear and realistic guidance for suppliers on what is required to determine the place of usual residence of their customers in a business-to-consumer context.

3.126. In the business-to-consumer context, jurisdictions are encouraged to permit suppliers to rely, as much as possible, on information they routinely collect from their customers in the course of their normal business activity, as long as such information provides reasonably reliable evidence of the place of usual residence of their customers. In addition, jurisdictions could consider adopting rules that, if they are satisfied that a business is following these principles, this business should expect challenges only where there is misuse or abuse of such evidence. Any guidance provided by the tax authorities will need to take account of the law and practice in the relevant jurisdictions, including with regard to the protection of personal privacy, while maintaining flexibility for businesses.

3.127. Generally, the information provided by the customer may be considered as important evidence relevant to the determination of the jurisdiction of the customer's usual residence. This could include information collected within business processes (e.g. the ordering process), such as jurisdiction and address, bank details (notably country of the bank account), and credit card information. If needed jurisdictions may require that the reliability of such information be further supported through appropriate indicia of residence. In some cases, such indicia might be the only indication of the jurisdiction of the customer's usual residence. The available indicia will vary depending on the type of business or product involved, and might include the contact telephone number, the Internet Protocol address[18] of the device used to download digital content or the customer's trading history (which could, for example, include information on the predominant place of consumption, language of digital content supplied or billing address). These indicia are likely to evolve over time as technology and business practices develop.

C.3.2. VAT collection in cases where the supplier is not located in the jurisdiction of taxation

3.128. The correct charging, collection and remittance of VAT, and the associated reporting obligations are traditionally the responsibility of suppliers. While requiring suppliers to carry out these responsibilities is relatively straightforward in cases where the supplier is located in the jurisdiction of taxation, the matter could be more complex in cases where a business makes supplies that are taxable in a jurisdiction where it is not located. According to the traditional approach, the non-resident supplier is required to register in the jurisdiction of taxation and charge, collect and remit any tax due there. It is recognised, however, that it can often be complex and burdensome for non-resident suppliers to comply with such obligations in jurisdictions where they have no business presence, and equally difficult for tax administrations to enforce and administer them.

3.129. For cross-border business-to-business supplies of services and intangibles that are taxable in the jurisdiction where the customer is located in accordance with Guideline 3.2, these Guidelines recommend the implementation of a reverse charge mechanism to minimise the administrative burden and complexity for non-resident suppliers, where this is consistent with the overall design of the national VAT system. If the customer is entitled to full input tax credit in respect of this supply, it may be that the local VAT legislation does not require the reverse charge to be made. The reverse charge mechanism shifts the liability to pay the tax from the supplier to the customer. Where only business-to-business supplies are involved, the application of the reverse charge mechanism should relieve the non-resident supplier of any requirement to be identified for VAT or to account for tax in the jurisdiction of taxation.

3.130. The reverse charge mechanism does not offer an appropriate solution for collecting VAT on business-to-consumer supplies of services and intangibles from non-resident suppliers. The level of compliance with a reverse charge mechanism for business-to-consumer supplies is likely to be low, since private consumers have little incentive to declare and pay the tax due, at least in the absence of meaningful sanctions for failing to comply with such an obligation. Moreover, enforcing the collection of small amounts of VAT from large numbers of private consumers is likely to involve considerable costs that would outweigh the revenue involved.

3.131. Work carried out by the OECD and other international organisations, as well as individual country experience, indicate that, at the present time, the most effective and efficient approach to ensure the appropriate collection of VAT on cross-border business-to-consumer supplies is to require the non-resident supplier to register and account for the VAT in the jurisdiction of taxation.

3.132. When implementing a registration-based collection mechanism for non-resident suppliers, it is recommended that jurisdictions consider establishing a simplified registration and compliance regime to facilitate compliance for non-resident suppliers. The highest feasible levels of compliance by non-resident suppliers are likely to be achieved if compliance obligations in the jurisdiction of taxation are limited to what is strictly necessary for the effective collection of the tax. Appropriate simplification is particularly important to facilitate compliance for businesses faced with obligations in multiple jurisdictions. Where traditional registration and compliance procedures are complex, their application for non-resident suppliers of business-to-consumer services and intangibles would risk creating barriers that may lead to non-compliance or to certain suppliers declining to serve customers in jurisdictions that impose such burdens.

3.133. A simplified registration and compliance regime for non-resident suppliers of business-to-consumer services and intangibles would operate separately from the traditional registration and compliance regime, without the same rights (e.g. input tax recovery) and obligations (e.g. full reporting) as a traditional regime. Experience with such simplified registration and compliance regimes has shown that they provide a practical and relatively effective solution for securing VAT revenues on business-to-consumer supplies of services and intangibles by non-resident suppliers, while minimising economic distortions and preserving neutrality between resident and non-resident suppliers. Such mechanisms allow tax administrations to capture a significant proportion of tax revenues associated with supplies to final consumers within their jurisdiction while incurring relatively limited administrative costs.

3.134. It is recognised that a proper balance needs to be struck between simplification and the needs of tax administrations to safeguard the revenue. Tax administrations need to ensure that the right amount of tax is collected and remitted from suppliers with which they might have no jurisdictional relationship. Against this background, Section C.3.3 below sets out the possible main features of a simplified registration and compliance regime for non-resident suppliers of business-to-consumer services and intangibles, balancing the need for simplification and the need of tax administrations to safeguard the revenue. This is intended to assist taxing jurisdictions[19] in evaluating and developing their framework for collecting VAT on business-to-consumer supplies of services and intangibles from non-resident suppliers with a view to increasing consistency among compliance processes across jurisdictions. Greater consistency among country approaches will further facilitate compliance, particularly by businesses that are faced with multi-jurisdictional obligations, reduce compliance costs and improve the effectiveness and quality of compliance processes. For tax authorities, consistency is also likely to support the effective international co-operation in tax administration and enforcement.

C.3.3. Main features of a simplified registration and compliance regime for non-resident suppliers

3.135. This section explores the key measures that taxing jurisdictions could take to simplify the administrative and compliance process of a registration-based collection regime for business-to-consumer supplies of services and intangibles by non-resident suppliers.

3.136. This section is intended to assist jurisdictions in evaluating and developing their framework for collecting VAT on business-to-consumer supplies of services and intangibles by non-resident businesses and to suggest the possible main features of a simplified registration and compliance regime. It also considers whether the scope of such a simplified registration and compliance regime could be extended to cross-border business-to-business supplies and recalls the proportionality principle as a guiding principle for the operation of a registration-based collection mechanism for non-resident suppliers. It identifies the possible simplification measures for each of the following core elements of a simplified administrative and compliance regime:

- Registration
- Input tax recovery – Refunds
- Returns
- Payments
- Record keeping
- Invoicing
- Availability of information
- Use of third-party service providers.

3.137. This section recognises the important role of technology for the simplification of administration and compliance. Many tax administrations have taken steps to exploit the use of technology to develop a range of electronic services to support their operations, in particular those concerned with tax collection processes and the provision of basic services to taxpayers. The reasons for this are fairly obvious: applied effectively, these technologies can deliver considerable benefits both to tax administrations and taxpayers (e.g. lower compliance and administrative costs and faster and more accessible services for taxpayers). But the use of technology will be effective only if the core elements of the administrative and compliance process are sufficiently clear and simple. This section therefore focuses mainly on possible simplification of administrative and compliance procedures while devoting less attention to technological features, recognising that these technologies are likely to continue to evolve over time.

C.3.3.1. Registration procedure

3.138. Simple registration procedures can be an important incentive for non-resident suppliers to engage with the tax authority of a jurisdiction where they might have no link other than the supply of services or intangibles to final consumers. The information requested could be limited to necessary details, which could include:

- Name of business, including the trading name
- Name of contact person responsible for dealing with tax administrations
- Postal and/or registered address of the business and its contact person
- Telephone number of contact person
- Electronic address of contact person
- Web sites URL of non-resident suppliers through which business is conducted in the taxing jurisdiction
- National tax identification number, if such a number is issued to the supplier in the supplier's jurisdiction to conduct business in that jurisdiction.

3.139. The simplest way to engage with tax administrations from a remote location is most likely by electronic processes. An on-line registration application could be made accessible on the home page of the tax administration's web site, preferably available in the languages of the jurisdiction's major trading partners.

C.3.3.2. Input tax recovery – Refunds

3.140. It is reasonable for taxing jurisdictions to limit the scope of a simplified registration and compliance regime to the collection of VAT on business-to-consumer supplies of services and intangibles by non-resident suppliers without making the recovery of input tax available under the simplified regime. Where applicable, the input tax recovery could then remain available for non-resident suppliers under the normal VAT refund or registration and compliance procedure.

C.3.3.3. Return procedure

3.141. As requirements differ widely among jurisdictions, satisfying obligations to file tax returns in multiple jurisdictions is a complex process that often results in considerable compliance burdens for non-resident suppliers. Tax administrations could consider authorising non-resident businesses to file simplified returns, which would be less detailed than returns required for local businesses that are entitled to input tax credits. In establishing the requirements for information under such a simplified approach, it is desirable to strike a balance between the businesses' need for simplicity and the tax administrations' need to verify whether tax obligations have been correctly fulfilled. This information could be confined to:

- Supplier's registration identification number
- Tax period
- Currency and, where relevant, exchange rate used
- Taxable amount at the standard rate
- Taxable amount at reduced rate(s), if any
- Total tax amount payable.

3.142. The option to file electronically in a simple and commonly used format will be essential to facilitating compliance. Many tax administrations have already introduced or are introducing options to submit tax returns electronically.

C.3.3.4. Payments

3.143. The use of electronic payment methods is recommended, allowing non-resident suppliers to remit the tax due electronically. This not only reduces the burden and the cost of the payment process for the supplier, but it also reduces payment processing costs for tax administrations. Jurisdictions could consider accepting payments in the currencies of their main trading partners.

C.3.3.5. Record keeping

3.144. Tax administrations must be able to review data to ensure that the tax has been charged and accounted for correctly. Jurisdictions are encouraged to allow the use of electronic record keeping systems, as business processes have become increasingly automated and paper documents generally have been replaced by documents in an electronic format. Jurisdictions could consider limiting the data to be recorded to what is required to satisfy themselves that the tax for each supply has been charged and accounted for correctly and relying as much as possible on information that is available to suppliers in the course of their normal business activity. This could include the type of supply, the date of the supply, the VAT payable and the information used to determine the place where the customer has its usual residence. Taxing jurisdictions could require these records to be made available on request within a reasonable delay.

C.3.3.6. Invoicing

3.145. Invoicing requirements for VAT purposes are among the most burdensome responsibilities of VAT systems. Jurisdictions could therefore consider eliminating invoice requirements for business-to-consumer supplies that are covered by the simplified registration and compliance regime, in light of the fact that the customers involved generally will not be entitled to deduct the input VAT paid on these supplies.

3.146. If invoices are required, jurisdictions could consider allowing invoices to be issued in accordance with the rules of the supplier's jurisdiction or accepting commercial documentation that is issued for purposes other than VAT (e.g. electronic receipts). It is recommended that information on the invoice remain limited to the data required to administer the VAT regime (such as the identification of the customer, type and date of the supply(ies), the taxable amount and VAT amount per VAT rate and the total taxable amount). Jurisdictions could consider allowing this invoice to be submitted in the languages of their main trading partners.

C.3.3.7. Availability of information

3.147. Jurisdictions are encouraged to make available on-line all information necessary to register and comply with the simplified registration and compliance regime, preferably in the languages of their major trading partners. Jurisdictions are also encouraged to make accessible via the Internet the relevant and up-to-date information that non-resident businesses are likely to need in making their tax determinations. In particular, this would include information on tax rates and product classification.

C.3.3.8. Use of third-party service providers

3.148. Compliance for non-resident suppliers could be further facilitated by allowing such suppliers to appoint a third-party service provider to act on their behalf in carrying out certain procedures, such as submitting returns. This could be especially helpful for small and medium enterprises and businesses that are faced with multi-jurisdictional obligations.

C.3.3.9. Application in a business-to-business context

3.149. The implementation of a simplified registration and compliance regime for non-resident suppliers is recommended primarily in the context of business-to-consumer supplies of services and intangibles by non-resident suppliers. These Guidelines recommend the reverse charge mechanism for cross-border business-to-business supplies of services and intangibles that are taxable in the jurisdiction where the customer is located in accordance with Guideline 3.2. If the customer is entitled to full input tax credit in respect of this supply, it could be that the local VAT legislation does not require the reverse charge to be made. Jurisdictions whose general rules do not differentiate between business-to-business and business-to-consumers supplies in their national legislation may consider allowing the use of the simplified registration and compliance regime for both types of supplies.

C.3.3.10. Proportionality

3.150. Jurisdictions should aim to implement a registration-based collection mechanism for business-to-consumer supplies of services and intangibles by non-resident suppliers, without creating compliance and administrative burdens that are disproportionate to the revenues involved or to the objective of achieving neutrality between domestic and foreign suppliers (see also Guideline 2.6 on VAT neutrality in international trade; Chapter 2 of the International VAT/GST Guidelines).

3.151. This objective should be pursued primarily through the implementation of simplified registration and compliance mechanisms that are consistent across jurisdictions and that are sufficiently clear and accessible to allow easy compliance by non-resident suppliers, notably by small and medium enterprises. Some jurisdictions have implemented a threshold of supplies into the jurisdiction of taxation below which non-resident suppliers would be relieved of the obligation to collect and remit tax in that jurisdiction, with a view to further reducing compliance costs. Relieving suppliers of the obligation to register in jurisdictions where their sales are minimal in value may not lead to substantial net losses of revenue in light of the offsetting expenses of tax administration. The introduction of thresholds needs to be considered carefully. A balance will need to be struck between minimising compliance burdens for non-resident suppliers and costs of tax administration while ensuring that resident businesses are not placed at a competitive disadvantage.

C.3.4. International co-operation to support VAT collection in cases where the supplier is not located in the jurisdiction of taxation

3.152. While simplification is a key means of enhancing compliance by non-resident suppliers with a registration-based collection mechanism for cross-border business-to-consumer supplies of services and intangibles, it is necessary to reinforce taxing authorities' enforcement capacity through enhanced international co-operation in tax administration in the field of indirect taxes.

3.153. Improved international co-operation could focus on the exchange of information and on assistance in recovery. Mutual administrative assistance is a key means to achieve the proper collection and remittance of the tax on cross-border supplies of services and intangibles by non-resident suppliers. It will also be helpful in identifying suppliers, verifying the status of customers, monitoring the volume of supplies, and ensuring that the proper amount of tax is charged. The exchange of information between the tax authorities of the jurisdictions of supply and consumption has a key role to play. This could include the use of spontaneous exchanges of information.

3.154. Chapter 4, Section B of these Guidelines describes the principal existing OECD instruments for exchange of information and other forms of mutual administrative assistance that can assist jurisdictions in strengthening the international administrative co-operation in the field of indirect taxes. These Guidelines recommend that jurisdictions take appropriate steps towards making greater use of these and other available legal instruments for international administrative co-operation to ensure the effective collection of VAT on cross-border business-to-consumer supplies of services and intangibles by non-resident businesses. Such co-operation could be enhanced through the development of a common standard for the exchange of information that is simple, minimises the costs for tax administrations and businesses by limiting the amount of data that is exchanged, and which can be implemented in a short timeframe. Against this background, the OECD's Committee on Fiscal Affairs (CFA) intends to conduct work on further, detailed guidance for the effective exchange of information and other forms of mutual assistance between tax authorities in the field of indirect taxes.

D. Business-to-business and business-to-consumer supplies – Specific rules

D.1. Evaluation framework for assessing the desirability of a specific rule

> **Guideline 3.7**
>
> **The taxing rights over internationally traded services or intangibles supplied between businesses may be allocated by reference to a proxy other than the customer's location as laid down in Guideline 3.2, when both the following conditions are met:**
>
> **a. The allocation of taxing rights by reference to the customer's location does not lead to an appropriate result when considered under the following criteria:**
>
> - **Neutrality**
> - **Efficiency of compliance and administration**
> - **Certainty and simplicity**
> - **Effectiveness**
> - **Fairness.**
>
> **b. A proxy other than the customer's location would lead to a significantly better result when considered under the same criteria.**
>
> **Similarly, the taxing rights over internationally traded business-to-consumer supplies of services or intangibles may be allocated by reference to a proxy other than the place of performance as laid down in Guideline 3.5 and the usual residence of the customer as laid down in Guideline 3.6, when both the conditions are met as set out in a. and b. above.**

3.155. According to Guideline 3.2, the jurisdiction where the customer is located has the taxing rights over services or intangibles supplied across international borders in a business-to-business context. This is the general rule for determining the place of taxation for business-to-business supplies of services and intangibles. In a business-to-consumer context, two general rules are set out in Guidelines 3.5 and 3.6 respectively for two main types of supplies of services and intangibles:

- According to Guideline 3.5, the jurisdiction in which the supply is physically performed has the taxing rights over business-to-consumer on-the-spot supplies of services and intangibles.[20]
- According to Guideline 3.6, the jurisdiction in which the customer has its usual residence has the taxing rights over business-to-consumer supplies of services and intangibles other than those covered by Guideline 3.5.

3.156. It is recognised that these general rules might not give an appropriate tax result in every situation and, where this is the case, the allocation of taxing rights by reference to another proxy might be justified. A rule that allocates taxing rights using a proxy other than those recommended by Guideline 3.2 (for business-to-business supplies) or Guidelines 3.5 and 3.6 (for business-to consumer supplies), is referred to in these Guidelines as a "specific rule". Such a rule will use a different proxy (e.g. location of movable or immovable tangible property, actual location of the customer, or place of effective use and enjoyment) to determine which jurisdiction has the taxing rights over a supply of a service or intangible that is covered by the rule. Any such specific rule should be supported by clear criteria and its application should remain limited. Guideline 3.7 describes these criteria and sets out how they may justify the implementation of a specific rule.

3.157. Under Guideline 3.7, a two-step approach is recommended to determine whether a specific rule is justified:

- The first step is to test whether the relevant general rule leads to an appropriate result under the criteria set out under Guideline 3.7. Where this is the case, there is no need for a specific rule. Where the analysis suggests that the relevant general rule would not lead to an appropriate result, the use of a specific rule might be justified. In such case, a second step is required.
- The second step is to test the proposed specific rule against the criteria of Guideline 3.7. The use of a specific rule will be justified only when this analysis suggests that it would lead to a significantly better result than the use of the relevant general rule.

3.158. These Guidelines do not aim to identify the types of supplies of services or intangibles, nor the particular circumstances or factors, for which a specific rule might be justified. Rather, they provide an evaluation framework for jurisdictions to assess the desirability of a specific rule against the background of a constantly changing technological and commercial environment. The next paragraphs describe this framework in further detail.

3.159. The evaluation framework for assessing the desirability of a specific rule builds on the overall objective of the Guidelines on place of taxation, as described in paragraph 3.3. In accordance with this objective, the evaluation framework for assessing the desirability of a specific rule on place of taxation consists of the following criteria:

- Neutrality: The six Guidelines on neutrality and their comments (Guidelines 2.1 to 2.6; Chapter 2 of the International VAT/GST Guidelines).
- Efficiency of compliance and administration: Compliance costs for taxpayers and administrative costs for the tax authorities should be minimised as far as possible.
- Certainty and simplicity: The tax rules should be clear and simple to understand so that taxpayers can anticipate the tax consequences in advance of a transaction, including knowing when, where and how to account for the tax.
- Effectiveness: The tax rules should produce the right amount of tax at the right time and the right place.
- Fairness: The potential for tax evasion and avoidance should be minimised while keeping counteractive measures proportionate to the risks involved.

3.160. Ensuring that the tax treatment of internationally traded supplies is in accordance with these criteria requires a consistent definition and implementation of place of taxation rules. The general rules in Guidelines 3.2, 3.5 and 3.6 set out recommended approaches for ensuring a consistent determination of place of taxation for internationally traded services and intangibles. The use of specific rules that use different proxies from these main approaches should be limited to the greatest possible extent, since the existence of specific rules will increase the risk of differences in interpretation and application between jurisdictions and thereby increase the risks of double taxation and unintended non-taxation.[21]

3.161. When assessing the desirability of a specific rule on the basis of the evaluation framework set out above, one should consider each of the criteria while also recognising that they form a package. No single criterion can be considered in isolation as the criteria are all interconnected. For example, neutrality, as described in the Guidelines on neutrality, and efficiency of compliance and administration are complementary to one another.

Similarly, efficiency depends on the degree of certainty and simplicity, whereas certainty and simplicity are also fundamental to achieving effectiveness and fairness. It is therefore unlikely that evaluating the performance of a general rule (or an alternative specific rule) in a particular scenario would result in a very low ranking when judged against one or two criteria but in a much higher ranking when judged against the other criteria. Rather, it is expected that the evaluation will reveal either a good or a poor outcome overall.

3.162. Consequently, it is recommended that jurisdictions consider implementing a specific rule for the allocation of taxing rights on internationally traded services and intangibles only if the overall outcome of the evaluation on the basis of the criteria set out in Guideline 3.7 suggests that the relevant general rule would not lead to an appropriate result and an evaluation on the basis of the same criteria suggests that the proposed specific rule would lead to a significantly better result.

3.163. While there remains a level of subjectivity as to what is and what is not an "appropriate result" and what is "a significantly better result", Guideline 3.7 provides a framework for assessing the desirability of a specific rule that should make the adoption of such a rule more transparent, systematic and verifiable. It is neither feasible nor desirable to provide more prescriptive instructions on what should be the outcome of the evaluation for all supplies of services and intangibles. However, the paragraphs below provide further guidance and specific considerations for particular supplies of services and intangibles for which a specific rule might be appropriate in some circumstances and conditions. The evaluation should be considered from the perspective of both businesses and tax administrations.

D.2. Circumstances where a specific rule may be desirable

3.164. It is recognised that the general rules on place of taxation as set out in Guideline 3.2, for business-to-business supplies, and in Guidelines 3.5 and 3.6, for business-to-consumer supplies, will lead to an appropriate result when considered against the criteria set out in Guideline 3.7 in most circumstances. However, the following paragraphs describe a number of specific circumstances where jurisdictions might find that the application of these general rules is likely to lead to an inappropriate result when considered against these criteria and that a specific rule might lead to a significantly better result.

D.2.1. Examples of circumstances where a specific rule might be desirable in a business-to-business context

3.165. In a business-to-business context, the general rule based on the customer's location might not lead to an appropriate result when considered against the criteria of Guideline 3.7 and a specific rule could lead to a significantly better result in situations where all the following circumstances are met:

- particular services or intangibles are typically supplied to both businesses and final consumers
- the service requires, in some way, the physical presence of both the person providing the supply and the person receiving the supply, and
- the service is used at a readily identifiable location.

3.166. If businesses that usually supply services or intangibles to a large number of customers for relatively small amounts in a short period of time (e.g. restaurant services) were required to follow the general rule based on the customer's location for business-to-business supplies, it would impose a significant compliance burden on suppliers. Any customer, business or non-business, could simply state that it was a business located in another country and request that no VAT be charged. It would put the supplier at considerable risk of having to bear the under-declared tax if it was subsequently shown that the customer was not a business located in another country (breach of certainty and simplicity). This would also make tax administration controls more difficult as evidence of location might be difficult to produce (breach of efficiency). The same considerations could apply to services that consist of granting the right to access events such as a concert, a sports game, or even a trade fair or exhibition that is designed primarily for businesses. If a ticket can be purchased at the entrance of the building where the event takes place, businesses as well as final consumers can be recipients of the service. In these cases, under the general rule based on the customer's location for business-to-business supplies, the supplier is confronted with the difficulty and risk of identifying and providing evidence of the customer's status and location. Efficiency, as well as certainty and simplicity, might then not be met. Fairness could be at risk. The adoption of a specific rule allocating the taxing rights to the jurisdiction where the event takes place could lead to a significantly better result when considered against the criteria of Guideline 3.7. In such circumstances, jurisdictions might consider using a proxy based on the place of physical performance, which would apply both for business-to-business supplies and business-to-consumer supplies (see Guideline 3.5).

D.2.2. Examples of circumstances where a specific rule might be desirable in a business-to-consumer context

3.167. In a business-to-consumer context, jurisdictions might find that the general rules set out in Guidelines 3.5 and 3.6 do not lead to an appropriate result when considered against the criteria of Guideline 3.7 in certain specific circumstances, where they lead to an allocation of taxing rights that is inefficient and overly burdensome from an administrative standpoint (breach of efficiency and of certainty and simplicity) and/or are not sufficiently accurate in predicting the likely place of final consumption (breach of effectiveness and of neutrality). For example, this might occur in the following circumstances:

- The general rule based on the place of physical performance (Guideline 3.5), in respect of on-the-spot supplies of services and intangibles, might not lead to an appropriate result when considered against the criteria of Guideline 3.7 in cases where the physical performance occurs in multiple jurisdictions because tax obligations could arise in multiple jurisdictions (breach of the efficiency and the certainty and simplicity requirements). An example is the international transport of persons.
- In cases where consumption is most likely to occur somewhere other than in the customer's usual place of residence, the general rule based on the place of the usual residence of the customer for supplies of services and intangibles not covered by Guideline 3.5 (Guideline 3.6) might not be sufficiently accurate in predicting the place of final consumption (breach of the effectiveness and the neutrality requirements). Examples could include services and intangibles that are performed at a readily identifiable location and that require the physical presence of the person consuming the supply but not the physical presence of the person performing it, such as the provision of Internet access in an Internet café or a hotel lobby, the use of a telephone booth to make a phone call or the access to television channels for a fee in a hotel room.[22] In such cases, it is reasonable to assume that suppliers will know or are capable of knowing the actual location of the customer at the likely time of consumption and jurisdictions may then consider using the actual location of the consumer at the time of the supply as a proxy for place of consumption.

D.3. Special considerations for supplies of services and intangibles directly connected with tangible property

3.168. Jurisdictions often choose to rely on the location of tangible property for determining the place of taxation for supplies of services and intangibles connected with tangible property or with the supply of such property. The business use or final consumption of such services is then considered to be so connected with the business use or the final consumption of the tangible property that the location of this tangible property is considered as the most appropriate place of taxation.

3.169. The following sections look specifically at services and intangibles connected with immovable property, as this is a particularly complex area where a specific rule is already applied by many jurisdictions both in a business-to-business context and in a business-to-consumer context (Sections D.3.1-D.3.4). This is complemented by a section on services and intangibles connected with movable tangible property, which explains that a rule based on the location of the movable tangible property might be particularly appropriate for identifying the place of taxation in a business-to-consumer context (Section D.3.5).

D.3.1. Specific rule for supplies of services and intangibles directly connected with immovable property

Guideline 3.8

For internationally traded supplies of services and intangibles directly connected with immovable property, the taxing rights may be allocated to the jurisdiction where the immovable property is located.

3.170. According to this specific rule, taxing rights are allocated to the jurisdiction where the immovable property is located.

3.171. This Guideline does not list particular supplies of services and intangibles that may or may not fall under such a specific rule. Instead, it identifies their common features and establishes categories of supplies of services and intangibles for which the conditions set out in Guideline 3.7 might be met and for which implementation of such a specific rule might therefore be justified.

D.3.2. Circumstances where a specific rule for supplies of services and intangibles directly connected with immovable property might be appropriate

3.172. When internationally traded services and intangibles are directly connected with immovable property, there may be circumstances where a specific rule allocating the taxing rights to the jurisdiction where the immovable property is located might be appropriate.

3.173. This is most likely to be the case when there is a supply of services or intangibles falling within one of the following categories:

- the transfer, sale, lease or the right to use, occupy, enjoy or exploit immovable property
- supplies of services that are physically provided to the immovable property itself, such as constructing, altering and maintaining the immovable property, or

- other supplies of services and intangibles that do not fall within the first two categories but where there is a very close, clear and obvious link or association with the immovable property.

3.174. The second condition for the implementation of a specific rule under Guideline 3.7 requires that such a specific rule would lead to a significantly better result than the relevant general rule when evaluated against the criteria of Guideline 3.7. While it is reasonable to assume that this second condition is met for the first two categories of supplies identified above, its fulfilment for the supplies mentioned in the last category above is likely to require an evaluation as set out in Guideline 3.7 before the implementation of a specific rule can be considered.

D.3.3. Common features of supplies of services and intangibles directly connected with immovable property

3.175. The supplies of services and intangibles for which Guideline 3.8 may apply are referred to as "services directly connected with immovable property". This expression does not have an independent meaning but aims simply to narrow the scope of the specific rule in the sense that it contemplates that there should be a very close, clear and obvious link or association between the supply and the immovable property. This very close, clear and obvious link or association is considered to exist only when the immovable property is clearly identifiable.

3.176. For the supply to be considered as directly connected with immovable property, it is not sufficient that a connection with immovable property be merely one aspect of the supply among many others: the connection with immovable property must be at the heart of the supply and must constitute its predominant characteristic. This is particularly relevant with respect to composite supplies involving immovable property. If a connection with immovable property is only one part of the supply, this will not be sufficient for the supply to fall under one of the three categories.

D.3.4. Further description of the supplies of services and intangibles directly connected with immovable property for which a specific rule might be appropriate

3.177. The transfer, sale, lease, or the right to use, occupy, enjoy or exploit immovable property, encompasses all kinds of utilisation of immovable property, i.e. supplies of services and intangibles "derived from" the immovable property (as opposed to other circumstances where the supplies are directed to the immovable property). The terms "transfer", "sale", "lease", and "right to use, occupy, enjoy or exploit" therefore should not be understood narrowly within the meaning of national civil laws. It should be noted however, that these supplies fall under this Guideline only when they are considered to be supplies of services or intangibles under national law, i.e. when they are not considered to be supplies of goods or of immovable property.[23]

3.178. Supplies of services such as the construction, alteration and maintenance of immovable property cover services that are typically physical in nature, as opposed, for example, to intellectual services. Such supplies of services are physically provided to immovable property. These are services that aim to change or maintain the physical status of the immovable property. Typical cases in practice will include, for example, the construction of a building[24] as well as its renovation or demolition, the painting of a building or even the cleaning of it (inside or outside).

3.179. In addition to the utilisation of immovable property and services that are physically performed on immovable property, there might be other supplies of services and intangibles where there is a very close, clear and obvious link or association with immovable property and where taxation in the jurisdiction of the immovable property leads to a significantly better result than the relevant general rule when considered under the criteria defined in Guideline 3.7. When considering the adoption of a specific rule, jurisdictions may in particular wish to take into account, in addition to the requirement of a very close, clear and obvious link or association between the supply and the immovable property, whether such a specific rule has a sufficiently high potential to be manageable and enforceable in practice. For example, certain intellectual services,[25] such as architectural services that relate to clearly identifiable, specific immovable property, could be considered to have a sufficiently close connection with immovable property.

D.3.5. Services and intangibles connected with movable tangible property

3.180. Examples of services and intangibles connected with movable property include services that are physically carried out on specific movable property such as repairing, altering or maintaining the property, and the rental of specific movable property where this is considered a service. Jurisdictions might consider implementing an approach based on the location of movable tangible property for identifying the place of taxation of such supplies of services and intangibles connected with movable tangible property. Such an approach ensures that the place of taxation rules for such supplies provide a reasonably accurate reflection of the place where the consumption of the services or intangibles is likely to take place and is relatively straightforward for suppliers to apply in practice, particularly in the case of business-to-consumer supplies. Services or intangibles connected with movable tangible property supplied to final consumers, such as repair services, will generally be consumed in the jurisdiction where the property is located. Movable tangible property that is shipped abroad after the service is performed will generally be subject to import VAT under standard customs rules when crossing the customs border. This ensures that the taxing rights accrue to the jurisdiction of consumption when the tangible property moves across the customs border. Jurisdictions generally complement these rules by giving temporary VAT relief in the jurisdiction where the supply is performed and where the movable property is temporarily located, if this property is subsequently exported. This treatment lies outside the scope of these Guidelines.[26]

3.181. For business-to-business supplies of services and intangibles connected with movable property, the application of the general rule based on the customer's location will generally lead to an appropriate result.

Annex 1

Examples to illustrate the application of the general rule on place of taxation for business-to-business supplies of services and intangibles to Single location Entities

The examples in this annex are illustrative of the principles set out in the Guidelines and consequently are not intended to be exhaustive. The place of taxation of internationally traded services and intangibles will be determined according to the facts of each individual supply.

Example 1: Supply between 2 separate legal entities (whether related by common ownership or not)

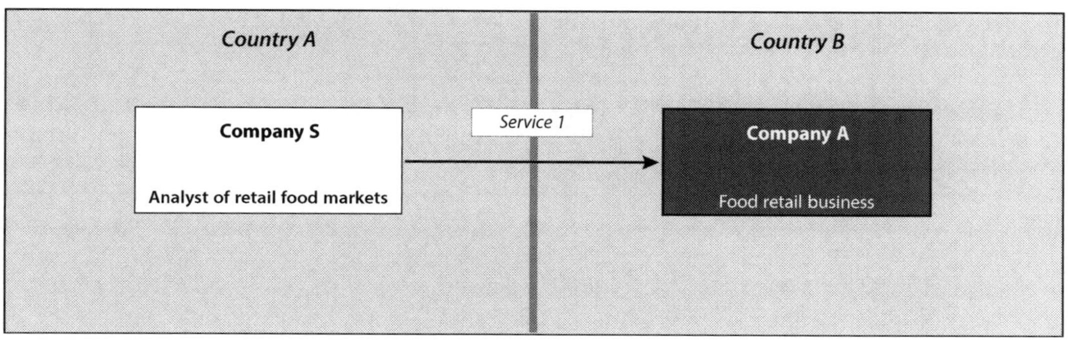

Facts

Company S is a business located in Country A specialising in analysing retail food markets, Company A is a food retail business located in Country B. Neither Company S nor Company A has other establishments for VAT purposes. Company A is considering expanding its retailing activities beyond Country B and approaches Company S. The two companies enter into a business agreement under which Company S will provide an analysis of market conditions in Country A to Company A. Company A will pay Company S a sum of money in return for Company S performing its obligations under this business agreement.

Place of taxation

According to the business agreement, Company S will be the supplier and Company B will be the customer. There will be a supply of a service provided by the supplier to the customer for consideration. In accordance with the general rule for business-to-business supplies (Guideline 3.2), the place of taxation will be Country B, which is the country where the customer is located.

The result remains the same even where the supplier and customer are two separate legal entities related by ownership.

Example 2: Two separate supplies involving three separate legal entities

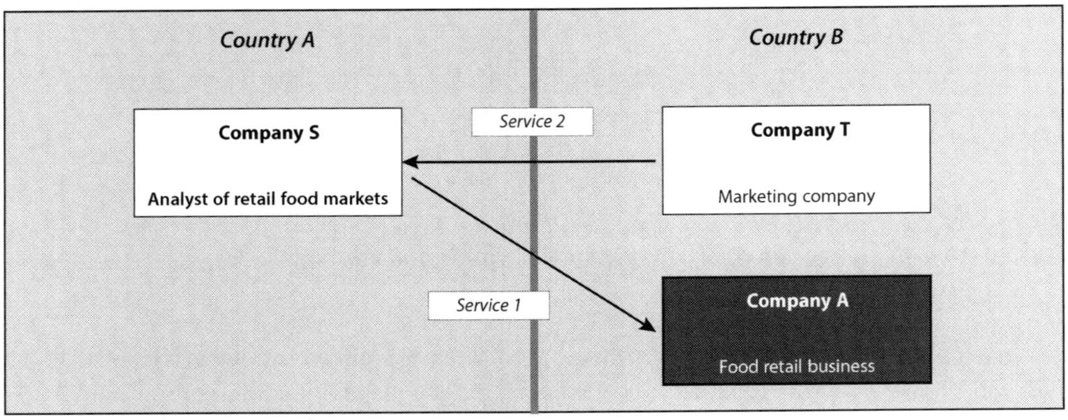

Facts

As Company A subsequently requested Company S to also perform studies on its own market in Country B, Company S engages the services of a marketing company in Country B, Company T. This company has no ownership connection with Company S or Company A.

Company T supplies its services of marketing to Company S under a business agreement (Service 2). The supply of Service 1 between Company S and Company A (as outlined in Example 1 – analysis of the market conditions in Country A) continues as before.

Place of taxation

According to the business agreement Company T is the supplier and Company S the customer. There is a supply of services for consideration. Therefore, in accordance with the general rule for business-to-business supplies (Guideline 3.2), the supply by Company T will be subject to taxation in Country A because that is the country where the customer is located. These are two independent supplies and are treated accordingly.

The outcome of Service 1 as outlined in Example 1 remains unaffected.

Example 3: A global agreement

This example illustrates the supplies that occur when a global agreement for a supply of auditing services is entered into between the parent company of an audit group and a centralised purchasing company of the group requiring audit services for other group members in various countries.

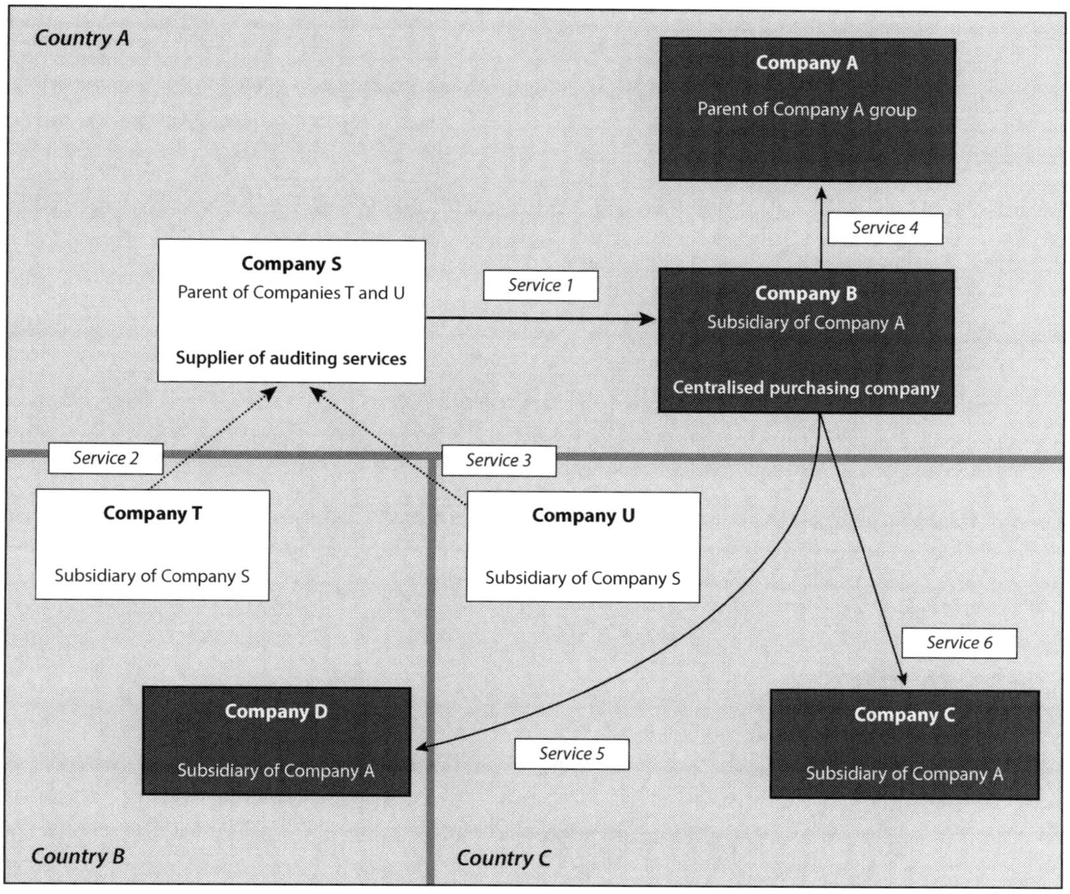

Facts

Company B is a centralised purchasing company in Country A. It belongs to a multinational company group with subsidiaries around the world, notably Company D in Country B and Company C in Country C. The parent company of Company B is Company A, also located in Country A.

Company S in Country A is the parent company of a multinational auditing company group with subsidiaries around the world, notably Company T in Country B and Company U in Country C.

Company A Group requires a global auditing service to meet legal requirements for the companies in Country A and its subsidiaries in Countries B and C. The global auditing service is purchased for the whole group by Company B, which therefore concludes a centralised purchasing agreement with Company S to supply auditing services to the whole Company A Group. Payment will follow each business agreement.

The global auditing service is supplied by Company S to Company B in return for consideration. While this service includes the supply of all components of the global agreement, Company S is able to actually perform only part of the services itself, namely the services to Companies A and B that are located in Country A. To be able to fulfil the rest of the agreement, Company S enters into business agreements with its two subsidiaries, Company T and Company U, under which these companies supply auditing services to their parent Company S. Companies S and T provide these services directly to the subsidiaries of Company A. These subsidiaries, Companies C and D, are in the same countries as the subsidiaries of Company A that provide the auditing service to them.

Company B enters into separate business agreements with its parent Company A and Company A's subsidiaries C and D. Under these business agreements, Company B supplies the auditing services that it has acquired from Company S, to Company A and to Company A's subsidiaries C and D.

There are six separate business agreements in this example, each leading to a supply of a service for consideration:

- Company S is the supplier and Company B is the customer under the centralised purchase agreement (Service 1).
- Companies T and U are the suppliers and Company S is the customer under two different business agreements (Service 2 and Service 3).
- Company B is the supplier and Company A is the customer under a different agreement (Service 4).
- Company B is the supplier and Company D and Company C are the customers under two different business agreements (Service 5 and Service 6).

The place of taxation will be decided for each supply individually.

Place of taxation

In accordance with the general rule for business-to-business supplies (Guideline 3.2), the place of taxation for the supply of Service 1 between Company S and Company B will be Country A as Company B is in Country A. In accordance with the general rule for business-to-business supplies (Guideline 3.2), the place of taxation for the supply of Services 2 and 3 between Company T and Company U as suppliers and Company S as a customer is Country A for both supplies. In accordance with the general rule for business-to-business supplies (Guideline 3.2) the place of taxation for the supply of Service 4 between Company B and Company A will be Country A as Company A is in Country A. In accordance with the general rule for business-to-business supplies (Guideline 3.2), the place of taxation for the supply of Service 5 between Company B and Company D will be Country B because Country B is the country where the customer is located. In accordance with the general rule for business-to-business supplies (Guideline 3.2), the place of taxation for the supply of Service 6 between Company B and Company C will be Country C because Country C is the country where the customer is located.

It should be noted that the auditing services by Company T and Company U are "supplied to" Company S, while they are "provided" directly to Company D and Company C. The fact that the services are *"supplied to"* someone different from those to which the services are directly "provided" is not relevant in this example to determine the place of taxation, as the place of taxation will still be the customer location as determined in accordance with the general rule for business-to-business supplies (Guideline 3.2) and not where or to whom the services are directly provided.

The reason for this is that, at each stage of this example, all supplies will be subject to the taxation rules in the jurisdiction where the customer is located and the services are deemed to be used by the business in accordance with the destination principle as implemented by the general rule for business-to-business supplies (Guideline 3.2). There is neither double taxation nor unintended non-taxation in Countries A, B and C. In particular, the tax that accrues to Countries B and C reflects the business use of the services in those countries in accordance with the general rule for business-to-business supplies (Guideline 3.2) that treats customer location as the appropriate proxy for the jurisdiction of business use thereby implementing the destination principle. There is no reason to depart from the business agreements e.g. by following the interaction between Company T and Company D or between Company U and Company C.

In developing this example, care has been taken to avoid any "stewardship" issues that may exist with respect to Company A.[27] Company A, as the parent, may also be seen as deriving an element of benefit from the audit activities in Countries A, B and C, for example because such audit included an additional review of financial statements under the parent company's country accounting standards, rather than only per local subsidiary country accounting standards. Stewardship issues are assumed not to arise in Example 3 due to the inclusion of Service 4, where Company B supplies auditing services to Company A. Further, any questions concerning valuation for VAT/GST purposes and the possible identification of supplies existing, other than those shown, are also ignored.

Example 4: Alternative global agreement – Framework agreement

In this example the parent company of the group requiring audit services enters into a global agreement described as a "framework agreement" with the parent company of the audit group (both in the same country) in order to provide audit services in a number of countries.[28]

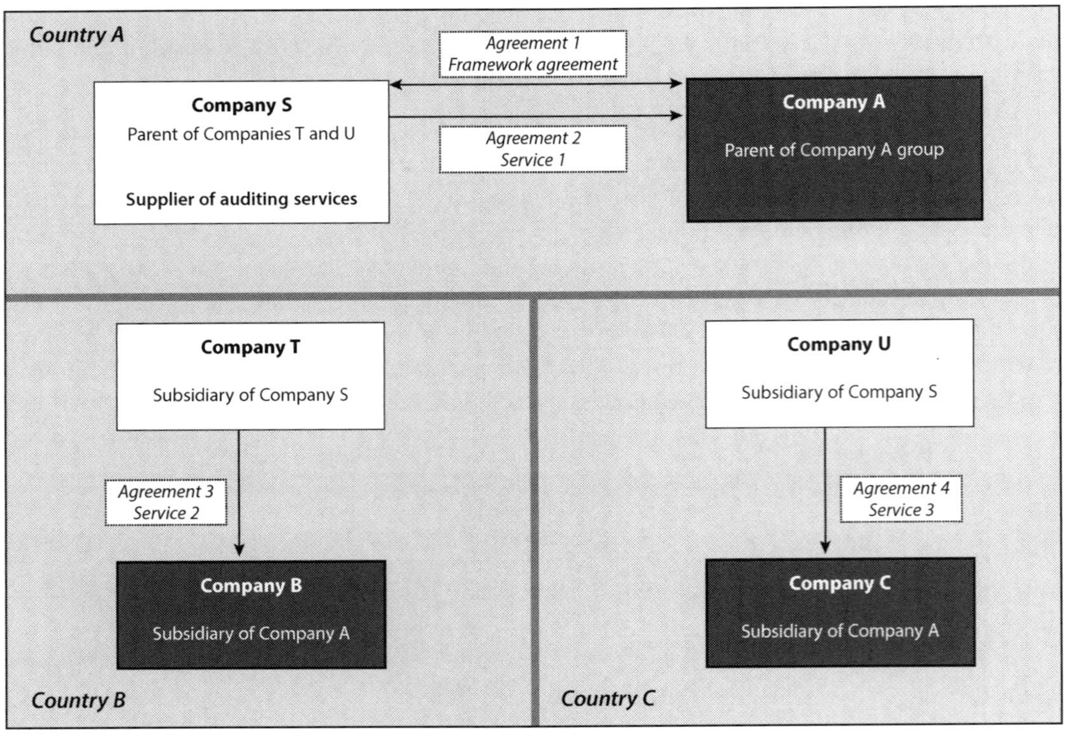

Facts

Company A is a parent company in Country A. It belongs to a multinational company group with subsidiaries around the world, for example Company B in Country B and Company C in Country C.

Company S is a parent company in Country A belonging to a multinational auditing company group with subsidiaries around the world, for example Company T in Country B and Company U in Country C.

Company A Group requires a global auditing service to meet legal requirements for its companies in Country A and its subsidiaries in Countries B and C. Company A concludes a framework agreement with Company S (Agreement 1). The framework agreement covers definitions, obligations relating to confidentiality, warranties, due dates for payment and limitations of liability, that would only apply if and when members of Company S and Company A enter into separate agreements referring to this framework agreement. The agreement also provides that companies that are affiliated with Company A and the auditing companies that are affiliated with Company S may enter into business agreements that will incorporate the terms of the framework agreement by reference. The agreement, however, does not oblige any member of Company A Group or Company S Group to enter into such business agreements.

Company A enters into a separate business agreement with Company S for the audit of Company A (Agreement 2); Company B enters into a business agreement with Company T for the audit of Company B (Agreement 3); and Company C enters into a business agreement with Company U for the audit of Company C (Agreement 4). In each of these three separate agreements (i.e. Agreements 2-4), an article is included where the parties agree to incorporate the terms included in the framework agreement (Agreement 1). Payment will follow each business agreement.

There are four separate agreements in this example, only three of which constitute business agreements that lead to supplies of services for consideration:

- Agreement 1 is not transactional, has no consideration and does not create a supply. Agreement 1 stipulates terms and conditions that become activated only when parties agree to separate business agreements as specified in the framework agreement.
- Under Agreement 2, Company S is the supplier and Company A is the customer (Service 1).
- Under Agreement 3, Company T is the supplier and Company B is the customer (Service 2).
- Under Agreement 4, Company U is the supplier and Company C is the customer (Service 3).

The place of taxation will be decided for each supply individually.

Place of taxation

In accordance with the general rule for business-to-business supplies (Guideline 3.2), the place of taxation for the supply of Service 1 between Company S and Company A will be Country A as Company A is in Country A. In accordance with the general rule for business-to-business supplies (Guideline 3.2), the place of taxation for the supply of Service 2 between Company T and Company U will be Country B as Company B is in Country B. Further, and again in accordance with the general rule for business-to-business supplies (Guideline 3.2), the place of taxation for the supply of Service 3 between Company U and Company C will be Country C as Company C is in Country C.

All three supplies are subject to the taxation rules in the jurisdiction where the customer is located and is the appropriate proxy for the jurisdiction of business use under the general rule for business-to-business supplies (Guideline 3.2). There is neither double taxation nor unintended non-taxation in Countries A, B or C. There is no reason to depart from the business agreements. In particular, no supplies take place under the framework agreement (Agreement 1) itself in this example. Consequently, no supplies are made under that agreement and no place of taxation issue arises.

Example 5: Alternative global agreement – Different flow of payments

This example expands upon example 4 by introducing payment flows that are different from the flows of the services as set out in the underlying business agreement.

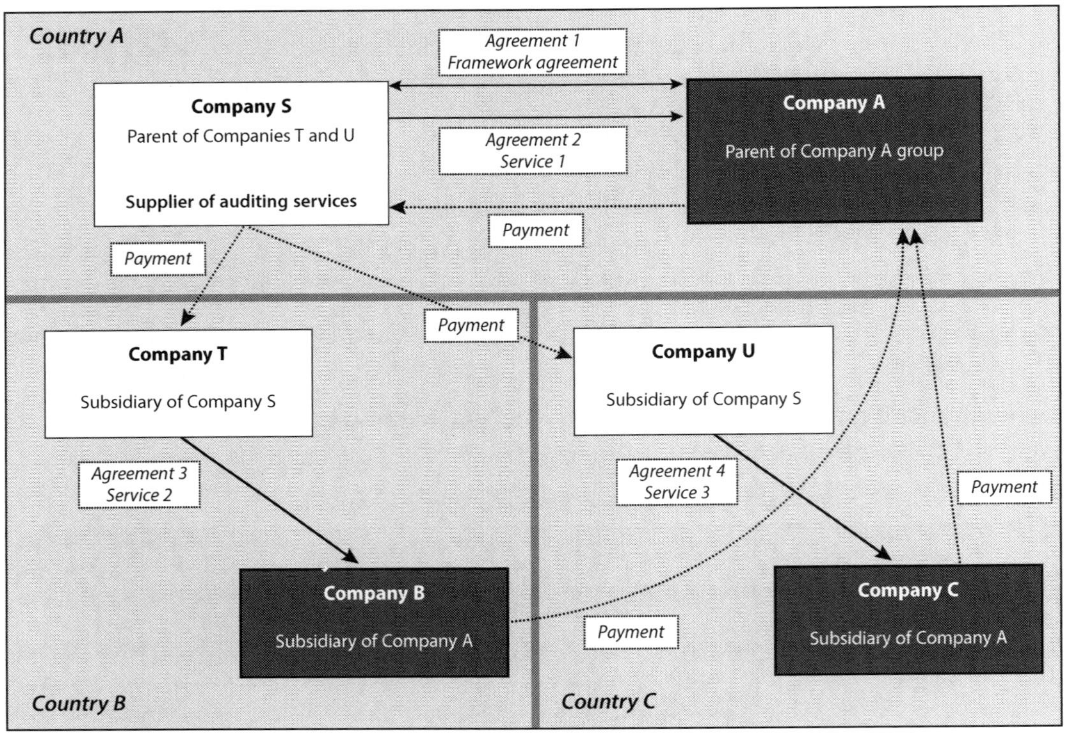

Facts

This example is similar to Example 4 except that the Company A group has put in place a system for settling inter-company supplies between group members. As a result, the Company A group decides to reduce the costs associated with cash disbursements by appointing Company A as the common paymaster for the group.[29] The framework agreement in this example is similar to Example 4 except that it specifies that the payments for the services supplied under the locally concluded business agreements will be handled by Company A directly with Company S for the whole Company A group.

For the audit services supplied under the three business agreements Company S, Company T and Company U will follow the general invoicing process and issue invoices respectively to Company A, Company B and Company C. For payment purposes, however, Company S will issue a collective statement (with copies attached of the invoices issued for the services supplied) to Company A. Based on the collective statement Company A will pay the requested amount to Company S and will on the same day collect the respective amounts from Company B and Company C. Similarly, Company S will transfer the respective amounts over to Company T and Company U on the same day it receives the payment from Company A.

The movements of payment are simply cash or account entries. The payment Company A makes to Company S represents consideration for the services supplied from Company S to Company A, from Company T to Company B and from Company U to Company C.

Place of taxation

The conclusions reached in Example 4 about the place of taxation of the supplies made under the business agreements (Agreements 2, 3 and 4) remain valid. The fact that payments are transferred via Company A and Company S has no impact on those conclusions.

All supplies under the business agreements are subject to the taxation rules in the jurisdiction where the customer is located according to the general rule for business-to-business supplies (Guideline 3.2). There is neither double nor unintended non-taxation in Countries A, B or C. There is no reason to depart from the business agreements e.g. by following the cash flows. The cash flows between Company A and its subsidiaries, between Company A and Company S, and between Company S and its subsidiaries are consideration for services supplied under the business agreements but do not in themselves create additional supplies, nor alter the supplies, nor identify the customer or customer location.

Annex 2

Example to illustrate the application of the recharge method under the general rule on place of taxation for business-to-business supplies of services and intangibles to multiple location Entities

Supply of payroll services

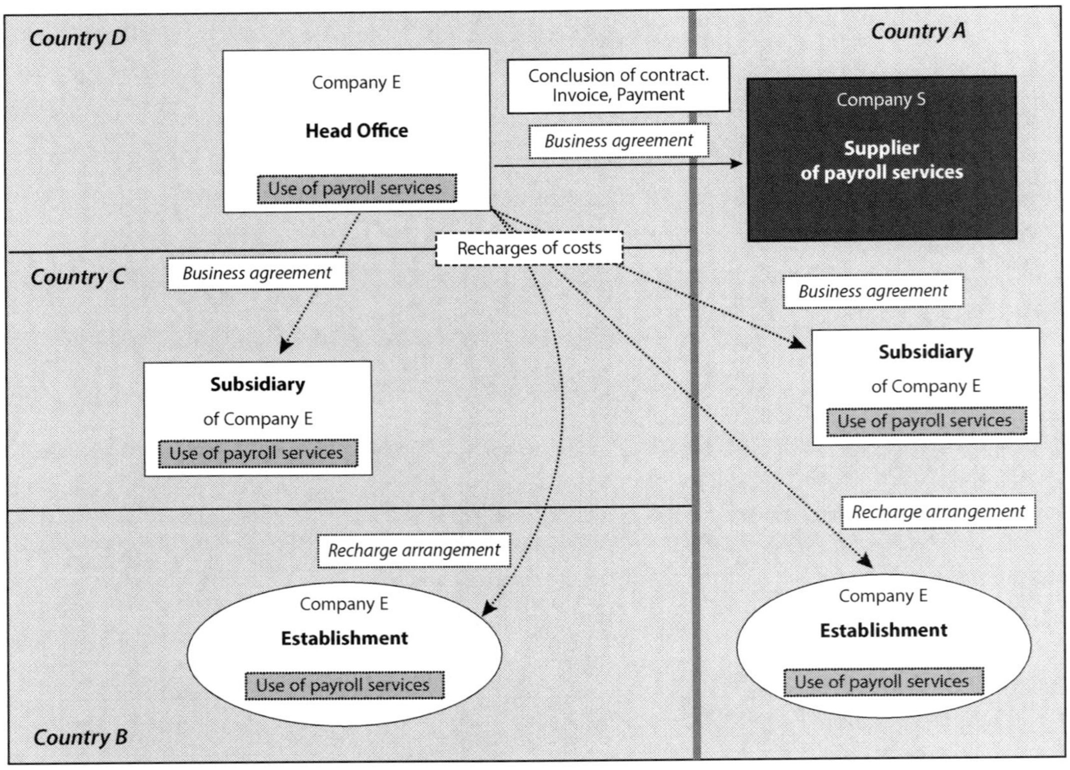

Facts

Company E is a multiple location entity located in three different countries: a head office in Country D ("Head Office") and trading establishments ("Establishments") in Countries A and B. It is the parent company of a multinational group with subsidiaries ("Subsidiaries") in Countries A and C. Company E's Head Office and Establishments as well as its Subsidiaries are all registered for VAT purposes.

Company E, represented by its Head Office, enters into a business agreement with Supplier S, located in Country A, for the supply of payroll management services. In this example, the payroll management services[30] relate to staff of Company E's Head Office and of its Establishments in Countries A and B and its Subsidiaries in Country A and C.

At its Head Office, Company E has business agreements in place with its Subsidiaries and recharge arrangements with its Establishments, setting out the terms and conditions for the transactions between them.

The business agreement between Supplier S and Company E establishes a fixed fee per month if the number of employees is within a given range. The fees for the services supplied under this business agreement are paid to Supplier S by Company E's Head Office on receipt of an invoice from Supplier S.

The agreed fee is 20 000. Supplier S issues an invoice for this amount to the Head Office of Company E, from which it receives payment of the entire amount.

Supplier

Supplier S in Country A has entered into a business agreement with Company E. It was negotiated and concluded for Company E by its Head Office in Country D, to which all invoices are addressed and which is responsible for payment. The business agreement provides the evidence allowing the supplier to supply the service free of VAT and to issue an invoice to Company E's Head Office in Country D without VAT.

Customer group[31]

After having represented Company E in the business agreement with Supplier S, the Head Office of Company E will typically have set up this supplier within the "supplier master data" of its ERP system[32] and will have created a cost centre to capture and pool the relevant costs. In this example, the Head Office has represented Company E in a business agreement to purchase services for its own use and for Company E's Establishments in Countries A and B and its Subsidiaries in Countries A and C. The Head Office of Company E will therefore consider the appropriate methodology for allocating the costs of these services to the Head Office and to its Establishments and Subsidiaries. In this example, the allocation will be based on the number of employees (or "headcount"). In this case headcount presents a fair and reasonable picture of the use of the payroll management services, by Company E's Head Office and its Establishments and Subsidiaries that employ the staff to which these services relate. Headcount is thus considered as an acceptable cost allocation key for these services.

The terms and conditions for the cost allocations to the Establishments and Subsidiaries will be reflected in business agreements between Company E and its Subsidiaries and in the recharge arrangements between the Head Office of Company E and its Establishments.

Upon receipt of the invoice from Supplier S, the accounts payable team in the Head Office of Company E will enter this invoice into the cost centre for invoices that have to be allocated on the basis of headcount for the onward supplies.

Next, the appropriate VAT treatment ("coding") will be assigned to this entry. This is typically based on a "decision tree", considering the various possible VAT scenarios. The conclusion for Company E's Head Office in this case will be that the invoice received from Supplier S should show no VAT and that the Head Office should account for the VAT in Country D under a reverse charge mechanism.[33] Once approved, the invoice will be processed for payment by the Head Office directly to Supplier S and the Head Office will account for the VAT in Country D under a reverse charge mechanism. Company E's Head Office in Country D will deduct the related input tax in line with its normal right to deduct.

Next, the Head Office of Company E will recharge part of the cost of the payroll services to the Establishments and Subsidiaries that employ the staff to which these services relate. This action is usually part of the regular "accounting close" that would for instance be run at the end of each month, quarter, semester or accounting year. In many cases, this will be done on the basis of an "allocation key table" maintained in the accounting software, highlighting for each account or range of accounts the percentage to be used to allocate the amounts that have been identified for recharge earlier in the process. This close out routine will calculate the amount per Establishment and Subsidiary, produce documentation and place the accounting entries.

In this example, the allocation key is based on headcount. The Head Office of Company E will identify the number of employees on payroll in each of the relevant Establishments and Subsidiaries, typically on the basis of budget data. In this example, budget data show that the Head Office employs 100 staff, the Establishments in Countries A and B employ respectively 10 and 30 staff and its Subsidiaries in Countries A and C respectively have 20 and 40 employees.

The allocation key table will attribute 50% to the Head Office in Country D, 5% to the Establishment in Country A, 15% to the Establishment in Country B, 10 % to the Subsidiary in Country A and 20% to the Subsidiary in Country C. The accounting system at the Head Office of Company E will produce two invoices for the onward supply to its Subsidiaries, one for 2 000 to the Subsidiary in Country A and one for 4 000 to the Subsidiary in Country C.[34] Based on the general rule for business-to-business supplies (Guideline 3.2), these invoices will be issued free of VAT since these Subsidiaries are single location entities located outside Country D where the Head Office of Company E is located. The accounting system will also generate two internal documents equivalent to invoices for the allocation of 1 000 to its Establishment in Country A and of 3 000 to its Establishment in Country B. Under the recharge method, these documents will receive the same treatment as if they were invoices to a separate legal entity, and will be issued free of VAT since both Establishments are located outside Country D where the Head Office of Company E is located.

Upon receipt of the invoices, the Subsidiaries in Countries A and C will account for the VAT through the reverse charge. The Establishments in Countries A and B will account for VAT through the reverse charge upon receipt of the documents for the costs allocated to them by their Head Office.

This process will be repeated throughout the accounting year. It may be possible in certain cases that allocation keys would remain unchanged in the course of the accounting year, even if the number of employees by entity would fluctuate during that period. In such a case, companies will typically, at year end, perform a "true up" calculation. The cost allocation will then be reconsidered on the basis of the more precise headcount, taking into account fluctuations in the course of the accounting year. Correcting credit notes or invoices/documents will then be created for the difference between the amount actually charged and the amount as calculated on the basis of actual headcount. These additional invoices or credit notes will follow a VAT treatment similar to the underlying invoices/documents.

Tax administrations

The supplier in Country A should hold all the relevant information that constitutes the business agreement to demonstrate that he has correctly supplied the service free of VAT to Company E's Head Office.

The tax administration in Country D should be able to ensure that the reverse charge is brought to account correctly by Company E's Head Office on the invoice received from Supplier S. It should also be able to ensure a correct tax treatment of the recharges made by Company E's Head Office to its Establishments and Subsidiaries. Company E's Head Office should hold all the relevant information that constitutes the business agreement with Supplier S. It should also hold the business agreements with its Subsidiaries and the recharge arrangements with its Establishments demonstrating how the recharges were allocated.

The tax administrations in Country A, B and C should be able to ensure that the reverse charge is brought to account correctly by the Subsidiaries and Establishments of Company E on the recharges made by the Head Office. The Subsidiaries should hold all the relevant information that constitutes their business agreement with Company E through its Head Office and the Establishments should hold the relevant information that constitutes their recharge arrangement with their Head Office. In particular, the tax administrations in Countries A and B should be able to verify that the Establishments have accounted for tax at the correct time of taxation under the normal domestic rules (e.g. date of internal recharge documents, date consideration is paid to the Head Office).

In order to audit the recharges, the tax administrations will need to be able to see all the relevant commercial documentation down to transaction level in order to identify the nature of the individual service that is recharged and so determine its place of taxation and the applicable rate.

Notes

1. For the purposes of these Guidelines, a supply of services or intangibles for VAT purposes takes place where one party does something for, or gives something **(other than something tangible) to another party** or refrains from doing something for another party, in exchange for consideration. It is recognised that a supply of services or intangibles in one country may in certain instances be regarded as a supply of goods (or some other category of supply) in another country. Where this is the case, and while these Guidelines deal only with supplies of services and intangibles, countries are encouraged to ensure that the rules for identifying the place of taxation of such supplies lead to a result that is consistent with these Guidelines.

2. See Guideline 3.7.

3. When a supply is made to a legal entity that has establishments in more than one jurisdiction (a "multiple location entity", "MLE"), an additional analysis is required to determine which of the jurisdictions where this MLE has establishments has taxing rights over the service or intangible acquired by the MLE. See Section B.3 below.

4. An illustration of this is the Centralised Purchasing Agreement in Example 3 and the Framework Agreement in Examples 4 and 5 in Annex 1 to this chapter.

5. Legal entities can include natural persons and non-commercial institutions such as governments, non-profit organisations and other institutions. The key point is that such entities, or certain of their activities, are recognised as "businesses" in national law. Such recognition may include the treatment for VAT purposes specifically or in national law more generally (notably in jurisdictions that have not implemented a VAT). See also paragraph 3.7.

6. For the purpose of these Guidelines, it is assumed that an establishment comprises a fixed place of business with a sufficient level of infrastructure in terms of people, systems and assets to be able to receive and/or make supplies. Registration for VAT purposes by itself does not constitute an establishment for the purposes of these Guidelines. Countries are encouraged to publicise what constitutes an "establishment" under their domestic VAT legislation.

7. "Use of a service or intangible" in this context differs from the concept of "use and enjoyment" existing in some national laws, which can refer to actual use by a customer in a jurisdiction irrespective of the presence of any customer establishment. See also Section D. on the use of specific rules for determining the place of taxation…

8. For the purposes of these Guidelines, the "reverse charge mechanism" is a tax mechanism that switches the liability to pay the tax from the supplier to the customer. If the customer is entitled to full input tax credit in respect of this supply, it may be that local VAT legislation does not require the reverse charge to be made. Tax administrations are encouraged to publicise their approach.

9. For the purposes of these Guidelines, a third party is an entity recognised as a "business". "Third party" refers to a party other than the supplier or the customer and has no necessary correlation to its meaning in other contexts, including direct taxation.

10. This company may be referred to as a "paymaster", "cash clearing agent", "billing agent" or some other such term. These Guidelines use the term "paymaster".

11. In cases where a customer omits to account properly for such a reverse charge, but is still, nevertheless, entitled to full input tax deduction in respect of that supply, it is recommended that any penalties that might be applied should be proportionate and linked to the gravity of the failure made, where the gravity of the failure is a consideration, bearing in mind there is no net revenue loss.

12. Netting occurs when establishments that have mutual obligations, e.g. because they have each made recharges to each other, agree to compensate the value of both obligations and to pay only the net amount that is still owed by one of the establishments after this compensation. Where netting has taken place, VAT should in principle be applied on the taxable amount of each recharge and not just the net value.

13. For the purposes of the Guidelines, business-to-consumer supplies are assumed to be supplies where the customer is not recognised as a business. Such recognition may include the treatment for VAT purposes specifically or in national law more generally (notably in jurisdictions that have not implemented a VAT). See also paragraphs 3.7 and 3.8.

14. This paragraph refers only to supplies of services rather than to supplies of services and intangibles, because services constituted the overwhelming proportion of such supplies to final consumers in the past.

15. Under the general rule for business-to-business supplies of services and intangibles set out in Guideline 3.2 and under the general rule for business-to-consumer supplies of services and intangibles set out in Guideline 3.6, the place of taxation is thus determined by reference to the customer's location. The customer's location is determined by reference to the customer's business establishment in the business-to-business context (in accordance with Guideline 3.2) and to the customer's usual residence in the business-to-consumer context (in accordance with Guideline 3.6).

16. Jurisdictions that treat some of these items (such as accommodation and restaurant meals) as a supply of goods or some other category are encouraged to ensure consistency with these

Guidelines by ensuring that such supplies are taxed at the place where they are performed. Similarly, where countries treat the supply of a ticket or right of entry as a separate supply, they are encouraged to determine the place of taxation by reference to place where the underlying supply of service is performed. See also note 1.

17. This should not be read as requiring countries to adopt such a categorisation approach to determining the place of taxation. Countries using an iterative approach may choose to use a series of rules that are applied consecutively to determine the appropriate place of taxation in an order the leads to the same end result as that recommended by Guideline 3.5.

18. An Internet Protocol address, also known as an IP address, is a numerical label assigned to each device (e.g. computer, mobile phone) participating in a computer network that uses the Internet Protocol for communication.

19. For the purposes of these Guidelines, the taxing jurisdiction is the jurisdiction that is identified as the place of taxation in accordance with these Guidelines

20. On-the-spot supplies are services and intangibles that are normally physically performed at a readily identifiable location and that are ordinarily consumed at the same time and place where they are physically performed, in the presence of both the person performing the supply and the person consuming it (see para. 3.116).

21. This should not be taken to suggest that countries must change their law to literally incorporate Guidelines 3.2, 3.5 and 3.6 as legal rules in national legislation. Rather, these Guidelines recommend what should be the end result of the national place of taxation rules, however they are described in the relevant laws, without predicting precisely by which means that result is achieved.

22. The supplies in these examples are performed at a readily identifiable location and require the physical presence of the person consuming the supply but they do not require the physical presence of the person performing them. These are therefore not "on-the-spot" supplies covered by Guideline 3.5 and their place of taxation is in principle determined by reference to the customer's usual residence, in accordance with Guideline 3.6.

23. Other rules will be applicable to such supplies, although they might lead to the same result.

24. If this is not treated as a supply of goods or of immovable property, for which other rules might apply, although they could lead to the same result.

25. The adjective "intellectual" has a broad meaning and is not limited to regulated professions.

26. Also the treatment of services that are incidental to the export or import of goods (e.g. packaging, loading, transport, insurance etc.) is outside the scope of these Guidelines.

27. Stewardship expenses are broadly the costs incurred by the parent company of the group for administrative and other services provided to subsidiaries and other affiliates for the benefit of the parent, as a shareholder, rather than for the individual benefit of the subsidiary or affiliate. These costs can be incurred directly by the parent or by the subsidiary and passed on to the parent. Typically, these are treated as expenses which ought to be absorbed by the parent company because they must be regarded as stewardship or shareholders' expenses benefiting the shareholders or the group as a whole and not a subsidiary or affiliate individually.

28. The expression "framework agreement" is used solely to distinguish it from the separate business agreement for audit services to the parent trading company. The Guidelines do not attempt to define in any way what a "framework agreement" might be.

29. It is recognised that, in some cases, the paymaster function could create a separate supply, or supplies, between Company A and its subsidiaries. For the purposes of this example this is not the case.

30. Payroll management services include multiple steps such as data collection, master data input in systems, tracking of legislation changes, calculation of taxes, issuance of pay sheets, preparation of accounting entries, preparation of bank transfer files, issue of summary reports, etc.

31. In the context of this example, the term "customer group" refers to Company E and its Establishments and Subsidiaries that employ the staff to which the services supplied by Supplier S relate.

32. Enterprise resource planning ("ERP") systems integrate internal and external management flows and information across an entire organisation, embracing finance and accounting functions, manufacturing, sales and services, customer relationship management, etc. ERP systems automate this activity with an integrated software application. Their purpose is to facilitate the flow of information between all business functions within an organisation and to manage the connections to outside stakeholders such as suppliers and customers. See Bidgoli, Hossein (2004). *The Internet Encyclopedia*, Volume 1, John Wiley & Sons, Inc. p. 707.

33. For the purpose of this example, it is assumed that all countries apply a "reverse charge mechanism" that switches the liability to pay the tax from the supplier to the customer. It is recognised that some countries do not require the customer to account for the tax under the reverse charge mechanism when entitled to full input tax credit.

34. See Section B.4 of Chapter 3.

Annex E

Economic incidence of the options to address the broader direct tax challenges of the digital economy

This annex contains an overview of the expected economic incidence on consumers, capital owners (including shareholders) and labour (workers) of three options to address the broader tax challenges of the digital economy.

1. The key policy question addressed in this annex is: *"How would the distribution of the change in tax burden differ under the three tax policy options?"* To answer this question, the following sections provide an overview of the expected economic incidence in open-border economies, but with particular attention paid to the fact that the options represent tax changes only for foreign providers without a permanent establishment (PE) making remote sales of digital goods and services to in-country customers. The results are summarised in terms of the distribution of tax burdens among consumers, capital owners and labour in both producing and consuming countries.

E.1. Proposals to be analysed

2. The three tax change options are:

- a corporate income tax on the net income generated from remote sales of digital goods and services to in-country customers by a foreign producer without a PE to which such income is attributed under current law
- an equalisation levy ("excise tax") imposed on the remote sales of digital goods and services to in-country customers by the same providers, and
- a withholding tax on the gross receipts from the remote sale of digital goods and services to in-country customers by the same providers.

E.2. Description of taxes

3. Table E.1 provides a brief overview of the general characteristics of the three types of taxes that will be included in the tax incidence analysis. This provides a framework for comparing the tax types.

4. *Corporate income tax.* The corporate income tax (CIT) is levied on the net income of businesses, calculated as the difference between gross receipts and the costs of generating the income. In the case of cross-border income, most countries apply a territorial CIT system in which tax is imposed on income attributable to economic activity within the country (a "source-based" tax); a few countries adopt worldwide CIT systems which also tax resident corporations on their world-wide income (a "residence-based" tax), though in most cases taxation of foreign-sourced profits of foreign subsidiaries is deferred until repatriation with a credit for foreign taxes.

5. *Excise tax.* The excise tax is commonly imposed on the sale of specifically listed products, such as alcohol, tobacco, motor fuels and insurance. It is generally designed as a tax on final consumption but the seller is responsible for collecting and remitting the tax. It shares common features with sales taxes, except that an excise tax may not vary with the price of the product being sold. Instead it may be levied on a specific basis, such as the unit of weight or volume of products sold. The tax basis is however flexible in practice, and may include the fair market value of products sold or gross receipts from sales, as presented in the option discussed above in Chapter 7. It can also be designed to impose a tax on a single stage in the production process (e.g. retail sale in the country where consumption occurs).

6. *Withholding tax.* The withholding tax (WT) option described in the Report is a tax, in concept, that would apply to digital sales to in-country consumers from non-resident suppliers without a PE. It can be described as a gross receipts tax (GRT) or excise tax on these sales to consumers. The WT could apply to sales to final consumers only or it could also apply to business-to-business digital sales.[1] As discussed in the Report, the WT could be collected from financial intermediaries that process the transactions used to pay for the digital purchases.

Table E.1. **Description of taxes included in the incidence analysis**

	Corporate income tax	Excise tax	Withholding tax
Type of tax	Net income tax imposed on corporations	Tax on final consumption	Tax on final consumption
Tax base	Net income of the business (gross receipts minus costs)	Gross receipts on sales to customers	Gross receipts on sales to customers
Geographic concept	Residence (where firm is headquartered) and/or source (where economic activity is located)	Destination (where customer is located)	Destination (where consumer is located)
Scope of tax	Applies to 1) income earned within the taxing country, or 2) world-wide income	Limited to final consumer purchases	Limited to final consumer purchases

E.3. What is tax incidence analysis?

7. Tax incidence analysis is designed to determine who bears the burden of a tax. The burden of the tax is defined to be the ultimate resting point of the tax after recognising any tax shifting that might occur after the tax is imposed. Shifting is the process by which the taxpayers bearing the legal responsibility for paying the tax ("legal incidence") alter their behaviour and, as a result, shift the burden of the tax to other parties though changes in output or input prices. The final resting point for the tax is the "economic incidence" of the tax.

8. The economic theory of tax incidence starts with the fundamental premise that all taxes are ultimately borne by individuals. The standard tax incidence analysis identifies three categories of economic actors that can bear the ultimate burden of a tax: households as consumers through higher prices for goods and services they buy, workers through reduced wages and salaries, and capital owners, including shareholders, through lower returns on capital investments.

9. The corporate income tax provides an example of the mechanics of tax shifting. While the CIT is the legal liability of a corporation, in response to the tax the firm may charge consumers higher prices for the firm's output, pay labour less, or reduce the dividends paid to shareholders on their capital investments. The extent of shifting depends upon the market conditions faced by the corporation, including how sensitive consumers are to price changes, the presence of competition, and how responsive the supply of labour and capital are to changes in compensation and the return on investment. The market conditions facing the firm paying the CIT will determine whether the tax burden will be primarily shifted forward to consumers and/or backward to labour and capital.

E.4. Tax incidence analysis

10. This section describes the expected shifting process that determines the expected economic incidence of each tax option. The more complicated corporate income tax incidence analysis is discussed first.

11. The amount of taxes to be collected from the excise tax and withholding tax is assumed to be equivalent to the corporate income tax that would be imposed on the economic activities of the remote seller sourced to the sales destination country. The incidence results depend on the specific details of each policy option.

E.4.1. Incidence of the corporate income tax option

12. There is an extensive body of literature on the theory of corporate income tax incidence, as well as a number of empirical studies estimating key parameters in the tax shifting process. An important determinant of the incidence of the corporate income tax is the degree of competition in the market where tax changes occur. The incidence results will differ between perfectly competitive markets, where sellers take market prices as given (beyond their control), and imperfectly competitive markets, where sellers have some control over market prices. Both cases are analysed in this paper.

13. The incidence of a corporate income tax increase will also depend on how extensive the tax increase is in terms of corporate sector activities subject to the increase. In the standard corporate income tax incidence analysis, it is assumed that all corporate taxpayers are subject to the increase in tax. In contrast, the corporate income tax proposal included in this analysis would increase corporate income tax liability only for foreign corporations without a PE selling digital goods and services to in-country customers, as domestic suppliers of such services are currently subject to corporate income tax on such income. In this case, the tax increase is more accurately analysed as a "selective excise" tax applying only to a select group of corporate suppliers selling in a specific market. This dimension affects the incidence of the corporate income tax increase, compared to the standard analysis of a broad corporate income tax increase.[2]

E.4.1.1. Key assumptions

14. The corporate income tax incidence analysis of the extension of the CIT to foreign providers without a PE selling digital goods and services into a country under current law is based on the following key assumptions:

- The digital goods and services are sold by both foreign corporations without a PE in the country and currently taxable corporations, including domestic corporations and foreign corporations with a PE.
- There is a worldwide market for capital; labour is substantially less mobile internationally.
- The time horizon for the analysis allows for cross-border adjustments in response to the tax changes, involving changes in both input and output markets.
- Any increase in corporate income tax collections from foreign suppliers of digital products without a current PE will be part of a CIT balanced budget change (e.g. used to reduce the countries' general corporate income tax rate).[3]

15. The incidence of tax changes in a single country depends upon what happens to tax rates in other countries. *Relative* tax rates determine the degree of shifting across industries within a single country, as well as shifting across countries. This CIT incidence analysis assumes that a significant number of countries impose these changes in a global co-ordinated step. It does not include an analysis of the expected incidence if only one or several countries impose the change. Thus, there are not significant relative tax changes between countries as a result of the co-ordinated action. However, as explained later, the size of the tax change may differ by country because of differences in statutory CIT rates.

E.4.1.2. Shifting process

16. The initial imposition of the CIT on remote sellers of digital products without a PE will increase the CIT liabilities of those firms.[4] This is the legal incidence of the tax. Although their tax payments to a country will increase, the owners of affected providers may not bear the ultimate burden (economic incidence) of the tax increase. This is due to the fact that the affected taxpayers are expected to respond to the tax increase by changing the level of production, the demand for inputs used in production and distribution, and, potentially output prices, in a process that can result in shifting the tax forward in consumer prices or backward in lower payments to the key factors of production, labour and capital.

17. The initial impact of the CIT tax increase on remote sellers of digital products without a PE is to reduce their after-tax rate of return on capital invested in producing digital products in the production country. In the short-run, with no change in the before-tax price charged to customers or payments to labour, the after-tax rate-of-return to capital invested in the production country by those affected companies will fall by the amount of the tax "wedge" between the before-tax and after-tax rates of return on the capital invested in producing digital products. For example, if the pre-tax rate of return is 10% and the CIT rate to be applied is 20%, the after-tax rate of return will be 8%.

18. With time to adjust to the changes, the suppliers without a PE will respond to the reduction in the after-tax rate of return through possible output price adjustments, changes in the level of output and changes in input prices. The types of adjustments will depend upon the market structure facing the remote sellers without a PE of digital goods and services. The following sections compare the expected corporate income tax incidence for two types of markets: perfectly competitive and imperfectly competitive markets.

E.4.1.3. Perfectly competitive market

19. In a perfectly competitive market, producers are viewed as "price takers" reacting to a market-determined price that is beyond their control. If the remote suppliers without a PE of digital goods and services are operating in a competitive market, the adjustment to the lower after-tax rate of return (relative to other investment opportunities) will occur through reductions in the affected remote suppliers' sales into the market where they don't have PE. In a competitive market, other suppliers would be expected to replace the sales reduced by the affected suppliers. Assuming that capital is mobile between industries and countries, equity investors in the affected remote suppliers will shift capital out of the production of digital goods and services for the market without PE, and other suppliers with PE will shift output and capital to produce the replacement sales.[5] The shifting will continue until the pre-tax rate of return on capital used by affected remote increases sufficiently to restore the after-tax rate of return to the world-wide rate.

20. The new worldwide after-tax rate of return may be relatively unchanged if the capital shifted away from the remote sellers with no PE is a relatively small share of worldwide capital.[6] If so, the shifted capital will bear little of the burden of the corporate income tax increase because the after-tax rate of return for equity investors will be almost unchanged. However, as capital is shifted to other uses, the output level of the foreign producers of digital goods and services without a PE will be reduced while the output of other suppliers will increase.

21. The reduced output by the affected foreign suppliers will result in less labour employed by the affected firms. To the extent that affected foreign producers of digital

goods and services employ specialised labour, it is possible that their wages could be reduced as labour shifts into other sectors where this type of labour is not as productive. The magnitude of any wage reduction is expected to vary across countries where the affected foreign suppliers are located given variations in labour market conditions. To the extent that wages are reduced, displaced labour would bear a portion of the corporate income tax increase on remote sellers without a PE.

22. The remaining question is whether the price of digital goods and services will increase as remote sellers affected by the tax increase reduce their output. The extent to which market prices in consumer countries increase will depend upon how important the output of the remote sellers without a PE is relative to the country sales. Assuming that the affected remote sellers account for a significant share of the worldwide market output, it is expected that the price of digital goods and services would increase and a portion of the tax increase would be shifted forward to consumers. The availability of other suppliers with similar pre-tax costs and the availability of substitutes for the digital goods and services will be a factor in determining the magnitude of the consumer price increase.

23. As a result, in the case of perfect competition, the incidence of the corporate income tax increase on remote sellers of digital goods and services is likely to be borne by labour in the production country and consumers in the market country. The combination of higher consumer prices in the digital goods and services market and reductions in wages for workers in affected production countries will reduce the real income of residents in both production countries and consuming countries. Without further information about the economic characteristics of the affected remote producers and the overall market for digital goods and services, the specific labour and consumer shares of the tax increase cannot be determined.

24. It should be noted that the tax shifting process described above may extend over a significant period of time. The incidence conclusions should be interpreted as the long-run results after the economic adjustments have occurred. It should also be noted that producers of digital goods and services, a relatively new industry, may be making excess profits, beyond a competitive rate of return, in the short- to intermediate-period, even in a competitive market due to cost efficiencies relative to the marginal supplier. In this situation, the initial reduction in the after-tax rate of return for capital invested by the affected foreign producers may not lead to an immediate reduction in their level of sales and capital. This is because the lower after-tax rate of return may still be higher than the next best alternative investment of the capital. In this case, capital may temporarily bear the burden of the tax increase. However, in the long-run (unlike in the example of an imperfectly competitive market below) these excess profits will be eliminated by competition and all capital will earn only a competitive rate of return; at this point the above analysis (assuming perfect competition) would apply.[7]

E.4.1.4. Imperfectly competitive market

25. The incidence of the corporate income tax increase will differ if the market for digital goods and services is not perfectly competitive. As used in this analysis, imperfect competition refers to a market where producers earn excess profits above the competitive rate of return. In this case, the affected producers are price setters, not price takers, and the affected foreign suppliers have enough market power to set the price of digital goods and services sold in the market countries. The lack of competition (at least in the short or medium term) may be due to unique factors of production, including intangibles, that are owned or used by the affected producers.

26. In this situation, in response to the higher CIT on the income of foreign suppliers without a PE, the affected foreign suppliers are less likely to reduce significantly their long-run level of output or capital investment. This is the case because the capital is earning excess profits above-and-beyond the competitive rate of return. In other words, there may be no alternative investment that could generate an after-tax rate of return higher than the after-tax rate of return, including the CIT, earned by the affected producers. In this case, the increased corporate income tax would be borne primarily by owners of equity capital invested in the affected foreign producers of digital goods and services without a PE in the consumer country.[8]

27. There is one more dimension of the shifting process that should be noted. Given that CIT rates differ across countries, the extension of the corporate income tax to foreign sellers without a PE will result in different relative reductions in the after-tax rate of return on capital in different countries. It is possible that the reduction in the rate of return in high-tax rate countries may be high enough to drive the after-tax rate of return of affected digital suppliers down below the competitive worldwide after-tax rate of return.[9] If this happens, there could be a shift away from those high-tax market countries unless prices of digital goods and services increase to offset the relative tax increases. In this case, a portion of the tax increase on the remote suppliers could be borne by consumers in the high-tax countries.

28. In summary, the expected incidence of the corporate income tax increase on foreign suppliers without a PE of digital goods and services is as follows:

- In the case of a perfectly competitive market for digital goods and services, the incidence of the corporate income tax increase is likely to be borne by labour in the affected foreign suppliers' production country and consumers in market countries. Consumers in the market countries are more likely to face higher prices if the affected suppliers sell a significant percentage in a particular market and there are not alternative suppliers with similar cost structures or there are not close product substitutes.
- If the market for digital goods and services provided by foreign suppliers without a PE is characterised as imperfectly competitive, the corporate income tax increase is likely to be borne principally by the equity owners of the affected foreign suppliers.

E.4.2. Incidence of the excise tax option

29. A second tax policy option identified for analysis is to impose, in place of the corporate income tax, an excise tax on the gross receipts paid by in-country customers in consideration for sales of digital products by remote sellers without a PE.[10] It is assumed that the excise tax rate would be calculated to raise an equivalent amount of revenue as the CIT on the related income of the remote sellers without a PE.[11]

30. The standard assumption in the incidence analysis of consumption taxes (i.e. taxes designed to tax final consumption of households) is that a general consumption tax, such as a VAT, will be passed forward in higher prices to consumers.

31. There are, however, important conditions that need to be satisfied to support this conclusion. The most important is that the consumption tax increase must be effectively collected from all sellers of the goods and services, whether domestic or foreign sellers. A second is that the same tax rate applies to all sellers of the product. Under these conditions, buyers cannot avoid paying the tax through higher prices by buying from a seller that is collecting a lower (or no) tax.

32. However, in the case of the proposal to adopt an excise tax equivalent to the CIT that would be imposed on foreign sellers without a PE, the tax increase is only affecting a subset of suppliers to the domestic market. Therefore, the degree of shifting of the tax depends upon the reactions of only a small number of suppliers, remote sellers without a PE, not responses from all market suppliers.

33. As in the case for the corporate income tax increase discussed above, the ability of remote suppliers without a PE to shift the excise tax forward to consumers will be influenced by the degree of competition in the market for digital goods and services. The analysis differs under the two assumed market possibilities: 1) the market is perfectly competitive, or 2) the market is imperfectly competitive. As in the case of the corporate income tax incidence analysis, these are distinguished by the presence or absence of excess profits.

34. If the affected foreign suppliers without a PE are operating in a competitive market, the initial impact of the excise tax on affected foreign suppliers will be the same reduction in the after-tax rate of return on capital invested by the affected foreign suppliers, as seen in the corporate income tax increase case. As the affected foreign suppliers attempt to increase consumer prices, the *relative* price of their sales of digital goods and products in consumer countries will increase. Because their customers can choose from substitute suppliers and/or alternative goods and services where the price has not increased, the ability of the affected foreign suppliers to pass the tax on to consumers in higher prices will be limited. As a result, the tax is not expected to be passed forward in higher prices as would be the case with a general consumption tax rate increase; any shifting to consumers will depend on the portion of the market of the affected suppliers and the availability of alternative suppliers with similar cost structures and the availability of alternative products.

35. As in the case of the CIT increase under perfect competition, capital will have to shift from the affected foreign suppliers to replacement suppliers or to other industries and countries. With competitive capital markets, the after-tax rate of return of the affected digital goods and services providers will have to be pushed back up to the unchanged worldwide after-tax rate of return though price increases of digital goods and services or reductions in wages for specialised labour used by the affected foreign suppliers or they will have to exit the market. Similar to the CIT analysis, the burden of the excise tax is expected to be borne by labour in the affected foreign suppliers' production country and by consumers in market countries. As noted above, the extent of shifting to consumers will depend on the portion of the market of the affected suppliers, the availability of alternative suppliers with similar cost structures, and the availability of alternative products.

36. The incidence of the excise tax will also be similar to the incidence of the corporate income tax increase on affected foreign suppliers of digital goods and services if the market is imperfectly competitive. When affected suppliers earn excess profits, the tax increase is expected to be borne by the equity investors in the affected suppliers through a reduction in their rates of return, which will still exceed a competitive rate of return.

37. In summary, the conclusion is that the excise tax is expected to have the same pattern of economic incidence as the extension of the corporate income tax to foreign suppliers without a PE.

E.4.3. Incidence of the withholding tax option

38. A third option identified for analysis is a withholding tax on the gross receipts from the sale of digital goods and services by foreign suppliers without a PE. As in the case of the excise tax, the withholding tax rate would be set to raise an amount of revenue equal

to the CIT that would be paid on the income generated by the remote sales to in-country customers.

39. The withholding tax is a gross receipts tax on the total sales to in-country consumers of digital products sold by foreign suppliers without a PE. In other words, it would also operate as a "selective excise" tax on the consumption of this category of goods and services. Because all three of the tax options are operating as selective excise taxes from an economic standpoint, the incidence of the withholding tax should be the same as the incidence pattern under the CIT extension and the excise tax.

40. If the market for digital goods and services is competitive, then the burden of the withholding tax on foreign suppliers without a PE is expected to fall on specialised labour used by the affected foreign suppliers and consumers of digital products, depending on the importance of the affected suppliers in the particular market and the availability of replacement suppliers with similar cost structures and the availability of alternative goods and services. In the case of imperfectly competitive markets, the withholding tax would be borne primarily by equity investors in the affected foreign suppliers.[12]

E.5. Conclusion

41. Given the assumptions described above, the expected economic incidence of the three tax options for taxing the activities related to the sales of digital goods and services by foreign suppliers without a PE would be the same.

- In the case of a perfectly competitive market for digital goods and services, the incidence of the corporate income tax increase is likely to be borne by labour in the affected foreign suppliers' production country and consumers in market countries, depending on the importance of the affected suppliers in the particular market and the availability of replacement suppliers with similar cost structures and the availability of alternative goods and services.
- If the market is imperfectly competitive, the corporate income tax increase is likely to be borne principally by the equity owners of the affected foreign suppliers.

42. It should be noted that there will be a difference in the geographic distributions of the tax burdens borne by capital owners, labour and consumers. Any portion of a CIT increase that would be borne by reductions in the income of equity shareholders of foreign suppliers without a PE will occur in countries where the shareholders are located. The distribution of the burden on labour will reflect the geographic distribution of production by the affected suppliers. In contrast, any portion of the tax burden borne by consumers will be spread over market countries where the foreign producers without a PE have market power in setting the domestic price of particular digital goods and services. Therefore, the share of the total worldwide increase in tax burdens borne by consumers, workers and capital owners will vary from country-to-country.

43. As a final point, further analysis of the economic characteristics of the affected remote producers and the market for particular digital goods and services would need to be analysed to determine whether perfect competition or imperfect competition, in the short and medium term is the most accurate to use in the incidence analysis. The analysis also does not provide any insights into the distribution of tax burdens by household income levels. In addition, the incidence results for the three tax policy options depend heavily upon the key assumptions about the responsiveness of foreign suppliers of digital goods and services without a PE that will become subject to the alternative tax options.

Notes

1. This incidence analysis assumes the excise tax and withholding tax only apply to final consumer sales. If these taxes were applied to business purchases, they could create "pyramiding" of taxes with incidence effects beyond the scope of this analysis.

2. The standard corporate income tax incidence analysis is based on the "Harberger Model" of the incidence of changes in a general corporate income tax. For a fairly easy-to-follow explanation of the model, see Arnold C. Harberger, "The ABCs of Corporation Tax Incidence: Insights into the Open-Economy Case," Chapter 2, American Council for Capital Formation, Policy and Economic Growth (April 1995). In this article, Harberger explains how his original closed-economy model has to be modified to analyse CIT incidence in the international setting. William C. Randolph, "International Burdens of the Corporate Income Tax," Congressional Budget Office, Washington, DC. (2006) provides a more detailed analysis of the expected incidence of the general corporate income tax. Other economic incidence analyses of note include Alan Auerbach, "Who Bears the Corporate Tax? A Review of What We Know," Tax Policy and the Economy 20 (2006) and Kimberly C. Clausing, "Who Pays the Corporate Tax in a Global Economy?", National Tax Journal, volume 66, no. 1, 2013.

3. This is a simplifying assumption. Assuming there is no change in overall corporate income taxes avoids the need to consider possible macroeconomic impacts from the tax options.

4. To simplify the analysis, it is assumed that the foreign suppliers of digital goods and services without a PE are not taxable on the income related to the sales in the production country. In this case, the change in corporate taxes will equal the increase imposed by the consumer country. If the supplier is subject to a corporate income tax in the production country under a residence-based tax with credits for taxes paid in other countries, the net change in corporate income taxes will depend upon the relative size of the tax rates in the production and consumer countries.

5. A clientele effect might occur where affected suppliers no longer provide goods and services in the country and shift output to other countries, while other suppliers with PE shift their output to the country with no economic effects other than geographic redistribution of the sales.

6. It should be noted that the average worldwide increase in the CIT is expected to be borne by worldwide capital. However, under the proposal this increase is expected to be relatively small.

7. The tax incidence of the corporate tax increase, in theory, can also be affected by what happens to the additional CIT collected from foreign suppliers of digital goods and services without a PE. In this analysis, it is assumed that any increased CIT collections will be offset by an equal decrease in the general CIT rate to hold CIT tax collections constant. This is a simplifying assumption.

8. There is a growing body of empirical studies estimating the incidence of the corporate income tax that supports this view. For a good review of the literature, see William M. Gentry, "A Review of the Evidence on the Incidence of the corporate Income Tax," U.S. Department of Treasury, OTA Paper 101 (December 2007). The studies suggest that the corporate income tax imposed on "supernormal" profits (economic rents) in excess of the normal rate of return is borne primarily by capital owners.

9. Given the assumption that total CIT collections are unchanged as a result of the balance budget adjustment in CIT revenues, there should be no net reduction in the worldwide after-tax rate of return up to this point. In other words, except for this final possibility, capital investment in other sectors of the economy should not be affected by the extension of the CIT to foreign suppliers without a permanent establishment.

10. In this analysis it is assumed that the excise tax (as well as the withholding tax) is only imposed on final consumers of digital goods and services purchased from foreign suppliers without a PE.

11. The mechanics of determining the amount of the excise tax have not been specified, but would likely be an industry rate rather than varying by company.

12. Note that as with the CIT and excise tax options, if the after-tax rate of return of affected digital suppliers is driven below the competitive worldwide after-tax rate of return, there could be a shift away from those high-tax market countries unless prices of digital goods and services increase to offset the relative tax increases. In this case, a portion of the tax increase on the remote suppliers could be shared with consumers in the high-tax countries.

ORGANISATION FOR ECONOMIC CO-OPERATION AND DEVELOPMENT

The OECD is a unique forum where governments work together to address the economic, social and environmental challenges of globalisation. The OECD is also at the forefront of efforts to understand and to help governments respond to new developments and concerns, such as corporate governance, the information economy and the challenges of an ageing population. The Organisation provides a setting where governments can compare policy experiences, seek answers to common problems, identify good practice and work to co-ordinate domestic and international policies.

The OECD member countries are: Australia, Austria, Belgium, Canada, Chile, the Czech Republic, Denmark, Estonia, Finland, France, Germany, Greece, Hungary, Iceland, Ireland, Israel, Italy, Japan, Korea, Luxembourg, Mexico, the Netherlands, New Zealand, Norway, Poland, Portugal, the Slovak Republic, Slovenia, Spain, Sweden, Switzerland, Turkey, the United Kingdom and the United States. The European Union takes part in the work of the OECD.

OECD Publishing disseminates widely the results of the Organisation's statistics gathering and research on economic, social and environmental issues, as well as the conventions, guidelines and standards agreed by its members.

OECD PUBLISHING, 2, rue André-Pascal, 75775 PARIS CEDEX 16
(23 2015 28 1 P) ISBN 978-92-64-24102-2 – 2015-18

Made in the USA
Coppell, TX
02 December 2022

87591787R00160